Children's Writer®
Guide to 2009

**Writer's Institute
Publications** ™

Editor in Chief: Susan M. Tierney

Contributing Writers:

Pamela Holtz Beres
Molly Blaisdell

Jacqueline Adams
Judy Bradbury
Chris Eboch
Sue Bradford Edwards
Christina Hamlett
Mindy Hardwick

Mark Haverstock
Jacqueline Horsfall
Jane Landreth
Amanda Norelli
Mary Northrup
Susan Sundwall
Katherine Swarts
Leslie J. Wyatt

Contributing Editor: Marni McNiff

Copy Editor: Meredith DeSousa

Production: Joanna Horvath

Cover Art: Guy Francis

Publisher: Prescott V. Kelly

International Standard Book Number 978-1-889715-44-5

1-800-443-6078. www.writersbookstore.com
e-mail: services@writersbookstore.com

Printed and bound in Canada.

Table of Contents

Markets

The Ever-Transforming Landscape of Children's Books

By Molly Blaisdell

The landscape of the children's book publishing industry is as fluid and dynamic as the geography of the Earth itself. Constant changes transform the panorama in sometimes dramatic and sometimes subtle ways. Editors move to new houses, others retire, imprints fold, new ones are born, once hot topics fade, sluggish sales improve, sobering turns of events depress the industry, and hopeful events refresh it. Last year, like every year, had its own set of dynamics, adding another unique layer to the geography of children's books.

Two-Way Streets

One pervasive force shaping the landscape is the unifying of media. Speaking from 25 years of publishing experience, David Saylor, Vice President and Creative Director of Hardcover Books, and of the Graphix imprint at Scholastic, Inc., encapsulates this movement: "The biggest trends in publishing are about creating multimedia content that expands the world of the book into other areas simultaneously with the actual book release. *The 39 Clues: Maze of Bones*, by Rick Riordan, and *Skeleton Creek*, by Patrick Carman, are examples of this."

The 39 Clues is described by Scholastic as "a multi-platform adventure series for ages 8 to 12." Along with the simultaneous release of the first book in the U.S., U.K., Canada, Australia, and New Zealand, Scholastic Media launched an online game based on the book—"a globe-trotting treasure hunt"—and published collectible cards. *Skeleton*

Creek is a ghost story series the company describes as a "novel/Web-video hybrid."

Many other large publishing houses have expanded into multimedia

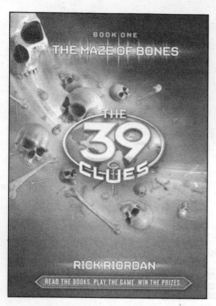

through formal arrangements with film companies: Random House has partnered with Focus Features on Random House Films; HarperCollins established Sharp Independent Pictures; and Simon & Schuster paired up with the Gotham Group. These kinds of agreements are generally two-way streets, bringing book properties to film and also turning film properties into books. These and other publishers also have alliances with audio production, toy, and gaming companies. The publishers have some form of graphic novel divisions, e-book divisions, audiobook divisions, and licensed character imprints, in addition to the various and more traditional multicultural, science fiction and fantasy, faith-based, educational, nonfiction, and general fiction imprints.

The crux is that children's book publishers today prefer to retain creative control of intellectual property—books and all of the other media a book spawns—within the parameters of one publishing program.

Writers are wise to consider their place in these complex publishing structures. The complexity, for instance, explains why many major houses will only look at agented writers, a policy that benefits the writer as much as the house. Agents help ensure that the writers receive equitable contracts that address multiple media formats.

Publisher David Fickling offered some guidance to writers during a telephone interview from his office in Oxford. Fickling is a 30-year industry veteran with his own imprint at Random House, and has been the editor of such luminaries as Philip Pullman and Mark Haddon. When asked if his imprint considers media tie-ins in the development of books, Fickling's answer was definitive: "Stories are chosen first." His firm belief is that other media forms unfold from meaningful stories that spark the imaginations of creative people. He stresses, "I'm not a filmmaker. Moral, ethical, informational, valuable, and profound materials are in stories and cannot be found elsewhere really. In the end, books are about good stories that ask the question, 'What happens next?' I'm interested in the answer." His advice is golden for writers. Place emphasis on writing good stories and let media spring from there.

"Children's book publishing has become more of a frontlist business than it ever was before."

Still, as the media opportunities widen for some books, the window of time for other books to succeed is smaller. With 25 years in the business, Allyn Johnston is Vice President and Publisher of her own Simon & Schuster imprint, Beach Lane Books. She says of the far-reaching changes in the children's market, "For a number of reasons, children's book publishing has become more of a frontlist business than it ever was before, which means that our books have much less time in which to succeed. Because of this, it can be tougher for us to take risks on books that may start more slowly, but that could have backlisted well and sold steadily in the school and library market for years." She offers insights into the challenges editors face. "The decision to acquire a book these days is more often accompanied by rigorous financial projections than it ever used to be, and we can't depend on the consistency of backlist sales as much as we used to when figuring out the financial picture of a book before we decide to buy it."

Financial challenges in the current economic climate impact small houses too. While they may not be able to extend their products to as wide a variety of media, small presses can still strategize to reduce risk. Donna German, Publisher and Editor of Sylvan Dell Publishing, acknowledges, "Bookstore sales are tough this year with the economy. We find that it is all the more imperative that each title we publish fit the niche and educational markets, which are stronger."

5

Book Marketing GPS

The creative use of technology to reach readers is a direction that will continue indefinitely. Tracking current marketing possibilities well can be like using a GPS. You may already know some of the established routes, but you could also find new paths through a new tool—and find a scenic, shorter, or more effective personal travelling plan.

Namrata Tripathi, Senior Editor of the Disney imprints Hyperion and Jump at the Sun, points to the new avenues of exploration: "With advances in new technologies, publishers are thinking about ways to enhance the reader's experience by using multiplatform approaches where appropriate—using MP3 play lists, online games, text message clues or updates, etc."

Vice President and Editorial Director David Gale explains a successful marketing program: "Simon & Schuster pioneered a teen author blog called Blogfest, in which teens posed questions each day for a few weeks. More than 125 teen authors posted their responses. We will continue to do this going forward as an annual online event."

New approaches also merge with old routes, according to Susan Van Metre, Editorial Director of Amulet Books. She says, "The Internet is connecting readers with authors in an unprecedented way. Using that tool, plus getting authors on the road [for marketing], has really helped us build a steady audience for our books, particularly for series such as the Sisters Grimm."

Author Justina Chen Headley also forged a new marketing path, as Alvina Ling, Senior Editor of Little, Brown Books for Young Readers, explains. "Justina has such a strong marketing background, and is able to think outside the box. She came to us with strong ideas, some of which she'd done the legwork for already, and strong contacts." One of the ideas was a tour she did with

Nina Hess is Senior Editor of Mirrorstone Books, the children's imprint of the fantasy fiction publisher Wizards of the Coast. She looks at the forces affecting mass-market publishers. "Walmart, Target, Costco, and other big box retailers are driving more book sales than ever before, and therefore publishers are developing projects that appeal to their demographics and needs."

Hess discusses the risk/reward ratio: "Publishing is the only industry where, if a retailer doesn't sell a product, they can return it to the producer at no cost. So, while a mass-market retailer can sell a lot of books,

Book Marketing GPS

Olympic Gold Medalist Hannah Teter for *Girl Overboard,* sponsored by Burton Snowboards. The tour and promotion included a challenge grant: a grant given to winners who "find the best youth-led ideas to change the world." But Ling cautions, "Unless you come from a marketing background, it would be best to leave the job to the publisher's marketing team."

Headley is also one of the founders of Readergirlz (www.readergirlz. com), along with Janet Lee Carey, Dia Calhoun, and Lorie Ann Grover, who have been joined by Mitali Perkins and Holly Cupala. Author of *A Light that Never Goes Out* (HarperCollins), Cupala offers a quick look at this pioneering program. "Our goal is to read great books celebrating gutsy girls, bring authors to readers, and reach out to our communities." Readergirlz accomplishes its goal by "hosting authors each month and during Teen Read Week in October; chatting in the Readergirlz forums; and in our newest venture, rgz TV: YouTube, [presenting] interviews with authors."

Readergirlz is an author platform much like Guys Read, the Web-based nonprofit literacy initiative for boys founded about ten years ago by National Ambassador for Young People's Literature, Jon Scieszka.

Cupala stresses the importance of an author's platform. "In this day and age, it's important to connect with readers on issues meaningful to them, on more than just a superficial level. It's not enough to say, 'Here's my book, hope you read it.' Teens want to know you care about more than just their credit card." Ling agrees about the importance of writers putting themselves out there for readers. "It's not crucial, but it sure helps! I think any way an author can raise their profile and get people to know their name and the names of their books is great."

there's also the potential for them to return a high number of books, which means the publisher is out a lot of money for printing more books than could be sold. For us, this means that going forward we're going to be investing in a smaller number of books so that we can give them all the marketing they need to succeed in the mass market."

Across the Planet

Beyond global changes that happen over years, one-time events create peaks and valleys in the publishing scenery. The merger of

Harcourt with Houghton Mifflin led to a cascade of new configurations. Harcourt was reborn as a Houghton Mifflin imprint, with Betsy Groban

> ## "We're acquiring across all ages and genres, but our primary focus is lyrical, emotionally engaging, highly visual picture books."

as the Senior Vice President and Publisher. Jeannette Larson was promoted to Editorial Director, Picture Books, and Kathy Dawson became Editorial Director, Fiction.

This merger also ultimately led Simon & Schuster to hire Johnston, the longtime Harcourt Editor in Chief, to head her Beach Lane Books imprint. Johnston's aim is to publish 18 to 20 books a year with a specific focus: "My colleague Andrea Welch and I will be acquiring across all ages and genres, with a primary focus on lyrical, emotionally engaging, highly visual picture books for young children—and the adults who love them."

Another shift in the landscape was the move of some of Hyperion's editorial staff to HarperCollins. Brenda Bowen formed her own HarperCollins imprint, Bowen Press. Its first list appeared in winter 2009, but the first single title was released earlier, for Earth Day. *MySpace/OurPlanet: Change Is Possible* is an innovative YA paperback that was printed on 100 percent post-consumer waste paper with soy-based inks. It was also the first MySpace-branded title, with the door open for more collaboration between Bowen Press and MySpace.

Two other former Hyperion editors also made the HarperCollins

New Imprints, Expanding Companies

➤ **Audible.com**'s new science fiction and fantasy imprint is **Audible Frontiers**.

➤ **Balzer & Bray** is a new **HarperCollins** imprint.

➤ **Barefoot Books** started a new Young Fiction Program featuring books about different cultures.

➤ **Beach Lane Books** is a new imprint of **Simon & Schuster**.

➤ **Bowen Press** is a new **HarperCollins** imprint.

➤ **Egmont USA** is the American line of the international company, **Egmont**.

➤ **Flash Point** is a new middle-grade and YA **Roaring Brook Press** imprint.

➤ **HarperCollins** and **Marvel Comics** joined to launch a new reading program based on Spider-Man.

➤ **Henry Holt** has a new imprint in the form of **Christy Ottaviano Books**.

➤ **Houghton Mifflin** restarted the **Sandpiper** paperback imprint for picture books and middle-grade books.

➤ **IDW** has started a new imprint called **Worthwhile Books**.

➤ **Kensington Publishing** has a new multicultural imprint, **Marimba Books**.

➤ **Little Simon** launched **Little Green Books**, on environmental subjects.

➤ **David Macaulay Studio** is also being launched by **Roaring Brook Press**.

➤ **MacKenzie Smiles** is a new U.S. publisher focusing on other cultures and countries.

➤ **Octopus Books** is a Hachette European-based company starting up in North America.

➤ **Mathew Price Ltd.** closed its U.K. office and moved to Texas.

➤ **Scholastic Trade** has started **Fourth Story Media**, integrating books and the Internet.

➤ **Sterling Publishing** and **Begin Smart Books** joined to start a new developmental reading program.

➤ **Stone Arch Books** has a new licensed book line based on **DC Comics** superheroes, targeting reluctant readers.

➤ **Tor Books** has a new manga imprint called **Seven Seas**.

move. Alessandra Balzer and Donna Bray joined as Co-Publishers of a new imprint, Balzer & Bray. According to Bray, "Our launch list is fall 2009, miraculously, with seven books—two picture books, one middle-grade, and three young adult novels." She is looking "for strong voices, fresh approaches, and original concepts—authentic, child-centered stories. I love humor even in a mostly serious book, and I appreciate stories that are a little irreverent and even subversive."

A bookend to these new HarperCollins imprints is a farewell to Joanna Cotler Books. Cotler ended a successful three-year run as publisher of her eponymous imprint. She will continue to edit a select few books as an Editor at Large.

Recent years have seen a flow of European publishing companies moving to the U.S., including Bloomsbury and Holtzbrink. Two of the latest pond jumpers are the Danish publisher Egmont and Britain's Mathew Price Ltd.

Now part of one of Europe's largest publishing companies, Egmont USA presents its first list of YA and middle-grade fiction, and picture books, as a division of Egmont UK. Elizabeth Law moved from Simon & Schuster to become Egmont USA's Vice President and Publisher, and Regina Griffin left her position as Editor in Chief at Holiday House to join as Executive Editor. Random House is handling the American distribution.

Griffin shares the company perspective: "Egmont's philosophy is to turn writers into authors, artists into illustrators, and children into passionate readers." The company also highly values philanthropy. "Egmont is committed to publish as ethically as we can. Many years ago our founder, Egmont Petersen, left the company to a foundation that supports children's and family issues and each year the profits that are not turned back into the companies go to the foundation." Environmental concerns are also carefully considered. "Not only a philanthropic company, Egmont also takes being green seriously. The head of production of our U.K. office recently received an award because she is a leader in that area among all publishers."

In its move, Mathew Price Ltd. closed its U.K. office and is making its global home in Denton, Texas. The company's initial U.S. list of 11 books is being distributed by Consortium. With a longtime motto of "education through delight," the company traditionally produces a list

that includes many pop-up and lift-the-flap books.

Aside from the European transplants, a couple of homegrown imprints have also appeared on the horizon. At Henry Holt Books for Young Readers, Christy Ottaviano is heading up an imprint that will publish literary and commercial picture books and fiction for all ages. When Christy Ottaviano Books was announced, she said, "The kinds of books that hold appeal are those that encourage imagination and free-thinking, foster a sense of family and community, target the feelings of children, and speak directly to children's interests as they explore various milestones." Ottaviano is looking for "fiction and nonfiction that make kids think, imagine, and question the world around them; books that speak to emotion, differences, and finding one's place and voice."

Another new imprint, which the Macmillan division Roaring Brook Press announced will launch in 2011, is David Macaulay Studio. The immediate impetus was the retirement of Walter Lorraine, Macaulay's editor at Houghton. The Studio will publish Creative Director Macaulay's own books, and titles by other authors and illustrators.

Roaring Brook Publisher Simon Boughton told *Publishers Weekly* that the Macaulay imprint is another step in Macmillan's recent effort to build its children's publishing business generally, and Roaring Brook's nonfiction specifically. Nancy Mercado joined Roaring Brook as Executive Editor, and Deirdre Langeland heads up the new Flash Point imprint, which publishes middle-grade and YA trade nonfiction. The first books on the imprint's list included *KidChat*, by Bret Nicholaus and Paul Lowrie, which pulls together interesting facts and questions, and a picture book biography by Catherine Brighton, *Keep Your Eye on the Kid: The Early Years of Buster Keaton.* Flash Point has also begun a history series with *King George: What Was His Problem? Everything Your*

New Story Visions

Every industry has its trends, and those in publishing are helpful markers for writers and editors; it is always wise to be informed. But many editors are not moved by trends in the market—they make them. Publisher of his eponymous Random House imprint, David Fickling thinks that the business world, including publishing, has it the wrong way around. Publishers should not put "the economic plow in front of the story horse," he says. Fickling finds the idea of marketing a book as a product just to make a profit abhorrent, and he feels it is "doom" to go out and try to create the next Harry Potter.

Patricia Lee Gauch, Vice President and Editor at Large of Philomel Books, also gives little weight to fashionable reading. "I have never been one for publishing to trends. My answer to such questions has always been, and still is, that a good book is a good book. The trend may not be historical fiction, but if it's fine historical fiction, it's time for a good book!" Joining the chorus is Molly O'Neill, Assistant Editor of HarperCollins's Bowen Press. "Trends come and go. Good writing is what never goes out of style, and no matter how complex the marketing and publicity plans created for any book, in the end, you always have to have a good story at the heart of it all in order for a book to truly endure."

Practicality and wisdom enter in, too. As Charlesbridge Publishing Senior Editor and Contracts Manager Emily Mitchell says, "By the time you notice a trend, it's too late to capitalize on it—the wheels of publishing move too slowly to piggyback on existing trends. We try to focus on the basics: good stories by great authors and illustrators. If we're lucky and catch a hot topic, great, but if we made that our business model, we'd all go crazy." Louise May, Editor in Chief of Lee & Low Books, wisely stresses, "To write to some perceived market need or trend, and not about something that really engages you, will not be fulfilling and will not yield your best writing. If your work has passion and authenticity, it will find its place and its champion."

"Atheneum doesn't publish topic-of-the-week books," says Caitlyn Dlouhy, Editorial Director. Her hope for titles is that readers would "feel forlorn when they are turning the last page, knowing they have to leave that world," and that readers feel an urgency to then share that book with their friends. "An ultimate goal is for emotional connections with Atheneum books to last through generations."

Schoolbooks Didn't Tell You About the American Revolution, by Steve Sheinkin.

Some existing lines are also growing and changing. Emily Mitchell, Senior Editor of Charlesbridge Publishing, says its latest list includes

"We've been acquiring more novels in the last five years, and I expect our list will soon become an even mix of picture books and novels."

"15 new titles. We have been ramping up our lists in recent years, from around 24 titles per year to 36 per year by 2010. The fall list was about evenly split between fiction and nonfiction, though historically the balance has been one-third fiction to two-thirds nonfiction. Eleven of our titles are picture books, and the remaining four are bridge books, our in-house term for longer books for older readers."

Lauri Hornik, Vice President and Publisher of Dial Books for Young Readers, works especially closely with her four editors, deciding with them which projects to acquire and offering feedback on all of the books in progress. "We have a new Senior Editor named Kate Harrison, who came to us from Harcourt," says Hornik. "She's very talented at both picture book and novel editing, and is interested in hybrids of the two. Kate is the editor of a super-fun summer 2009 book called *Dragonbreath,* by Ursula Vernon, which combines narrative, illustration, and comic book panels to tell its story."

Hornik says that Dial will publish about 55 books this year, about 60 percent of them picture books. She also provided a peek into the future. "We've been acquiring more and more novels in the last five years or so, and I expect that our list will soon become an even mix of picture books and novels (with the occasional nonfiction title thrown in too)."

Books on diversity continue to be a strong trend in the wide landscape of children's publishing, whatever the age. Namrata Tripathi, Senior Editor at the Hyperion imprint Jump at the Sun, which publishes books celebrating black culture, enthusiastically says, "Books reflect the changing face of the world and recently I've been happy to see more

Recent Print Runs

➤ James Patterson and Michael Ledwidge, *The Dangerous Days of Daniel X* (Little, Brown): 500,000 initial print run for a YA novel from the writer of blockbuster adult thrillers.

➤ Stephenie Meyer, *Breaking Dawn* (Little, Brown): 3.2 million first printing for the fourth and final book in the Twilight series; the largest first printing for a Hachette company book.

➤ Christopher Paolini, *Brisingr* (Alfred A. Knopf): 2.5 million, the largest first run ever for a children's book from Random House.

➤ Lisi Harrison, Clique Summer Collection, series (Poppy/Little, Brown): 350,000 first printing for each of five novellas.

➤ Roderick Gordon and Brian Williams, *Tunnels* (Scholastic/Chicken House): 100,000 first printing, three subsequent printings for a total of 250,000 copies in print.

➤ John Flanagan, *The Battle for Skandia* (Philomel): 150,000 first printing for the fourth book in the Ranger's Apprentice series.

➤ Sara Shepard, *Unbelievable* (HarperTeen): 150,000 first printing for book four in the Pretty Little Liars series.

➤ Michael Scott, *The Magician* (Random House): 150,000 first printing for the second book in the Secrets of the Immortal Nicholas Flamel series.

➤ Jay Asher, *Thirteen Reasons Why* (Penguin/Razorbill): First printing of 18,000 copies for this first novel, but after nine more press runs has sold more than 100,000.

➤ Ted Bell, *Nick of Time* (St. Martin's Press): 100,000 first printing for this first children's novel from the best-selling author of adult suspense.

books showing the diversity of the U.S. population and addressing important issues such as immigration."

YA Literature: Magnificent Mountains

Over the past decade, the field of young adult literature has transformed from a pastoral backwater into a series of magnificent mountains. With midnight book parties becoming the norm for blockbusters, numerous adult writers jumping into the YA fray, first print runs of more than than 100,000 becoming almost commonplace, and runs of more than a million books more frequent, it's clear to see that YA has reached the heights.

Among the reasons are gifted, caring editors who support authors as they grow. Another is the crossover adult appeal stemming from wider and more sophisticated treatment of important subject matter. The great reader interest in fantasy, which may now be shifting, is a third.

Alvina Ling, Senior Editor of Little, Brown Books for Young Readers, says, "I'm excited about Justina Chen Headley's third novel, *North of Beautiful*. I feel she's absolutely blossomed as a writer, and this is her best work yet." Ling shares her thoughts about the respect YA literature now receives in literary circles. "I think that with more adult authors writing children's books, and books such as the Harry Potter series, the Twilight series, *The Absolutely True Diary of a Part-time Indian*, by Sherman Alexie, and *The Book Thief*, by Markus Zusak, more readers [of all ages] are looking to the YA and children's section as a valid place to find good books to read. Children's books and young adult books are gradually gaining the respect they deserve from the literary world as a whole."

The increasing number of hard-hitting, controversial subjects in YA literature provides high potential for crossover adult appeal, says Ling. "We don't shy away from controversial topics and some content people might consider to be adult. I just acquired a young adult novel called *Freaks and Revelations*, by Davida Wills Hurwin. It is about two teenagers—one a homeless gay prostitute, the other a skinhead punk." The story follows the main characters through violence, sex, drugs, and strong language, and yet has a powerful redemptive core. Ling believes the book has "a lot of potential for crossover adult appeal, but the fact

that everyone involved thought that this should be published as a novel for teens says a lot about the respect for the genre."

The fantasy genre has also been a YA powerhouse for several years and added life to the market. That may be changing, however. David Gale, Vice President and Editorial Director of Simon & Schuster Books for Young Readers, says, "I think horror books are beginning to replace fantasy, which has been dominating the market."

Karen Wojtyla, Editorial Director of the Simon & Schuster imprint Margaret K. McElderry Books, is "seeing a lot of teen fantasy right now, understandably, but I'd like to see more reality-based fiction and more middle-grade novels. We publish pretty selectively, as our list is not large. But we don't limit ourselves to literary fiction, whatever that really means! I like books that present something intriguing that I might not know about, culturally or historically. But I also like zingy di-

"I'll be on the lookout for work-for-hire writers with a background in traditional epic fantasy for middle-graders and young adults."

alogue and fun characters, and comedies. For all three, you can check out Hilary McKay's Casson family books."

Even with some sense the fantasy market is reaching a saturation point, there still seems to be room for a good fantasy title, especially at fantasy niche publishers such as Wizards of the Coast. At its Mirrorstone Books imprint, Senior Editor Nina Hess discusses an upcoming book, *The Stowaway: Stone of Tymora, Volume I,* by R. A. and Geno Salvatore. "R. A. Salvatore is a huge name in adult fantasy fiction with his best-selling Legend of Drizzt series. Now, he's partnered with his son to write his first book for young readers. The book has all the elements of a classic fantasy adventure," says Hess.

Mirrorstone is undergoing a shift in its publishing program, however. "Our list will focus more exclusively on publishing books for young readers inspired by the lore of the Dungeons & Dragons game (produced by Wizards of the Coast), to take advantage of the cross-marketing potential," says Hess. "I'll be on the lookout for work-for-hire writers with a background in writing traditional epic fantasy for middle-graders and young adults. Many writers have the misconception that they need to know something about the Dungeons & Dragons game to work with us. It's appreciated for sure, but it's not a requirement."

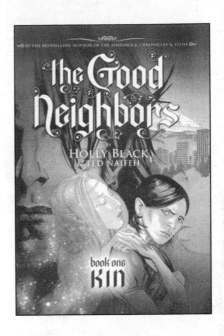

Lee & Low Books, known for its children's books on cultural diversity, is just entering the teen market. Editor in Chief Louise May says, "This fall we published our first original YA release—*Alicia Afterimage*, by Lulu Delacre. It is an exploration of teen grief after the death of the author's 16-year-old daughter in a car accident."

Graphic Novels Terraform the Environment

The awarding of the Caldecott Medal last year to Brian Selznick's *The Invention of Hugo Cabret*—a unique melding of picture book and novel—was a formal acknowledgement of the literary merit to be found in graphic novels. The eruption of the graphic novel form in traditional children's publishing has virtually terraformed the industry.

"While kids have always loved comics, the change over the last three years is that every major publisher is now creating comics for kids. This is a category of mainstream children's publishing that didn't really exist pre-2005," says Scholastic's Saylor, who heads up the graphic novel imprint Graphix. He touches on the trend for established authors to create

Graphic Novel Publishers

➤ **Amulet Books:** Abrams Books imprint. *Nat Turner,* Kyle Baker.

➤ **Bowen Press:** HarperCollins imprint. *Gettysburg: The Graphic Novel,* C. M. Butzer; *Emily the Strange,* Rob Reger.

➤ **Candlewick Press:** *Beowulf,* Gareth Hinds.

➤ **Charlesbridge Publishing:** *The Legend of Hong Kil Dong: The Robin Hood of Korea,* Anne Sibley O'Brien.

➤ **DK Graphic Readers:** Historical fiction: *The Price of Victory* and *The Terror Trail,* Stewart Ross.

➤ **First Second Books:** Roaring Brook Press (Macmillan) graphic novel imprint. *American Born Chinese,* Gene Luen Yang; *Slow Storm,* Danica Novgorodoff; *Gus,* Chris Blain.

➤ **Graphic Universe:** Lerner Publishing imprint. Graphic Myths and Legends series: *Ali Baba,* Marie P. Croall, illus., Clint Hilinski.

➤ **Graphix:** Scholastic imprint. Graphic novel versions of the Baby-Sitters Club, Goosebumps, and Bone series. Scholastic's Arthur A. Levine imprint also published Australian author Shaun Tan's graphic novels, *The Arrival* and *Tales from Outer Suburbia.*

➤ **HarperCollins:** Converted series such as the Time Warp Trio.

➤ **Holiday House:** *Wuv Bunnies from Outers Pace,* David Elliott and Ethan Long.

➤ **Hyperion:** Elizabeth Lenhard's graphic W.I.T.C.H. series; *Houdini: The Handcuff King,* Jason Lutes, illus., Nick Bertozzi.

➤ **Penny-Farthing Press:** Small press for comics and children's books. The Loch Trilogy, Marlaine Maddux; Captain Gravity series, Stephen Vrattos.

➤ **Random House Books for Young Readers:** Babymouse series, Jennifer and Matt Holm.

➤ **Seven Seas:** Tor Books imprint. Science fiction and fantasy series such as Hollow Fields, Madeleine Rosca; Amazing Agent Luna, Nunzio DeFilippis and Christina Weir; and others.

➤ **Simon & Schuster:** *A House Divided* (Turning Points American history series), Marshall Poe, illus., Leland Purvis; *Chiggers,* Hope Larson.

➤ **Stone Arch Books:** Partnership with DC Comics. Tiger Moth series, Aaron Reynolds.

➤ **Yen Press:** Little, Brown manga and graphic novels. *Sarasah,* Ryang Ruy; *One Fine Day,* Sirial; adaptations of Cirque du Freak series.

graphic novels. "Graphix has published Holly Black's first graphic novel, *The Good Neighbors,* illustrated by Ted Naifeh. Holly is very well-known for her middle-grade and young adult novels, but she's also now ventured into the graphic novel area with an exciting fantasy about a teenager caught between two worlds, her mother's faerie realm and the human world of her father."

Many other houses have wholeheartedly embraced graphic novels. Susan Van Metre, Editorial Director of the Amulet Books imprint of Abrams Books for Young Readers, says her company is developing a broad list of graphic novels that includes *Meanwhile*, by Jason Shiga, and *Hereville: How Mirka Got Her Sword,* by Barry Deutsch.

Mitchell cites Charlesbridge Publishing's *Unite or Die*, written by Jacqueline Jules and illustrated by Jef Czekaj. It "tells the story of the writing of the U.S. Constitution using the conceit of a school play. Thirteen kid characters play the parts of each state, and there are a whole lotta word balloons going on."

Graphic *novels* aren't all fiction, in fact. Molly O'Neill, Assistant Editor at Bowen Press, describes a title with a strong nonfiction slant. *"Gettysburg: The Graphic Novel,* by C. M. Butzer, is a graphic novel-style portrayal of the Gettysburg address and the events of the Civil War leading up to it. It shows the relevance of an age-old battle in a stunning new way."

Another trend is the creation of graphic versions of successful novels. Little, Brown's Ling says, "Although I don't work on these books myself, with the launch of our graphic novel/manga imprint Yen Press last year, we've started to look at our books and adapt them into graphic novels. Examples are the horror series Cirque du Freak, Gossip Girl, and James Patterson's Maximum Ride."

Caitlyn Dlouhy, Editorial Director of Atheneum Books for Young Readers, has an insightful take on the emergence—or re-emergence—of graphic novels for children. She points out that in the past, many younger middle-grade books were beautifully illustrated, a format that had since almost disappeared. "Graphic novels are making an old idea new again," Dlouhy says, "in that suddenly more and more books for younger readers, such as *The Underneath, The Tale of Despereaux,* and *The Seven Wonders of Sassafras Springs* are illustrated with black-and-white art."

Science fiction and fantasy publisher Tor Books entered the U.S. manga market last year, and is publishing the Japanese-style comics under its Seven Seas Entertainment imprint. Its titles will primarily be licensed from popular Japanese series.

Holiday House has produced an entry in the graphic novel arena as well. Mary Cash, Vice President and Editor in Chief, says, "We just published our first graphic novel, *Wuv Bunnies from Outers Pace*, by humorist David Elliott with art by illustrator and animator Ethan Long. This project started out as a chapter book. However, the illustrator's interpretation of the story led him to make it into a longer and more visual work. Fortunately, when the author saw the direction the illustrator was taking, he was thrilled. These are the kind of talent-driven evolutions that can be very exciting."

Exploring Middle-Grade Country

While YAs have flourished in recent years, middle-grade fiction has languished some, but the vista for readers from about age eight to the teen years may be changing. Many industry insiders are feeling new energy in what has become undiscovered country.

At Lee & Low Books, May says simply, "For several years YA has been the hot genre. Now middle-grade is the genre that is receiving more attention." McElderry's Wojtyla echoes the sentiment, and wants to see more middle-grade novel submissions.

"Middle-grade fiction is strong right now, particularly fantasy," says Rosemary Brosnan, Executive Editor of HarperCollins Children's Books. She thinks that middle-grade fiction is picking up, and she is interested in acquiring more. "That's a genre I love (I edit the wonderful Gail Carson Levine), and so I am looking for more of it. It's something I enjoy

very much that is doing well. I'm not doing many picture books at all, but mainly focusing on fiction for middle-graders and young adults."

Hornik notes a favorite middle-grade title and its new sequel. "The novel *Emma-Jean Lazarus Fell Out of a Tree*, by Lauren Tarshis, is one of my favorite Dial books in a very long time. It's a middle-grade novel with a unique but fully believable and lovable main character, and such universality to the emotions and relationships, despite Emma-Jean's quirkiness." The follow-up title is *Emma-Jean Lazarus Fell in Love*.

A subgenre of middle-grade that also crosses into younger books,

"For several years, YA has been the hot genre. Now, middle-grade is the genre that is receiving more attention."

chapter books generally span ages six to ten. The short chapters bridge the river between early readers and the fluency needed for novels with longer chapters. An upcoming example from Charlesbridge weaves illustration with text in a style that is both old and new, says Mitchell. "I'm working on a chapter book by Janet Wong, *Me and Rolly Maloo*, that includes traditional chapter book text and spot illustrations, as well as intertextual graphic *novel-y* sections offering the back story on different characters. Elizabeth Buttler is the illustrator; she's just working on sketches now, and I think it's going to be a beautiful, brilliant book."

At the Canadian publisher Fitzhenry & Whiteside, Editor Ann Featherstone is excited about the innovations in a new upper middle-grade title. "The free verse novel is hardly innovative in the U.S., but we have seen only a few published in Canada, so Alma Fullerton's *Libertad* represents an exciting direction for us."

Vibrancy is the word for middle-grade fiction today, says Griffin. One of her favorites on Egmont's inaugural list is by Kristin Venuti. "*Leaving the Bellweathers* is a middle-grade debut novel about a charmingly odd family that lives in a lighthouse and their much aggrieved and very proper butler, who is desperate to leave them. That novel combines the

Recent Picture Book Bestsellers

➤ *Alphabet,* Matthew Van Fleet (Paula Wiseman/Simon & Schuster)

➤ *Barack Obama: Son of Promise, Child of Hope,* Nikki Grimes, illus., Bryan Collier (Simon & Schuster)

➤ *Big Words for Little People,* Jamie Lee Curtis (Joanna Cotler/HarperCollins)

➤ *Born to Read,* Judy Sierra, illus., Marc Brown (Knopf/Random House)

➤ *Fairies and Magical Creatures,* Matthew Reinhart, Robert Sabuda (Candlewick)

➤ *Fancy Nancy: Bonjour Butterfly,* Jane O'Connor, illus., Robin Preiss Glasser (HarperCollins)

➤ *Gallop!,* Rufus Butler Seder (Workman)

➤ *Gingerbread Friends,* Jan Brett (Putnam)

➤ *Goodnight Goon: A Petrifying Parody,* Michael Rex (Putnam)

➤ *Knuffle Bunny Too,* Mo Willems (Hyperion/Disney)

➤ *Ladybug Girl,* Jacky Davis, illus., David Soman (Dial Books)

➤ *Let's Dance, Little Pookie,* Sandra Boynton (Random House)

➤ *Louise, The Adventures of a Chicken,* Kate DiCamillo, illus., Harry Bliss (Joanna Cotler/HarperCollins)

➤ *My Dad, John McCain,* Meghan McCain (Aladdin/Simon & Schuster)

➤ *On a Scary Scary Night* (Can You See What I See?), Walter Wick (Cartwheel Books/Scholastic)

➤ *The 7 Habits of Happy Kids,* Sean Covey, illus., Stacy Curtis (Simon & Schuster)

➤ *Smash! Crash!,* Jon Scieszka, illus., David Shannon, Loren Long, David Gordon (Simon & Schuster)

➤ *Splat the Cat,* Rob Scotton (HarperCollins)

➤ *Tea for Ruby,* Sarah Ferguson (Paula Wiseman Books/Simon & Schuster)

➤ *Ten Little Fingers and Ten Little Toes,* Mem Fox, illus., Helen Oxenbury (Harcourt)

➤ *Too Many Toys,* David Shannon (Blue Sky Press/Scholastic)

➤ *A Visitor for Bear,* Bonny Becker, illus., Kady Macdonald Denton (Candlewick)

➤ *We the People: The Story of Our Constitution,* Lynne Cheney, illus., Greg Herlin (Simon & Schuster)

➤ *Zen Ties,* Jon J. Muth (Scholastic Press)

spirit of the great old Elizabeth Enright, or Eleanor Estes books, with the arch, modern tone of Lemony Snicket."

Picture Book Flatlands

The picture book landscape has been in a long-term drought. Sales of picture books have remained sluggish, and those titles that make the most news, and achieve the highest numbers, tend to be celebrity

> "Even though the prevailing wisdom is that picture books are not doing well, illustrated books are our mainstay and they are thriving."

books and popular series. Notably, author and actress Jamie Lee Curtis's latest picture book, *Big Words for Little People* (Joanna Cotler/Harper-Collins), had a print run of 500,000 copies. *If You Give a Cat a Cupcake* (Laura Geringer/HarperCollins), the new entry in Laura Numeroff and Felicia Bond's ever popular If You Give . . . series, had an initial print run of a million copies.

Simon & Schuster's Gale succinctly says, "Yes, although some individual picture books do well, overall the market is flat, so we are publishing fewer picture books and more novels, which are still selling well." Griffin has a similar take: "Picture books, alas, still remain flat—if they're not sinking, and it is partly due to that reason that Egmont USA will focus on middle-grade books and up for its first few lists."

Though the prospects may seem disheartening, remember that picture books are still selling and some houses are still interested in stories for younger children. Johnston's Beach Lane Books is focusing mainly on picture books. "We will be publishing 18 to 20 titles per year, most of which will be picture books. We will be publishing books by established authors and illustrators such as Mem Fox, Marla Frazee, Lois Ehlert, Douglas Florian, and Cynthia Rylant, as well as people newer to the field, such as Brian Biggs, Jan Thomas, and Liz Garton Scanlon."

23

Nonfiction-Only Publishers

- **Adams Media:** YA self-help and inspirational titles.
- **Avocus Publishing:** Homeschooling books.
- **Benchmark Books/Marshall Cavendish:** Educational books, all grades.
- **Capstone Press:** Reading-development books on all curriculum topics.
- **Chelsea House:** Curriculum-based titles for middle and high school.
- **Children's Press:** Scholastic. School and library series for grades K-8.
- **Creative Learning Press:** Creative thinking skills at all grade levels.
- **Crown Books:** Random House. Educational children's and YA nonfiction.
- **Dawn Publications:** Nature.
- **DK Publishing:** Children's reference books and other nonfiction.
- **Douglas & McIntyre:** Canadian regional and natural history, First Nations art and culture.
- **Enslow Publishers:** Curriculum-based series for all ages.
- **Facts on File:** Reference books and curriculum-based nonfiction. The Ferguson imprint publishes books on careers.
- **Franklin Watts:** Scholastic imprint. Middle-grade and YA.
- **Fairview Press:** Physical, emotional, spiritual health.
- **Free Spirit Publishing:** Solution-based learning to support emotional and social development.
- **Gifted Education Press:** Materials for gifted students.
- **Globe Pequot Press:** Nature, regional, sports.
- **Goodheart-Willcox:** Technical/trades/technology education and how-to.
- **Greenhaven Press:** Thomson Gale. YA history, social issues, biography, literary criticism.
- **Hazelden Foundation:** Substance abuse.
- **HCI Books:** Life issues, recovery, personal growth.
- **Hunter House:** YA personal growth, health and wellness.
- **Impact Publishers:** Middle-grade and YA psychology, self-esteem, life issues, behavior.
- **Jossey-Bass:** John Wiley. Unusual topics, innovative formats on many subjects for beginning readers to YA.
- **KidHaven Press:** Thomson Gale. Middle-grade educational nonfiction.

Nonfiction-Only Publishers

➤ **Lark Books:** Wide variety of fun nonfiction for preK to YA.

➤ **Leadership Publishers:** Accelerated and enrichment materials, K-12.

➤ **Learning Horizons:** Educational material for preK-6.

➤ **Lucent Books:** Thomson Gale. Middle and high school nonfiction.

➤ **Maple Tree Press:** Science, nature, humor, crafts. Canadian authors.

➤ **Millbrook Press:** Lerner Publishing. Elementary school math, science, social studies, multicultural.

➤ **Mitchell Lane:** Nonfiction for reluctant readers.

➤ **Morgan Reynolds:** Middle-grade and YA biographies and other nonfiction.

➤ **Mountain Press:** Nature, history, Earth science.

➤ **National Geographic Society:** Exploring the world, ages four to YA.

➤ **Newmarket Press:** Health and nutrition, middle-grade and YA.

➤ **Perigee Books:** Penguin. Self-help, how-to, reference.

➤ **Peter Pauper Press:** Activity books on natural history and science.

➤ **Phoenix Learning Resources:** Educational skill development.

➤ **PowerKids Press:** Rosen Publishing. Elementary and middle-grade educational series.

➤ **Prometheus Books:** Critical thinking, social, moral, sexual, religious, scientific issues for elementary and middle school children.

➤ **Rosen Publishing:** Middle-grade and YA guidance and curriculum-based subjects.

➤ **Science, Naturally!:** Science and math in everyday life.

➤ **Stemmer House:** Illustrated nonfiction on art, history, geography.

➤ **Twenty-First Century Books:** Lerner Publishing. Middle-grade and high school series.

➤ **Two-Can Publishing:** History, science, math, culture.

➤ **UXL:** Thomson Gale. Reference for upper-elementary to high school.

➤ **J. Weston Walch:** Teaching aids for middle and high school subjects.

➤ **Watson-Guptill:** Art, architecture, entertainment, middle-grade and YA.

➤ **Weigl Publishers:** Visual, integrated resources on science, social studies, language arts, sports.

➤ **Wiley Children's Books:** John Wiley. Science, math, history, nature.

Christy Ottaviano's imprint at Henry Holt is publishing about 20 books a year, half of them picture books and the remaining half middle-grade and YA fiction. Ottaviano says, "In terms of picture books, I like preschool stories, those that are concept-driven, projects with an underlying curriculum connection, as well as those that feature quirky humor."

Dial Books continues to have a strong picture book list, but the focus has changed over the last few years. "We're most interested in stories that speak to universal preschooler experiences, and that are written in a boppy, concise way," Hornik explains. "This is a recent departure from Dial's previous focus, which had been on longer, more informational picture books. Those books are quite rare on our list now."

Wojtyla describes the qualities she looks for at Margaret K. McElderry. "For picture books, we look for kid-friendly books with lively stories and fun art. We also publish books that have more of an educational component, but only if that comes in a way that's engagingly written and illustrated."

Allison Remcheck, Editorial Assistant, offers examples illustrative of the Macmillan imprint Feiwel and Friends. "In the picture book category, our fall list includes *The Happiness Tree: Celebrating the Gifts of Trees We Treasure,* by Andrea Gosline and illustrated by Lisa Burnett Bossi, and *Splash! A Little Book about Bouncing Back,* by Maria van Lieshout. These books, as well as other picture books on our list, represent the kind of fresh and enduring content, art, and format of our picture books."

Small presses support the genre too. Illumination Arts is a regional press that specializes in inspirational picture books. President John Thompson says, "One of our upcoming titles is *Sparky and the Magic Blue Ribbon,* the story of Helice (Sparky) Bridges, whose foundation has assisted in more than 30 million people worldwide being honored with blue ribbons that say 'Who I Am Makes a Difference.'" Illumination Arts currently has an acquisitions logjam, however. "Right now we are backed up about two years on moving forward with new manuscripts."

Thompson believes one of the great successes in children's publishing also negatively affected picture book sales, especially those for older readers. "The picture book market was set back a bit by the Harry Potter craze. There is an all too common feeling that 'My child is reading

Harry Potter so he or she is not interested in picture books.'"

May tempers the negative with hopeful daring. "Even though the prevailing wisdom in trade markets is that picture books are not doing as well as books for older readers, illustrated books are our mainstay and they are thriving. We push the envelope with the kinds of stories we tell in this format, for both fiction and nonfiction topics." Her view is revealing. Authors need to strive to create lively, groundbreaking picture books.

Nonfiction's Well-Kept Garden

The volcanic transformation in children's nonfiction is now two decades old, and the soil produced is the basis of a still fertile garden. The nonfiction eruption was marked in part by the striking quality and innovation of Russell Freedman's *Lincoln: A Photobiography* (Houghton Mifflin) and by the rapid growth of Dorling Kindersley, now DK Publishing and owned by the Penguin Group, and especially by its line of Eyewitness Books.

The flourishing nonfiction garden is varied, well-cultivated, and even artfully arranged. Nonfiction today has come to be all about specializing and refining facts in ways that engage children immediately and imaginatively, and is increasingly full of innovative, hybridized plants. An example comes from Fickling: "*Aidan Potts Takes on Recycling* is a new way to look at nonfiction that invites participation and thinking."

Lee & Low's unique titles range from picture book biographies to graphic novel treatments of nonfiction, all reflecting the company's focus on multiculturalism and diversity. "We have several exciting picture book biographies—Isamu Noguchi, Bob Marley, Anna May Wong, to name a few. The most innovative is a middle-grade graphic novel based on the life of a 12-year-old gang member," says May. Other recent biographies from the company are *The Last Black King of the Kentucky Derby,* by Crystal Hubbard, illustrated by Robert McGuire, and *Honda: The Boy Who Dreamed of Cars,* by Mark Weston, illustrated by Katie Yamasaki.

"*Lincoln Shot: A President's Life Remembered,* written by Barry Denenberg and illustrated by Christopher Bing, is a unique package," says Remcheck. The Feiwel and Friends biography is "a large (12 x 18 inches) hardcover book, presented as a newspaper published one year after Lincoln's death. The design reflects an 1860s newspaper, and it includes actual Civil War-era photographs, as well as stunning art from Caldecott honoree Christopher Bing."

Mitchell remarks on the flurries of nonfiction books on the same topics released in the same time-

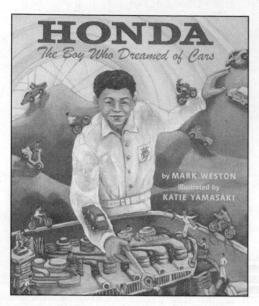

frame. "I think a lot of emphasis is placed on anniversaries these days: lots of Wright Brothers books in 2003, lots of Lincoln books in 2009," on the two-hundreth anniversary of his birth. "That's not necessarily a bad thing—when done right, you can get a sales boost on first publication, and become a steady backlist seller on that topic—but it can tempt people to push a book through too quickly, before it's really as good as it can be, to meet that anniversary date." Charlesbridge's recent nonfiction titles include *Reign of the Sea Dragons*, by Sneed Collard III, illustrated by Andrew Plant, and *Asian Art*, by Kimberly Lane.

Hybrids of nonfiction and fiction are popular today, with editors and readers. Small press Sylvan Dell Publishing offers books with a unique blend, says Editor and Publisher Donna German. "The picture books that we publish are usually, but not always, fictional stories that relate to animals, nature, the environment, and science. All books should subtly convey an educational theme through a warm story that is fun to read and will grab a child's attention. Each book has a three- to five-page section called For Creative Minds to reinforce the educational component of the book itself."

German is full of the enthusiasm for Sylvan Dell's books and authors that perhaps only a small house can offer. "As a small press, we have to believe 100 percent in each of the ten titles we publish a year. Of the ten 2009 titles, three are math- and nature-based, one marine-related, four about animal adaptation and survival, one an animal rescue, and—new to us—a retelling of Mother Goose tales from a marine perspective."

Black Dog & Leventhal, a Workman Publishing imprint, publishes "beautifully (and often cleverly or innovatively) produced nonfiction books that will reach a wide audience," says Elizabeth Van Doren, Editor in Chief of the children's book line. She looks for "innovative nonfiction, either as a series or as single titles. The series we've been very successful with is Get Ready for School. We just published three more titles in that series with write-on/wipe-off pages, pens, memory cards, and stickers."

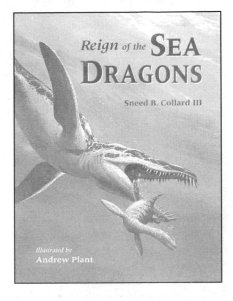

Cash discusses Holiday House's nonfiction forte: "Our school and library market is our greatest strength. We view teachers and librarians as our colleagues and want to provide the kinds of books that will support them. The nonfiction we publish reflects this." Inventive design is central. "I think that the design of all books continues to become more important. People can get pure information online. They often want reading a book to be a more aesthetic experience. Nonfiction, in particular, is becoming more visual."

She finished by explaining how this new emphasis on design is affecting the production process. "We are paying more attention to our designs and illustrations. We are looking for innovative approaches to nonfiction. We are letting our illustrators and authors lead the way to new formats and design ideas."

From long range trends to one-time events, and including snapshots of various genres, this whirlwind tour of the landscape of children's books reveals the current vibrancy of the children's book industry. Writing and submitting in this environment may seem like charting a course across impassable terrain. Consider this market overview a jumping-off place. Journey on, focusing on learning the breadth and depth of your favorite genres. Read the books that interest you, pass on books that do not, and educate yourself with a goal to be an expert navigator in your field.

Keep an eye on burgeoning multimedia. There will always be a place for books, but writers must recognize the forces vying for reader attention. Do not underestimate the abilities and interests of your audience; infuse your work with vigor in answer to their sophisticated, if young, tastes. Avoid the vapid currents of trends and write your own original stories as only you can tell them. Finally, never lose sight of the greatest part of your journey—writing a story that is a reflection of your essential voice. Be keenly aware that your creation is your corner of the children's publishing landscape, a place only you can carve out.

Staying Afloat: Magazines Launch, Adapt, & Survive in Changing Times

By Pamela Holtz Beres

G ood news is hard to find. With gas prices topping out in excess of $4.00 a gallon for a time, death knells ringing for major financial institutions, and the mortgage industry a mess, economic news dominates the headlines. Airline, automotive, and related industries have been hard hit, and unemployment and inflation are rising nationwide. While families struggle to feed their families, heat their homes, and pay their bills, tough times have befallen the magazine industry.

Consumers are cutting back on extras, including impulse buys such as magazines picked up in the checkout aisle. That fact, stated an Audit Bureau of Circulations (ABC) report, is among the reasons newsstand magazine sales fell 6.3 percent in the first half of last year. ABC tracks 467 consumer magazines, using ad pages and circulation figures as indicators of magazine health. When subscription and newsstand sales are down, advertising rates go down too. While there had been a general feeling that there would be better news to report later in the year, that hope faded when figures began emerging.

Yet, undaunted by industry news and predictions of declines, a large number of new magazines have also debuted, and several begun within the last several years are flourishing. Commonalities among the successful publications are the founders' passion, a tight focus on a particular market, and a clear plan for moving forward.

31

The Ups and Downs of Children's Numbers

While many children's magazines do not rely on advertising or newsstand sales, if the big, glossy publications are having a difficult time keeping sales figures up, smaller children's magazines dependent on subscriptions may also be struggling to maintain circulation or find necessary funding.

Even the robust teen market figures fell. ABC reported that circulation at *CosmoGirl!* and *Seventeen* was down 1.4 percent, and *J-14* was down 4.7 percent. By the end of the year, Hearst Magazines had announced it would close *CosmoGirl!* and fold its subscribers into *Seventeen*. Only *Teen Vogue* saw an increase of 4.5 percent. The year-to-date

> Credit one magazine's longevity to its willingness to improve content to meet readers' needs—and to its shift toward a younger market with increased purchasing power.

numbers reported by the Publishers Information Bureau (PIB), an affiliate of the Magazine Publishers of America (MPA), showed parallel news concerning advertising revenues. *Nickelodeon* and *National Geographic Kids* were both down almost 40 percent in ad pages; the decline at *Sports Illustrated for Kids* was about 30 percent; at *Boys' Life*, 9.4 percent; *Twist*, 8.1 percent; and *Seventeen*, down 5.7 percent. Parenting magazine *FamilyFun*, however, was up 7.1 percent and *Scholastic Parent & Child* up 55.7 percent.

Yet Nina B. Link, MPA President and Chief Executive, told the *New York Times* in September, "We feel magazines are holding their own, relative to the state of the economy." Writers can hold their own, too, but that means a combination of putting more effort into the business side of their careers, and continuing to improve their writing and overall ability to meet editor needs at the right times and in the right ways.

In tough economic times, it's especially critical to keep up with market news—to track changes; dig deeply to discover the impact on

Identifying Healthy Markets

➤ What categories are flourishing?

➤ What categories are seeing new launches?

➤ Which magazines have cut their staff or had changes in staff?

➤ Which magazines have redesigned their formats?

➤ Which markets have changed their submissions guidelines, and in what way?

➤ What markets are buying more material than in the past? What markets are buying less?

➤ In markets that are buying, what type of material are they most receptive to seeing from freelancers?

market segments and on individual publications; and then tailor ideas, research, and submissions appropriately. Writers must ask questions such as those listed in the sidebar to identify the healthiest markets and keep their freelance careers alive.

Good news comes from Karen Bokram, CEO of *GL* (*Girls' Life*), for instance. She says that despite gloomy industrywide reports, she would describe her year as successful. "Our sales are up by 16 percent," she says. Aimed at girls ages 10 to 15, *GL* offers its readers advice on friends, fashion, and beauty, as well as celebrity interviews and quizzes. Keeping its finger on the pulse of readers' changing needs, the bimonthly introduced a redesign with its August/September issue. Bokram notes that no content has been omitted, but fashion and beauty pages have been added. *GL* now has more of a focus on style trends, advice for finding fashion on a budget, and fashions that enhance the reader's body type.

While Bokram credits the magazine's longevity—15 years in print—to a willingness to improve content as needed to meet readers' needs, *GL*'s success may also be attributed partially to a shift toward a younger market with increased purchasing power.

The current icons of tween power may be Miley Cyrus and the Jonas Brothers, but market strength is really in the kids themselves. According to U.S. Census Bureau estimates, teens 15 to 19 comprise 7.2 percent of the population (second only to the Boomer generation) and tweens, ages 10 to 14, are right behind at 6.9 percent. As long as the adult world continues to fill kids' wants and needs—perhaps more questionable in the current economic climate—the magazine market may reap the benefits as attention focuses on tweens as an age group and the spending follows them through to young adulthood and beyond.

Bright New Markets

The girl market is strong enough that Pamela Holley-Bright saw an opportunity for a new magazine for African American teens. *Faithful Sister* targets ages 11 to 22. Holley-Bright created the magazine as a senior in high school. "It was prom time and I didn't find any magazines that catered to African American girls. I was also tired of seeing celebrities on magazine covers." While the magazine covers fashion, beauty, and health, it aims to go much deeper. "*Faithful Sister* was created to empower young African American women and discuss issues in our community—real issues. They love reading about other women who have faced what they face, and they love reading spiritual and inspirational stories." Recent articles have covered body image, academic success among black students, and the serious side of flirting.

The success of any magazine is ultimately dependent on the publisher knowing its readership and editors fulfilling audience interests and needs. Start-ups therefore look for unfilled segments of the market,

as Holley-Bright did.

Jacquitta McManus also identified a specific audience and genre she thinks is underserved in creating *Labyrinth's Door*, a middle-grade fantasy and adventure magazine featuring African American characters and writers. Her decision to write children's stories, and eventually to publish *Labyrinth's Door,* sprang from a desire to create characters to whom her daughter could relate. McManus's research for a children's series led her to discover that most titles for African American children are biographies, historical fiction, contemporary fiction, and concept books. Realizing, too, that writing and publishing a book series was a long-range goal, she devised a plan that would help her realize her dreams sooner: Launch a magazine.

"The goal was to develop a fantasy/adventure magazine with great stories. In connection with that, I also hope to feature African American writers, and there will be stories with African American characters." McManus developed a business plan that fit her purpose and would allow her to begin publishing quickly; she presented the plan to a business counselor, got a positive response, and moved forward.

The bimonthly targets ages 8 to 14 with imaginative stories that allow readers to adventure through enchanted worlds. *Labyrinth's Door* looks for fantasy adventure and science fiction submissions in lengths that range from 500 to 5,000 words, and poetry to 50 lines. McManus prefers to receive a query first, indicating word count, and a one-page writing sample. Payment is up to 20 cents a word on publication.

Passion for the future and the well-being of young adults led Bryan Sims to begin *brass* magazine. "Prior to launching *brass,* I had created a teen investment club in high school, and saw what a void there was for making money interesting to young adults." Based on the premise that it is crucial that teens know how money affects their lives, *brass* aims at college students and those beginning their careers, and is also distributed to high school students nationwide. "We view our demographic as 16 to 25 years of age, the time period when people are just starting to go through their firsts in life: first job, first car, college, etc.," says Sims.

Behind the bold and glossy *brass* package are articles that help young readers plan for retirement, throw parties, and everything in between. Subjects include issues that impact young adults' ability to make money; personal improvement topics such as time management, goal-setting, leadership, and motivation; professional advancement; educational progress; issues concerning what young adults choose to do with their money, and getting the most out of it, whether with gear (technology, equipment), fashion, sports and recreation, entertainment, relationships, health and fitness, or travel; using money to make more money; and profiles of inspiring young adults.

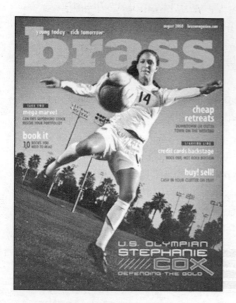

Sims credits the magazine's success after a couple of years to his employees, customers, investors, and readers, but also says, "The foundation of *brass* is that we're dedicated to helping young adults better understand money, and that's something people can get behind universally." He believes it is also key to fill the magazine with content written, photographed, and designed by peers, so that readers feel the magazine is meeting them eye to eye in their own world. Sims is actively looking for contributors.

From things of the world to things of the spirit: Elizabeth Dabney Hochman has put her passion and plan into producing a new, nondenominational, spiritual magazine, *KidSpirit*. The first quarterly issue was timed for back-to-school. "I started *KidSpirit* because I felt that in our society, the media reflects the values we pass on to teens," says Dabney Hochman, who argues that too many magazines are low on substance. "I believe [young readers] need a new vehicle. *KidSpirit* is one way to empower kids from many backgrounds and traditions to explore values, spirituality, and big ideas. In our pluralistic society, it is particularly exciting to offer a high-quality publication that is probing life's big questions in a nonaffiliated forum." *KidSpirit* addresses kids 11 to 15 who are "curious about the meaning of life" and "eager to connect with other deep thinkers." Her goal is to help young people develop into global citizens who are aware of the values and spirit that connect us all.

Publications from religious and nonprofit organizations often struggle with resources, especially in a national economic downturn. Similarly, library and classroom magazines may be early casualties when school districts face tight budgets. The key word is *may*. For instance, funding has been problematic for *Junior Shooters,* says Editor in Chief Andy Fink. But Managing Editor Stephanie Lile reports the opposite at *COLUMBIAKids*, which debuted in August. "We hadn't planned to launch so soon, but the idea took off and we got funding on our first try," says Lile.

When preschool magazine *Tessy & Tab* began about seven years ago, its founders quickly learned that traditional marketing techniques such as advertising and direct mail were expensive and did not work well for them. Yet the magazine flourishes through grassroots marketing efforts. Judy Johnston, CEO and Co-Founder, explains, "Once people try *Tessy & Tab,* they love it, and they tell their friends about it. It is a slower growth path, but it has worked very well for us."

Reaching Readers Where They Live: Regionals

Zeroing in geographically and giving readers a magazine that focuses on where they live remains another recipe for success that includes the ingredients of knowing the market demographically and geographically, and knowing readers' needs. *Kidz Rule USA* targets preschoolers through tweens and their parents in the New Hampshire area. Publisher Kristen Pare declares the publication a success: "*Kidz Rule USA* has been in production for just over a year. In that time, we have doubled in circulation and page count." The bimonthly covers arts and crafts, activities, party ideas, health, money, and the outdoors for parents, and also offers stories, articles, and puzzles for children.

Conservationist for Kids, published by the New York State Department of Environmental Conservation, is another success story. The fourth-grade classroom magazine motivates kids to go out into New York's natural world, and Editor Gina Jack sees the audience expanding beyond its school distribution. "We have found that our readers include more than just a fourth-grade audience. We've been contacted by grandparents who say that they're enjoying reading *Conservationist for Kids* with their grandchildren and taking it with them when they explore outdoors together. To make it more broadly available, *Conservationist*

Magazine Start-ups of Interest

➤ *Bloghology:* www.bloghology.org. A quarterly online resource for bloggers, including articles on improving writing skills, making money online, trends in the blogging industry, and more.

➤ *bNets@vvy:* www.bnetsavvy.org. A bimonthly online publication offering tools to help kids ages 9 to 14 stay safe on the Internet.

➤ *Brass:* www.brassmagazine.com. Published quarterly with a focus on providing financial information to young adults.

➤ *COLUMBIAKids:* http://columbia.washingtonhistory.org/kids/index.html. An online publication on Pacific Northwest history, for ages 4 to 14.

➤ *Dane County Parent:* www.danecountyparent.com. Biannual publication with practical information for families in Dane County, Wisconsin.

➤ *ESPN Rise:* http://sports.espn.go.com/highschool/rise/index. A relaunching of the high school athletics magazine *Rise*, for ages 12 to 17.

➤ *Ethical Living:* www.ethical-living.org. Bimonthly focusing on environmental and social concerns, and lifestyle.

➤ *Evoke:* www.evokemagazine.ca. Canadian magazine "for and by" young people that encourages them to take their place in the larger world.

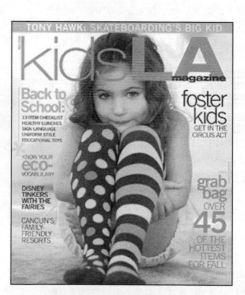

➤ *Faithful Sister:* www.faithfulsismag.com. Quarterly magazine for African American teens that includes empowering stories and articles.

➤ *Footprint Eco:* www.footprintecomagazine.com. Information and resources about sustainable living, distributed bimonthly in North Carolina.

➤ *Good Life Living Green:* www.goodlifelivinggreen.com. Canadian lifestyle and business magazine focused on ecological issues.

➤ *KidsLA:* www.kidslamagazine.com. For Los Angeles parents and their children, ages 4 to 14. Started

Magazine Start-ups of Interest

as a quarterly, with plans to go bimonthly.

➤ *Kidz Rule USA:* www.kidzruleusa.com. Bimonthly for kids and their parents in New Hampshire.

➤ *KidSpirit:* www.kidspiritmagazine.com. A quarterly spiritual magazine targeting 11- to 15-year-olds, with a focus on nature, science, arts, global issues, book reviews, spiritual issues, and more.

➤ *Kidzine:* www.kidzine.ca. New regional magazine for ages 6 to 12 in the Brampton/Mississauga area, Canada.

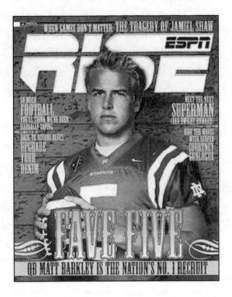

➤ *Labyrinth's Door:* www.labyrinthsdoor.com. A bimonthly, full-color, advertising-free fantasy adventure magazine for ages 8 to 14.

➤ *Mindful Mama:* www.mindfulmamamagazine.com. Combines subjects related to motherhood and living a green lifestyle, and provides an online social community.

➤ *Peppermint:* www.peppermintmag.com. Published quarterly, targets individuals interested in sustainable living.

➤ *RGVSports:* www.rgvsports.com. Regional high school athletics quarterly, located in the Rio Grande Valley.

➤ *St. Mary's Messenger:* http://stmarysmessenger.com. The publishers of this still-under-development magazine call it a Catholic version of *Highlights*.

➤ *Secular Homeschooling:* www.secular-homeschooling.com. A quarterly "committed to the idea that religious belief is a personal matter rather than a prerequisite of homeschooling."

➤ *WWEKids:* www.wwekids.com. From World Wrestling Entertainment, this bimonthly for ages 6 to 14 covers wrestling, nutrition, geography, games, and more.

for Kids is now featured as a pull-out insert in *Conservationist* magazine three times during the academic year, in October, February, and April." It is also entirely downloadable.

"*Conservationist for Kids* is one of our answers to 'Leave no child inside,'" says Jack. "It encourages kids to explore the outdoors at their own pace. The outdoor activities we suggest are great for kids to try on their own, with classmates and friends, or at home with their family. A one-page supplement for teachers encourages integrating *Conservationist for Kids* into lessons in the classroom." A recent issue covered various state symbols, such as the striped bass, beaver, ladybug, and pending bills in the legislature to name the state butterfly.

Kids can relate to a magazine with a sharp geographical focus and

content, feeling that it is published just for them in the place they live. Keeping the active nature of middle-grade readers in mind, both magazines feature bright photos and images, including children involved in local or regional activities. "The launch was inspired by a need for local children to have their own magazine," says Pare. "Kids love the magazine for the photos, stories, activities, and contests, and parents love the magazine for the [lists of] things to do in the area and the articles, tips, and recipes. *Kidz Rule USA* includes suggestions for outdoor activities for children to complete on their own, with classmates, or at home with their family."

Children in the Pacific Northwest now also have their own magazine. Springing from a one-page, back-of-the-book kids' feature idea in *Columbia Magazine*, *COLUMBIAKids* was developed in response to "teachers who bemoaned the fact that there was so little short, easy-to-read information about Pacific Northwest history," says Lile. Both are published by the Washington State Historical Society. The online kids' magazine targets ages 4 to 14 with stories that are readable by beginning

and struggling readers and that make "history fun, engaging, and relevant." Stories "have to be short, to the point, yet intriguing, and present unexpected viewpoints into the Pacific Northwest's past." *COLUMBIAKids* was also developed to integrate seamlessly into language arts classes, many of which incorporate regional history. Only two departments are written by staff, and Lile depends on freelancers for the remainder. She advises writers, "We're sticklers for good research. Angle is key, as well. For example, we're more likely to take a story if it is written from a kid's point of view rather than an adult's." She cites the One Day in History department's "Capture at Penn Cove," historical fiction by Sharon Mentyka, and the article "Grub for Giants," by Joni Sensel, as good examples.

Pare plans to make *Kidz Rule USA* available in New Hampshire schools as well. She says one goal is to prepare kids to succeed in the world. "We strive to achieve this commitment by providing content children enjoy. We focus on a variety of fun yet educational and informative subjects to help them prepare for the many aspects of life, such as sports, arts and crafts, money, recipes, outdoors, health, activities, stories, poems, contests, and much more." Most content is supplied by freelancers. *Kidz Rule USA* also features a Parents' Page, which offers insightful tips and articles to help with common topics such as sibling rivalry, online safety, and more.

Regional parenting publications universally give readers resources they can't find in national publications. When the only one in Dane County, Wisconsin, folded a couple of years ago, an opportunity arose. Georgia Beaverson, who edits *Dane County Parent,* says, "My publisher was convinced it was a good time to start a new one since the market was wide open." She is proud of "editing a quality, full-color publication with an extensive local resource directory in every issue, instead of a throwaway piece on newsprint. We've had very good responses from area readers." Beaverson hopes to increase frequency from the current two issues a year, and has already expanded content. "We added a cooking column, a book review column for books by Wisconsin authors, and at least one family-centered article." While national publications have their strengths, Beaverson says *Dane County Parent's* strength is "growing a magazine with strong local roots."

Debuting early last year, *KidsLA* addresses "affluent, educated parents

Green and Thriving

As concern for ecological issues continues to rise, the magazine industry responds both in content coverage and in practical physical ways. The Magazine Publishers of America (MPA) launched the Please Recycle campaign to educate and encourage readers about the ability to recycle magazines in many communities. MPA has also announced that it is "pursuing several initiatives to improve magazines' environmental performance. These include improving retail sales efficiency for magazines sold at newsstands and other retail outlets, and encouraging an increase in the availability and use of magazine papers certified for sustainable forestry harvesting practices."

Children's magazines have long had nature and the environment prominent on the list of high-interest topics. The Christian magazine *Pockets*, for example, has long published issues carrying themes on caring for the Earth. *Highlights for Children* has

encouraged readers to recycle and reuse by featuring craft projects using everyday items such as egg cartons and milk jugs. *Highlights* also publishes science articles that encourage an appreciation for nature and good stewardship of the Earth. (See a list of children's magazines interested in the topic on page 44.)

Now, green topics are gaining more special attention in adult consumer lifestyle, family, and women's markets. The new *Boho* targets ecologically conscious young women, focusing on fashion, beauty, the home, and travel (http://bohomag.com). From Nashville Interiors magazines comes *Positively Green*, which also targets women and offers sensible solutions to living green and healthier (www.positivelygreen.com). *Footprint Eco* targets readers in North Carolina with advice on living a green life, covering

Green and Thriving

everything from architecture to cars, fashion, technology, kids, and pets (www.footprintecomagazine.com).

The Green Guide newsletter was purchased by the National Geographic Society and last year was relaunched as a magazine with national distribution. By offering a digital version as well as a print version, publishing no more than quarterly, and striving to include content that consumers will keep and refer to, *Green Guide* minimizes its eco-footprint. Its website offers a number of interactive features, including quizzes, blogs, and buying guides. (www.thegreenguide.com)

Good Life Living Green was distributed across Canada twice last year and is going quarterly. Editor Connie Eklund says of the decision to launch *Good Life Living Green,* "The need was obvious as *green* is such a part of our everyday lives. People want to be as green as possible but have not had anywhere to source the information." *Good Life Living Green* also calls itself a *virtual company.* Eklund explains, "Being virtual means that we do not have a bricks and mortar office that houses employees. Everyone who works with us is an independent contractor and works from their home. Some of our people are in Australia, Texas, New Jersey, Alberta, England, and of course beautiful British Columbia." (www.goodlifelivinggreen.com)

Other new green-minded magazines include *Mindful Mama* (www.mindfulmamamagazine.com), which merges issues of motherhood and environmentalism; and *Green Lifestyles on Planet Paradise,* a quarterly, Sedona, Arizona-based magazine (www.greenplanetparadise.com).

Ecology, Environment, and Nature in Children's Magazines

The following general interest and other magazines regularly publish pieces on nature and the environment.

➤ *AppleSeeds, Dig, Odyssey:* www.cobblestonepub.com
➤ *ASK, Ladybug, Muse, Spider:* www.cricketmag.com
➤ *Boys' Life:* www.boyslife.org
➤ *Boys' Quest:* www.boysquest.com
➤ *Brilliant Star:* www.brilliantstarmagazine.org
➤ *Children's Playmate:* www.childrensplaymatemag.org
➤ *Chirp, Chickadee,* and *Owl:* http://owlkids.com
➤ *Cousteau Kids:* www.cousteaukids.org
➤ *Crinkles:* www.crinkles.com
➤ *Edutopia:* www.edutopia.org
➤ *Focus on the Family Clubhouse, Clubhouse Jr.:* www.clubhousemagazine.com
➤ *Fun For Kidz:* www.funforkidz.com
➤ *Green Teacher:* www.greenteacher.com
➤ *Highlights for Children:* www.highlights.com
➤ *Hopscotch:* www.hopscotchmagazine.com
➤ *Humpty Dumpty:* www.humptydumptymag.org
➤ *JAKES:* www.nwtf.org/jakes
➤ *Kansas School Naturalist:* www.emporia.edu/ksn
➤ *Kid Zone:* http://scottpublications.com
➤ *Know:* www.knowmag.ca
➤ *National Geographic Kids, National Geographic Little Kids, National Geographic Explorer:* http://kids.nationalgeographic.com
➤ *Organic Family Magazine:* www.organicfamilymagazine.com
➤ *Ranger Rick:* www.nwf.org/gowild
➤ *Scholastic Choices:* www.scholastic.com
➤ *Science Activities:* www.heldref.org
➤ *Science and Children:* www.nsta.org/elementaryschool
➤ *Scouting:* www.scoutingmagazine.org
➤ *U Mag:* www.usaa.com
➤ *VegFamily:* www.vegfamily.com
➤ *Young Bucks Outdoors:* www.youngbucksoutdoors.com

of children between the ages of 4 and 14" in Los Angeles with articles on travel, finance, media, fashion, and more. Originally issued quarterly, it has gone bimonthly.

For freelancers, regional publications often offer opportunities—at the least to get some clips and make contacts, and at the best to begin to establish a regular writing relationship. While some, such as *Conservationist for Kids,* are primarily staff-written, others, including *Dane County Parent,* rely on outside writers to fill their pages. The key is to check the market carefully. Often, writers who live within the geographic region of the magazine's coverage have an edge in submissions. "We only use local writers and sources," says Beaverson.

Weaving the Web

Near the end of the first decade of the twenty-first century, magazine publishers are certain of one thing: Electronic media are not just here to stay, they are an essential component of any readership. The MPA reported that traffic to consumer magazine websites in the second quarter of last year rose by 8.5 percent compared to the previous year—more than double the increase for websites generally in the U.S.

A study done by ROI Research also found that tweens now prefer the Web to television; 48 percent spend three or more hours a day online, and 35 percent watch TV for that time. About 61 percent reported spending an hour or less a week with a magazine, and 83 percent spend less than an hour a week reading a newspaper.

Publishers are taking note and increasing their Web presence. Last year, Hearst announced a cross-promotional partnership with the social music site Jango to develop "co-branded online music widgets" for *Seventeen's* website. *Seventeen* also partnered with Exercise TV to produce online workout videos, available for free at www.seventeen.com. Bonnier Corporation's *Parenting* magazine announced a partnership with AudibleKids.com, owned by Amazon.com, to provide *Parenting* readers and online users with downloadable resources to encourage children to read. (Note that *Parenting* is splitting into two publications, *Parenting Early Years,* for parents of newborns and preschoolers, and *Parenting School Years,* for parents of children in kindergarden to grade five.)

Clearly, publishers have learned to co-exist with modern technology, and are finding ways to use media in new ways, to improve and enhance their readers' experiences and even bring a new audience of readers to their magazines. A Generation Y member himself, Sims recognizes that technology is part of *brass* readers' everyday lives. He uses digital resources extensively in publishing. "We recently launched a video podcast titled *brass*/SHOW, where we deliver the same information in the magazine through online video. We've also created a social network for teachers to share ideas on how to use *brass* in the classroom; we host a blog at blog.brassmagazine.com; and people can become a fan of *brass* through Facebook," he says.

Writers would be hard-pressed to find a magazine that doesn't have, at the very least, a website giving visitors a taste of a magazine's content; a glance at the readership; and, for publications that use freelancers, guidelines, editorial calendars, and contact information. Most publishers change the content of their websites on a regular basis, and many of them are expanding their sites and implementing interactive features to keep visitors at the site longer, and encourage them to return often.

Bokram notes that the content on the *GL* website is different than the content of the magazine, but both target the same core audience and carry the same mission. She compares the magazine/website connection to a chicken or egg dilemma. "Some girls will read the magazine and then try the website; other girls will find the website and then buy the magazine." If readers like what they see on the website, they'll buy the magazine. On the other hand, an attractive website can keep readers loyal and engaged as they wait for the next issue to arrive at the newsstand or in their mailbox.

At Children's Better Health Institute (CBHI), Editor Daniel Lee notes that the past year has been one of change and new directions, and its website will soon reflect this forward movement. "The Internet will play a larger role. We're redesigning our landing page to make it more interactive and exciting for kids." Lee also says the site's redesign could be good news for writers, too. "Eventually, I'm sure we'll be buying material that is designed explicitly for the Web."

Carus Publishing began launching redesigned websites as well. Eventually, each of its 14 children's magazines will have an individual site with content aimed at the readers of the magazines. Sites for *Cricket, Ladybug,* and *Spider* launched last summer, and the *Click,*

Babybug, and *Cicada* sites in the fall. Interaction is a key ingredient with *Cicada* offering The Slam, which allows teen readers to submit po-etry and microfiction for posting and comment by visitors to the site. Deborah Vetter, *Cicada* Editor, says the launching of the new websites is "very exciting for us. There's lots of interaction, and that's proving very popular." She notes that the response to The Slam has been particularly posi-tive, and says that another feature, Call for Creative Endeavors, is so-liciting responses, too. "Readers are asked to submit poetry, art, or photos on a particular theme, which changes from issue to issue." The call is put out to both the website and the magazine, with a number of selections appearing in print.

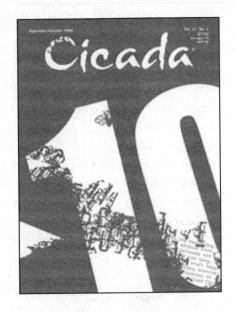

Associate Managing Editor Judy Burke of *Highlights for Children* says, "We use HighlightsKids.com (our free website for kids) as an av-enue for enhancing the content of *Highlights.* For example, when we published a science article about different prairie-dog calls, kids were able to listen to the various calls on HighlightsKids.com and hear the differences for themselves." Besides featuring magazine tie-ins, Burke says the company is excited about exploring new ways of using its website and other new media to serve kids in general.

Today, the belief that a strong Web presence is essential to survival is so widely held that new publications launch a website before the maga-zine appears in print. Dabney Hochman says, "We developed our web-site months before we launched the print magazine, knowing that the Web would provide a crucial way to connect with our age group." Since most of the content in *KidSpirit* is provided by readers, the site plays a vital role. "We have an open submission process online that invites kids anywhere in the world to contribute their work electronically, or if they prefer, via snail mail. Our goal is to have an ever-expanding web of

A Winning Market

While some magazines come and go and others share the spotlight as longtime favorites, still other publications quietly carry out their mission, sticking to a tried and true formula, succeeding on their own merits.

Devoted to keeping teens and kids off drugs, *Listen* and *Winner* have been around for decades, with teen-targeted *Listen* rolling off the presses in 1948 and the middle-grade *Winner* following ten years later. While the content has changed over the years as drugs overtook alcohol as the substance of concern, the goal has always been to inform readers of the dangers of abuse and serve as a measure of prevention. Editor Jan Schleifer says *Winner* helps kids have a healthy concept about themselves.

Winner "is the only magazine out there that talks to younger kids about being drug-free." Used in public, private, and homeschools, it includes teacher guides that feature worksheets written by an educator and an expert in drug prevention. Each issue focuses on a specific drug, or a negative behavior such as bullying or video game addiction. Schleifer says, "We give readers the tools to stand up to peer

Liv and Belle
Gerasole
see page 10

February 2009

Smart Choices for the Game of Life

pressure, and give them ideas for other interesting things to do." The 16-page magazine is published monthly during the school year. Parents, grandparents, or aunts and uncles often subscribe to give a child in their life a magazine that will have a positive influence.

Schleifer always appreciates submissions from freelancers, but notes that *Winner* has moved toward making assignments. "Material had been straying from the focus of the magazine, primarily because we weren't getting properly targeted submissions." Occasionally, Schleifer will have something come in over the transom that is suited to her needs, but often submissions are too general, featuring a topic that is not related to substance abuse or negative behavior issues addressed by the magazine. Submissions are usually missing the required three *thought questions* and *pencil activity*. "About two or three pieces each year will come in complete," explains Schleifer. "That will often lead to a working relationship where more work is assigned."

Writers who are able to adhere to specific guidelines and are looking for steady markets, might make a winning combination with these publications.

young writers and artists from all corners of the globe engaged in an open dialogue about their values, dreams, and inner spirits." Dabney Hochman holds to the belief, however, that while the Web is an essential part of reaching kids from divergent backgrounds, holding a beautifully crafted print magazine has pleasures of its own. "We want to create a synergy between the magazine and the Web that will energize both."

McManus launched her website for *Labyrinth's Door* four months before the scheduled launch of the magazine. She notes that she, too, will use features of the website to engage young readers and keep them coming back. "The monthly Keeper's Journal is a mini version of things to come in the magazine. It will contain a micro story, a puzzle, etc. It will hopefully also give the subscribers something to look forward to while they wait for the bimonthly magazine."

While the need for Web interaction seems vital to most, Johnston has intentionally limited the amount of online material for the preschool readers of *Tessy & Tab*. "We strongly agree with the American Academy of Pediatrics that it is best that children under two years of age have no screen time (TV, video, computer) and that between two and six years old, excessive screen time hampers vocabulary and social skills." She notes that they've "held their own" against electronic media by doubling their frequency to two issues per month and keeping the content fun and appealing to young readers. While the website contains a Fun Stuff for Kids section, it is limited to games that are "short, related to building reading and cognitive skills and are not meant to be addictive (keeping scores, etc.)."

If websites are vital to the health and sustainability of print magazines, what about online magazines with no print counterpart? After eight years in existence, *Wee Ones* has closed down. Editor Jennifer Reed names the greatest challenge of maintaining an online magazine: "Probably, as with most online publications, money. We paid our contributors out of our own pockets for many years. Keeping a magazine like this viable online is very difficult. It's hard to make enough money to support the magazine, let alone pay a staff." Still, Reed feels that there is a future for online magazines, and offers advice to those who may consider it. "Create a business plan: Know your theme, your mission, and try to pay contributors. Businesses who buy articles and stories from magazines will only work with magazines that are *official*.

This means getting an ISSN and paying your contributors." She says that longevity will build credibility and adds, "Make your website as professional as possible and work with top-notch writers."

Solid and Staying the Course

While the children's magazine industry saw the demise of some favorite publications, like the *Guideposts* magazines for kids and teens, in the last couple years, *Highlights*, the Carus publications, and the CBHI magazines all report good news for writers.

Lee says, "After several years in which we weren't buying new material, we're back in the market now, looking for great stories and activities." While CBHI is still interested in health and fitness, it's also broadening its focus so that features don't always have an explicitly health-related connection. "We're running a school-year art contest that is closely tied to classroom art curriculum elements," Lee explains. Other notable changes include the redesign of *Jack And Jill*, which targets ages seven to ten. "We've been redesigning with an eye toward bringing the title characters into a more prominent role, along with a neighborhood of new kid pals with varying interests and backgrounds." He advises writers to check the website (www.jackandjillmag.org) for more information.

Burke says *Highlights* is becoming more selective in order to do a better job of using what's acquired in a timelier manner. "However," she adds, "we still have a need for quality work that feels right for *Highlights* and its own unique flavor at the same time." The preschool publication, *High Five*, remains closed to freelancers.

Vetter was also happy to report that the news for freelancers with an interest in *Cicada* is brighter than it has been in the recent past. "We're open to submissions from readers between the ages of 14 and 23. We've also opened up general submissions for adults on a limited basis. Please see www.cricketmag.com for updates." She would also like writers to note the new format. *Cicada* is now a 48-page magazine measuring 8 x 10 $\frac{1}{2}$-inches. "While it features the same high-quality fiction and poetry as before, we have added bold new graphics and features that encourage reader interaction."

When the economy is sluggish, it can be tough to ignore the signs of struggle within the magazine industry. Yet writers on top of their game who look beyond the headlines and optimize available resources to track preferred markets may be surprised by what they find. Magazines, and the way they connect with readers, may be changing, but they are not going away. There will always be readers seeking the information and entertainment they provide, and there will always be those who delight in the feel of a real paper and ink magazine in their hands. There will also always be a need for writers to fill those pages.

Those Mellow, Magnificent, Misunderstood Middle-Graders

By Pamela Holtz Beres

Picture the proverbial middle child: One moment, they're hanging with the older sibling, acting cool, hip, smart. The next moment, they're playing with a younger brother or sister, watching the younger child's movies, playing their games, and connecting on a completely different level. One day, the middle child laments, "No one pays any attention to me! No one cares what I do, what happens to me, or how I feel!" The next day, they're happy to exist unnoticed, relieved that they don't shoulder the expectations of the oldest and glad that they're not fawned over or coddled like the younger child. Some days the middle child feels ignored or misunderstood; other days they're mellow and happy in their own world.

In children's publishing, the middle-grade market and the readers themselves display many of the same characteristics. The audience begins at about age eight on one end and moves into the tweens on the other. That range covers miles of development physically, socially, emotionally, and intellectually—and with developments in one area not always keeping pace with another, the middle-grader's behavior varies from child to child, time to time, day to day. Yet, while the publishing community keeps a close eye on an uncertain picture book market and rejoices in a booming YA market, the middle-grade segment hums along steady and secure.

The Spectrum

Traditionally defined as serving readers between the ages of 8 and 12, the middle-grade category has expanded in range as publishers try to reach children on all those multiple levels of development. On the older end, middle-grade books can now even appeal to readers as old as 14.

Fiction for the younger end is often limited to a single plot line; story problems are smaller; and the focus is on universal topics such as school, friendships, and family. Parents play a larger role than in stories for older children. As readers move up the age ladder, so do the characters' ages and the plots' complexity. Issues are explored in greater depth, reflecting readers' expanding experiences. Tween books often mirror the audience's budding interest in romance; problems and themes may be more controversial.

Madeline Smoot, Editorial Director of Blooming Tree Press, notes that series fiction appeals to younger middle-graders. Classics include Nancy Drew; Beverly Cleary's several series about Ramona, Henry, and Ralph S. Mouse; and the Spiderwick Chronicles, by Holly Black. Smoot points to the Harry Potter books as an example of a series that runs the entire gamut of middle-grade, even slipping into YA toward the end. "In the first book, the plot is a fairly simple quest with some reading time devoted to exploration of the new world. As the books progress, the plots become more complex and subplots between secondary characters develop," she says. "By the time the reader reaches book five, which has a plot almost identical to the quest plot in book one, the writing is radically different in tone and quality than in the first book."

While book editors can bounce from one end of the age range to the other, like the proverbial middle child, magazine editors usually find their choices fixed on one end of the age group or the other. *Hopscotch*, *Boys' Quest*, and *Fun For Kidz* all include middle-graders in their audiences, but as magazines that avoid fads, trends, fashion, make-up, and romance, their pitch is toward the innocence of childhood. They attract readers as young as six or seven. *Discovery Girls* editors, however, recognize that their older middle-grade, or tween, audience straddles the line between childhood and the teen years, and is concerned about such subjects as appearance and fitting in. If this need to zero in on a specific audience seems restrictive, *Jack And Jill* Editor Daniel Lee would disagree. Lee says that although middle-grade magazines compete with so much else that clamors for kids' attention—friendships, other media, and the increasing complexities of their lives—the focus on middle-grade readers also provides opportunities for a wider range of topics. "Kids this age are experiencing the rapid expansion of their world, and if you keep your magazine interesting, it can be one of the sources they'll look to for information," he says.

Finding topics to keep a magazine interesting for this age group isn't a problem, especially for the editors who focus on nonfiction. "Middle-graders are often curious about a wide variety of things," says Joëlle Dujardin, Associate Editor at *Highlights for Children.* "Because they have longer attention spans and a larger frame of reference, middle-graders are able to delve deeper into a subject area" than *Highlights*'s younger readers. The magazine's readers top out at about age 12.

Cobblestone Publishing has a number of magazines that focus on the older end of the middle-grade range, including *Cobblestone, Dig,* and *Faces.* Managing Editor Lou Waryncia says writing nonfiction for middle-graders, particularly those at the upper end, isn't much different than writing for adults. "Our goal at Cobblestone Publishing is to present the whole story— whatever the topic may be—in a clear, lively, and understandable manner that is age-appropriate." He believes that any topic can be interesting to this age group. "Kids are always fascinated by heroic figures, great events, mysterious places and situations. Anything wild and a bit crazy also gets their attention."

Bethany Shank is Co-editor of *Nature Friend,* which has a Christian point of view. She believes that the adventurous side of nonfiction appeals to middle-grade children and that they are interested in the "strange and interesting parts of creation, and the strange and interesting parts of common things." She gives as an example the way baby spiders get from one place to another by *flying*. Dujardin notes that middle-graders are increasingly aware of other people and they notice what needs fixing in the world, such as the environment. They appreciate reading about kids who make a difference in the world, as well as stories about scientists working in the field or historians working on a case. "As kids become more aware of their own interests and ideas, they seem to appreciate the impact individuals can have on the world," says Dujardin.

Middle-grade readers who find a topic interesting will go to lengths to learn more. As Shank puts it, "They latch onto whatever they can find out about that topic." Exploration expands the reader's world. Waryncia says, "Introducing a topic such as mummies can then lead to life in ancient civilizations, which can lead to customs, inventions, foods, religion, and so on down the line until you've covered everything about and related to a topic."

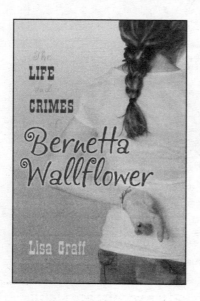

The Heart

Despite middle-grade readers' wide developmental variation, authors and editors have no problem finding common traits among them. Assistant Editor Molly O'Neill of Bowen Press uses three words to describe children this age: *savvy, connected,* and *busy*. Lisa Graff, Associate Editor at Farrar, Straus and Giroux and author of the middle-grade novels *The Thing About Georgie* and *The Life and Crimes of Bernetta Wallflower* (both from Laura Geringer/HarperCollins), uses *smart* and *skeptical* in her description, while Delacorte Senior Editor Krista Marino adds that middle-graders are "hard to fool."

O'Neill says they are savvy "because young readers can find information about anything in a few short seconds: They're smart and aware of the world going on around them and they're learning how to be a part of it." O'Neill notes that they are also just as connected to worlds of friends online as offline, and, thanks to the Internet, they have an easier

time finding communities of kids who share their interests and experiences.

"Friends are hugely important to them, as are caring adults who truly listen and respect their ideas," says Julie Bowe, author of *My Last Best Friend* and *My New Best Friend* (Harcourt).

Cynthia Lord, the author of the Newbery Honor book *Rules* (Scholastic), sees her middle-grade audience as "exuberant," often writing her e-mails full of smiley icons and exclamation points. She says that they care about justice, people, and animals and that they also believe in big

> "Middle-graders are exuberant. Their writing is full of smileys and exclamation points. They also care about justice and animals and believe in big possibilities and dreams coming true."

possibilities and dreams coming true. "Middle-grade is a very hopeful, funny, and thoughtful age."

Editor of the new middle-grade fantasy magazine *Labyrinth's Door*, Jacquitta McManus sees the curious, imaginative, and adventurous side of middle-grade readers. Their curiosity, she says, "is the unconscious asset that excites readers when they follow a character into unknown places and adventures." Their imaginative nature allows them to believe in talking trees and magical books, while a sense of adventure drives them to seek out new stories and follow the characters into new places, says McManus, who has a background in film. She recalls her own childhood memories when explaining her decision to target middle-grade readers with her magazine. "Right around ten was the age I fell in love with fantasy and adventure stories; plus, I feel that the middle-grade/tween audience is open to worlds of fantasy without judgment. They welcome adventure and the opportunity to be amazed."

Joy Neaves, until recently Editor in the North Carolina office of Front Street Books, believes that discovery is part of the adventure. Readers

Middle-Grade Markets

Books

➤ **Amulet Books:** www.amuletbooks.com. Abrams Books imprint.

➤ **Annick Press:** www.annickpress.com. Canadian authors.

➤ **Augsburg Books:** www.augsburgbooks.com. Christian.

➤ **Barefoot Books:** www.barefootbooks.com. Ages, birth to 12.

➤ **Bloomsbury USA:** www.bloomsburyusa.com. Divisions include Walker & Co., www.walkerbooks.com

➤ **Boyds Mills Press:** www.boydsmillspress.com. Imprints include Calkins Creek, www.calkinscreekbooks.com (American history); and Front Street, www.frontstreetbooks.com.

➤ **Candlewick Press:** www.candlewickpress.com

➤ **Carolrhoda Books:** www.lernerbooks.com. Fiction only.

➤ **Marshall Cavendish:** www.marshallcavendish.us

➤ **Chelsea House:** www.chelseahouse.com. Educational.

➤ **Chronicle Books:** www.chroniclebooks.com

➤ **Clarion Books:** www.clarionbooks.com. Houghton Mifflin imprint.

➤ **Cooper Square Publishing:** www.coopersquarepublishing.com. Imprints include Luna Rising, Northland, NorthWord, Rising Moon, Two-Can.

➤ **Coteau Books:** www.coteaubooks.com. Canadian authors.

➤ **Joanna Cotler Books:** www.harperchildrens.com

➤ **Darby Creek Publishing:** www.darbycreekpublishing.com

➤ **DK Publishing:** www.dk.com. Reference.

➤ **DNA Press:** www.dnapress.com. Science.

➤ **Down East Books:** www.downeastbooks.com. New England.

➤ **Eakin Press:** www.eakinpress.com. American Southwest.

➤ **Eerdmans Books:** www.eerdmans.com/youngreaders

➤ **Egmont USA:** www.egmont-us.com

➤ **Farrar, Straus and Giroux:** www.fsgkidsbooks.com. Macmillan division.

➤ **David Fickling Books:** www.davidficklingbooks.co.usa. British and American; Random House imprint.

➤ **Groundwood Books:** www.groundwoodbooks.com. Canadian authors.

➤ **Hard Shell Word Factory:** www.hardshell.com

➤ **HarperCollins:** www.harperchildrens.com. Imprints include Bowen Press, Laura Geringer Books.

Middle-Grade Markets

➤ **Hendrick-Long Publishing:** www.hendricklongpublishing. Texas and the Southwest.

➤ **History Compass:** www.historycompass.com. American history.

➤ **Just Us Books:** www.justusbooks.com. African American culture.

➤ **Kids Can Press:** www.kidscanpress.com. Canadian authors.

➤ **Lark Books:** www.larkbooks.com. Nonfiction only.

➤ **Lerner Books:** www.lernerbooks.com. Divisions include Kar-Ben (Jewish themes); Millbrook Press (nonfiction).

➤ **Little, Brown:** www.lb-kids.com, www.lb-teens.com

➤ **Llewellyn Publications:** www.llewellyn. Alternative spirituality and health.

➤ **Magination Press:** www.maginationpress.com. Self-help fiction and nonfiction.

➤ **Meriwether Publishing:** www.contemporarydrama.com. Theater.

➤ **Mirrorstone Books:** www.mirrorstonebooks.com. Fantasy and adventure.

➤ **National Geographic Society:** www.nationalgeographic.com/books

➤ **Naturegraph Publishers:** www.naturegraph.com. Native American.

➤ **Newmarket Press:** www.newmarketpress.com. Health.

➤ **Overmountain Press:** www.overmountainpress.com. Appalachia.

➤ **Richard C. Owen:** www.rcowen.com. Literary education.

➤ **Peachtree Publishers:** www.peachtree-online.com

➤ **Pelican Publishing:** www.pelicanpub.com. Louisiana and the Gulf Coast.

➤ **Penguin Books:** www.penguin.com/young readers. Divisions include Dial, Dutton, Philomel, G. P. Putnam's Sons, Razorbill, Viking.

➤ **Random House Books:** www.randomhouse.com/kids. Divisions include Crown Books, Delacorte, Alfred A. Knopf.

➤ **Rosen Publishing:** www.rosenpublishing.com. Curriculum and guidance nonfiction.

➤ **RP Books/Reagent Press:** www.reagentpress.com. Fantasy, science fiction, mystery.

➤ **Saint Mary's Press:** www.smp.org. Catholic themes.

➤ **Sandlapper Publishing:** www.sandlapperpublishing.com. South Carolina.

➤ **Scholastic:** www.scholastic.com. Imprints include Blue Sky Press, Arthur A. Levine Books, Orchard Books.

➤ **Scobre Press:** www.scobre.com. Hi-lo books.

Middle-Grade Markets

➤ **Simon & Schuster:** www.simonsayskids.com. Divisions and imprints include Atheneum Books, Margaret K. McElderry.

➤ **Sports Publishing:** www.sportspublishingllc.com.

➤ **Star Bright Books:** www.starbrightbooks.com. Multicultural.

➤ **Tanglewood Press:** www.tanglewoodbooks.com

➤ **Texas Tech University:** www.ttup.ttu.edu. Great Plains, West, Southwest.

➤ **TokyoPop:** www.tokyopop.com. Manga.

➤ **Tommy Nelson:** www.thomasnelson.com. Christian.

➤ **Tor Books:** www.tor-forge.com. Science fiction and fantasy.

➤ **Tricycle Press:** www.tenspeedpress.com

➤ **White Mane:** www.whitemane.com. American history.

➤ **Albert Whitman:** www.albertwhitman.com

➤ **John Wiley:** www.wiley.com/children

Magazines

➤ *American Girl:* www.americangirl.com

➤ *Ask, Calliope, Cobblestone, Cricket, Dig, Faces, Muse, Odyssey:* www.cricketmag.com. Carus Publishing. *Ask* explores science and history; *Calliope*, world history; *Cobblestone*, American history; *Dig*, archaeology; *Faces*, people and cultures; *Odyssey*, science. *Cricket* and *Muse* are literary magazines.

➤ *BabagaNewz:* www.babaganewz.com. Jewish.

➤ *Blaze:* www.blazekids.com. Horses.

➤ *Boys' Life:* www.boyslife.org. Boy Scouts.

➤ *Boys' Quest, Fun For Kidz, Hopscotch:* www.boysquest.com; www.funforkidz.com; www.hopscotchmagazine.com (girls)

➤ *Brilliant Star:* www.brilliantstarmagazine.org. Bahá'i.

➤ *Cadet Quest:* www.calvinistcadets.org. Christian boys.

➤ *Chess Life for Kids:* www.uschess.org

➤ *Children's Digest, Jack And Jill:* Children's Better Health Institute magazines, www.childrensdigestmag.org, www.jackandjill.org

➤ *Cousteau Kids:* www.cousteaukids.org. Oceans, rivers, lakes.

➤ *Crinkles:* www.crinkles.com. Critical thinking and activities.

➤ *Current Health 1:* www.weeklyreader.com/ch1

Middle-Grade Markets

➤ *Dogs for Kids:* www.dogsforkids.com
➤ *Focus on the Family Clubhouse:* www.clubhousemagazine.com. Christian.
➤ *The Friend:* www.lds.org. Latter-Day Saints.
➤ *GL (Girls' Life):* www.girlslife.com
➤ *Highlights for Children:* www.highlights.com
➤ *Horsepower:* www.horse-canada.com
➤ *JuniorWay:* www.urbanministries.com. Christian, African American.
➤ *Keys for Kids:* www.keysforkids.org. Christian.
➤ *Kids Discover:* www.kidsdiscover.com. Science, history, ecology.
➤ *Kid Zone:* www.scottpublications.com
➤ *National Geographic Explorer, National Geographic Kids:* http://kids.nationalgeographic.com
➤ *Nature Friend:* www.naturefriendmagazine.com. Christian; nature.
➤ *New Moon:* www.newmoon.org
➤ *Partners:* www.clp.org. Mennonite.
➤ *Passport:* www.wordaction.com. Christian.
➤ *Pockets:* www.pockets.org. Christian.
➤ *Ranger Rick:* www.nwf.org/gowild. National Wildlife Federation.
➤ *Science Weekly:* www.scienceweekly.com
➤ *Shine Brightly:* www.gemsgc.org. Christian girls.
➤ *Skipping Stones:* www.skippingstones.org
➤ *Sports Illustrated for Kids:* www.sikids.com
➤ *Stone Soup:* www.stonesoup.com. Written by kids.
➤ *SuperScience:* www.scholastic.com/superscience
➤ *U Mag:* www.usaa.com. U.S. Automobile Association.
➤ *Winner:* www.winnermagazine.org. Substance abuse education.
➤ *Worlds to Discover:* www.worldstodiscover.com
➤ *Yes Mag:* www.yesmag.ca. Science. Canadian.
➤ *Young Bucks Outdoors:* www.youngbucksoutdoors.com. Wildlife and the outdoors.
➤ *Young Rider:* www.youngrider.com. Horses and riding.

look for the *aha* moment that provides insight, adding substance to an experience. Whether reading is an adventure through inner thoughts and emotions or an action-packed trek across the globe, Neaves believes that "in the process they usually discover something important about themselves or those around them."

Carefree or Conflicted?

Sandwiched between the younger years—when help and supervision are required for many aspects of life from school to sports to friends to family dynamics—and the often turbulent and angst-filled teen years, middle-graders are often seen as easy, even mellow. But experienced authors and editors (and many a parent and teacher) quickly diffuse that myth.

"I'm not sure that kids would describe these years as easy," says Bowe, whose novels focus on the joys and heartaches of middle-grade friendships. "Most middle-grade kids are experiencing lots of change—

physical, intellectual, social, and emotional." Lee agrees. "They've got their own set of concerns that are just as real and troubling to them as any looming credit card payment or office project is to an adult."

Middle-graders are learning where they fit into their families and into the world. "They look outward at injustice, prejudice, differences, and learn that the answers are not as simple as they once believed," says Lord. "There is much joy and wonder, but also disillusionment in middle-grade." She recalls one conversation with a third-grade class where the ending of her middle-grade novel came up again and again. Lord finally asked one boy how he wished the story had ended. He pondered and answered that he wanted the bully to "turn nice" and the main character "to be friends with everyone."

Mary Ann Rodman, author of the middle-grade novels *Yankee Girl* and *Jimmy's Stars* (both from Farrar, Straus and Giroux) strives to tell kids the truth in her historical fiction. She recalls that as a middle-grade reader herself, her discoveries about the world around her resulted in frustration when the books she read were "prettified" and "white-washed" with happy endings. "I can remember being 11 and being so mad at yet another unrealistic happy ending that I threw the book against the wall. I screamed, 'Real life isn't like this!'" Now some kids write to her wanting happy endings but then usually add, "But the book ended just right. It's just different."

Discovery can be painful, and acceptance isn't always easy. Middle-grade readers may want happy endings, but they are beginning to see that life isn't a neatly wrapped package. Rodman recognizes that today's 10- to 14-year-olds are far more socially and emotionally informed and worldly than she was at the same age. She believes that if her novels "show the grittier side of American history, their sophistication (relative to mine) allows them to accept it."

The reality of what middle-grade kids cope with in their daily lives discounts what some believe about these years being easy. As Lord concludes, "Coming to terms with a world that won't always turn nice isn't carefree."

Joys and Challenges

Still, a report by Scholastic found that most middle-grade kids do read for fun, according to *Publishers Weekly* (www.publishersweekly.com/eNewsletter/CA6569801/2788.html). While they foresee a future where reading and technology continue to be intertwined, nearly two-thirds of kids say they prefer to read books of paper and ink rather than on digital screen. Yet writers are wise to consider the large role of technology in kids' lives today. As O'Neill notes, technology "extends into their lives in every way—cell phone, MySpace, Facebook, e-mail, IMing, etc.—and they find it odd if that world isn't reflected in books, too."

If meeting kids in their world is one challenge, keeping them engaged is another. Lee says, "Kids are acutely sensitive to any hint that you're talking down to them. Even when you're introducing material they may know nothing about, you have to avoid sounding like a teacher or parent." All editors and successful authors agree. Marino says, "They will know if the writer is patronizing them, if the voice doesn't feel authentic." Graff says, "The worst thing you can do in a children's book is talk down to your audience or try to impart a message."

Suggested Middle-Grade Reading

Reading middle-grade books published within the last five years will give you a good idea of what's being published today, while reading older classics will provide clues to what makes a story transcend time. Here's a sampling of titles found on the favorites lists of some editors and authors.

➤ Julie Bowe, author of *My Last Best Friend* and *My New Best Friend:*
- *Dear Mr. Henshaw* and *Ramona Quimby, Age 8,* Beverly Cleary
- *Leepike Ridge,* N. D. Wilson
- *Love That Dog,* Sharon Creech
- *Number the Stars,* Lois Lowry
- *Tales of a Fourth Grade Nothing,* Judy Blume
- *The View From Saturday,* E. L. Konigsburg
- *The Wednesday Wars,* Gary D. Schmidt
- *Where I Live,* Eileen Spinelli
- *Wringer,* Jerry Spinelli

➤ Lisa Graff, Associate Editor at Farrar, Straus and Giroux:
- Graff calls *A Corner of the Universe,* by Ann M. Martin, and *The Great Gilly Hopkins,* by Katherine Paterson, "quiet books with very real characters in slightly quirky settings."
- She says Cynthia Lord's *Rules* and Ruth White's *Way Down Deep* "both combine sadness and humor which kids appreciate, and the two always go down better together."

➤ Cynthia Lord, author of *Rules:*
- *The Best Christmas Pageant Ever,* by Barbara Robinson, "never ceases to make me laugh and move me, and remains a favorite through many readings," says Lord.
- Of *Holes,* by Louis Sachar, she notes, "So much done so well and with a splash of humor."
- *Toys Go Out,* by Emily Jenkins, is a favorite of Lord's "for pacing, characterization, and the author's respect for children's sensibilities."

➤ Joy Neaves, editor:
- *The Higher Power of Lucky,* Susan Patron

Suggested Middle-Grade Reading

- *Inkspell*, Cornelia Funke
- *The Invention of Hugo Cabret,* Brian Selznick

➤ Molly O'Neill, Assistant Editor, Bowen Press:
- *Love That Dog* and *Hate That Cat,* Sharon Creech. O'Neill says, "The characters are nuanced and deftly drawn."
- The Lightning Thief series, Rick Riordan. "Rollicking fun, full of humor."
- *Savvy,* Ingrid Law. "A totally original premise, delightfully appealing characters."
- *The Secret Language of Girls,* Frances O'Roark Dowell. "Characters of depth and honesty; the story perfectly portrays pains of growing up."

➤ Mary Ann Rodman, author of *Yankee Girl* and *Jimmy's Stars:*
- *Bird Springs*, Carolyn Marsden. "The writing is lyrical yet gritty," says Rodman.
- *Firegirl*, Tony Abbott. "Another outsider book but from the point of view of the insider."
- *Isabel and the Miracle Baby*, Emily Smith Pearce. Rodman describes this title with, "Southern working class setting, and a main character with a traditional nuclear family."
- *Keeping Corner*, Kashmira Sheth. "A book I lived inside and have read and re-read."
- *Reaching for the Sun*, Tracie Vaughn Zimmer. "Essential being-the-outsider book."
- *Rules*, Cynthia Lord. "A completely satisfying book."

➤ Madeline Smoot, Editorial Director of Blooming Tree Press:
- *House of Many Ways*, Diana Wynne Jones. "Howl and Sophie are my favorite of Jones's characters," says Smoot.
- *Julia Gillian and the Art of Knowing*, Alison McGhee. Smoot calls this a "sweet younger book with a classic feel."
- *The Night Tourist,* by Katherine Marsh, is "a lovely, inventive reworking of the Orpheus myth."
- *The 39 Clues*, Rick Riordan. "Enjoyable first book in a Scholastic series with multiple authors."

Neaves has often seen authors struggle to pick a protagonist age that is right for both the subject and the audience. This issue surfaced with a book Front Street published called *Isabel and the Miracle Baby,* by Emily Smith Pearce. "The story was infused with the voice of a very naive young kid, but the story itself was for older readers."

Bowe finds it a challenge to get the voice and the humor right—not too young and not too old. "It's also challenging," she says, "to write concisely (short paragraphs and chapters) and still provide plenty of interesting detail."

Lord recently conducted a survey of middle-grade readers and found pacing/tension and clarity were the two primary issues. "Both of these challenges are related to the fact that we are adults, and sometimes we forget what we can and can't take for granted." She explains that as adult writers, we sometimes focus on our characters' inner lives (because that's what adults are often most interested in), but her middle-grade readers have said that they want more action and excitement and less talking and thinking in their books. For clarity, it's important to remember that adult authors obviously have more life experience and if the author doesn't clarify enough—through showing, not telling or lecturing or patronizing—to keep the readers' confidence, they'll give up on the book.

But with challenge comes joy. When kids reach an age when they truly can choose their own reading material, Graff says, "They can be very enthusiastic about books and stories, and they are already developing very definite opinions about what kind of books they like to read in terms of genre or character."

Rodman says, "This age group is such a treasure to write for because, having achieved the skills to stop worrying about puzzling out the words, they will find a character in the book and literally crawl inside the skin of that character." Middle-graders will often read a book they like repeatedly, believing that the author is talking just to them.

O'Neill says, "There's an intense loyalty among this age group, which explains the cult following that develops for certain series, like Erin Hunter's Warriors books (HarperCollins) or Angie Sage's Septimus Heap books (Katherine Tegen/HarperCollins)." This group is also heavily influenced by their friends and peers, and when they like something, including good books, O'Neill says, "Well, word travels fast!"

With a broad spectrum covering a wide expanse of development the middle-grade market can feel like a moving target—much like the on-the-go and ever-busy kids themselves. At times they're mellow, other times misunderstood. But with an enthusiasm that outshines any other age group, middle-grade readers are always one thing: magnificent. And a marvelous market for writers.

Regional Realities: Narrow Focus and Broad Readership

By Sue Bradford Edwards

There are large states and small states, metropolises and compact cities. There are cities and regions with enormous breadth of opportunities to explore art or sports or history or business or the sciences, and others that are more focused or low-key or slower-moving. Similarly, there are regional publishers that offer useful publications for a narrowly targeted audience, and regional publishers that offer a whole range of publications that may not compete directly with the capacity of a big house but that aren't small potatoes either.

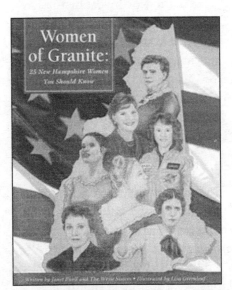

Muriel Dubois, Publisher of Apprentice Shop Books, explains, "As a small press, we can carry books that continue to be popular, even when larger publishers need to trim their lists. We believe that child readers are a renewable resource, so reprints are a good investment." Dubois points out that Apprentice's New England-focused books, such as the recent children's title *Women of Granite: 25 New Hampshire Women You Should Know*, are written to fill a very specific need. "These books are meant to appeal to a finite audience. In the case of *25 Women*, the books sell primarily to schools, libraries, museum stores, etc., in a particular state. Most large publishers cannot devote time to books that have this kind of limited range."

Michael Long, President of Hendrick-Long Publishing Company, which concentrates on Texas history, agrees. "Our titles don't have as broad an appeal as [titles from] a large trade publisher, and because of that, sales won't be rich enough for a big corporation," he says. Yet it would be a mistake to believe that the readers of books from regional presses are bound into a tight geographic area.

Tight Focus & Broad Readership

Although regional publishers are willing to think smaller in terms of sales, and topics are related to a smaller geographic area, their books or magazines can still reach a nationwide audience.

For some regional publishers, this broad reach results from modern

technology. This is the case with *COLUMBIAKids*, an online magazine that features Pacific Northwest history. "The lines between regional and national publications are getting blurred," says Managing Editor Stephanie Lile. "We are certainly regionally focused and aim to present the highest-quality information about the Pacific Northwest to kids all over the world." Available online, the magazine focuses substantively on the region but pulls in readers worldwide.

Other regional publishers keep topics and sales plan within one region, but link into a national readership through tourism and adult buyers interested in educational activities. An example is Hendrick-

Regional Markets

Books
➤ **Alaska Northwest Books:** www.alaskanorthwestbooks.com
➤ **Apprentice Shop Books:** www.apprenticeshopbooks.com
➤ **Down East Books:** www.downeastbooks.com. New England.
➤ **Eakin Press:** www.eakinpress.com. American Southwest.
➤ **Hendrick-Long Publishing:** www.hendricklongpublishing.com. Texas and the Southwest.
➤ **Overmountain Press:** www.overmountainpress.com. Appalachia.
➤ **Pelican Publishing:** www.pelicanpub.com. Louisiana and the Gulf Coast.
➤ **Sandlapper Publishing:** www.sandlapperpublishing.com. South Carolina.
➤ **Sasquatch Books:** www.sasquatchbooks.com
➤ **Texas Tech University Press:** www.ttup.ttu.edu. Great Plains, West, Southwest.

Magazines
➤ *COLUMBIAKids:* http://columbia.washingtonhistory.org/kids/index.html
➤ *Conservationist for Kids:* www.dec.ny.gov/education/40248.html. New York State.
➤ *Tar Heel Junior Historian:* www.ncmuseumofhistory.org/thjha/magazine.html. North Carolina.
➤ *Texas Cheerleader:* www.texascheerleadermagazine.com

The universe of regional magazines geared toward parents and kids is virtually limitless. For a listing of many, see *Magazine Markets for Children's Writers 2009* (www.writersbookstore.com). Writers may also purchase a roster of the members of Parenting Publications of America (PPA), or join as associate members (www.parentingpublications.org).

Long's workbook, *Plays & Poems from Texas History*. With placement in bookstores and gift shops throughout the state, Long points out that many of the company's workbook sales are a result of "family giving through tourism." He says, "Aunt Betty and Uncle Tom come down from Wisconsin and want to bring little Ned and Nancy a book. Bob and

Betty come down from Cape Cod and discover the third coast—the Gulf Coast!" Long also advises writers interested in Texas, "*Plays & Poems* is a workbook and I always need good workbooks."

Denise Martin, Editorial Director of *Texas Cheerleader Magazine*, extends her sales beyond the Lone Star State by virtue of the magazine's topic. "We look for just about anything related to the sport of cheerleading. We include articles that are relevant to the state of Texas but we also include articles that anyone would want to read. We've received requests from cheer gyms in New York, Illinois, and Florida," says Martin. "Because Texas is the largest cheerleading state in the world, people look at Texas." Interested readers can link into this high-energy magazine that, though regional, offers content for any cheerleader. "If you are a cheerleader and you wear a uniform, we are concerned about you as a person," says Martin.

Regional book publishers also make use of broad subject appeal, or multiple interests. "*The Black Regiment of the Revolutionary War* is a book set primarily in Rhode Island," says Dubois, "but it also appeals to anyone interested in African American history."

This doesn't mean that just any article or book with broad appeal will succeed with regional publishers. The writing must have more than a simple regional setting.

Giving Life to Region X

To sell to Alaska Northwest Books, a book must be Alaskan through and through. "Our books must be rooted in Alaska, providing insight

into some aspect of life here that helps others better understand the place and the people who live here," says Sara Juday, Associate Publisher. "Rich wildlife, diverse landscape, remote living, extremes of temperature and light, and our distance from the rest of the United States all impact living in Alaska. Underlying everything is the very rich, vibrant, and diverse cultural heritage. Our hope is that our books will take readers beyond the surface and expose them to an informed and accurate truth

Successful regional writing "is all about your lens."

of what Alaska is. One of our best-selling books is *Recess at 20 Below,* by Cindy Aillaud. Through photos and text, the book shares what kids like about recess and what they do to go outside at 20 degrees below zero." This book simply could not take place anywhere else.

Lile discusses the profiles she looks for at *COLUMBIAKids* as one way to understand what it means to write for a regional publisher. Whether the author is writing for Notorious NWesterners, a column about people from the past, or Making History, a column about contemporary artists, craftspeople, scientists, and scholars, the Pacific Northwest must play a significant role. Lile explains that a piece has "to make a kid in rural Texas or New York City understand how and why this person's experiences in the Northwest influenced his or her actions in the world."

This means bringing out appropriate details. "It's all about your lens," says Lile. "While a national magazine might want a piece that describes Elvis's whole life or the broad sweep of a particular album tour, we'd want a very specific chunk of that story to relate directly to the Pacific Northwest. We'd want the story about Elvis performing in the Stadium Bowl in Tacoma. The point of our magazine is to get kids to understand the connections between the Pacific Northwest and the world."

Regional Inspiration

The connection is often strongest when an author hails from that region. This was the case with Elizabeth Rusch's *Will It Blow? Become a*

A Shift of Focus

For some regional publishers, a time comes to branch out.

"Right now, Apprentice Shop Books is focusing on nonfiction, historical titles. All our titles have a New England basis," says Publisher Muriel Dubois. "That will change in the coming year. Our newest title, *Women of Granite: 25 New Hampshire Women You Should Know*, is the first in a series of collected short profiles of women from every state." Upcoming volumes will focus on women from Massachusetts, California, Texas, and New York. These books will shift Apprentice Shop Books from being strictly a regional publisher to a small publisher, still specializing in historical nonfiction.

Such a shift offers a rare opportunity for the author poised to take advantage of it. Author Elizabeth Rusch's *The Planet Hunter: The Story Behind What Happened to Pluto* and *A Day with No Crayons* sold to publisher Rising Moon when the company was shifting from a regional to a broader focus. "If you look at the catalogue, it is very heavily skewed toward the Southwest," says Rusch. Rising Moon's "guidelines said for many years that it would only take submissions on Southwest topics." Rusch made contact with her Rising Moon editor through a picture book critique session at the national Society of Children's Book Writers and Illustrators (SCBWI) conference. For a manuscript critique, says Rusch, "I was assigned Theresa Howell at Rising Moon and she said, 'I want to take this to acquisitions. We have greatly increased our children's book sales and we've started doing books with more national appeal.'"

Although Howell passed on the original manuscript, Rusch didn't give up. "I told her about *A Day with No Crayons* and she bought that. Then when Pluto was being kicked out of the planetary club, I e-mailed her and said, 'All the children's books are going to be out of date,'" says Rusch. "I did both of those for Rising Moon. I was very excited to be a part of a regional publisher going national."

Take advantage of the opportunities before you, and you may find yourself in print with both regional and large-scale publishers.

Volcano Detective at Mount St. Helens. "In October 2004, walking
around my neighborhood, we could see steam coming from the Mount
St. Helens crater," says Rusch. "Here is a volcano looming over
a major city with over a million people." She and her son took a trip to
Mount St. Helens National Volcanic Monument. "While we were there,
there was another steam eruption." The park rangers invited people to
stand on a patio to watch the event and handed her son a volcanic rock
that had been formed the previous day. "My son said with wonder,
'Mom, this rock is younger than me.' I went to the gift shop to buy a
book and feed this interest. But I couldn't find any and thought they
were sold out." A trip to the library resulted in a pile of about 20 books
on volcanoes, only one of which was on Mount St. Helens and it was
over 10 years old.

Rusch saved newspaper and magazine clippings, but hadn't started
writing when another event sparked the process. At the Western Washington Society of Children's Book Writers and Illustrators conference in
Seattle, she was assigned to Gary Luke, Editor of Sasquatch Books, for a
manuscript critique. Sasquatch calls itself a publisher of "regional
books without boundaries." It publishes titles about the Pacific Northwest, Alaska, and California. The manuscript Rusch had submitted had
no regional focus. "I went in and said, 'I am really interested in your
comments on this submitted manuscript, but I have to tell you that I
have another idea for a children's book on Mount St. Helens,'" says
Rusch. "He handed me his card and said, 'Call me, let's talk about it.' We
met at the monument and spent the day talking to rangers and talking
to each other. I wrote up a proposal and got a contract." Although she
might have tried to market her manuscript to a national publisher, the
fit with Sasquatch was perfect.

Other times the fit is perfect because the publisher pitches the initial
idea. Nancy Warren Ferrell, author of *Alaska's Heroes: A Call to Courage*,
met a regional editor over lunch because he was considering publishing
a book of her husband's. "The publisher mentioned that he thought the
Alaska Medal of Honor members would make a good subject for a book,"
says Ferrell. "I started researching and was amazed at the courage of
these medal winners—young, old, women, men, different cultures."
Ferrell wrote several accounts and pitched the piece to the publisher,
but he passed. "I mentioned the project to a publishing representative

from another regional company, and she was interested," she says. Because she had fallen in love with the project, Ferrell might have taken it to a national publisher, but the fit with a regional house was obvious to author and publisher alike.

Writers write with such love for their topics, but it takes an audience to bring their work to life fully. The key is to find a regional publisher that shares your vision. "*Texas Cheerleader Magazine* is down home, country, Texas-style, and personal. From the time readers open the magazine and read my Letter from the Editor," says Martin, they find a magazine filled with "articles that people are really going to read. I try to stay away from coaching cheerleaders. I focus on inspiration." This inspiration goes beyond success in cheerleading. The personal values found in the magazine include developing a strong work ethic and independence.

Does this pairing of cheerleading and Martin's own strong values succeed? Just ask the cheerleaders, coaches, and parents nationwide who, according to recent surveys, eagerly await each issue of *Texas Cheerleader Magazine*. They are just a few of the readers you can reach through a regional publisher.

Genres in the Balance: Magazine Editor Fiction Preferences

By Katherine Swarts

Short isn't easy, as many a fiction writer has found out. But a great short story appeals to youngsters. Fortunately for those who write for children, children's magazines are "among the few periodicals that regularly publish fiction," says Suzanne Hadley, Editor of *Focus on the Family Clubhouse Jr.*

Children's magazines publish all kinds of stories for all kinds of kids. At *Highlights for Children*, Associate Editor Joëlle Dujardin says, "Because we have such a wide range of readers, we try to publish many different genres over the course of a year to ensure that every reader finds something that appeals. We currently need funny stories, sports stories, holiday stories, adventure, mysteries, 500-word folktales, and historical fiction."

Some publications prefer certain genres over others, and some specialize. A new children's publication dedicated to a particular kind of story, for example, is *Labyrinth's Door*, a "fantasy adventure magazine for children ages 8 to 14. Our primary mission is to provide great and exciting original African American-written fantasy adventure stories that push the imagination and that create worlds of enchantment for children around the world," says founder Jacquitta McManus.

The preferences of other publications vary depending on editorial calendars and recent submissions. "*Cricket* and *Cicada* need more than a steady diet of fantasy and folklore," says Deborah Vetter, Senior Contributing Editor of *Cricket* and Executive Editor of *Cicada*. "We'd like to see science fiction, historical fiction, adventure, and modern-day stories set in other countries or within specific cultures in the United States."

Successfully choosing a genre means taking the measure of several dimensions: writer interest, reader interest, and editor interest. Balancing those is key to story and sales success. "Have a good reason for writing in a particular genre, other than the genre's popularity," says Dujardin. "In science fiction, for example, it's not enough to say the year is 2510 and the kids ride the hoverbus to school. The fact that it's 2510 should be important to the action."

That means story integrity: fiction that is true to itself, true to good storytelling, and true to the qualities distinctive to a given genre.

Contemporary Fiction

Many editors consider contemporary fiction a genre in itself. "We would like to publish more contemporary, realistic stories about children," says Jenny Gillespie, Submissions Editor of the Cricket Magazine Group's *Ladybug*. "Narratives with a dash of adventure are especially welcome. But such stories for three- to six-year-olds [*Ladybug*'s audience] are difficult to write. Developing a realistic story is a balancing act" of staying at the preschooler's comprehension level, "while taking risks with nuance and humor to create something unique. A good example is [the picture book] *Knuffle Bunny*, by Mo Willems, an entirely realistic narrative enhanced by irreverent humor."

Another ingredient of story integrity is authenticity. For any genre—mystery, adventure, or comic—with a modern setting, that means immersing yourself in the world of modern kids. If you have none directly at hand, at least spend time observing them in their public haunts; your own memories of being a given age are not enough. "Avoid setting a contemporary story in your own childhood," says Marileta Robinson,

Highlights Senior Editor. "Make your settings and characters reflect the world of today's readers."

"You have to get it exactly right," says *GL* (*Girls' Life*) Editor in Chief Karen Bokram. "If you're off in your cultural references, if you're off in how characters relate to each other, it comes off as fake."

Other Times, Other Places

Your own childhood memories could be helpful in writing some historical or multicultural fiction—setting stories in an earlier decade or a particular ethnic, religious, or other setting. Genres involving past times and specific or unfamiliar cultures remain much sought after. "We receive many stories about middle-class, white, suburban households," says Hadley, at *Clubhouse Jr.* "While we certainly won't reject a great story in this genre, we would like to publish more fiction about other parts of the world or different cultures within America."

The editor of the companion publication for older children, *Focus on the Family Clubhouse,* agrees. "We get too many stories set in modern-day, white suburban neighborhoods," says Jesse Florea. "We believe in educating and entertaining our readers. Exotic settings, and short historical fiction" of about 1,000 words are ideal. "Kids learn a lesson—there must be strong character-based take-away value—and learn something about another country or time."

If you don't have firsthand experience, then writing about real but unfamiliar cultures requires *visiting* the time and place. That can be done through letters, diaries, and other primary resources, including, whenever possible, people with direct knowledge or experts. Reading the exact words of those who have lived earlier or elsewhere helps "keep dialogue realistic to setting and time period," Florea advises. Hadley cites an upcoming piece in *Clubhouse Jr.* "We just received a

Kids Rule

Whatever your preference or your own age, start by reading several dozen stories recently published for your target readership. Aspiring writers, says GL (*Girls' Life*) Editor in Chief Karen Bokram, "often don't have a clue what appeals to 10- to 14-year-old girls. Many write something they think parents would approve of: The kid learns to obey her parents, and everybody lives happily ever after—I mean, *gag!*"

Jesse Florea, of *Focus on the Family Clubhouse*, echoes the sentiment: "Don't have adults come to the rescue. In over half of *Clubhouse* submissions, a grandma or parent swoops in and saves the day. Let your child characters figure things out."

"We prefer stories whose young protagonists inspire children to be curious, adventurous, and independent thinkers," says Jenny Gillespie, Submissions Editor of the Cricket Magazine Group's *Ladybug*. "We get many 'Mommy and Me' stories in which didacticism and sentimentality overwhelm the narrative."

"Don't overload your stories with awfulness, either," adds Deborah Vetter, Senior Contributing Editor of *Cricket* and Executive Editor of *Cicada*. "What you can handle in a novel is overwhelming in a short story. Remember hope at the bottom of Pandora's box—and remember the leavening effect of humor."

beautiful piece set in Hungary during World War II. The writer's knowledge of the time period showed through in wonderful details, like traditions and clothing styles."

"For historical fiction," says Vetter, "do your research and create a fully imagined world, as Christy Lenzi does in 'Ball and Mallet,' an Assyrian sports story (*Cricket*, July/August 2008). Geraldine McCaughrean's 'Casting the Gods Adrift,' (serialized from May to November 2002), made Eighteenth Dynasty Egypt seem like a world we could inhabit."

Whether modern-day or historical, if fiction is set in a foreign place, "an author steeped within a particular culture" is very desirable, says Vetter. "A single visit to, say, a village in Kenya does not make an author an expert. I remember one piece [about China] that sounded authentic.

After we accepted it, the illustrator, who was Chinese, kept pretty busy straightening us all out. Fortunately, the fixes were doable, but we're more careful now. Recently, Marnie K. Jorenby teamed up with Bineshii Hermes-Roach, an Ojibwe girl, to write 'A Gift from the Rabbit Nation.' That story appeared in the January 2008 *Cricket* and, in authentic detail, explored cultural conflict over hunting."

Small details can trip up authors. The writer intimately familiar with a setting drops in relevant items naturally; the writer with only a casual acquaintance tends to get minor, but still important, points wrong or to create text that feels forced. "Use cultural details and vocabulary sparingly," advises Robinson. Work in just enough so readers can visualize the setting accurately; subtly spread out information to keep the story from reading like a textbook.

"*Cicada* has run a number of stories by Tish Farrell, who offers an unsparing yet nuanced and humorous look at contemporary African life," says Vetter. One example is "El Niño and the Bomb" (November/December 2008). In *Cricket*'s "The Henna Boys," by Indian author Deepa Agarwal (April 2009), "The 12-year-old protagonist, Jagga, is worried that his well-to-do aunt will adopt his little sister and take her away from the shantytown where they live."

Other Worlds

Then there are the genres set apart from any real culture, past or present. "I think skilled children's writers have a lot of fun writing fantasy," says Gillespie, "because they can create a richer universe."

But fantasy is also challenging. "It's hard to do teen fiction well as it is," says Bokram, and fantasy is "a very specific thing, very hard to write in short story form."

Credibility is one of the challenges. "Be sure to create a believable world," says Dujardin. "It can be tempting to assume anything goes with fantasy, but every world must have its own rules and logic so readers don't get lost. Overuse of fantastic elements can distance kids from a story."

Hadley agrees: "Fantasy is the most difficult genre to write, in my opinion. It must ring true and yet carry the reader to another world. Much children's fantasy is overwrought, garish, or silly." Many writers' wildest fantasies are their dreams of becoming rich and famous through the genre: "Everybody wants to be the next C. S. Lewis or J. K. Rowling," says Florea.

Yet, fantasy writing can simply mean a story that is realistic except that it features animals acting (or just thinking) with human capabilities. This approach can in fact help solve the problem of portraying characters doing adult things such as driving or living alone, without leaving child readers thinking "this story is just about grown-ups." Robinson finds, "Talking animal stories are usually humorous, although sometimes they are serious, as in 'Goose Says Good-Bye' (*Highlights*, March 2007), in which a migrating goose says good-bye to her friends and learns that most of them don't really understand why she's going."

For older readers, the magical and fabulous have become familiar and the conventions more understood. "Many of us never outgrow childhood fairy tales," says Vetter. "They just grow up with us. So it's not surprising that fantasy rules with teens, too; Charles de Lint and Neil Gaiman are especially popular. The best fantasy allows readers to wander beyond the borders of our own prosaic world. Yet along the way we face real-life issues as well and learn about courage, friendship, and perseverance."

"The world the story takes place in," says McManus, "is the silent character of the story and should get the same attention as any other main character."

But when setting a story in another dimension or on another planet, "don't make it so alien that readers lose their way. Introduce new vocabulary and concepts slowly rather than dumping them on your reader in the first paragraph," says Vetter. Remember: "Good fantasy and science fiction explore the same themes as other genres: friendship, loneliness, belonging, courage."

Indeed, even alien stories must never be so alien as to hamper reader empathy. Whether your protagonist is a Harry Potter who travels back and forth between magical and real worlds, or is a totally non-human being on a distant planet, the character must be someone of whom the reader can think, "He or she (or it?) is just like me!"

Genres can present the danger of falling into stereotypes if a writer adheres too closely to the category's conventions. This hazard can be especially precarious in fantasy. "Avoid clichés and formulaic plots and characters," says Vetter. "Even when retelling a folktale, inject your own voice and style. Our readers do love fantasy and folklore, from fresh retellings of the familiar Cinderella story (see Janni Lee Simner's 'Heart's Desire' in the October 2006 *Cricket*) to less familiar folktales such as Phillis Gershator's sprightly Chinese tale, 'Ancestor Dog' (September 2008) or Deborah Gee Zigenis's Serbian folktale 'One Horse, One Bird, Two Brothers' (April 2008). *Cricket* has recently run 'The Star Shard,' a year-long fantasy by Frederic S. Durbin."

Adventure Fiction and Mysteries

You may even want to consider interactive stories, which allow the reader to choose among multiple plot lines. "Study the genre and stick to a couple of main storylines," says Florea. "Choose Your Own Adventure stories are difficult to write, especially in our allotted 1,800 words, because writing one is like putting together a puzzle. Often authors write themselves into a never-ending loop where the reader will never reach a conclusion."

Even puzzles with set solutions have their pitfalls: "It can be hard to create a mystery that conveys just enough information," says Dujardin, "so that a reader can follow clues while not finding out too much too soon. Certain traps are easy to fall into: making the outcome too predictable from the get-go; letting a character remain passive as the mystery unfolds around him or her; attributing the mystery to someone or something that is not introduced until the end."

"The hardest thing about writing mysteries," says Vetter, "is planting clues and red herrings without giving anything away until the end, when the pieces fall neatly together." Second hardest may be not succumbing to the temptation of using a plot element that's been done again and again: "One of the most overused plot devices revolves around kids who have a treehouse detective agency, run around solving mystery after mystery, and talk like Joe Friday from *Dragnet*. Another cliché is the raccoon in the attic."

Tired settings are another peril to be avoided. "Authors who write mysteries frequently think of haunted houses and ghosts, and these are always welcome because kids gobble them up," says Vetter. "However, mysteries come in many guises. What about true history mysteries (the two princes in the tower or the fate of the Roanoke colony), or historical fiction mysteries, or one-off mysteries in which modern-day kids unravel

Please Don't

Relatively few magazine editors buy long stories to break into installments, so don't be tempted to suggest the option. "We do not want to publish the first chapter of someone's book," says *GL* (*Girls' Life*) Editor in Chief Karen Bokram, who gets many submissions of that nature. "I want concise short stories written as short stories." If you want to write short fiction, make it short; and send it to an editor who publishes fiction.

All writers of fiction should also remember that there is hardly a prominent nonfiction-only magazine that, however often and explicitly it states that fact, doesn't receive hundreds of fiction submissions every year.

a perplexing situation: How does the escape artist horse manage to get out every day? Why do the neighbor's lights flicker on and off three times every evening at eight o'clock? Who are those men who beach their boat on the sand at dusk and disappear again at daybreak? What do the mysterious signs mean on the fence post at the end of the road?"

Crime and violence are not allowed at *Highlights*, and virtually all children's magazines, "and that can seem daunting to a mystery writer," says Robinson. "However, many entertaining mysteries meet this criterion. A puzzling situation, a child who is curious and observant, plus a surprising, yet logical outcome can produce a satisfying story. For younger readers, this may be enough. For older readers, the mystery should involve something at stake for the characters."

On writing genre fiction, Hadley perhaps sums it up best: "Don't get too caught up in the genre itself. Adhere first and foremost to the principles of good children's writing: plot-driven stories with strong, relatable protagonists, a primary conflict, and lots of action. The genre should simply enhance what is already a well-told story."

Blending the Hip and Traditional for Girls

By Sue Bradford Edwards

G irls want more than just fun. But teen girls certainly do look for fun in their reading, and that has helped drive the still-going-strong young adult market. The label *chick lit* may be over-applied, but it does highlight the fact that fiction for young women over the last decade has had a large cast of star performances, and those have benefitted publishers, writers, and readers alike.

Chick lit carries some negative connotations—lightweight, pop, for-mulaic, even opportunistic—but it wouldn't be a label that stuck or was criticized or debated so much without reason. The genre wouldn't be so successful if the writing didn't often have substance, art, and solid appeal.

Delacorte Press Senior Editor Krista Marino calls chick lit "a fun, fast, and accessible read." Accessibility comes in the form of both the char-acters and stories, and the ability to purchase the books. Popular fiction for teen girls largely sells to the readers themselves, not to their parents or other gatekeepers. A teen won't pick up a book or keep reading if the story doesn't feel real. "No matter what," says Marino of fiction for teen girls, "it must be authentic."

Flux Editor Andrew Karre agrees that the story must have a teen real-ity check. Chick lit "is concerned with the immediate YA experience," he says. Think contemporary teen concerns and sensibilities. Karre reminds writers that fiction for girls isn't about adult characters reflecting on how their teen years affected marriage or other experiences in later life. It is about the now, about real, live teens.

Not Everything Goes

With so many traditional plot types and tales up for inspirational grabs, is there anything that doesn't work for chick lit?

"High fantasy is really tricky," says Flux Editor Andrew Karre. "It is usually written in the third-person omniscient, with huge, arching stories." This epic scale doesn't work well with the character-driven focus of most chick lit. Nor does anything else epic, be it a quest or an adventure. As author Mary Wilcox points out, many chick lit novels are written in the first person and are relationship-driven. Chick lit goes for the close-up shot, not the panorama of an epic.

Another limiter comes with the fact that adolescent chick lit is first and foremost YA. You can't write a YA story about a time or place that doesn't recognize teens as separate from both adults and children. These adolescents also need to have their own culture. "This is a shared experience of general idleness where you aren't working for a living," says Karre. "It's a modern thing." This rules out most historical fiction, since few if any past cultures recognized adolescence as a separate developmental period. While historical fiction can feature strong female characters, so far chick lit and historical fiction have yet to mesh.

Despite this immediacy, chick lit is ultimately traditional. For every book structured around instant messages, there is an old-time tale newly explored. Many authors selling YA for girls today rely on story-telling forms such as quests, vampire legends, epistolary novels (IMs rather than letters, perhaps), stories of alienation, and fairy tales.

I Spy a Princess

The titles may not be subtle: *Cindy Ella* (Speak), by Robin Palmer; *The Frog Prince* (Simon Pulse), by Gillian McKnight; Francesca Lia Block's *The Rose and the Beast: Fairy Tales Retold* (Simon Pulse). Chick lit is fresh and new. So where did all the fairy tale princesses come from?

Author Robin Palmer offers her insight: "You walk around on Halloween and see all these princesses. Fairy tales are the first stories you are read [as a child] and they become deeply engrained in your psyche."

Little girls dress up in pink gowns and sparkly tiaras, and big girls

dream in their own ways about their own personal happily ever after. Fairy tale-inspired stories enliven the dream, but often with real life convincingly woven through the story. "There are always good versus evil themes, but I think Cinderella is the most popular form," says Marino, who cites examples of fairy-tale inspired novels for teen girls from Delacorte. "Read a few titles and you'll find the underdog, or unpopular girl, getting the hot guy (*Top Ten Uses for an Unworn Prom Dress,* by Tina Ferraro), making the cheer squad, or overcoming obstacles (*Hot Mess,* by Julie Kraut and Shallon Lester) so that a character's self-esteem is improved in the end."

Many teen girl novels are not like the elaborately embroidered expansions that Donna Jo Napoli created in *Beast,* a reworking of Beauty and the Beast, or *Zel,* based on Rapunzel (both from Simon Pulse). Instead, they may be well-written, page-turning, identifiable but straightforward modern reconstructions. Why bother with the fairy tale at all if you are going to modernize it? Because the stories have withstood the test of time. They are about relationships and good and evil and people finding their way through life. Modern fairy tales explore the same truths and troubles as good fiction always has.

In *Cindy Ella* and its new companion title *Geek Charming,* Palmer purposefully maintains similarities between her work and the traditional tales of Cinderella and the Frog Prince. "I wanted to give myself the leeway to use the form but riff

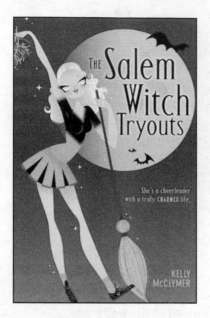

THE Salem Witch Tryouts

She's a cheerleader with a truly CHARMED life.

KELLY McCLYMER

on it," says Palmer. "I have anti-princesses. *Cindy Ella* is all about the flip flops, not the high heels." Cinderella's family has also changed. "I didn't want to make the evil people really evil. That's boring and people aren't really like that. They are just self-involved. Their values aren't Cindy's values, but they aren't horrible people."

Cindy and her love interest end up together, but in many twenty-first century tales, Prince Charming and the lovely princess do not end in each other's arms. "Part of the process may be realizing that *she* doesn't want this prince and doesn't need this prince. This is a huge change in the traditional Cinderella story," says Marino. "It's not necessarily happily ever after, but that's okay, as the protagonist has learned she can handle that."

A variation on the Cinderella theme is the fish-out-of-water story, in which the protagonist is a girl who who just doesn't fit in. Alternatively, think Ugly Duckling. The duckling doesn't want a prince or a handsome young man of any type. The duckling simply wants to belong. The main character longs for acceptance and security.

Author Kelly McClymer composes out-of-place characters in the Simon Pulse books *Getting to Third Date* and the Salem Witch series, which features a gifted young witch named Pru. "When you want to use this form, you come up with either a situation or a character, and then imagine the 180-degree opposite," says McClymer. "I set Pru up as a witch who had grown up in the mortal world being forbidden to use her powers, but doing well in her mortal high school and on her cheerleading squad." Pru has adapted to life without magic, so McClymer throws in another twist. "Then I sent her to a witch school where all her peers use magic, even in cheering."

Quests

A fish-out-of-water character may want to be reunited with a parent or could be having trouble adjusting to high school. An ugly duckling

Walk the Modern Walk

You may have a story idea that takes advantage of a traditional form. It may be set here and now and feature a strong female protagonist. But it won't be publishable if your character isn't truly modern.

"Early on, my editor at Flux pointed out that I was writing YA novels that felt 'old-fashioned.' He gave me a reading list of contemporary YA lit, and boy was that an eye-opener!" says author Susan Thompson Underdahl. "I learned that I had to make my characters more sophisticated in order to make them relatable to today's YA audience. The lives of today's teens involve elements of sex, addiction, violence, death, so many overwhelming, complicated things. Teens today cope with adult issues at a very young age."

Underdahl doesn't focus on all of these things in her novels, but they inform the world in which her characters live. Her characters are believably complex and as sophisticated as any teen roaming the mall today. Make sure your own chick lit character can walk the modern walk, whether they do it in sports flip flops, unbelievably high heels, or the latest athletic shoe.

character who wants something tangible may be on a quest, another traditional storytelling form that adapts well to teen fiction. In a quest, the main character searches for a person, place, or thing of vital importance.

Author Mary Wilcox sets up a quest in *Backstage Pass* (Delacorte), the first book in her series, the Hollywood Sisters. In these books, the main character, Jessica, must find the person who is planting lies in the press about her TV-star sister. Unlike the archetypal quester Odysseus, Jessica doesn't encounter Sirens or Cyclops. She does carry a modern burden. "I've given Jessica an ongoing celebrity jinx that engulfs her in high-profile trouble with the set's guest stars, as well as the ongoing challenges of being a young teenager trying to emerge from a more

successful sister's shadow," says Wilcox. Jessica has her own Scylla and Charybdis.

Another variation from classical quests is the nature of Jessica's reward: no enchanted sword, golden fleece, or singing harp, but instead something less tangible and more in keeping with the current trends in chick lit. "Her reward hasn't ever been material," says Wilcox. "Her rewards have been the gaining of self-confidence and wisdom."

Susan Thompson Underdahl also uses quests in her teen fiction and rewards her successful protagonists in terms of character development. "In both *The Other Sister* (Flux) and *Remember This* (Flux), the modern-day quest of my characters is for self-acceptance and mastery of a new situation," she says.

In an age of self-help, it isn't surprising that often this success comes in terms of self-empowerment. "The form works because of the inherent interest that people have in stories that feature goal-setting, facing challenges, and finding success," says Wilcox, "especially if that success has a different definition than it did in the goal-setting stage."

Thoroughly Modern

Whether the traditional form you adapt is a fairy tale or a story type such as a quest or an adventure, your heroine must be thoroughly modern. Even Cinderella has been updated from a wide-eyed, childlike innocent. "The protagonist isn't perfect because that's not really something a teen reader can identify with. Who likes perfect people?" says Marino. "But evil and nastiness shouldn't be rewarded, nor should it be glorified. It's just a bad message to send. And how could you be happy for a protagonist who is mean?"

Wilcox agrees and has written Jessica the Hollywood sister as good but not innocent. "She is good-hearted, but jumps to the wrong conclusions, retreats, gets mad, but she is ultimately sympathetic."

In addition to creating realistically imperfect characters, happiness is found someplace other than in the arms of the perfect man, even if he is the most popular guy in school. "Girls have goals outside of getting a dance with Prince Charming," says McClymer. The *Salem Witch Tryouts'* "Pru is ambitious, and she doesn't want or need to hide it from anyone. She's proud of her ambition." Ambition does not make a chick lit character unappealing. It simply gives her goals and the drive to attain

them. After all, these are characters for today.

When you think chick lit, don't forget to consider the classic forms your story might take. You might work up a *rescue plot* in which the boy must be saved from the wrong girl. What about a *riddle plot* in which things are not as they seem and the protagonist is tricked into working against her own best interests? These plot types have been around for so long because they work. Pair them with an independent young woman who is believably imperfect and start looking for an editor. If your character also has a good manicure and a sporty convertible, no one is going to complain as long as she learns something about herself in the end.

The Realities of Faith Writing for Teens

By Susan Sundwall

I t was a wonderful moment for me as a children's playwright when my friend's young grandson, Andrew, played the lead role in the Christmas play I'd written, *Bartholomew the Clueless Shepherd.* That was six years ago and the play later went on to publication, but I often think about Andrew, now a teenager. How had that role affected him, or had it at all? I don't see him in church often now. Maybe the ideas in my play seem childish or irrelevant to him today. Still, as an author, I wrote for a positive and lasting effect. As a person of faith, I hope this young man's faith has grown and not stagnated or simply faded in the glare of all that distracts in the teen years.

There's a common desire among believing writers to impart the reality of the hope and comfort that faith offers. The challenge is to meet readers where their need is greatest. This goes double or triple for teens. Having faith in an invisible, all-caring God can be difficult at times, even for a seasoned believer, so imagine writing about faith convincingly enough to reach the skeptical young.

Count the Ways

Writer/director John Cosper uses the medium of plays and skits when writing for teens. His skit booklet, *Righteous Insanity,* was the inspiration for his website of the same name. "My skits were about God and Christianity, hence the word *righteous.* And *insanity* because the skits were a little over-the-edge crazy," he says. Cosper understands the cathartic effect that taking a role onstage can have for teens. "If I can draw them in, pick at an old wound, or raise a question they themselves might be afraid to ask, then they're going to be more attentive to what follows."

Another effective path for faith expression lets the teens do the talking. Whether ghostwritten by an adult or written teen to teen, there's much to learn from the process. T. Suzanne Eller featured 39 true-life

stories in her book *Real Teens, Real Stories, Real Life* (River Oak/Cook Communications). When the book was published, someone critiqued the book as "just stories," as if they had no real draw. "And yet I watched several teens one night after a conference," Eller says. "They were completely absorbed. I receive e-mails all the time from teens who identify with one of the people in the book." The words of fellow teens pack a punch. "It's a fundamental rule for any writer: show don't tell. But it's key with this audience. There is power in story."

Teen Editorial Assistant at Randall House's *Clear Horizon* and *Clear Direction* magazines, Tanya Shallahamer, agrees. "True life stories are vital. Aside from the Bible studies, they are the lifeblood of the magazines. We have a regular column called Changing Lanes in which teens tell stories of how God is working in their lives and we usually have at least one more true life general article."

It's been true for centuries that teens often feel misunderstood and resent taking guidance from adults, especially those in direct authority over them, like parents and teachers. But if someone their own age has gone through a faith crisis or awakening, the chances of the spiritual message being heard is far greater. The best writers, according to Shallahamer, write it real. "They don't just say, 'Hey, life is tough but Jesus will get you through.' They show readers how God has come through for them. They give specifics rather than generalizations." She adds, "We're always on the lookout for adult freelancers for general articles and feature articles relating to the quarterly themes. We're more

than happy to provide a list of themes to writers who ask."

Profiling the faith life of popular sports figures is another avenue for putting a positive spin on faith while exploring the natural competitive instincts of teens. Teens can see that having faith and loving sports are not incompatible. *Sharing the Victory* is a ministry tool of the Fellowship of Christian Athletes (FCA). Editor Jill Ewert says the staff there discovers much from teen feedback. "We learn that our readers have a desire to be made better, whether that is by learning from the examples of those we profile or through ministry-related articles that we print. Either way, our readers want to go deeper into their faith." Sports have always had a strong youth following; teaming sports with faith has proven to be a real faith enhancer, especially for young men. For writers who want to utilize the broad spectrum of sports to connect with teens Ewert says, "Our best writers are the ones who know the FCA ministry and are familiar with what we do. That helps them to communicate with our audience." For her magazine she suggests that writers "plug in with a local FCA Huddle. If they have interviewed FCA staff from around the country as part of the story, we will likely do something with it, whether online or in the magazine."

Similarly, in a recent story in *Connected*, "Hamilton and Griffey Jr.: Baseball Metaphors for Life," readers are invited to compare the career paths of the two baseball greats (http://connected.christianrecord.org/editor/343/). Ken Griffey Jr., who was recently traded by the Cincinnati Reds to the Chicago White Sox, seems to have his life all pulled together while Josh Hamilton of the Texas Rangers fell from grace in a big way but, through faith, worked his way back to the top. Editor Bert Williams sees the value in such comparison. "Many teens struggle with the sense that life doesn't seem fair. If life isn't fair, that calls into question the character of God." Again, we see the age-old problem of why God allows bad things to happen to people. "For a Christian teen, it is a challenge to comprehend the interplay between God's free grace and the continuing importance of living a moral and ethical life." *Connected* is affiliated with Christian Record Services for the Blind. Its editors are always on the lookout for fresh voices to write stories and articles for the magazine.

Application of Truth

Communication and *relevance* are two buzz words that put faith writers on alert. Shallahamer says, "Above all, teens look for relevance. They may believe what you say, but unless you show them the relevance, they will never apply it to their lives."

> "In any good writing, content is king. And in faith writing, relevance is the point: to make spirituality matter in everyday life."

Speaking of Christian teens Eller says, "They are looking for someone to show them Christ, not necessarily to talk about it, but to live it. So, when we try to write at them about the *don'ts* and fail to show them the *do's* we miss an opportunity to come alongside a teen. I meet too many writers (as I speak at writers' conferences) who are writing pieces that are sermons. They address the ills of youth culture or try to fix teens, forgetting that these teens have lived only 13 to 18 years. The teens didn't create the culture; they simply live in it. So, rather than trying to fix teens, let's show them the way."

"In any good writing, content is king," says Williams. "The writer must first have something to say." Focusing on one key idea and making that idea work in contemporary life is crucial. "Relevance is an overused term, but it's still the point: To make spirituality matter in everyday life is my goal."

"No matter what theme an article is about," says Shallahamer, "the writer should be able to lead the students in how to apply the truths

in the article to their own lives, and then show what they can do to respond to how the truths should touch their lives. Again, without showing them how it's relevant to their lives, nothing will change."

Nothing smacks of relevance for teens like issues of social justice, love, the environment, poverty, and other intense, all-consuming subjects. People of faith have always involved themselves with such matters, and the concern often begins in the teen years. Being exposed to or involved in something beyond their immediate environment that reels them into a group of like-minded young adults has great appeal. They then want to move a step closer to faith-based solutions. With more than 15 years of working with teens, Eller says, "Their insight on faith, family, life, and the tougher issues was profound. This is such an intelligent generation. They want to impact the world in tangible ways."

Shallahamer delves deeply, saying, "They want to move beyond the simple Sunday School answers and really get to the meat of who God is, what He's done, why He's done it, and what He'll continue to do. Then they want to feel how that impacts them personally."

Speaking of the teens he's worked with, Cosper says, "Everyone brings different experiences and insights into the faith journey. I learn about God from them, about how to love others, how to reach out to the world, everything you can imagine."

Faith and Fun

Humor resounds with every age group, and teens are no exception. The faith/humor combo can be a freeing eye-opener for teens. One of the most moving religious services I ever attended was a clown service. Teens dressed in bright, baggy clothes, wearing fright wigs and clown makeup, performed mime. They not only made their audience laugh but, a few times, brought us to tears. This kind of scripting is a departure from traditional church services but shows innovation in reaching a younger generation of believers. (And it has tradition behind it in the form of the medieval Troubadour legend of *le Jongleur de Dieu*, which influenced Francis of Assisi, and which some young readers may know through Tomie dePaola's picture book, *The Clown of God* (Harcourt).)

"I write a lot more comedy than I do drama," Cosper states, "so I'm always looking for some way to bring it in. Humor's a great way to loosen up any audience. What gets some going is finding a good image

Teen Religious Markets

Books

➢ **Augsburg Books:** www.augsburg.com. Christian.
➢ **Bahá'i Publishing Trust:** http://bahai.us
➢ **B & H Publishing Group:** www.bhpublishinggroup.com. Christian.
➢ **Behrman House:** www.behrmanhouse.com. Jewish.
➢ **Bethany House:** www.bethanyhouse.com. Evangelical Christian.
➢ **David C. Cook:** www.davidccook.com. River Oak imprint. Christian.
➢ **Deseret Book Co.:** www.deseretbook.com. Latter-day Saints.
➢ **Jewish Publication Society:** www.jewishpub.org
➢ **Moody Publishers:** www.moodypublishers.com. Conservative Christian.
➢ **New Hope:** www.newhopepublishers.com. Christian.
➢ **Our Sunday Visitor:** www.osv.com. Catholic.
➢ **Paulist Press:** www.paulistpress.com. Catholic.
➢ **St. Anthony Messenger Press:** www.americancatholic.org. Catholic.
➢ **Saint Mary's Press:** www.smp.org. Catholic.
➢ **Skinner House:** www.uua.org. Unitarian.
➢ **Standard Publishing:** www.standardpub.com. Christian.

Magazines

➢ **General Assemblies of God:** www.gospelpublishing.com. Publishes many books and magazines, including *On Course,* www.oncourse.ag.org, and *Take Five Plus* for teens.

or metaphor to play with in my scripts."

"We know that God has a sense of humor," says Ewert. "If He has demonstrated a great lesson in a humorous way, we are certainly open to telling it that way."

Williams says he would definitely like to see more humor in *Connected.* "Very serious topics can be grappled with much more effectively if done good naturedly. If a writer has a sparkling wit, the otherwise mundane or shrill becomes winsome and compelling," he states. "Humor should always be in good taste and above reproach—and not every occasion calls for it—but, I think spiritual things are so important that we must use the tool of humor, when it is appropriate, to drive a point home."

Teen Religious Markets

➤ *Connected:* http://connected.christianrecord.org, Christian Record Services for the Blind.

➤ *Devozine:* www.devozine.org. For and by teens.

➤ *Focus on the Family:* www.focusonthefamily.com. Evangelical Christian; publishes numerous books and magazines for all ages.

➤ *Higher Things:* www.higherthings.org. Lutheran.

➤ *Ignite Your Faith:* www.igniteyourfaith.com. Christian.

➤ *Inside Out:* http://pentecostalyouth.org. United Pentecostal.

➤ *InTeen:* www.urbanministries.com. African American, Christian.

➤ *Muslim Girl:* www.muslimgirlworld.com

➤ *On Course:* www.oncourse.ag.org. Assemblies of God.

➤ **Pacific Press Association:** www.pacificpress.com. Seventh-Day Adventist; publishes numerous magazines for all ages.

➤ **Randall House:** www.randallhouse.com. Baptist; publishes books, and *Clear Direction* and *Clear Horizon* magazines.

➤ **Review and Herald Publishing:** Seventh-Day Adventist; publishes many products, including *Guide,* www.guidemagazine.org and *Insight,* www.insight-magazine.org, for teens.

➤ *Sharing the Victory:* www.sharingthevictory.com. Fellowship of Christian Athletes.

➤ *Teenage Christian:* www.tcmagazine.org

➤ *Young Salvationist:* Salvation Army, 615 Slaters Lane, Alexandria, VA 22314.

Watch Your Tongue!

Cosper and Eller have similar thoughts on language in writing about faith. "Avoid pop references at all costs," says Cosper. "That means slang, popular bands, whatever. You'll date yourself and look like a moron so just leave it out."

Eller says, "The most challenging part is to stay ahead of the curve. Language changes quickly. I have to be current, but also look ahead to what is next. If a book goes to print one year after I write it, some things may already be passé."

Shallahamer expresses herself very strongly when it comes to adults writing for teens. "If the writers are not teens, then don't try to sound like teens. Write on their level without talking down to them. Teens are real people and don't want to be treated as though they're half-programmed robots."

Williams, referring to the latest hip terminology as the teenage "mother tongue," says, "Most of us will make fools of ourselves if we attempt to write in that idiom when it is not our own mother tongue. Authenticity is far more important to teens than any attempt to mimic the latest flavor in trendy words."

All writers seek to understand the subject about which they write. But for faith writers it's important to bring something of their own faith to the table. It can inform every aspect of his or her writing and thus bring out the best in the piece. Some publications even require a faith statement.

Shallahamer says, "Many times we will request a 200-word testimony from inquiring writers; not only does this give us a faith statement, but it also gives us a sample of their writing."

The faith of the writer does indeed play an important role. "Plus, we have an obligation to our readers to take them deeper into the faith," says Ewert, "and the best way to do that is through gifted writers who share the same belief. We would like to see more articles that minister to student-athletes and coaches by covering tough topics and issues that they face." Some of her suggestions are prayer in sports and handling athletic injuries.

"When it comes to writing about their faith, a strong faith of their own is absolutely essential," says Williams. "But that does not mean their lives are not messy or that some days aren't just filled with trouble and discouragement. If a writer is ultimately concerned about the life of faith, that person will have something authentic to say."

The teen years are relatively short and the window for influencing them slams down suddenly with the coming of age. Writers who keep in mind the constant changes in the teen world coupled with the understanding that there's really nothing new under the sun will do well in writing about faith for teens. Teens are, after all, just people in transition. It's a rough one, for sure, but as we were helped through the often shark-infested waters between 12 and 20, so now, on the other side of those years, we can help others.

Miss Manners in Flip-Flops: Children's Reference Books Get Goofy Good

By Judy Bradbury

From pitch to publication, the creative picture book look at our 50 states, *Go, Go America* (Scholastic), written and illustrated by Dan Yaccarino, took five years and saw three editors come and go. Although the compendium is appealingly lighthearted, filled with fun facts, weird festivals, and antiquated laws, it also contains plenty of hard facts.

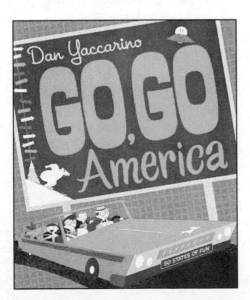

Yaccarino testifies to the laborious task of creating such a seriously silly book. "It's so much more than the writing. It's the fact-checking. Every item was investigated five different ways and had to be located in more than one source. And if a fact was disputed, that started us down a whole other path searching for verification." An editor at Scholastic Press when the book was being worked on, Leslie Budnick recalls, "If a fact couldn't be properly verified, it was replaced. Sometimes that required Dan to create new artwork. He sketched and re-sketched. Then the incredible design team, Art Director Marijka Kostiw and Designer Kristina Albertson, along with Dan, brought it all into focus. It was a collaborative, non-linear effort guided by Dan's vision, his one-of-a-kind illustrations, and sense of humor." The seasoned author/illustrator says he is indebted to Budnick (who saw the project through to publication) and "an army of Scholastic librarians" who assisted him in the vetting of the entertaining facts that trip across the pages of his book. "I would not go lightly into nonfiction," he cautions.

> **"Books are called on to provide what the Internet does not: an aesthetic experience, stunning art, something tactile, and are to be savored rather than raced through."**

Fun and Factual

Today's creative nonfiction for children is indeed fun, frolicsome, and at times fantastical, appealing to a child's sense of adventure and offering healthy doses of humor in an altogether appealing package.

"Authors, illustrators, editors, and design teams are trying new approaches, topics, ways to organize material, layouts, formats, trim sizes, and types of illustrations," attests Mary Cash, Vice President and Editor in Chief of Holiday House. "Nonfiction is more heavily illustrated and more carefully designed and packaged [than ever before]. It's also more innovative. Today's young people are visually sophisticated and likely to be visual learners. Books are being called on to provide things the Internet cannot—an aesthetic experience, stunning art, something tactile, and something to be savored rather than raced through like an online video game. If people invest in a book, they want to be able to use it again and again."

As an example of an author (and illustrator) of a successful string of books in this realm, Christy Ottaviano, Editorial Director of her own imprint at Henry Holt Books for Young Readers, points to Laurie Keller.

Keller's creations include *The Scrambled States of America, The Scrambled States of America Talent Show,* and *Do Unto Otters: A Book About Manners.*

Of Keller and her decade of success with such books, Ottaviano reflects, "Laurie is consistently in tune with kids. She is intuitive about how they learn and what excites them. I see her Scrambled States books as primers—introductions to geography that offer more than just dry facts. In the case of *Do Unto Otters,* kids have heard it all before, but Laurie presents etiquette in a fresh and humorous way."

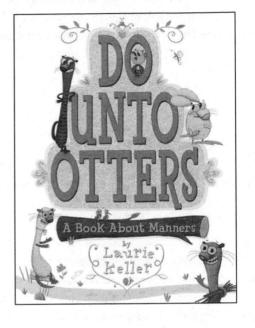

Go, Go America is similarly "fun, fun, fun!" confirms Budnick. "But it's also thoughtfully created with an eye to balancing facts with fun. The illustrations and the design have loads of kid appeal. They're meant to attract and hold the attention of kids and to show them that facts can be intriguing (and silly). We also wanted to include some basic information about the states that kids need for reports and that teachers are looking for, so we included this in the backmatter of the book. Again, though, it's presented in a lively and unique format. Even the brief source notes in the back of the book are presented in a light way."

Tweet Curriculum Success

"At Holt we are always interested in presenting curriculum topics in new and accessible ways," says Ottaviano. At Holiday House, too, "because of our strong ties to the school and library market, topics that are taught in school work well for us," says Cash.

"We're all looking at different topics with a curriculum connection," agrees Susan Kochan, Associate Editorial Director at G. P. Putnam's Sons. One of her favorite geography-related books is *United Tweets of America: 50 State Birds, Their Stories, Their Glories,* written and illustrated by the

Reference Publishers

➤ **Barron's Educational:** www.barronseduc.com

➤ **Borealis Press:** www.borealispress.com. Canadian history.

➤ **Candlewick Press:** www.candlewick.com

➤ **DK Publishing:** www.dk.com

➤ **Facts on File:** www.factsonfile.com. Ferguson imprint, career references.

➤ **Gale/Cengage Learning:** www.gale.cengage.com, www.galeschools. com/teachers.htm. Imprints include Blackbirch Press, Greenhaven Press, Greenwood Publishing, KidHaven Press, Lucent Books, Macmillan Reference, Thorndike Press, and U-X-L.

➤ **Holiday House:** www.holidayhouse.com

➤ **JIST Publishing:** www.jist.com. Careers, life skills.

➤ **Libraries Unlimited:** www.lu.com

➤ **Macmillan:** http://us.macmillan.com. Imprints that publish reference include Henry Holt, Kingfisher Books.

➤ **Meriwether Publishing:** www.meriwetherpublishing.com. Theater reference books.

➤ **National Geographic Children's Books:** www.ngchildrensbooks.org

➤ **Neal-Schuman Publishers:** www.neal-schuman.com

➤ **Penguin Putnam:** http://us.penguingroup.com

➤ **Scholastic:** http://librarypublishing.scholastic.com. Scholastic's reference imprints include Children's Press, Franklin Watts, and Grolier.

➤ **School Specialty Publishing:** www.schoolspecialtypublishing.com

➤ **Simon & Schuster:** www.simonsays.com

➤ **Sterling Publishing:** www.sterlingpub.com

➤ **Workman Publishing:** www.workman.com

award-winning Hudson Talbott. Here, factoids about each state are offered by the birds you'd be likely to meet in those states. Cardinals— the bird seven states claim as their own (now, did you know that?)—are center stage and uproarious. Consider this line from the page about Kentucky: "The northern cardinal would be a standout anywhere, but he knows that nothing sets off his red color better than Kentucky's blue-grass." On another page, the cardinal argues across the spread with an American goldfinch about who owns Washington (the state/the person). "It's funny," says Kochan, "but aside from that, readers are treated to lots of information. There's some geography, of course, but it's irreverent and entertaining. What's important in these kinds of books is taking something that can be dry and boring and making it appealing to young readers. It can be silly and humorous and entertaining for kids while also being instructive."

Trade Books that Tickle and Teach

Elizabeth Bicknell, Associate Publisher and Editorial Director at Candlewick Press, looks beyond curriculum to the bookstore consumer. "Candlewick does not have a large nonfiction list, yet we bring our trade sensibilities to these books just as we do to fiction titles. Publishers can't rely on school and library as the sole market for nonfiction; they need to have a broader sales base. The books we publish need not only meet curriculum needs, but also attract a browser or casual bookstore customer. The way I would think about it is this: If there isn't an institutional look to our fiction or picture book list, why should nonfiction be treated any differently?"

Bicknell is the editor of the wildly popular Charlie and Lola series by Lauren Child, about manners, feelings, and other childhood hurdles, as well as the blockbuster pop-up books, *Encyclopedia Prehistorica: Dinosaurs* and *Encyclopedia Prehistorica: Sharks and Other Sea Monsters*,

Sample Reference Titles

Not Your Grandma's Grammar

➤ *Dear Deer: A Book of Homophones,* Gene Barretta (Henry Holt).

➤ *Eats, Shoots & Leaves: Why, Commas Do Make a Difference!; The Girl's Like Spaghetti: Why, You Can't Manage without Apostrophes!; Twenty-Odd Ducks: Why, Every Punctuation Mark Counts!* Lynne Truss; illus., Bonnie Timmons (Putnam Juvenile).

➤ *Nouns and Verbs Have a Field Day; Punctuation Takes a Vacation; Silent Letters Loud and Clear,* Robin Pulver; illus., Lynn Rowe Reed (Holiday House).

➤ *Woe Is I Jr.: The Younger Grammarphobe's Guide to Better English in Plain English,* Patricia T. O'Conner; illus., Tom Stiglich (Putnam Juvenile).

Goofy Good Geography

➤ *Go, Go America,* Dan Yaccarino (Scholastic).

➤ *Scrambled States of America; Scrambled States of America Talent Show,* Laurie Keller (Henry Holt).

➤ *United Tweets of America: 50 State Birds, Their Stories, Their Glories* Hudson Talbott (Putnam Juvenile).

Mind over Manners

➤ *Are You Quite Polite? Silly Dilly Manners Songs,* Alan Katz; illus., David Catrow (Margaret K. McElderry).

➤ *But Excuse Me That Is My Book* (Charlie and Lola series), Lauren Child (Dial).

Sample Reference Titles

➤ *Don't Say That Word!*, Alan Katz; illus., David Catrow (McElderry).

➤ *Do Unto Otters: A Book About Manners*, Laurie Keller (Henry Holt).

➤ *Mind Your Manners, B. B. Wolf*, Judy Sierra; illus., J. Otto Seibold (Knopf).

➤ *17 Things I'm Not Allowed to Do Anymore*, Jenny Offill; illus., Nancy Carpenter (Schwartz & Wade).

<u>Eye-Popping Perspective</u>

➤ *ABC3D*, Marion Bataille (Roaring Brook).

➤ *Encyclopedia Prehistorica: Dinosaurs; Encyclopedia Prehistorica: Sharks and Other Sea Monsters*, Robert Sabuda and Matthew Reinhart (Candlewick).

➤ *Mosque*, David Macaulay (Houghton Mifflin/Walter Lorraine).

<u>High-Energy History and Bodacious Biography</u>

➤ *Fartiste: An Explosively Funny, Mostly True Story*, Kathleen Krull and Paul Brewer; illus., Boris Kulikov (Simon & Schuster).

➤ *Independent Dames: What You Never Knew About the Women and Girls of the American Revolution*, Laurie Halse Anderson; illus., Matt Faulkner (Simon & Schuster).

➤ *Leonardo's Horse*, Jean Fritz; illus., Hudson Talbott (Putnam Juvenile).

➤ *Now & Ben: The Modern Inventions of Benjamin Franklin; Neo Leo: The Ageless Ideas of Leonardo Da Vinci*, Gene Barretta (Henry Holt).

➤ *The Trouble Begins at 8: A Life of Mark Twain in the Wild, Wild West*, Sid Fleischman (HarperCollins).

created by Robert Sabuda and Matthew Reinhart. What drew her to these projects? "I like the enthusiastic tone of the text, the humorous headlines, and the sense of wonder that the creators bring to their work. Their passions show clearly, and that is contagious—not to mention the power of having a dinosaur or shark lunge out at you in pop-up form!"

Grammar Grabs Attention

Examples of other books that have nailed this concept of *entertaining instruction* are the successful grammar books on Putnam's list: *Eats, Shoots & Leaves: Why, Commas Really Do Make a Difference!; The Girl's Like Spaghetti: Why, You Can't Manage without Apostrophes!;* and *Twenty-Odd Ducks: Why, Every Punctuation Mark Counts!,* written by Lynne Truss and illustrated by Bonnie Timmons. Truss, the author of the national bestselling adult version of *Eats, Shoots & Leaves,* and illustrator Timmons "managed to answer the question, 'What can we do with this subject so there is a bit more going on to entertain kids while they learn?'" says Kochan. The treatment of grammar in this trio of books is simple, straightforward, engaging, and thus winningly effective. Punctuation placement within a sentence is comically illustrated, demonstrating to kids the effects of a misplaced or misappropriated punctuation mark.

Woe is I Jr., by Patricia T. O'Conner, is the middle-grade version of an-

other popular adult grammar book, also from Penguin Putnam. Here, a conversational approach and humorous examples make grammar approachable and less noxious to kids. "The tone is adapted for sixth to eighth graders," notes Kochan, "and provides teachers the opportunity to present a not so popular subject in a fun way."

On the list at Holiday House is a trio of grammar books written by Robin Pulver and illustrated by Lynn Rowe

Reed, the most recent of which is *Silent Letters Loud and Clear*. "Robin comes up with truly unorthodox approaches and has a delightful sense of the absurd," says Cash. "She writes hilarious dialogue that has lots of clever touches. Lynn Rowe Reed has an uncanny ability to conceptualize abstract concepts as well as an extraordinary sense of color and a zany sense of humor. Robin has punctuation marks writing postcards to students in *Punctuation Takes a Vacation;* Lynn puts arms, legs, and heads on verbs in *Nouns and Verbs Have a Field Day*. These books are about how far you can stretch the rules. You can ignore all punctuation; you don't have to put nouns together with verbs; and you can get rid of all the silent letters. However, the irony is that these books are also about why you actually need rules: If you don't use standard punctuation and spelling, people can't understand your writing. Kids enjoy the freedom and chaos of these books, but they come away understanding why it's important to follow certain precedents." As Cash sees it, that's a winning combination. "The trick," stresses Kochan, "is to use humor, fun, and lightheartedness so kids aren't viewing it as a lesson."

Biography Gets a Life

In biography, too, young readers are being treated to intriguing subjects, creative formats, and fresh slants. David Gale, Vice President and Editorial Director at Simon & Schuster Books for Young Readers, doesn't publish very much nonfiction, but *Fartiste*, written by Kathleen Krull and Paul Brewer and illustrated by Boris Kulikov, caught his attention. "First and foremost, *Fartiste* is a very funny book. That it is based on a real person is a plus, but I was not looking for a biography, and I would not have published a picture book biography of Joseph Pujol just to publish a book about him. I published *Fartiste* because it tells its story in a very funny way. Additionally, one of the book's great strengths is the additional humor that Boris Kulikov brought to the already funny text through his witty and beautiful illustrations."

Bicknell likes to see that an author "has found a story or narrative thread in the material that engages the reader and prevents the text from being too dry." As an example, she offers Kathryn Lasky's picture book biography, *John Muir: America's First Environmentalist*, illustrated by Stan Fellows. Primary source material is essential. "And, of course, I like to see a good bibliography!"

Gale agrees that backmatter is important. "Because Pujol was a real person, Kathy and Paul added an extensive authors' note explaining more about the actual Fartiste. I think that sort of reference material is critical in any informational book." Mostly, though, Bicknell, like Gale, seeks what is now widely called the *wow factor*. "I have to find the material of interest, since it takes at least two years to make a nonfiction book. I want to spend that time learning and being engaged myself."

Says Ottaviano, "Biographies that catch my attention are not usually traditional narrative. There are plenty of those around. Today's readers are drawn to more interesting treatments. When done well, these more specialized, often shorter approaches can offer greater impact because they focus on a specific time or point in the subject's life." Ottaviano lists *Elizabeth Leads the Way*, written by Tanya Lee Stone and illustrated by Rebecca Gibbon, as an example of a vibrant "slice" of women's history.

Kochan calls *Leonardo's Horse*, by Jean Fritz, "fantastic nonfiction" that's less straightforward than some of this prolific author's more traditional biographies.

Bicknell believes, "Despite the growth in picture book biographies of women or people of color, I still think this is an area that should be developed. And in an era when established science (in the form of evolution) is being challenged by intelligent design proponents, we should be offering children interesting, credible, low-key defenses of Darwin's work."

Tough Market No Joke

As original and fun and deeply researched as reference books and other nonfiction works are in contemporary children's publishing, authors must step up their games.

Kochan finds, "One of the challenges of nonfiction in the marketplace today is getting it looked at. It must be top-notch and eye-catching in its approach and design." Ottaviano and Yaccarino caution authors about tackling nontraditional treatments of nonfiction. Ottaviano says, "It seems effortless to write, but it's hard to do well."

In evaluating manuscripts, Kochan looks for projects that offer "humor, cleverness, and an approach that is different, fresh, and effective." Cash lists "original ideas, clear and crisp writing, and a firm grasp of the topic" as top priorities when evaluating a project. "I need nonfiction that has a hook, takes an unusual approach, and offers a unique

perspective. There is a reason why *Mistakes that Worked: 40 Familiar Inventions and How They Came to Be,* by Charlotte Foltz Jones, has been in print for nearly 20 years, but other books about inventions have not stuck around."

Ottaviano, whose eponymous imprint at Holt typically consists of about 50 percent picture books, seeks biography, history, and other subjects that support the curriculum. "Kids love history, so our job is to find new and exciting ways of presenting history to them." Not only does Ottaviano have a personal interest in such subjects, but, she claims, "Holt knows how to sell these books. The continued success of these titles on our backlist testifies to that. In today's publishing climate, the market is challenging; books are at an advantage if they speak to a niche."

Cash comments, "Authors need to find out what's missing yet needed." Budnick sums it up: "Well-written, thoughtfully organized, original nonfiction is something that editors are always looking for. I think more than ever those in publishing are interested in approaches that look outside the box—unusual formats with a distinct point of view."

Today's successful nonfiction is fresh, appealing, and contemporary in format and design, even if the topic is as old as history. But as nonfiction of merit always has done, these books stand solidly on mountains of investigative research and substantiated fact.

News of the Year

Anniversaries

➤ April marked the seventy-fifth anniversary of Viking's Junior Books division. Junior Books began under May Massee, who worked with such writers as Ludwig Bemelsmans, Munro Leaf, and Robert McCloskey.

➤ J. K. Rowling's Harry Potter series marked its ten-year anniversary. The first title in the seven-book series, *Harry Potter and the Sorcerer's Stone,* was published in 1998.

➤ This year marked the twenty-first anniversary of Martin Handford's Waldo, the bespectacled character who gained fame by getting lost in a crowd, prompting the catch-phrase "Where's Waldo?" The anniversary brings two new titles and a wealth of merchandise targeting the twenty-somethings who grew up with the character.

➤ Vermont-based Tuttle Publishing celebrated its sixtieth anniversary. The press, founded by Charles Tuttle Jr., marked the occasion by publishing new editions of its first titles. The titles from Tuttle Publishing focus on bridging East and West cultures.

➤ Sleeping Bear Press marked the tenth anniversary of its first children's title, *The Legend of Sleeping Bear.* The Michigan-based company launched in 1994 as a publisher of regional titles and became exclusively a children's book publisher in 1998.

➤ Running Press Kids celebrated its fifth anniversary this year. The imprint, which has seen much growth in the past two years, started licensed publishing this year with its first line of John Deere books.

113

➤ Abbeville Press marked its thirtieth anniversary by launching a new division, Abbeville Family. The division includes the Abbeville Kids imprint, as well as Abbeville titles for parents and families.

➤ Don Freeman's popular children's book about a toy bear with a button missing from its trousers, *Corduroy*, celebrated its fortieth anniversary.

➤ MadLibs, the popular game of inserting nouns, adjectives, and verbs, turned 50 this year. Price Stern Sloan celebrated the occasion with the publication of a new deluxe oversized edition featuring over 125 new MadLibs.

Awards

➤ The John Newbery Medal was presented to Laura Amy Schlitz for *Good Masters! Sweet Ladies! Voices from a Medieval Village* (Candlewick). Newbery Honor Books were *Elijah of Buxton*, by Christopher Paul Curtis (Scholastic Press); *The Wednesday Wars*, by Gary D. Schmidt (Clarion); and *Feathers*, by Jacqueline Woodson (Putnam).

➤ The Randolph Caldecott Medal went to Brian Selznick for *The Invention of Hugo Cabret* (Scholastic Press). The win marks the first time the medal has been presented to an illustrated novel.

➤ Orson Scott Card was the recipient of the Margaret A. Edwards Award, honoring his lifetime achievement in writing for teens.

➤ The Michael L. Printz Award was presented to *The White Darkness*, by Geraldine McCaughrean (HarperTempest). The Printz Honor books were *Dreamquake: Book Two of the Dreamhunter Duet*, by Elizabeth Knox (Frances Foster); *One Whole and Perfect Day*, by Judith Clarke (Front Street); *Repossessed*, by A. M. Jenkins (HarperTeen); and *Your Own, Sylvia: A Verse Portrait of Sylvia Plath*, by Stephanie Hemphill (Knopf).

➤ The Scott O'Dell Award for Historical Fiction was presented to Christopher Paul Curtis for *Elijah of Buxton* (Scholastic Press).

➤ The James Madison Book Award was presented to James Cross Giblin for *The Many Rides of Paul Revere*.

➤ The Boston Globe-Horn Book Awards went to *The Absolutely True Diary of a Part-Time Indian*, by Sherman Alexie (Little, Brown), for fiction/poetry; *At Night*, by Jonathan Bean (FSG), for picture book; and

The Wall, by Peter Sís (FSG/Foster), for nonfiction.

➤ Mystery Writers of America presented its Edgar Award to Katherine Marsh for *The Night Tourist* (Disney/Hyperion) for the best juvenile novel and to *Rat Life,* by Tedd Arnold (Dial), for the best young adult novel.

➤ The Américas Award for Children's and Young Adult Literature was presented to *Red Glass,* by Laura Resau (Delacorte), and *Yum! ¡Mmmm! ¡Que Rico! America's Sproutings,* by Pat Mora.

➤ British author Philip Reeve won the Los Angeles Times Book Prize in the young adult category for *A Darkling Plain* (HarperCollins/EOS).

➤ The Canadian Library Association presented its Book of the Year for Children Award to Christopher Paul Curtis for *Elijah of Buxton.* The CLA Young Adult Canadian Book Award went to *Mistik Lake,* by Martha Brooks.

➤ The Jane Addams Childrens Book Awards went to *The Escape of Oney Judge: Martha Washington's Slave Finds Freedom,* by Emily Arnold McCully (FSG), in the Books for Younger Children category; and *We Are One: The Story of Bayard Rustin,* by Larry Dane Brimner (Calkins Creek), in the Books for Older Children category.

➤ Swiss author Jürg Schubiger and Italian illustrator Robert Innocenti won the Hans Christian Andersen Award, which is presented every other year to a living author and illustrator whose complete works have made an important contribution to children's literature.

➤ The Ezra Jack Keats Book Award was presented to author David Ezra Stein for his picture book *Leaves* (Putnam) and to illustrator Jonathan Bean for *The Apple Pie that Papa Baked* (Simon & Schuster).

➤ The fifty-ninth annual Christopher Awards were presented to *Taking a Bath with the Dog and Other Things That Make Me Happy,* by Scott Menchin (Candlewick) for preschool; *How Many Seeds in a Pumpkin?* by Margaret McNamara (Schwartz & Wade) for ages 6 to 8; *Owen & Mzee: The Language of Friendship* by Isabella Hatkoff, Craig Hatkoff, and Dr. Paula Kahumbu (Scholastic Press) for ages 8 to 10; *The Wild Girls,* by Pat Murphy (Viking) for ages 10 to 12; and *Diamonds in the Shadow,* by Caroline B. Cooney for young adult.

➤ Jon Scieszka was named the United States' first National Ambassador for Young People's Literature. He is the author of *The Stinky Cheese Man and Other Fairly Stupid Tales, The True Story of the Three*

Little Pigs, and *The Frog Prince, Continued.*

➤ The Costa Book Award (formerly the Whitbread Award) went to *The Bower Bird,* by Ann Kelley (Luath Press) in the children's book category.

➤ Lee & Low Books' New Voices Award was presented to Pamela M. Tuck for her novel, *A Fly in a Bowl of Milk.*

➤ *M. L. K.: Journey of a King,* by Tonya Bolden (Abrams) was awarded the Orbis Pictus Award for Outstanding Nonfiction for Children. Five honor titles were also announced: *Black and White Airmen: Their True History,* by John Fleischman (Houghton Mifflin); *Helen Keller: Her Life in Pictures,* by George Sullivan (Scholastic); *Muckrakers,* by Ann Bausum (National Geographic); *Spiders,* by Nic Bishop (Scholastic); and *Venom,* by Marilyn Singer (Darby Creek).

➤ The Society of Children's Book Writers and Illustrators (SCBWI) announced the winners of its Golden Kite Award, which recognizes excellence in children's literature. This year's winners are Katherine Applegate for *Home of the Brave* (Feiwel and Friends) for fiction; *Muckrakers,* by Ann Bausum (National Geographic) for nonfiction; *Pierre in Love,* by Sara Pennypacker (Orchard) for picture book text; and *Little Night,* by Yuyi Morales (Roaring Brook) for picture book illustration.

➤ Mary Ann Hoberman was selected by the Poetry Foundation as Children's Poet Laureate.

➤ The Guardian Children's Fiction Prize went to *The Knife of Never Letting Go,* by Patrick Ness (Walker Books).

➤ The finalists for the National Book Award in the category of Young People's Literature were *Chains,* by Laurie Halse Anderson (Simon & Schuster); *The Underneath,* by Kathi Appelt (Atheneum); *What I Saw and How I Lied,* by Judy Blundell (Scholastic); *The Disreputable History of Frankie Landau-Banks,* by E. Lockhart (Hyperion); and *The Spectacular Now,* by Tim Tharp (Knopf).

Mergers, Acquisitions, & Reorganizations

➤ Houghton Mifflin purchased Harcourt's Education Group. The acquisition includes Harcourt's el-hi operations, as well as its trade and reference division. Harcourt closed its San Diego trade division in June as part of restructuring changes in the integration of Harcourt and

Houghton Mifflin trade operations into Houghton Mifflin Harcourt Trade & Reference Publishers division.

Houghton Mifflin sold its college division to Cengage Learning. As part of their agreement, Houghton Mifflin will sell Cengage's college titles into the high school advanced placement market.

➢ Mathew Price Ltd. closed up shop in the United Kingdom and moved its home to Texas this year. Its titles will continue to be published in both countries.

➢ Cloth book and play set publisher SoftPlay, Inc. acquired Boston-based Kidsbooks. Kidsbooks will remain a separate entity with its editorial, product development, and sales offices remaining in the Boston area. Kidsbooks publishes approximately 100 titles annually with a backlist of more than 500 titles.

➢ Chronicle Books acquired the New York-based Handprint Books. Handprint became a Chronicle imprint, beginning with its fall 2008 list.

➢ Lerner Publishing Group inked a deal with *USA Today* to create a high-quality, educational series for upper elementary, middle-grade, and high school students. Its first four titles are biographies of Oprah Winfrey, Tiger Woods, Bill Gates, and Vera Wang. The titles resulting from this deal will be released under Lerner's Twenty-First Century Books division.

➢ Raincoast Books closed its Canadian publishing operations. Raincoast continues to operate as a distributor.

➢ Los Angeles-based Tokyopop reorganized by creating two divisions, the Tokyopop Inc. publishing division and Tokyopop Media, a digital and comics-to-film unit. The restructuring resulted in layoffs of close to 40 staff members.

➢ Marvel Comics and HarperCollins joined forces to launch a reading program based on the popular Marvel Comics superhero Spider-Man. The new line features titles in a variety of formats.

➢ New Harbinger Publications acquired Instant Help Books, a Connecticut publisher of workbooks used by mental health professionals and educators to help treat the emotional and psychological issues of children and teens.

➢ Random House acquired Tamarind Ltd., strengthening its position as a multicultural publisher. Tamarind Ltd. was founded by Verna Wilkins, who remains its director. The list from Tamarind includes picture books featuring children of all backgrounds and cultures.

➤ Kensington Publishing acquired most of the assets of Holloway House Publishing, including approximately 400 backlist titles. The titles will now be published under Kensington's Holloway House Classics imprint.

➤ After failing to meet its fiscal 2008 goals, Scholastic sold its direct-to-home continuities unit to the Norwegian publisher and distributor Sandvik.

➤ Actress Julie Andrews has moved her imprint, the Julie Andrews Collection, to Little, Brown. The imprint, which Andrews founded with her daughter Emma Walton Hamilton, is now overseen by Liza Baker. Its 25-title backlist remains at HarperCollins.

Launches & Ventures

Books

➤ Beach Lane Books is the new Simon & Schuster imprint from former Harcourt Editor in Chief Allyn Johnston. The San Diego-based imprint will produce 18 to 20 titles yearly. It will primarily focus on picture books for young children, but will also offer titles for middle-grade and young adult readers.

➤ IDW, a graphic novel, horror, and science fiction publisher, launched its new children's imprint, Worthwhile Books. The imprint will publish under IDW's new Jonas Publishing Division.

➤ Struggling readers are the target audience of the new licensed book line from Stone Arch Books. The fiction imprint of Capstone Press debuts its licensed book line, which features popular superheroes from DC Comics. The line will be distributed in the school and library market and will include 48 titles over four seasons.

➤ MacKenzie Smiles is a new, San Francisco-based children's publisher co-founded by Christina Turner and Brenda McLaughlin. The company focuses on bringing other countries and cultures to children living in the U.S.

➤ Kensington Publishing expanded its presence in the children's market with the introduction of its Marimba Books imprint. The multicultural imprint was established in partnership with Hudson Publishing Group.

➤ Fourth Story Media is the brainchild of former Scholastic Trade Publishing and Book Fairs president, Lisa Holton. Holton's plan for this new studio is to integrate books and the Internet to develop children's properties. Fourth Story plans to produce material in multiple formats including books, websites, games, and DVDs.

➤ Barefoot Books launched its Young Fiction Program, a new fiction line of stories that focus on various cultures and traditions. Its debut title, *Little Leap Forward: A Boy in Beijing,* is based on co-author Guo Yue's experience growing up during the Cultural Revolution in China. Primarily a picture book publisher, Barefoot Books plans to make illustrations a prominent part of its new program.

➤ Begin Smart is the new developmental reading program resulting from the partnership between Begin Smart Books and Sterling. The program targets children from birth to two with titles that are leveled by age and ability in six-month increments. Begin Smart offers titles in several formats, including board books and lift-the-flap titles.

➤ Christy Ottaviano, former Executive Editor at Henry Holt Books for Young Readers, started her own eponymous imprint at Holt. The imprint will publish approximately 20 titles annually ranging from preschool readers through young adult titles.

➤ Science fiction and fantasy publisher Tor Books joined with Seven Seas Entertainment this year to create a new Tor imprint, Tor/Seven Seas. The imprint is Tor's first step into the U.S. manga market and will publish both original and licensed-character material.

➤ Egmont USA is the new American subsidiary of the Egmont Group. Douglas Pocock heads the subsidiary that will publish its inaugural list in fall 2009. Egmont USA will focus primarily on middle-grade fiction, an area of strength for Egmont in the United Kingdom, but will also publish picture books and young adult titles.

➤ Audible Frontiers is the new science fiction and fantasy imprint from Audible. Its digital titles are available only at audible.com/scifi.

➤ David Macaulay Studio is the new imprint at Roaring Brook Press set to launch in 2011. It will publish future titles by Macaulay, as well as titles from other authors and illustrators.

➤ Little Simon launched its eco-friendly line of children's books targeting parents and children interested in environmental awareness. Little Green Books publishes titles in several formats including cloth books, board books, and novelty formats.

➤ Former Sterling Publishing Executive Editor Julie Trelstad launched White Plains Press, a venture she started from her home.

➤ Hachette-owned European publisher Octopus Books formed its own North American group. Octopus Books USA announced a January 2009 start-up.

➤ The Houghton Mifflin Harcourt Children's Publishing Group re-launched the Sandpiper paperback imprint. The imprint targets younger readers, with picture books to middle-grade titles.

Magazines

➤ *Kidzine* targets children ages 6 to 12 in the Toronto, Canada, region. Sharon Foster is Editor of the monthly, which offers games, stories, and activities.

➤ *WWE Kids* is the new bimonthly from World Wrestling Entertainment that targets children ages 6 to 14.

➤ *Mindful Mama* is a green lifestyle magazine that debuted this year focusing on pregnancy, birth, and raising a family.

➤ Targeting fans of *Dora the Explorer,* the British and Italian joint venture GE Fabbri launched *Dora Dress Up and Go,* a biweekly that features Dora on new adventures with accompanying crafts and activities.

➤ *World of Cars* is a new title from Egmont Magazines that targets four- to seven-year-old boys and offers comic strips, puzzles, and games based on the Disney movie, *Cars.*

➤ *Shrek's Quests* targets fans of the popular ogre, offering adventures and activities inside each biweekly issue.

➤ The content in the newly launched *007* focuses on the action and villains from the adventures of the fictional spy.

➤ Attempting to step away from the many magazines for young adults that focus on appearance and shopping, new magazine *KidSpirit* focuses on nature, science, and spiritual and global issues targeting 11- to 15-year-old readers.

➤ *Brass* is a new quarterly for young adults interested in learning how to manage their finances.

➤ Young adults in Canada read *Cream World* for its information on fashion, music, movies, arts, and culture.

➤ *RGVSports.com* is a new quarterly magazine that covers high school sports and athletes in the Texas Rio Grande Valley.

➤ Young adults ages 16 to 34 are the target audience of *Gradient,* a new quarterly that launched this summer. The free publication for residents of New York City covers dining, travel, fashion, and the arts in the metropolitan area.

➤ Los Angeles parents of children 4 to 14 read *KidsLA,* launched as a quarterly this summer with plans to go bimonthly by the end of the year. It is distributed free in pediatric offices, private schools, and high-income neighborhoods.

➤ *Canadian Teen Girl* is an inspirational magazine that promotes a healthy and positive body image. Alexandra Kimball is the Editor in Chief of the quarterly that is distributed free in more than 500 Canadian high schools.

➤ *Conservationist for Kids* targets fourth-grade students in the state of New York with an interest in nature, the environment, and conservation.

Multimedia

➤ Penguin Books for Young Readers teamed up with national radio network, BusRadio, to provide content that will be broadcast daily to more than one million children during their bus rides to and from school. Each month a different Penguin title will be featured.

➤ Simon & Schuster Children's Publishing made a formal arrangement with the Gotham Group to ensure a bigger piece of the profits of its book-to-film deals.

➤ Macmillan Publishing Solutions subsidiary MPS Mobile teamed with Simon & Schuster to distribute over 500 of Simon & Schuster's titles through its Global Reader platform. Among the first titles to be released as e-books through MPS Mobile are the Nancy Drew mysteries.

Book Deals

➤ Ben Schrank at Razorbill acquired North American rights to *The Teen Vogue Handbook: An Insider's Guide to Careers in the Fashion Industry,* by Amy Astley with Lauren Waterman.

➤ Jake Parker sold two graphic novels featuring his character Missile Mouse to David Saylor for the Graphix imprint at Scholastic. The first title, *Missile Mouse: The Star Crusher,* will be released in spring 2010. Judy Hansen of Hansen Literary Agency organized the deal.

➤ Jennifer Lyons of the Jennifer Lyons Literary Agency orchestrated a deal with Howard Reeves from Abrams Books for Young Readers to publish the first two picture books from Angela Farris Watkins, niece of Dr. Martin Luther King Jr.

➤ HarperCollins purchased world rights to a new YA fiction series from the star of MTV's reality show, *The Hills.* Lauren Conrad's series, tentatively titled L.A. Candy, is loosely inspired by her life experiences.

➤ Margaret Raymo of Houghton Mifflin purchased world rights to Newbery medalist Lois Lowry's *Birthday Ball.* The middle-grade novel will be published in spring 2010.

➤ Razorbill's Jessica Rothenberg acquired *Strange Angels,* the debut novel from Lili St. Crow, in a three-book deal that was organized by Miriam Kriss at the Irene Goodman Literary Agency.

➤ Newbery winner Kate DiCamillo's new middle-grade novel, *The Magician's Elephant,* was acquired by Candlewick Press.

➤ Lexa Hillyer of Razorbill acquired Mandy Hubbard's debut novel *Prada and Prejudice.* A two-book deal was organized by Zoe Fishman of Lowenstein-Yost.

➤ The 2008 election was the focus of many new titles. Meghan McCain, daughter of Senator John McCain, released her first picture book, *My Dad, John McCain.* The book was acquired by Mark McVeigh at Aladdin Books. *Barack Obama: Son of Promise, Child of Hope,* by Nikki Grimes, and *Hillary Rodham Clinton: Dreams Taking Flight,* by Kathleen Krull, were acquired by Alexandra Cooper at Simon & Schuster Books for Young Readers.

➤ Hyperion acquired *Burning Up: On Tour with the Jonas Brothers,* the behind-the-scenes title by Disney's juggernaut boy band.

➤ Harlequin's Tracy Farrell acquired a new YA urban fantasy series by Gena Showalter that will launch the imprint's upcoming YA line.

➤ Regina Griffin at Egmont USA acquired two new titles by Walter Dean Myers set for publication in fall 2009.

➤ Miley Cyrus, of *Hannah Montana* fame, teamed with the Disney Book Group to publish her first book covering her rise to fame.

➤ Susan Van Metre of Amulet Books acquired Michael Buckley's middle-grade adventure series N.E.R.D.S.: National Espionage, Rescue, and Defense Society. The first three titles from the series will be published in fall 2009.

➤ A graphic edition of famous novelist James Patterson's new young adult series, Maximum Ride, will be published by Yen Press, the new graphic novel imprint at Hachette Book Group USA.

➤ Nancy Conescu at Little, Brown Books for Young Readers acquired *Thirteen Treasures*, a debut middle-grade novel by Michelle Harrison.

➤ Simon & Schuster Books for Young Readers released a picture book version of Bob Dylan's song, "Forever Young."

➤ Simon Boughton at Roaring Brook Press purchased *Applesauce Season,* by Eden Ross Lipson, former children's book editor of the *New York Times.*

➤ HarperCollins acquired the rights to Danielle Steele's *The Happiest Hippo in the World.* This is not the romance novelist's first experience in children's publishing. She published the Max and Martha picture book series with Delacorte.

➤ Coretta Scott King Award winner Javaka Steptoe sold her debut graphic novel, tentatively titled *Tupac Shakur: A Graphic Novel in Three Acts,* to Candlewick Press.

➤ Scholastic acquired a multiplatform middle-grade adventure series, the 39 Clues, from Rick Riordan, author of the bestselling Percy Jackson series.

➤ Candace Bushnell, author of *Sex and the City,* signed with Balzer & Bray in a two-book deal to write teen novels. The first book, *The Carrie Diaries,* is scheduled for release in fall 2010.

➤ Eoin Colfer, author of *Artemis Fowl,* was chosen to write the sixth book in the Hitchhiker's Guide to the Galaxy series. The first title is *And Another Thing . . . .*

➤ Scholastic acquired a picture book titled *March On! The Day My Brother Martin Changed the World,* by Christine King Farris, sister of Dr. Martin Luther King, Jr.

➤ Nancy Mercado at Roaring Brook Press purchased world rights to *Episodes,* a memoir by 20-year-old autistic student Blaze Ginsburg.

➤ Thomas Nelson acquired an unpublished manuscript by author Margaret Wise Brown. The manuscript of *The Moon Shines Down* was

123

found in Brown's sister's attic more than 30 years after her death.

➤ From her eponymous imprint, Paula Wiseman Books, at Simon & Schuster, Paula Wiseman acquired *Tea for Ruby* by the Duchess of York, Sarah Ferguson. The book is illustrated by Robin Preiss Glasser.

➤ Scholastic's Andrea Pinkney acquired world rights to a historical picture book by Lois Lowry titled *Crow Call.*

Other News

➤ A partial rough draft of Stephenie Meyer's upcoming novel was leaked online, prompting her to put the project on hold indefinitely. She is quoted as saying to *Publishers Weekly,* "I think it is important for everybody to understand that what happened was a huge violation of my rights as an author, not to mention a human being."

➤ Singer Dionne Warwick adds picture book writer to her résumé with the release of *Say a Little Prayer* from Running Press. The title is co-authored by David Freeman Wooley and Tonya Bolden.

➤ Beginning on September 14, the *New York Times* changed the criteria for the series category of its children's bestsellers list. All series with a minimum of three titles will now be listed in the section. Previously, at least one title had to have been published in hardcover, but the change comes in the wake of the onslaught of such series as Lisi Harrison's Clique, which has been released in paperback.

➤ Harry Potter author J. K. Rowling won her lawsuit against RDR Books, thus preventing the publication of *The Harry Potter Lexicon,* by Steven Vander Ark, which she maintained would infringe on her copyright to the popular series.

➤ Legendary creator of many classic children's titles Maurice Sendak turned 80 on June 10. Sendak's forthcoming title, *Bumble-Ardy,* will be released by Michael di Capua Books in 2010.

➤ Basketball players Larry Bird and Magic Johnson are teaming up to publish a new book chronicling both their rivalry and friendship. The title will be published by Houghton Mifflin Harcourt.

➤ *The Cat in the Hat, Horton Hears a Who!,* and *Green Eggs and Ham* are among the Dr. Seuss classics that were launched in digital versions this year resulting from a partnership between Dr. Seuss Enterprises and kidthing.com, a content distribution platform.

➤ Simon & Schuster Children's Publishing rejoined the Children's Book Council (CBC) just one year after its departure. According to *Publishers Weekly*, Publicity Director at Simon & Schuster Paul Crichton realigned with the CBC because it "made a few changes that are in line with our greater vision."

➤ Toymaker RC2 Corp. called off its purchase of Publications International's childrens publishing group, citing high financing as its main reason not to go through with the deal.

➤ Christopher Paolini's long-awaited third volume of the Inheritance Cycle, *Brisingr,* was released by Knopf in September, breaking Random House's sales record by selling 550,000 copies in its first day.

People

Books

➤ Brian Murray replaced Jane Friedman as President and CEO of HarperCollins.

➤ Stephanie Owens Lurie was named Editorial Director at Hyperion Books. The change in title has Lurie overseeing publishing programs at Disney's Hyperion and Jump at the Sun imprints.

➤ Ginee Seo resigned as Vice President and Editorial Director of Atheneum Books for Young Readers, leaving behind her own imprint. She is completing work on titles-in-progress, on a freelance basis.

➤ Laura Geringer stepped down from her eponymous imprint at HarperCollins to spend more time on her writing career and charity work with First Book. She was with HarperCollins for 28 years; her imprint sold more than 50 million books.

➤ Andrew Karre, formerly Acquiring Editor at Flux, the YA imprint of Llewellyn Worldwide, was hired as Editorial Director at Carolrhoda. His duties now include developing, acquiring, and editing fiction and nonfiction titles, along with picture books for the trade market.

➤ Stephen Roxburgh resigned as Publisher at Boyds Mills Press. Roxburgh has been with Boyds Mills since its 2004 acquisition of Front Street Books, which he founded in 1994. Boyds Mills closed its Asheville, N.C., office where Front Street Books was based. Editor Joy Neaves at the North Carolina office will not remain with the company on a full-time basis, and the status of the imprint is uncertain.

➤ Children's book Editor and Publisher Joanna Cotler, of the Joanna Cotler Books imprint at HarperCollins, stepped down from her current position. Her new title is Editor at Large and she will continue editing select titles under the Joanna Cotler imprint.

➤ HarperCollins announced its new imprint Balzer & Bray after the new hires of Alessandra Balzer and Donna Bray, former Editorial Director and Executive Editor at Hyperion Books for Children. Its inaugural list is set for fall 2009.

➤ Regina Griffin was hired as Executive Editor at Egmont USA. Griffin was formerly Editor in Chief at Holiday House.

➤ HarperCollins Children's Books hired Kelly Smith as Senior Editor.

➤ Houghton Mifflin Harcourt announced the appointments of Mary Wilcox to Vice President and Editorial Director, Franchise Publishing; and of Julia Richardson to Editorial Director, Paperback Publishing for all imprints within Houghton Mifflin Harcourt Children's Book Group.

➤ Carol Burrell was promoted to Editorial Director at Graphic Universe. She previously held the title of Senior Editor.

➤ Susan Van Metre was promoted from Executive Editor to Editorial Director at Amulet Books.

➤ Farrar, Straus, and Giroux hired Jill Davis as Executive Editor. She comes to the company from Bloomsbury Children's Books, where she was an executive editor.

➤ Andrea Welch joined Allyn Johnston's new imprint Beach Lane Books as Editor. Welch and Johnston previously worked together at Harcourt.

➤ Former Listening Library Publisher and Publisher at Large for Random House Audio Tim Ditlow joined Brillance Audio. Much of his focus will be on growing Brillance's children's audio market.

➤ John Rudolph was promoted from Senior Editor to Executive Editor at Putnam Books for Young Readers.

➤ Sally Doherty was hired as Executive Editor at Henry Holt Books for Young Readers.

➤ Jordan Brown was hired as Editor at Walden Pond Press, a new imprint at HarperCollins.

➤ Former Editorial Director at Harcourt Children's Books, Elizabeth Van Doren was named Editor in Chief at Black Dog & Leventhal, a publisher of titles for both children and adults.

➤ Liesa Abrams was promoted from Senior Editor to Executive Editor at Aladdin Books.

➤ Emily Meehan was promoted to Executive Editor at Simon & Schuster Books for Young Readers.

➤ Simon Pulse promoted Anica Rissi to Senior Editor.

➤ Greg Rutty was promoted to Associate Editor at Scholastic Press. He previously held the title of Assistant Editor at Scholastic Paperbacks.

➤ Scholastic Paperbacks hired Jonathan Valuckas as Editorial Coordinator; he was previously Executive Assistant at Scholastic.

➤ Bloomsbury Children's Books hired Margaret Miller as Editor. She comes to the company from HarperCollins Children's Books.

➤ Houghton Mifflin Harcourt Children's Books Group promoted Monica Perez to Senior Editor.

➤ Little, Brown Books for Young Readers named Joseph Monti Director of Paperbacks. The newly created position has Monti overseeing the imprint's middle-grade and young adult reissues.

➤ Jennifer Besser was promoted from Senior Editor to Executive Editor at the Disney Book Group. *The Night Tourist* and *The Runaway Dolls* are among the titles that she has edited.

➤ Arthur A. Levine was named Vice President and Publisher of Arthur A. Levine Books; his previous title was Vice President and Editorial Director at the 12-year-old imprint.

➤ At Penguin Young Readers Group, Nicole Kasprazak was promoted to Associate Editor at G. P. Putnam's Sons; and Kristin Ostby and Molly Kempf were both promoted to Associate Editor at Grosset & Dunlap/PSS!.

➤ Barbara Berson was let go from Penguin Group Canada as part of a company-wide restructuring. Nicole Winstanley assumed the responsibility of Penguin Group Canada's children's publishing.

➤ Ellen Kriet was promoted from Vice President to President at Puffin Books.

➤ After leaving his position at Harcourt Trade, Dan Farley was named interim President and Publisher at Macmillan's Henry Holt division. Farley replaces John Sterling, who now holds the title of Vice President at Macmillan.

➤ Philomel Books promoted Michael Green from Vice President to President and Publisher.

➢ The Egmont Group appointed Elizabeth Law Vice President and Publisher of its new American children's publishing subsidiary, Egmont USA. Law was most recently Vice President and Associate Publisher at Simon & Schuster Books for Young Readers.

➢ Suzanne Murphy was named Vice President and Publisher, Trade Publishing and Marketing. Ellen Berger, who previously held the title, was promoted to President of Scholastic's Trade Division. Since starting her position, Murphy named David Saylor to the newly created position of Vice President, Associate Publisher and Creative Director for hardcover books.

➢ Kate Harrison was named Senior Editor at Dial Books for Young Readers.

➢ Jessica Garrison was promoted to Editor at Dial Books for Young Readers; she was previously Assistant Editor.

➢ Kiley Fitzsimmons was promoted to Assistant Editor at Atheneum Books for Young Readers.

➢ HarperCollins laid off Adriana Dominguez, head of its Rayo children's imprint. The imprint will be maintained under Maria Gomez.

➢ Debra Dorfman was named Vice President and Publisher of paperbacks at Cartwheel and Licensed Publishing at Scholastic. Dorfman came to Scholastic from Penguin Books for Young Readers, where she held the title of President and Publisher of Grosset & Dunlap/Price Stern Sloan.

➢ Karen Wojtyla was promoted to Editorial Director at Margaret K. McElderry Books.

➢ Kelli Chipponeri was promoted to Associate Editorial Director at Running Press Kids and Running Press Miniature Editions.

➢ Hyperion's longtime President Bob Miller left the company for a position at HarperCollins. According to *Publishers Weekly,* Miller will head a publishing studio that produces 25 titles a year.

➢ Paula Hannigan was named Children's Editor at the Accord division of Andrews McMeel. Hannigan comes to Accord having previously worked at Klutz Press.

➢ Little, Brown Books for Young Readers saw several promotions this year with Jennifer Hunt promoted to Executive Editor; Alvina Ling promoted to Senior Editor; and Nancy Conescu promoted to Editor.

➢ Doug Whiteman was promoted to the newly created position of

Executive Vice President, Business Operations at Penguin Group USA. He is succeeded in his former title of President, Penguin Young Readers Group, by Don Weisberg. Weisberg formerly held the title of Executive Vice President and CFO for North America at Random House.

➤ Barbara Marcus, former president of Scholastic Children's Books Publishing and Distribution, joined Penguin as a strategic advisor to the children's group.

➤ Anne Hoppe was named Executive Editor at the Bowen Press imprint at HarperCollins.

➤ Jennifer Klonsky was promoted to Editorial Director at Simon Pulse. She was previously Executive Editor.

➤ Former Assistant Editor Michael del Rosario was promoted to Associate Editor at Simon Pulse.

➤ Courtney Bongiolatti was promoted to Associate Editor at Simon & Schuster Books for Young Readers.

➤ AnnMarie Harris left her position of editor at Scholastic's licensed publishing group to join the trade paperback group as senior editor.

➤ Paula Wiseman was promoted to Vice President and Publisher at Simon & Schuster Children's Books' Paula Wiseman Books imprint.

➤ Anne Zafian was promoted to deputy publisher of Simon & Schuster's trade imprints, including Simon & Schuster Books for Young Readers, Atheneum, Margaret K. McElderry Books, and Paula Wiseman Books.

➤ Little, Brown Books for Young Readers announced the promotion of Liza Baker to Editor in Chief for the Little, Brown and LB Kids imprints.

➤ Nancy Hinkel was named Vice President at Knopf & Crown Books for Young Readers. Hinkel joined Random House in 1996 and was named Publishing Director of the imprint in 2003.

➤ Jeff DeBalko was named President of Reed Publishing Group. The promotion places him in charge of *Publishers Weekly*, *Library Journal*, and *School Library Journal*.

➤ Zondervan named Maureen "Moe" Girkins President and CEO. She took over the position in January from Interim President Bruce Ryskamp.

➤ Abigail McAden was promoted to Publishing Director, Paperbacks at Scholastic Paperbacks and Point. Most recently she was Editorial Director at Point.

➤ Deb Futter left Random House/Bantam Doubleday Dell for a position as Vice President and Editor in Chief at the hardcover division of Grand Central Publishing, a Hachette company. She replaces Amy Einhorn, who left the company to move to Penguin.

➤ At HarperFestival, Jodi Harris was promoted from Executive Editor to Editorial Director, and Erin Stein was promoted from Senior Editor to Executive Editor.

➤ Jennifer Haller was named Vice President and Associate Publisher at Harcourt Children's Books, an imprint of Houghton Mifflin Harcourt Children's Book Group.

➤ Howard Reeves was promoted to Senior Vice President, Publisher at Abrams Books for Young Readers.

➤ Marcus Leaver was promoted to President at Sterling Publishing. The position was previously held by Charlie Nurnberg, who resigned in January.

➤ Gretchen Hirsch joined HarperCollins Children's Books as Associate Editor.

➤ HarperCollins' Editorial Director and Foreign Acquisitons Manager Michael Sterns left the company to become an agent. He joined Firebrand Literary Agency as a partner. Brenda Bowen will assume his responsibilities at HarperCollins.

➤ Kara Sargent was promoted to Editorial Director at Simon Spotlight and Simon Scribbles.

➤ Albert Whitman & Company saw major personnel changes this year with Joe Boyd, President and Richard Gutrich, Vice President retiring. The operations were sold to John Quattrochi and Patrick McPartland.

➤ Colin Dickerman was promoted from Editorial Director to Publisher at Bloomsbury. Dickerman succeeded Karen Rinaldi, who left the company for Rodale Press.

➤ Richard Charkin, Executive Director at Bloomsbury Publishing PLC, added President of Bloomsbury USA to his list of titles.

➤ Eve Adler was promoted to Associate Editor at Christy Ottaviano Books, an imprint at Henry Holt.

Magazines

➤ Lori Singer Moran was named Editor in Chief at *Babytalk*.

➤ Vicky Smith was named Children's Book Review Editor at *Kirkus Reviews*. The position was previously held by Karen Breen who has since retired.

➤ Lori Robinson replaced Denise Crittendon as Editor at *African American Family*.

➤ Mary Esselman joined *bNetS@vvy* as Editor.

➤ Deborah Vetter was named Executive Editor at *Cicada*.

➤ Erin King is the new Editor at *Current Health 1*.

➤ Adriane Dorr replaced Julie Stiegemeyer as Managing Editor at *Higher Things*.

➤ Jim Beecher took over the role of Editor/Publisher at *Junior Baseball*.

➤ Lenée Harvey was hired as Editor at *OC Family*.

➤ Dr. Rosa Sailes took over the position of Senior Editor at *Preschool Playhouse* and *Primary Street*.

Closings

Books

➤ Chippewa Publishing
➤ Denlinger's Publishers
➤ Forest House Publishing Company
➤ Jordan House
➤ Raincoast Books

Magazines

➤ *Big Country Peacock Chronicle*
➤ *Characters*
➤ *Child Life*
➤ *Child Welfare Report*
➤ *CosmoGirl!*
➤ *Daughters*

➤ *Fandangle*
➤ *Girlfriend*
➤ *InQuest Gamer*
➤ *Kids Hall of Fame News*
➤ *Know Your World Extra*
➤ *Loud Magazine*
➤ *MomsVoice.com*
➤ *No Crime*
➤ *Potluck Children's Literary Magazine*
➤ *Synapse*
➤ *Technology & Learning*
➤ *True Girl*
➤ *Vegetarian Baby & Child*
➤ *Vegetarianteen.com*
➤ *Wee Ones*
➤ *With*

Deaths

➤ Founding member of SCBWI and author of over 25 children's books Sue Alexander passed away July 3 at 74. Alexander created SCBWI's Sue Alexander Award, which recognizes the most promising manuscript submitted to the SCBWI summer conference in Los Angeles.

➤ Scholastic editor and author Ann Kleinman Reit passed away on August 7. She is famous for her work on several paperback series including Sunfire Romances, Girls of Canby Hall, and the Guardians of Ga'Hoole.

➤ Author of over 17 young adult novels, Jeannette Eyerly died on August 18. *Escape from Nowhere* and *He's My Baby Now* were among her titles, which frequently dealt with serious subject matters.

➤ Lenore Blegvard, author of more than 12 children's books, died on September 5. Many of her titles, including *A Sound of Leaves, First Friends,* and *Kitty and Mr. Kipling: Neighbors in Vermont* were illustrated by her husband, Erik Blegvard.

➤ YA author Hila Colman passed away on May 15 at 98. She authored more than 50 books including *The Girl from Puerto Rico* and *Forgotten Girl.*

➤ British illustrator Pauline Baynes died on August 1. An illustrator of more than 100 books, she was perhaps best known for her drawings for the Chronicles of Narnia, by C. S. Lewis.

➤ Author and illustrator Tasha Tudor died at the age of 92 with over 100 titles to her credit. Her first title, *Pumpkin Moonshine*, was published in 1938.

➤ Charles Ellis, former President and CEO at John Wiley & Sons, died at the age of 72. He was with Wiley from 1988 to 1998.

➤ Colleen Salley died at the age of 79. She was the author of *Epossumondas* and its two sequels.

➤ Illustrator Dirk Zimmer, best known for his work on *In a Dark, Dark Room and Other Scary Stories* and *Bony-Legs,* died at age 64.

Style

Once Upon a Time Revisited: Myth, the Bible, Fairy Tales, & Shakespeare in Children's Narrative

By Christina Hamlett

What does a catchy tune have in common with a great plot? They both have beginnings, middles, and endings with recurring themes and variations throughout. They can both be played in virtually any venue, interpreted at any level, and use as many or as few voices as their creator feels necessary. Most important, such works have the potential to transcend time and become classics that are as relevant in the modern era as they were when they were first written and to the generations since.

Listen closely to musicians playing pieces from classical to jazz to rock to film scores and you can hear the influences that musicians of earlier decades, and even centuries, had on their respective styles. Similarly, the plot elements of whatever book you're reading—including the latest installment of Cecily von Ziegesar's Gossip Girl series—can also most likely be traced back to a quartet of core sources: mythology, the Bible, fairy tales and legend, and Shakespeare.

Are the rules of narrative structure carved in stone, never meant to be broken? Or is there enough wiggle room within their framework to put a fresh spin on tales we've heard a hundred times before?

Spirit, Reality, Understanding

When Julianna Baggott (whose books under the pseudonym of N. E. Bode include *The Slippery Map* and the Anybodies trilogy, all for

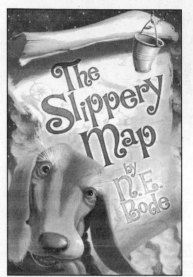

HarperCollins) was young, she was a reluctant reader, but she loved story tremendously. "Between the combination of Southern oral storytelling tradition and attending lots of my older sister's plays in New York, I definitely wasn't interested in realism. I was more excited by escape and adventure!" Now a successful author, she recalls hearing a comment by Kurt Vonnegut that no matter how much the advances in technology encouraged writers to challenge previous rules, writing still came down to the ongoing need for an old-fashioned plot.

But Baggott discovered that traditions may be adapted or even put aside. "I remember asking my editor what the rules were and was terrified to hear the reply, 'There are no rules.' What I discovered is that doors that had been closed for a long time were suddenly opening and allowing young readers to burst into the healthy, complex world they're right in the middle of, a world that's much different from what prior generations grew up with."

Baggott is fascinated by Stephenie Meyer's young adult Twilight series, for example. "What's so gripping to me is that it shows how the dark side of someone can poison you no matter how much you love them. It's a *magic realism*—minus a traditional happily ever after—that readers can apply to some of the dark chapters of their own lives such as divorce, separation, and loneliness."

Young readers may love the make-believe of fairy tales and myths, stories of times past, but they are also responsive to the underlying realities. Doris R. Wenzel, Publisher and Editor of Mayhaven Publishing, credits a long memory of childhood classics with how she evaluates new submissions. Yet breaking the rules of structure, she explains, is usually a good way to get her attention. "Children have always realized that nothing is happy ever after. When I read to children of all ages, they seem to connect, even in fantasy, with reality or the possibility of reality." As an illustration, she recommends the science fiction novel *A Doorway Through Space*, by Judith Bourassa Joy, as a plot abiding by classic story structure.

Wenzel also hits on another aspect of those four core sources that is found over and over again in fiction: the spiritual, moral, and physical

> # "It's a magic realism—minus a traditional happily ever after—that readers can apply to some of the dark chapters of their own lives."

quest. She cites *Pythagoras Eagle and the Music of the Spheres*, by Anne Carse Nolting, and *Following the Raven*, by Jenny Weaver, because they "mix reality with spiritual journeys where understanding is the goal and endings aren't necessarily happy."

Building Blocks of Modern Storytelling

It can be argued that the source and staying power of all fiction is the distinguishing of right from wrong, good from evil. Whether in the form of a biblical parable, a mythical epic, or chronicles of monarchs and mortals on the historical stage, classic story structure provides a template for moral behavior when people are confronted with temptation. In contemporary times the template underpins many genres.

Jason Schneider, Children's Publishing Manager of Dover Publications, believes it's hard to pinpoint just one aspect of fairy tales, folk stories, and legends that makes them so enduring, especially among children's stories. "Many tales have a long, rich history and were passed down by oral tradition through the years. Parents now pass these tales to their children, but with the addition of a printed medium. The stories have wonderful themes and ethical concepts that are important for children to learn, and many tales end with everyone living happily ever after."

Universal themes, ethical dilemmas, and satisfying resolutions from traditional storytelling still appeal in modern entertainment forms.

Websites and Blogs

➤ **Max Elliot Anderson:** www.maxbooks.9k.com,
http://booksandboys.blogspot.com
➤ **Julianna Baggott:** www.juliannabaggott.com
➤ **Baker Trittin Press:** www.bakertrittinpress.com
➤ **Cindy Hudson:** http://motherdaughterbookclub.com
➤ **Kar-Ben Publishing:** www.karben.com
➤ **Gabrielle Linnell:** www.innovativeteen.blogspot.com
➤ **Mayhaven Publishing:** www.mayhavenpublishing.com
➤ **Pamela Jaye Smith:** www.mythworks.net
➤ **Writer's Digest Books:** www.writersdigest.com/Books

Add to those qualities the appeal of characters. Schneider continues, "The influence of classic fairy tales and stories can be felt in today's popular movies, books, and programming for children. Whether elements such as the wicked witch are embodied by characters like Narnia's White Witch or *Star Wars*' Darth Vader, living happily ever after in an enchanted land (or with the whole fairy tale concept lampooned, as in *Shrek*), fairy tales are still the building blocks to modern storytelling and there will always be an audience for them."

Robert Lee Brewer, Editor of Writer's Digest Books, reflects on how his own childhood trio of favorite titles all adhere to conventional structure and underscore the timeless power of classics, and yet the three are so thoroughly different. They run the gamut from a French existentialist classic to a *Sesame Street* book to a novel by a master sports writer for children. Antoine de Saint-Exupery's "*The Little Prince* is still my favorite because I not only see something new in it, and myself, each time I read it, but it also reminds both children and adults of the importance of staying young mentally," says Brewer. "*The Monster at the End of This Book* (written by Jon Stone and published by Golden Books) is simple, cute, funny, and reminds us that our greatest fear is often ourselves. *Little Lefty,* by Matt Christopher (Little, Brown), is a classic story of a kid who overcomes adversity to become a good pitcher on his team. It's the only book I read multiple times as a multi-sport elementary school boy who preferred playing outside and studying stats on his baseball cards over reading books."

The remarkable thing about those four core sources—fairy tales, mythology, the Bible, and Shakespeare—Brewer says, is that they're applicable to any genre. "It often just takes a little creativity to see how to take a story and place it in the future or at a crime scene, etc. And as Shakespeare taught so well, the only thing that differentiates a drama from a comedy is whether everyone gets killed or hitched at the end."

Adventures and mysteries are among other genres that often incorporate traditional story arcs, heroic characters meeting challenges, and conflict between good and evil. Author of the Tweener Press Adventures for Christian publisher Baker Trittin Press, Max Elliot Anderson wasn't keen on reading books as a child—an odd condition, he quips, in light of the fact that his father, Ken, was a prolific author. But Anderson was immersed in storytelling.

"I grew up before many homes in America had a television. We used to listen to radio programs like *The Lone Ranger, Big John and Sparky,* and *The Shadow.* I can clearly remember how my imagination was engaged while listening to those shows and how we'd then go outside to create our own excitement," says Anderson. He relates that his dad, who also owned a film studio, would tell him original stories at night and allow him to visit the set during the day. "What I soaked up about character development, pacing, and classic plot structure came from watching him direct movies. When I began writing stories, they always came to me fully formed with a beginning, middle, and end—no doubt influenced by those childhood experiences."

It was natural for Anderson to find his writing home in adventures and mysteries for boys who are reluctant readers. The reluctant reader category, he explains, "wasn't popular when I started and it's still difficult to convince publishers there's a market for it today." Happily, his reviews for the Tweener Press books, including *Big-Rig Rustlers, Mountain Cabin Mystery,* and *Secret of Abbott's Cave,* demonstrate that what was hatched as a series that would appeal to young boys is now winning fans among females as well. The books incorporate biblical values, Christian perspectives on the environment and other issues, and the guidance and inspiration of God.

Culture and Character

Now the Editorial Director of Kar-Ben Publishing, Judye Groner was read to, and read avidly, from a very young age. Her adult career became connected to books that tell the stories of a culture, including its folktales, myths, and Bible stories. "Aside from a few didactic books [in my childhood], there were no children's stories that dealt with being Jewish." With the birth of her own children, Groner began writing Jewish books for them, a decision that launched Kar-Ben as a Jewish publisher.

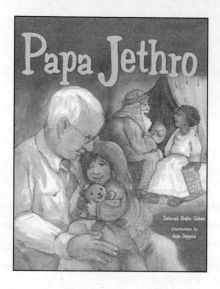

"Thirty years later, we continue to seek books that speak to today's Jewish community—the diversity of ethnic backgrounds, the variety of family structures, and the different modes of observance," says Groner. "What I think has made cultural myths endure is that kids like to imagine other worlds; they identify with the quest that is often part of folktales; and they particularly love tricksters and other humorous characters." She recommends *Papa Jethro*, by Deborah Bodin Cohen; and *The Hardest Word* and *Noah and the Ziz*, by Jacqueline Jules, as Kar-Ben titles that successfully integrate mythological and biblical themes into universal plots that resonate with contemporary readers.

As enticing as humorous characters or characters setting off on quests are villains, figures core to crafting classic standoffs between good and evil. But *Writer's Digest* Managing Editor Alice Pope says that writers often fall into a trap of making their villains one-dimensional. "That's so dull! We need villains we can sympathize with on some level—villains who are flawed, evil, and yet still human. Maybe even villains who have the capacity to learn and change. Villains need layers of complexity just like any character." While she believes there may indeed be nothing new under the sun, every writer has the freedom to bring a new twist to *old* characters and plots. "What's fresh is an author's unique voice, and ultimately that's what appeals to agents, editors, and readers."

A Contemporary Coliseum?

Contemporary times have seen a move toward reality-based plots with sad or ambiguous endings, and antiheroes with rebellious moral centers. Yet the classic master of these plots and characters is surely Shakespeare. Think of young Hamlet's angst, alienation, and rebellion against love and expected behavior. Or the adolescent, if not morally questionable, Prince Hal who plays hard with the clownish Falstaff and aggressively competes with Hotspur in *Henry IV*, but becomes the dynamic, honorable, inspirational young king delivering the Saint Crispin's Day speech at Agincourt in *Henry V*.

Author and mythology expert Pamela Jaye Smith believes the move toward the hard-edged character or plot is more the result of sociology than a major shift in story paradigms. "We saw the same thing in the late 1960s and 1970s as stories rebelled against the button-down, happy-ending Beaver Cleaver 1950s," she says. In films rebellion was expressed in the antiheroes of *Midnight Cowboy, Taxi Driver, The Wild Bunch,* and *Pretty Baby.* In books, the rebellion and darkness took the form of what came to be labelled *problem novels:* S. E. Hinton's *Outsiders* (1967), Paul Zindel's *The Pigman* (1968), Robert Cormier's *I Am the Cheese* (1977).

"It's a typical pendulum swing that alternating generations seem to spawn," says Smith. "Antiheroes give young people an inspiration not to be repressed by a contemporary culture that's dominated by imposed fear and rampant consumerism. The more rebel models we have in thinking and dreaming, the more exploration we'll do, the more things we'll discover, and the more adventures we'll dare."

With so much focus on realism in books for young readers, teens especially, Cindy Hudson feels it's sometimes easy to forget that children, and adults, also need to read for fun. The founder of the online Mother Daughter Book Club says, "When children inhabit fantasy worlds written on a page, they develop their ability to imagine creative solutions to life's challenges. It's likewise true that individuals who are experiencing real problems can benefit by discovering they're not alone when they read about someone else experiencing the same thing. Not only can these two approaches be balanced, but occasionally nudging us out of our comfort zones can be a rewarding journey as well."

At age 16, Gabrielle Linnell has already been published in many YA and writers' magazines and runs a website for teens. What shaped her storytelling style, she says, was a simultaneous introduction to the Bible and fairy tales. "I've never known a time where I didn't know both the stories of Jonah and John the Baptist as well as Cinderella and Sleeping Beauty. When I began writing, I wrote a lot of fantasy adventure stories that, at least in concept, were traditionally structured. Now I play around with structure more but that basic fairy tale framework is always in the back of my mind."

Linnell compares classic story structure to the Coliseum. "Every architect of great buildings since that time considers the Coliseum while planning: what makes it stand, what's given it such longevity, what makes it significant. The architect then either crafts a similar design (the White House) or goes in a completely opposite direction (the Eiffel Tower). Classic story structure is an influence that should always be considered, though not as a strict rule or old-fashioned model. It's simply one of the great ways to tell a story, and writers would be foolish not to study why it has worked in order to either use it or change it for their own style."

The Making of Memorable Nonfiction

By Judy Bradbury

"Each book demands its own research approach, and you have to discover it as you go along." So writes James Cross Giblin, author of more than 25 nonfiction books for children, in *The Giblin Guide to Writing Children's Books* (Writer's Institute).

Susan Campbell Bartoletti, author of the Newbery Honor book *Hitler Youth: Growing Up in Hitler's Shadow* (Scholastic); *The Flag Maker* (Houghton Mifflin); and numerous other nonfiction and historical fiction titles, agrees. "No writer writes a book the same way twice." She likens each nonfiction project to a puzzle that must be worked through: "Each book requires its own tricks."

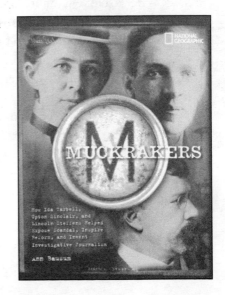

Golden Kite winner Ann Bausum, author of *Muckrakers: How Ida Tarbell, Upton Sinclair, and Lincoln Steffens Helped Expose Scandal, Inspire Reform, and Invent Investigative Journalism* (National Geographic), says the individual challenge of each nonfiction book "is what makes it fun."

Detective Work

The award-winning biographer Elizabeth Partridge claims her best

145

research technique is "insatiable curiosity." She explains, "I love doing research. I start by Googling the subject. That gives me a quick overview. But the problem, of course, is the unreliability factor, so I pretty quickly start looking at printed sources." Her titles include *John Lennon: All I Want Is the Truth* (Viking).

Bartoletti begins with exhaustive, careful notetaking. She pores over secondary sources, which she refers to as "standard works," culling for

> # "In the library, I look at the shelves nearby. I sit in the aisle and read, amassing a bibliography of my own."

"anything that makes my heart turn over." Her successful tackling of tough topics, and her delivery, have earned her a host of prestigious honors, including the Sibert Award.

Partridge's lifelong membership in her university alumni association allows her to check out books from the expansive library within walking distance of her home. "But the main way my research has changed" she says, is her use of www.abe.com—Advanced Book Exchange. "Anyone who has used books for sale, from small independent bookstores and Friends of Libraries groups to individuals, can post them here. It's amazing what I pick up for a few dollars!" Early in the process, Partridge "inhales information" by underlining, dog-earing pages, and taking notes.

Bausum calls this process detective work. "I begin by finding basic sources. These lead to the next layer, which includes scholarly books, anthologies, and articles. The tools embedded in these sources, such as the bibliography and footnotes, lead to additional resources and offer a variety of perspectives and slants on my subject. In the library I look at what books are shelved in the same proximity to those I've been led to. I sit in the aisle and read, amassing a bibliography of my own."

Although she consults secondary source materials, Partridge says, "I love primary sources. The material can be written (books, articles) or

interviews. It's fascinating to see what people say, how they express themselves, and the words they choose. I also love to conduct interviews with people who knew the person I'm writing about."

True Originals

Carole Boston Weatherford, award-winning poet and author of numerous works of historical fiction and fact-based historical verse, begins her process with a feeling, thought, or experience. For her latest picture book, *Becoming Billie Holiday* (Boyds Mills Press/WordSong), which she calls a "somewhat imagined verse memoir" of the singer's life from birth to age 25, Weatherford recalls listening to Holiday's music for months before writing a single line of the poetry that fills the book's pages. She read selectively from multiple biographies of Holiday, focusing on those sections that dealt specifically with details of the singer's childhood and young adult life. She delved into the discography and investigated oral histories, such as interviews of Holiday's contemporaries. Weatherford also read the singer's autobiography, but what impelled the author most in this project were her own memories. "I grew up on Billie Holiday's music," she reminisces. "I was meant to write this book."

Versatile nonfiction author Susan Goldman Rubin begins her art-related biographies with the art itself. Whenever possible she travels to view the original artwork. Then her work begins. "I never outline; it's too much like schoolwork," admits Rubin. She does, however, do the legwork, researching vigilantly before submitting a proposal to her publisher. "Preliminary research helps me find material that will be most interesting to my readers," says Rubin, who has written 15 art books for children, among them *Matisse: Dance for Joy*

Selected Nonfiction Publishers

➤ **Harry N. Abrams Books for Young Readers** and **Amulet Books:** The arts, history, nature and environment, relationships. www.abramsyoungreaders. com, www.amuletbooks.com

➤ **Absey & Company:** Educational. Activities, biography, history, religion, language arts. www.absey.biz

➤ **Annick Press:** Canadian culture, history, and contemporary issues. www.annickpress.com

➤ **Benchmark Books, Marshall Cavendish:** Educational. Animals, American studies, the arts, health, math, history, science, social studies, world cultures. www.marshallcavendish.com

➤ **Bess Press:** Hawaii and the Pacific Islands. Culture, history, language, natural history, literature, biography. www.besspress.com

➤ **Bloomsbury USA Children's Books:** Multicultural, autobiography. www.bloomsburyusa.com

➤ **Boyds Mills Press, Calkins Creek Books, Front Street Books:** Activities, geography, history, holidays, math, multicultural, nature, science. Calkins Creek is the American history imprint. www.boydsmillspress.com, www.calkinscreekbooks.com, www.frontstreetbooks.com

➤ **Charlesbridge Publishing:** Alphabet, animals, art, celebrations, math, multicultural, music, nature, science. www.charlesbridge.com

➤ **Chelsea House:** Curriculum-based, nonfiction only. American and world history, the arts, biography, careers, criminal justice, culture, drug education, health, nature and environment, reference, religion, science, sports, travel. www.chelseahouse.com

➤ **Chicago Review Press:** Animals, the arts, biography, history, how-to, humor, multicultural, natural history, science. www.chicagoreviewpress.com

➤ **Chronicle Books:** The arts, crafts, geography, health, history, holidays, multicultural, nature, reference, science, travel. www.chroniclebooks.com

➤ **Clear Light Books:** Native Americans, the Southwest, Hispanics, American and world history, cookbooks. www.clearlightbooks.com

➤ **Cooper Square Publishing, Luna Rising, Northland Books, NorthWord Books, Rising Moon, Two-Can Publishing:** Animals and nature, arts and crafts, biography, bilingual books, history, the Southwest, Mexican culture, science. www.coopersquarepublishing.com

➤ **The Creative Company:** Educational. Architecture, the arts, nature and the environment, explorers, geography, history, humanities, science, sports. www.thecreativecompany.us

➤ **Cricket Books:** History, math, science, social issues, sports. www.cricket-books.net

Selected Nonfiction Publishers

➤ **Dawn Publications:** Nature and the environment, family, multicultural. www.dawnpub.com

➤ **DK Publishing:** Nonfiction publisher with subjects across the spectrum. www.dk.com

➤ **DNA Press:** Science and technology. www.dnapress.com

➤ **Douglas & McIntyre Publishing:** Canadian regional and natural history, arts, culture. www.douglas-mcintyre.com

➤ **Dover Publications:** Botany, natural science, wildlife, science, regional. www.doverpublications.com

➤ **Eakin Press:** American Southwest. www.eakinpress.com

➤ **Eerdmans Books for Young Readers:** Biography, ecology, history, religion, social issues. www.eerdmans.com/youngreaders

➤ **Enslow Publishers:** Educational. Animals, arts and crafts, biography, careers, current issues, government, history, health, math, science projects, sports. www.enslow.com

➤ **Facts on File:** Current affairs, history, math, multicultural, politics, social issues, science. www.factsonfile.com

➤ **Fairview Press:** Physical, emotional, and spiritual health. www.fairview-press.org

➤ **Finney Company:** Middle-grade and YA educational and career guidance. www.finney-hobar.com

➤ **Fulcrum Publishing:** Conservation and the environment. www.fulcrum-books.com

➤ **Gale, Greenhaven Press, KidHaven Press, Lucent Books:** Gale is a large educational company with many imprints. www.gale.com/greenhaven, www.gale.com/kidhaven, www.gale.com/lucent

➤ **Gibbs Smith:** Activities, cookbooks, educational, nature. www.gibbs-smith.com

➤ **Globe Pequot Press:** Animals, nature, environment, regional, travel. www.globepequot.com

➤ **David R. Godine:** Wide range of topics, from study habits to the outdoors. www.godine.com

➤ **HarperCollins:** Large company with many imprints, including Amistad Press, Laura Geringer Books, Greenwillow, HarperTeen, and HarperTrophy, covering the entire range of nonfiction. www.harperchildrens.com

➤ **Hazelden Foundation:** Substance abuse, health, fitness, social issues. www.hazeldenbookplace.org

➤ **Health Press:** Wide variety of medical issues. www.healthpress.com

➤ **Hendrick-Long:** Texas and the Southwest. www.hendricklongpublishing.com

Selected Nonfiction Publishers

➤ **History Compass:** Biography, American history. www.historycompass.com

➤ **Holiday House:** Biography, history, social issues, science. www.holiday-house.com

➤ **Houghton Mifflin:** Large company with a wide range of nonfiction and imprints that include Clarion Books and Graphia. Purchased and integrated Harcourt over the last year. www.houghtonmifflinbooks.com, www.clarion-books.com, www.graphiabooks.com, www.harcourtbooks.com

➤ **Just Us Books:** African American biography, history, culture. www.justus-books.com

➤ **Lark Books:** Only nonfiction on a variety of subjects. www.larkbooks.com

➤ **Lee & Low Books:** Multicultural, ethnic issues and traditions, biography. www.leeandlow.com

➤ **Lerner Publishing Group, Millbrook Press, Twenty-First Century Books:** School and library books covering the curriculum. www.lernerbooks.com

➤ **Little, Brown and Company, Megan Tingley:** Division of Hachette. Covers many nonfiction subjects. www.hachettebookgroupusa.com/kids-teens.aspx

➤ **Macmillan; Farrar, Straus & Giroux; Feiwel & Friends; Henry Holt; Roaring Brook Press; Tor Books:** Wide range of topics from Macmillan USA. http://us.macmillan.com

➤ **Magination Press:** Family issues, grief, divorce, disabilities, medical issues. www.maginationpress.com

➤ **Mitchell Lane:** Nonfiction for reluctant readers. www.mitchelllane.com

➤ **Mondo Publishing:** Classroom literacy. www.mondopub.com

➤ **Morgan Reynolds:** High-quality, documented nonfiction on curriculum subjects and sports. www.morganreynolds.com

➤ **National Geographic Society:** Biography, culture, geography, history, nature and environment. www.nationalgeographic.com/books

➤ **Naturegraph:** Native Americans, birds, crafts, hiking, marine life, natural history, rocks, wildlife. www.naturegraph.com

➤ **North Country Books:** New York State, from the Hudson to the Adirondacks to the Finger Lakes. www.northcountrybooks.com

➤ **Richard C. Owen:** Educational, current events, geography, music, science, nature. www.rcowen.com

➤ **Peachtree Publishers:** Nature, recreation, travel. www.peachtree-online.com

➤ **Pelican Publishing:** Louisiana and Gulf Coast history, culture, travel, biography, self-help, cookbooks. www.pelicanpub.com

➤ **Penguin, Dial Books, Dutton Children's Books, Perigee Books, Philomel Books, Puffin, G. P. Putnam's, Viking:** Penguin Group imprints. Entire range of nonfiction subjects. www.penguin.com

➤ **Pineapple Press:** Subjects related to Florida. www.pineapplepress.com

➤ **Platypus Media; Science, Naturally!:** Health and fitness, math, multicultural,

Selected Nonfiction Publishers

nature, science and technology, social issues. www.platypusmedia.com

➤ **Prometheus Books:** Social, sexual, scientific, moral, religious issues. www.prometheusbooks.com

➤ **Random House, Crown Books, Alfred A. Knopf:** Random House imprints publish on a large array of nonfiction topics. www.randomhouse.com/kids

➤ **Raven Productions:** Natural history; North Woods, MN. www.ravenwords.com

➤ **Red Deer Press:** Canadian. Biography, field guides, nature, family activities. www.reddeerpress.com

➤ **Rosen Publishing Group, PowerKids Press:** Wide variety of standalone and series fiction. www.rosenpublishing.com

➤ **Sasquatch Books:** Alaska, California, Pacific Northwest themes. www.sasquatchbooks.com

➤ **Scholastic, Cartwheel Books, Arthur A. Levine Books, Children's Press, Franklin Watts:** Large children's publisher with imprints for all ages and books on many nonfiction topics. www.scholastic.com

➤ **Scobre Press:** Biography, sports, YA issues. www.scobre.com

➤ **Seedling Publications:** Animals, nature, math, science, technology. www.seedlingpub.com

➤ **Simon & Schuster, Atheneum Books, Margaret K. McElderry, Simon Pulse:** Simon & Schuster divisions and imprints cover a full range of nonfiction topics. www.simonsayskids.com

➤ **Sports Publishing:** Biography, sports. www.sportspublishingllc.com

➤ **Star Bright Books:** Multicultural, educational, bilingual. www.starbrightbooks.com

➤ **Sterling Publishing:** Exclusively nonfiction. Animals, cooking, crafts, games, poetry, science, sign language, vocabulary. www.sterlingpublishing.com

➤ **Third World Press:** Black and African themes. www.thirdworldpressinc.com

➤ **Tilbury House:** History, culture, nature, multicultural. www.tilburyhouse.com

➤ **Tricycle Press:** Food, gardening, math, life lessons, and social skills. www.ten-speedpress.com

➤ **J. Weston Walch:** Educational. www.walch.com

➤ **Walker Young Readers:** History, biography, nature, social issues. www.walkeryoungreaders.com/for_kids

➤ **Watson-Guptill:** Fine arts, drama, culture, crafts, social skills. www.watsonguptill.com

➤ **Weigl Publishers:** Educational. Nature, sports, critical thinking, global cultures, social and evironmental issues. www.weigl.com

➤ **Albert Whitman:** Family, social, multicultural. www.albertwhitman.com

➤ **Wiley, Jossey-Bass:** History, science, technology, sports, cookbooks. www.wiley.com

and *Delicious: The Art and Life of Wayne Thiebaud* (both from Chronicle Books). "For me, the art informs the text."

Weatherford, who describes her approach as "blurring the line between historical fiction, nonfiction, and poetry," often writes on spec, and claims, like Rubin, never to work with an outline "unless the publisher asks for one." She develops the structure for her books in her head, often on her long commutes to and from her full-time job as a university professor. "For me, the structure comes first; it's crucial for the pacing and artfulness. The idea doesn't always come immediately. The voice of the narrator has to speak to me first."

Heart-Turning Moments, Little Gems

Whether the research or the emotion comes first, "no book begins with a fact," says Bartoletti. "It begins with a feeling; a heart-turning moment."

Rubin digs for "grabby quotes," which often become her working titles. She revels in intriguing anecdotes, delighting in those times when serendipity joins hands with research and connections are made that impact the slant of the story. Occasionally, an offhand remark by a source leads Rubin down a path that reveals a new piece of information or offers a striking correction of a well-known *fact*.

Partridge, too, looks hard for "little gems that other biographers haven't included in their books." She admits, "It's part of the fun for me. After all, the main person I'm entertaining is myself. I have to enjoy the process, or why bother?" Rubin, who often spends big chunks of time with people who have been closely involved with her subject, agrees. She searches for anything that is "funny, quirky, or particularly significant to kids." Enlivening fact is the nonfiction essence of the writing rule to show, not tell. As Rubin aptly puts it, "Anecdotes are scenes that bring the story to life."

Bausum recounts "one of those rewarding surprises you hope for" in the research of her book, *Freedom Riders: John Lewis and Jim Zwerg on the Front Lines of the Civil Rights Movement* (National Geographic). After a year of developing rapport with Jim Zwerg, Bausum was delighted when he offered to let her read the diary he had written during his experience as a white man becoming involved in the civil rights movement. "He hadn't shared that with anyone outside of his family. It was invaluable to have his real-time perspective decades later."

Similarly, Partridge recalls, "When I was working on *This Land Was Made for You and Me: The Life and Songs of Woody Guthrie* (Viking), the Woody Guthrie Foundation and Archives had taped interviews with his childhood friends, recorded years after Woody died. His loyal best friend, Matt Jennings, stuck by Woody as his Huntington's worsened and his behavior became outrageous. The interviewer said, 'Wow, you must have had some really ambivalent feelings about him.' Matt said softly, 'Still do. Still do.' That response rings in my mind. It's not something I used in my book, but it helped me find the emotional core of Woody's life. I'd seen how his mother's mental and physical heath was destroyed by Huntington's, and gradually his life. He both knew and denied for many years that the disease was closing in on him. I taped a note on my computer that said, 'Haunted by Huntington's' and started writing."

Interior Life

Weatherford doesn't conduct many personal interviews; instead, she looks for "a project that hasn't been treated as I intend to treat it." She explores the subject's "interior life—what I imagine it to have been. That's often left out of picture books," believes Weatherford. "Even if I fictionalize part of the story, I try to be true to the spirit of the person."

Bartoletti, who labels herself both an "information gatherer" and a "social historian" feels a responsibility to "give the book over" to the people she's interviewed. "They need to have the strongest voice. I try never to let the narration overpower their story. It is their book."

Giblin discovers the "narrative line" as his research progresses. "The deeper I get into the research, the more I see connections between various aspects of the topic: the interconnectedness and thematic progression." Bartoletti is "always open for a revision or a look from a different angle. I dig for what breathes life into the story, what captures my breath." Bausum "digs, digs, and digs," and strives to build relationships with those connected to her subject.

"What I do is look for the emotional thread in the person's life that I find compelling," says Partridge. "With John Lennon, my early take on him was what a natural leader he was, always willing to be out there, willing to jump off a cliff. I assumed he was highly independent. But once I'd read widely and taken in enough, I realized he always had someone very strong who created boundaries for him. First it was his Aunt Mimi who raised him, then it was Paul McCartney, and finally Yoko Ono. He always needed someone who would keep him from jumping off the wrong cliffs."

Structuring the Story

Although outlining may not be at the top of the list for many authors successful at writing nonfiction, accuracy in collecting and disseminating facts is. Bausum is "committed" to index cards. "It's old-fashioned, but it really works." Using her computer, she transcribes what can be several hundred pages of notes onto index cards before she begins writing. Bausum works through extensive revisions before she has a draft that she feels is ready to share with her editor.

Bartoletti filled 12 legal pads with information for her current project on the Ku Klux Klan, for Houghton Mifflin. "I circled like a flow chart the themes that belonged together," Bartoletti recalls. "This gave me the rough order of the book." Next, she typed out all her notes, printed them on index cards, and organized them into piles according to topic. "Nonfiction doesn't have to be chronological. It can be thematic, with chronology occurring within themes." With about 50 piles, including subjects within chapters, Bartoletti "began at the beginning." She explains that when writing nonfiction, "I need a sense of the big picture, and then I can begin writing."

Telling the Story

Yet, Bartoletti believes that when composing the book, "It's best to order material as you would fiction, with rising action, falling action, and the eventual climax."

A nonfiction writer must be a storyteller. The concept is deceptively simple; the challenge, according to Giblin, is "writing a lively text while hewing closely to the facts." He explains, "I've approached this problem in a number of ways. When I'm researching the subject, I always look for the story line in the material. Every nonfiction topic has one, whether it's the aggressive moves Adolf Hitler made in his rise to power, or the way John Wilkes Booth plotted first to kidnap and then to murder Abraham Lincoln. Once I've settled on the story line, I use fictional techniques to shape the material in what I hope will be a dramatic and involving way. For instance, *Good Brother, Bad Brother: The Story of*

"People sometimes think nonfiction is non-emotional, but that's simply not true."

Edwin Booth and John Wilkes Booth (Clarion Books) begins with Edwin Booth on tour in Boston, getting the terrible news that his brother has shot the President. Then the narrative flashes back to Edwin's childhood, when he and John were growing up in Maryland as the sons of a famous actor father, Junius Brutus Booth."

"A long time ago biographer Henry Mayer taught me this," says Partridge: "Make sure every paragraph resonates emotionally. It's tough to do, but it is really important to keep in mind. People sometimes think nonfiction is non-emotional, but that's simply not true."

Penny Colman, award-winning author of books for all ages, says, "Oftentimes, I'll see an image in my mind or imagine something that I'd like to include in a book. That's when I set off with my camera." For her latest book, *Thanksgiving: The True Story* (Henry Holt), Colman attended Chusok, the Korean harvest festival; drove to Newport, New Hampshire, to photograph the historic marker for Sarah Josepha Hale; and visited the Sarah Josepha Hale Room at Richards Free Library to photograph "a less than pristine copy of the November 1865 issue of *Godey's Lady Book*" to give readers a sense of the wear and tear of history. "To convey the fact that history is everywhere, and because I like to include a few quirky images in my books," Colman also photographed street signs in Weymouth with the names Pilgrim, Squanto, and Massasoit.

Bausum does all her own photo research, which she considers "rewarding but time-consuming." Her projects require at least a year from germination to final proof. "It's all in the presentation. In the best of nonfiction, stories unfold on multiple levels, with the text and images enhancing the reader's understanding." The story's progression can occur naturally, as it did when Rubin wrote *Andy Warhol: Pop Art Painter* (Abrams Books). "The arc of the story is inherent in the chronicle of his childhood. Warhol was a poor kid who wanted to be an artist. He worked hard, got some breaks, emerged, and was eventually recognized as a fine artist."

Rubin has also written Judaica such as *Cat with the Yellow Star: Coming of Age in Terezin,* co-authored with Ela Weissberger, and *Fireflies in the Dark: The Story of Friedl Dicker-Brandeis and the Children of Terezin* (both for Holiday House) that deal with horrific history. It is often a tightrope walk when writing for young children about sensitive or emotionally wrought issues. "It's a challenge deciding what to include and what not to include. I want to be honest and give an absolutely accurate account, and I want to get across the drama and intensity of a situation, but as a mom and grandmother, I am also sensitive to how deeply I delve into challenging topics. I intentionally keep my audience in mind." Rubin benefits from "a consensus of thinking," relying on the advice of her editor, librarians, fellow authors, and historians. "I always have one goal in mind: Remember the children."

Join the Revolution in Art Forms and Reading

By Mark Haverstock

Since the first Bible emerged from Gutenberg's press more than 500 years ago, we've been literally bound to paper publishing as the standard for sharing written information. Sure, it takes a whole bunch of trees to make the process work, but think of the convenience and portability. Picture books fit easily in the hands of mom or dad while they read their toddler a bedtime story. Summer reading is portable, with several books tossed inside a beach bag along with a towel and sunscreen. Many paperbacks still fit comfortably in the back pocket of a pair of jeans, ready to be read at a moment's notice.

But today's technology-driven society demands newer and more modern solutions. Why can't books be made more interactive? Smaller and lighter? Easier to read? More economical? Easier to publish and distribute?

The technological creation of books and magazines today—the expression of story or gathered information through words or the interaction of words and pictures—is in a revolutionary period, no matter how one looks at it. It may be true that paper and ink will never be fully replaced. But new forms are joining and expanding them, just as print joined the illuminated manuscript. Writers and artists of all kinds are creating new styles, new forms, new effects in the reading experience.

Unfolding Forms

Authors and publishers have been tinkering with the paper-based book for years. Early attempts from the 1980s included plain text files that could be displayed on a computer screen. More ambitious versions followed in the 1990s, utilizing proprietary formats, popular word processor formats such as MS Word, and Adobe's PDF format.

In 1992, Broderbund software adapted several titles from authors like Mercer Mayer, Marc Brown, Dr. Seuss, and Stan and Jan Berenstain, converting them into what they described as interactive animated multimedia children's books. In these titles from the Living Books series, kids could click on specific page items to see animation and sound. More recently, Leapfrog makes a touch-and-talk device called Tag, that enables children to hear words and stories read aloud using their special books and hardware.

New LCD and E-Ink devices promise to deliver hundreds of books in a compact electronic reader. Cutting-edge computer animation programs promise to turn reading into an entirely new and engaging experience with motion and other special effects.

This roundup includes several examples of new or improved media for delivering books to young readers and adults. Each has its own unique capabilities, strengths, and the ability to hold the interest of today's generation of iPod listeners and computer users.

Picture Books in Motion

Jean Gralley is a picture book writer and illustrator who loves the traditional book form, but her newest books are unlike anything on paper or even on screen. "My digital picture books are all about motion and reading," she says. "This is what differentiates them from other digital picture books which, basically, are still paper-based." Her *middle way* between books and animation has gained some attention in the *Horn Book* and the Children's Book Council's (CBC) newsletter, *Features*. An animation she created to describe this new kind of book has been shown at the Eric Carle Museum of Picture Book Art and the Katonah Museum of Art. Called "Books Unbound," it can be viewed on her website (www.jeangralley.com), which is the current home base for her paper and digital work.

To truly understand the concept behind Books Unbound may take a change of mindset. Gralley's ideas involve more than just transferring paper stories to digital. "Authors frequently approach me, sure their published picture book would be great for this treatment," explains Gralley. "But books that work well on paper are rarely ideal. Weston Woods and other animating studios aside, this is not about animating a paper story. This is about imagining new kinds of stories from the start."

"This is not about animating a paper story. This is about imagining new kinds of stories from the start."

The first challenge—absolutely necessary to the process—is escaping an automatic kind of paper-thinking. Once we're free of that, the possibilities open up and the imagination can start visualizing a truly digital reading experience.

Adobe Flash software acts as the writer's and illustrator's pallet for text, drawings, and animation. "It allows me to create natural stop places and go buttons," says Gralley. "In this way, readers can read at their own pace and move ahead when they're ready. I also place buttons at ends of sequences so they can be repeated again and again." Gralley believes that the reader should be the prime mover of the reading experience. Just as with traditional picture books, and no matter what the digital book is capable of, the most important point is that the reader should direct the experience, determining the pace, backtracking, or moving ahead.

One of the temptations of using digital media is to want to exploit all its capabilities at once, adding as many gee-whiz features to the mix as possible. But Gralley's philosophy is to avoid the clutter; a book's charm is often its simplicity. "Ironically, I suspect my ideas are often rejected out-of-hand because they're assumed to include digital bells and whistles," she says. "If anything, I'm a little retro: I don't want to interrupt a storyline with a digital game; I'm not currently interested in choices; and my stories aren't even narrated—they're all about reading. The picture book aesthetic is my aesthetic: clean, simple story lines and a good story to tell. I want to use all digital offers to that end, and I want to get there in a way paper can't."

So what are publishers saying about this new kind of digital book? Do they understand the concept? Are any publishers buying or considering the potential of Gralley's new ideas? "One brave publisher has invited me in for a private presentation and many executives have written privately with support, encouragement, and even wistfulness," she says. "I think the spirit is willing but the industry's flesh turns goosebumpy at the thought of leaving the paper paradigm. There would be no need to leave it altogether, however. What I propose is creating a parallel universe to paper publishing, not overthrowing it. There are so many market indicators that make *thinking digital* very smart."

It's likely that digital forms such as Gralley's will find their niche in the publishing industry, complementing print and other still to be developed technologies. Gralley continues to move forward with her projects, and is in contact with other children's writers and illustrators who are eager to get on the bandwagon. "The paperbound book is a wonderful, enduring form that will roll on, like 'Old Man River.' But I believe I'm lucky enough to stand at a confluence, a new river formed by the best of the old flowing into something exciting and new," she says. "Others will dig their paddles in and go a lot farther down this new river than I will. It's going to be a great ride for our storytellers and for our readers."

Electronic Paper and Long-Form Reading

Three years ago, Amazon.com set out to design and build an entirely new class of device: a convenient, portable reader with the ability to wirelessly download books, blogs, magazines, and newspapers. The result is Amazon Kindle, a small and lightweight electronic book. Think of it as an iPod for books, one that has the capability of storing your home library in a 7.5 x 5.3 x 0.7-inch package that tips the scales at a little more than ten ounces. The unit has a storage capability of 200-plus books, which can be increased with optional memory cards.

Thanks to *electronic paper*, a new display technology, reading Kindle's

Gallop!

A new technology called Scanimation hit the shelves during the holiday season a year ago. It makes images appear to move across the pages of an otherwise typical-looking picture book. Workman Publishing introduced this invention to readers in the title *Gallop!,* by Rufus Butler Seder.

Animals and other living creatures seem to move, as though you were watching them on film instead of simply reading. Seder's picture book shows a horse at a full gallop and a turtle swimming up the page. A dog runs, a cat springs, and an eagle soars. Complementing the art is conventional rhyming text like, "Can you gallop like a horse? Giddyup-a-loo!"

Actually the "new" technology is based on the same principles as kinetoscopes, zoetropes, and other nineteenth-century toys that employed an optical illusion using persistence of memory to create the appearance of motion. There are no chips or electronic gadgets, just a striped acetate overlay that's flowed over a scrambled image underneath.

screen is much like reading ink on paper—without the strain and glare associated with computer screens. Kindle will support some graphics and pictures, but is really designed for long form reading. The screen is not back-lit, which saves power consumption but also requires some ambient light to see. You'll still need your flashlight while reading under the covers.

"We believe that long form reading should be freed from the limitations of analog," says Heather Huntoon, Public Relations Director for Amazon.com. "You can't order a physical book and have it delivered to your home in one minute. You can't carry hundreds of books with you everywhere you go. You can't access more than 140,000 new books wherever you are. With the immediacy of the Internet and the digital medium, these limitations on readers are no longer necessary." While

Amazon couldn't outbook the book, they could use existing technology to enhance the reading experience.

Authors and publishers alike see the potential of Kindle. "In general, they are very supportive and excited about Kindle," says Huntoon. "We work with them every day to get more books on the device for our customers. In fact, we launched with 90,000 books and today, have more than 140,000 available, and we're adding more every day." If you're an author who wants to self-publish for the Kindle, Amazon has a tool called Digital Text Platform that will allow you to upload your book directly into the Kindle store. Learn more at http://dtp.amazon.com.

Amazon wanted Kindle to be completely mobile and simple to use, so it is wireless, a significant selling point for a generation that tends to want instant gratification. Using the same 3G network as advanced cell phones, the device delivers content through Amazon Whispernet, which uses Sprint's national wireless data network. Think of the process as book-sized texting, but better. The wireless service comes free with the downloads—no service plans, yearly contracts, or monthly wireless bills are involved. No PC and no syncing are needed, though you can download via a computer with a standard USB cable, an option when out of range of the cellular network.

You can't judge a book by its cover, so Amazon allows users to download samples and read the beginning of a book for free. If you like it, simply buy and download right from your Kindle, and continue reading. You can also subscribe to major newspapers, magazines, and blogs, delivered to your Kindle each morning. The 22 newspapers currently available include the *Washington Post*, the *New York Times, Le Monde*, the *Atlantic, Time*, and *Newsweek*, among others. Book prices generally range from $.99 to $9.99; magazine and newspaper prices vary.

For those who would rather listen to their books than read them, Kindle can play audiobooks from Audible.com, which was recently purchased by Amazon. However, these must be downloaded to a computer, and then transferred to the Kindle using the USB port.

In addition to downloading content, Kindle contains some Web browsing and e-mail capabilities. A basic browser allows users to view Web pages, and access the *New Oxford American Dictionary* and Wikipedia, with all wireless costs bundled into the device's price. Kindle owners can send MS Word docs to their Kindle e-mail address (assigned when they purchase it) and it will convert to the Kindle format so they can read the document. Uploads of other e-book formats don't "officially" work at the present, though that could change in the future.

What impact will Kindle have on traditional print books and the publishing industry as we currently know it? Jeff Bezos, founder of Amazon.com, claims that customers continue to purchase the same

> ## "The world of reluctant readers is huge" and can be well-served by the medium of audiobooks.

number of paperbound books as they did before getting a Kindle and their total book purchases increase. The possibility that e-books will add to the bottom line rather than hurt print sales will certainly reassure publishers and kindle their interest.

Audiobooks for the iPod Generation

Nearly a third of children ages six to ten regularly listen to digital audio players, according to a survey by market research firm NPD Group. The same technology that brings the Jonas Brothers and Hannah Montana to young ears can also deliver kids' favorite books. Launched in spring 2008, Audiblekids.com has approximately 4,000 titles organized by age, grade, and subject that are downloadable in a matter of minutes.

Although many kids will pick up a book on their own and read, the underserved group of reluctant readers may be especially enticed by this digital audio medium. "The world of reluctant readers is huge," says Don Katz, founder, CEO, and Chairman of the Board of Audible. com. He notes that reading outcomes tend to fall apart around the third grade—which is often the same time that parents stop reading to their kids. Digital audiobooks, according to Katz, could extend that pleasure of being read to into the fifth, sixth, and seventh grades.

For iPods and other MP3 players that deliver color graphics, Audiblekids Enhanced can deliver both pictures and story narration. Children can watch the picture book illustrations appear as they listen to favorite titles, like *Owl Moon, Curious George Rides a Bike,* and *Stone Soup.* Graphic versions of classic novels such as *The Adventures of Tom Sawyer* and *The War of the Worlds* are brought to life through original illustrations on the player's display. Bringing literature to life in new forms—that's what storytelling has always been about, and what remarkably creative artists have embraced through all the centuries.

Extras! Extras! Read All About Them

By Katherine Swarts

The differences between a good and a great manuscript are often smaller than one might think. But when competing with thousands of others, writers may find it impossible to break into top markets with an article, story, or book that is merely good. It pays to understand how the *extras*—items complementing or supplementing the main text—can lift your good work into the great category.

Most extras take the form of sidebars, but may also be photos or illustrations, even suggestions for callouts or decks if a publication uses them. Sidebars may consist of additional information on a particular detail or related subject; glossaries; charts; lists of websites, books, experts, or other sources; or activities, crafts, recipes, or experiments. It pays to think about the extras even before starting to write your main text. Indeed, they can be a key factor in a well-written query or proposal. Consider how, from an editor's perspective, they might join with the main text to form a superior package for delivering a piece to readers.

Long popular in magazine nonfiction, sidebars now also appear regularly in books, and even fiction. It's no surprise that the current generation of young readers—raised on Internet sights and sounds, online links, and multiple computer screens—finds appeal in hardcopy *windows*.

Standing Alone

"Sidebar material should be fun or high-interest enough to stand on its own," says Emily Easton, Publisher of Walker Books for Young Readers. "If there's a visual element—a photo, a graph or chart, a political cartoon—all the better."

"Sidebars can make pages more visually interesting," agrees Tanya Kyi, author of one of the Science Squad Adventure novels for Whitecap Books. The series, written for middle-grade girls in cooperation with the Canadian Association for Girls in Science (CAGIS), includes nonfiction sidebars that "supplement the text with information directly

related to what is being explored in the story line," says CAGIS President Larissa Vingilis-Jaremko. "In our books, the sidebars are purely scientific (an experiment or did-you-know form) to supplement the story line."

Magazines tend to handle sidebars differently, says Vingilis-Jaremko. "In magazines, editors often prefer to have the sidebars looking at the topic from a different perspective; for example, a sidebar may look at the topic from a historical perspective or profile an interesting scientist within the field. The main text is mainly scientific—an experiment, or explanation of a scientific concept."

"Sidebars can accommodate lists, bullet points, and information more loosely related to the main text," says Kyi. "For example, in a story about modern makeup, a sidebar might offer information on how makeup was used in ancient Egypt."

Of course, a sidebar shouldn't be so loosely related as to make readers wonder what it's doing there at all. Before planning anything extra, says Maureen A. Doolan Boyle, Executive Director of Mothers of Supertwins (MOST), which publishes *Supertwins* magazine, "The first question to ask is what you want readers to take away from the whole story. That should be in the main text. Sidebars can further understanding of the topic, give additional resources, or share human-interest stories."

Sidebars should not simply reiterate or continue the main text. Many aren't even *text* in the standard sense, but rather bibliographies or notes with more information. *Listen,* a magazine that promotes a drug-free lifestyle for teens, "uses sidebars for various lists: websites, reading material, or organizations that can expand on the subject," says Editor Céleste Perrino-Walker. Or sidebars can provide additional information through quotes, anecdotes, or points of advice.

Avoid extensive detail, however; the extra material shouldn't smother the main text. "Make sure the sidebar will fit on a single typeset book

"A sidebar should be very high-interest, a fun break for the reader."

page," advises Easton. "One hundred words is generally a good target. A sidebar also should be very high-interest, a fun break for the reader."

"Most magazine sidebars are only a few sentences long," comments Kyi. Longer sidebars "in books often fall at the ends of sections or chapters, so when readers finish scanning the sidebar, they don't have to flip backwards to pick up the thread of the main text." Compilations of further resources are frequently presented at the end of a book. Book extras, notes Boyle, are "more supporting of narrative—versus bulleted—information than in a magazine."

Reliable Sources Say

Sidebars should never contradict that thread, either. Don't recommend an outside source that "doesn't reinforce your article—and the publisher's principles," says Perrino-Walker. It sounds obvious, but "I often have to scrap suggestions for this very reason. For example, be sure the website you're referencing doesn't 'leave it up to the teen' to decide whether he will participate in underage drinking. Underage drinking is illegal. Period."

Publisher understanding of reader preferences is equally significant. "I would recommend websites over books" as sources with additional information, says Perrino-Walker, "because our teen audience is more apt to log onto an Internet site." Wesley Adams, Executive Editor of Farrar, Straus, and Giroux Books for Young Readers, however, prefers "a list that refers kids mainly to actual books. Kids need to learn how to chase down books rather than just Google and click." Most editors do want some variety in recommended media. "Books or links that lead to visuals or animations can be especially useful," notes Vingilis-Jaremko, since "such visuals cannot always be included in print." Easton says, "We include a variety of media—books, magazines, websites, interview transcripts—and a diversity of opinions on all sides."

When compiling a resource list, remember that most published material is in the production stage for months. A year or more could pass between the submission of your final manuscript and the release of the published version; and it won't do much for your reputation if 75 percent of the sources you recommend have gone offline months before any reader tries to check them.

"Resources should be unlikely to change," says Kyi. "Websites should be respectable and stable. Otherwise, a reader who picks up the book six months after publication may find that the suggested sources have disappeared." The most reliable websites are hosted by well-established institutions and organizations, including the U. S. government. And the information such sites provide is also more likely to go beyond one person's unsubstantiated opinion.

"Know the reputations of the institutions or people behind the websites," says Easton. "Anyone can post information on the Web. For an animal book, the San Diego Zoo website would be a welcome resource, but not a blog by someone who raises wild animals in the backyard. For book resources, have they been well reviewed and do the authors have solid reputations? We also want the most recent copyright dates, to make sure knowledge and scholarship are current. The exception is primary sources, where origination date is not an issue."

Picture That

While hunting down your own research sources, you may find contact links on websites. For a nonfiction article or book, take this opportunity to ask about obtaining photos or other illustrations—another valuable extra.

"My first source for photos is always the Library of Congress," says

Easton. "Historical societies are also valuable. For a science book, I love authors who work directly with scientists" to obtain photos, "and there are many royalty-free photo sources on the Internet: Getty Images, Corbis, and Shutterstock, to name a few."

Some publishers also welcome writers who take their own photos. "I prefer to use photos that families have taken themselves," says Boyle. "They are real." This means reasonably professional-looking photos, of course. Before you make the offer, check the publisher's guidelines to make sure this particular market doesn't explicitly reject amateur photos; and if it doesn't, check the photo credits in its already published materials to see how many other writers have taken their own pictures.

Artwork is another good extra possibility. "With scientific experiments and sidebars," says Vingilis-Jaremko, "I often send draft images to illustrate a scientific concept or experiment."

With straight drawings—as opposed to photos, charts, or diagrams—don't even bother making the offer unless you have professional artist credentials. "Most editors prefer to match the writing with an illustrator of their own choosing," says Easton.

It does pay to think *illustratable* while writing for children. "It is important to consider the dynamic between text and art," says Jude Evans, Associate Publisher of British-based Little Tiger Press. "Illustrations can form a subplot, or create irony. If you are writing picture books, it is well worth considering the power and potential of the combination of text and art, and how you can craft your writing to make the most of this unique opportunity." You can briefly mention, in your proposal, any ideas you have in this area. Don't, however, get carried away and make a detailed list of instructions for the illustrator—editors see this as another mark of amateurism.

The First Thing You See

Often last in the actual writing, but first in any published item, comes that extra that is common to all published material: the title.

"It is well worth spending the time to seek out a title suitable for your intended audience," says Evans. "It is important to spark the editor's attention every way you can." She cautions, however, "We would not expect or recommend that alternate titles be provided."

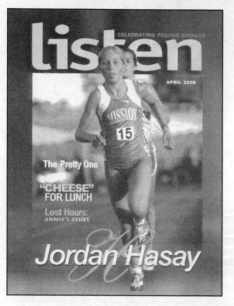

"I've never included alternate titles in a cover letter," agrees Kyi. "I think that information would be too cumbersome, and could also indicate a lack of confidence in the title you've chosen. But if I have other catchy phrases in mind, I will work them into the body text or subheads."

"Send in a manuscript with the best title you can come up with," says Easton. "Put your best foot forward and be confident about what you've submitted. Let the editor come to you if he or she thinks a title needs further work, and be willing to work with your editor to find the perfect title."

Not everyone concurs that one working title is enough. "If I received a list of possible alternate titles," says Perrino-Walker, "I'd be impressed that the writer took the time to give it some thought." Vingilis-Jaremko says that "it doesn't hurt" to suggest other possible titles.

The best approach: First, see if official guidelines mention title suggestions; if not, assume only one is needed. Then, give it some thought. Review the titles of your target market's already published pieces, and note what they have in common: Short and snappy? Humorous? Straightforward? With or without subtitles? Craft your own title to fit in while standing out. Don't get too attached to it, though; often, after your best efforts, editors will still change your working title before publication. But even then, they'll look on you more favorably if the original was neither dull and prosaic nor long and indecipherable.

Ideas on the Side

Sidebars can take on as many topics and forms as articles do. Done well, they can be like a party favor that makes the main event even more memorable. Consider these suggestions for adding something extra to articles, stories, and books—and always make sure the sidebars are truly relevant to the main text. Don't forget to provide a catchy title for the sidebar as well as the article.

➤ **Active:** Suggest related activities, crafts, experiments, recipes, puzzles, games, quizzes, practice exercises, songs, dance steps, places to go (museums, historical places, locations related to a science or nature subject, etc).

➤ **Additional:** Supplemental information can take the form of sources, relevant facts, other ideas, additional reading, anecdotes, an interesting related topic that doesn't fit in the main text, brief profile, contrary opinion, statistics, quotes, tips, humor, timeline, brief history, personal experience, expert advice, glossary, pronunciation guide, or recap in the form of a checklist that helps the reader absorb the information found in the main text.

➤ **Visuals:** While most editors arrange for the artwork, a writer's suggestions for photos, illustrations, graphs, or charts are usually very welcome. If you're going to include ideas for graphs or charts, make them colorful and visually interesting if possible (see the examples here). Sidebars could be bulleted lists, or brief paragraphs with striking subheads. The magazine or book designer will determine whether the sidebars will be presented in a different typeface, shaded or outlined boxes, and so on.

$4,838 Year 1
$4,925 Year 2
$4,947 Year 3
$5,001 Year 4

When all is said and done, the something extra that moves a specific manuscript from good to great—the sparkle in the text itself; the clever turns of phrase; the mannerism that makes a character that much more appealing—is often impossible to pinpoint. Don't try too hard here. If you spend your time searching for a sure-sale gimmick instead of developing your own style, chances are that everything you write will come out gimmicky-sounding and unsalable. Better to take the slow-and-steady, learn-by-doing approach. Read all you can; write all you can; and trust that, with time and diligence, something extra will emerge on its own.

"Concentrate on creating your own unique tone and voice," says Evans, "right from the first word."

The Revision Rainbow: Finding the Pot of Gold

By Jacqueline Adams

I n Beverly Cleary's beloved Ramona books, one of Ramona's many misadventures occurs when she sets off to find the pot of gold at the end of the rainbow. At first, the rainbow appears to end in the park. But when Ramona gets there, the rainbow seems to end behind the supermarket, and so on.

Writers can relate to Ramona's predicament. We spend hours, weeks, and months revising a manuscript until we believe it's perfect. Then, when we find an interested editor, he or she may request round after round of further revisions. We may wonder if we'll ever reach the pot of gold—a published book or magazine piece.

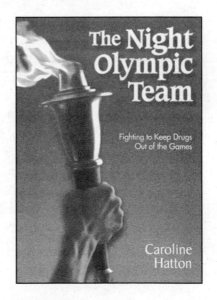

Three children's writers who've found the pot of gold share their winning strategies for pre- and post-submission revision. Their editors offer advice on self-revision and explain their expectations when they make a revision request.

The Anatomy of Revision

Caroline Hatton's nonfiction book, *The Night Olympic Team* (Boyds Mills Press), reveals how scientists catch Olympic athletes who use prohibited drugs. The fact that Hatton was one of these scientists was no guarantee that she could translate such a complicated subject into a strong manuscript for young readers. To achieve this, she relied on her tried-and-true, three-part revision strategy. "I revise from story backbone to flesh to fat," she says. "Align bones, add flesh, trim fat."

Aligning the backbone involves developing a story arc with a beginning, middle, and end. Referring to an outline during revision helps Hatton keep the story organized. She also asks herself: "Will escalating

> ## "I revise from story backbone to flesh to fat. Align bones, add flesh, trim fat."

tension keep the reader reading?" This step helped her avoid a problem that her editor, Andy Boyles, often sees in manuscripts and book proposals he receives as Science Editor at Boyds Mills Press. Boyles reports, "Even if the author is an expert in the subject, in many cases the book needs to be reorganized and rewritten. Usually the main shortcoming is the lack of a strong story line or organizing principle."

With the backbone in place, Hatton moves to step two: fleshing out the people, narrative, and setting. She checks that all the important ideas are in place. Then she revises to make each idea fun to read. She offers this example: In *The Night Olympic Team*, she originally wrote, "Discussions were confidential." That eventually became, "Some days, Don [one of the scientists] took a teammate for a drive beyond the last buildings on the fringes of Salt Lake City, into the wilderness, to talk privately where no one could hear them."

In the fleshing-out step, colored markers and highlighters help Hatton balance narrative or story elements. "To check pacing, I draw lines of different colors for action and narrative down the margins or make boxes around paragraphs. To check consistency, I highlight dialogue with a different color for each character."

Step three is to trim the fat. Hatton says, "I keep zooming in, asking myself, 'Is every single word necessary?' as I comb the manuscript from end to end."

Hatton also counts a middle-grade novel, easy readers, and magazine articles among her publishing credits, and she uses the same strategy for all these genres. The only difference comes when she must cut a great deal of material to fit a magazine's word limit. "I chop major parts or facets in big chunks, chosen perhaps by prioritizing big ideas. If it helps mechanically, I spread the manuscript on the floor and highlight lines corresponding to this and that, cut it up with scissors, and tape together rearranged parts."

A Manuscript Fit for an Illustrator

For picture books, a tight word count and the teamwork between text and illustrations present additional challenges. Lisa Wheeler, author of more than two dozen picture books and early readers, meets the challenges with a two-stage revision strategy. "First, I look to see if the story, as a whole, is working." To be sure it is, she asks, "How much time did I give to the beginning, middle, and end? Have I bogged down the middle? Have I stayed true to my original premise or have I strayed? Is my main character still the main character or was he hijacked by a sidekick? Do I wrap things up in a timely manner? Is the ending satisfactory?"

An important consideration at this point is the potential for illustrations. Jean Reynolds, the recently retired Executive Editor at Lerner Publishing who worked with Wheeler on *Dino-Hockey* and *Dino-Soccer* (Carolrhoda/Lerner), advises, "The writer should review a picture book manuscript from the point of view of the artist. Twenty lines of dialogue with no action doesn't give an artist much to work with!" She recommends that writers create a dummy in which they divide the text into spreads. "You will be able to see the rough spots that your artist will encounter—and then revise accordingly."

Next, Wheeler moves on to stage two, revising line by line. She asks, "Are my word choices strong? Does each line move the story forward? Do my sentences flow? How does it read aloud? Have I included picture book elements like repetition and the rule of threes? Is it too wordy?"

Since tight writing is essential for picture books, Wheeler removes anything that doesn't contribute to the story. "If something is fun and clever, but does not give the story forward momentum, cut it. You have to be brave and remove those idle lines—kill those darlings. It can be painful, but after a few days, read it again and you won't even miss them."

> ## "You have to be brave and remove those idle lines— kill those darlings."

Reynolds advises picture book writers to cut descriptive adjectives, which usurp the job of the illustrations. She says, "When you talk about the red bow in the little girl's hair, isn't that really your way of telling the artist that you think her bow should be red? In fact do you need to mention the bow at all, if it is obvious that she has one in the art?"

Never a Dull Moment

For novelist Kathleen O'Dell, revision goes hand in hand with the first draft. "During the first draft, I write daily in 400-word lumps," she says. "Every day, I go back and redo what I've done the day before and move ahead." She tightens at this point, but her main focus is characterization. "It's important to me to have every element of the story serve more than one purpose. If the plot calls for everyone in the family to come together for a conversation, for example, and I sit the characters down for dinner, I try to make sure that the way everyone behaves at the table illustrates aspects of character."

When the draft is complete, she goes through it over and over, fine-tuning details and cutting unnecessary words. "Most of all, I'm concerned about the parts of the book that bore me. Here's where I have to be ruthless with myself. Invariably, I'll find parts of the story where I'll

The Benefits of a Critique

Most of the writers and editors interviewed for this article emphasize the benefits of running a manuscript past a critique group, or at least a couple of savvy readers. Cecile Goyette, Executive Editor of Alfred A. Knopf Books for Young Readers, says, "If possible, have somebody smart, well-read, and incredibly blunt cold-read your draft for an instant reaction."

Boyds Mills Press and *Highlights for Children* Science Editor Andy Boyles points out that this is a special concern with science writing. "After investing a lot of time and energy in a book or article, the writer faces the danger of becoming so familiar with the subject that he or she may have failed to include some of the basics that non-scientists, and especially young readers, would need to understand what's been written. This happened to me once, and by *once* I mean a chronic condition that lasted eight years." To avoid this pitfall, he says, "I don't know of any substitute for at least two other readers who will tell you the truth in a civilized way." If they identify problem areas, revise and show them the manuscript again, until everything is clear. But Boyles warns that seeking reviewers' input doesn't mean relinquishing control of the manuscript. "The process of listening to reviewers is not so much about finding just the right words. It's more about discovering which parts are not working and considering various ways they might be made to work. In the end, the whole work should be written in the author's voice. It should not read like something written by committee."

Although the hectic schedules of author Caroline Hatton's writer friends preclude a regular critique group, she asks a few who specialize in the genre to read her manuscript. She says, "I ask them where tension slacks off, where they tune out, where the science is unclear." When she thinks self-revision is complete, she runs the manuscript past one more reader—herself. "The last thing I do before submission is to record myself reading the manuscript aloud, let at least 48 hours pass, and listen."

When Is It Time to Submit?

Self-revision can turn into an endless cycle, as a writer continually tinkers with a manuscript out of fear that it's not "ready." How can writers know when to stop revising and start submitting?

Author Lisa Wheeler says, "For me there are two ways: (1) When I think it is perfect, and (2) when my critique group says it's perfect. I like to run it by them just in case I am delusional."

Kathleen O'Dell explains, "When I can read through the book feeling engaged all the way through, I'm ready to show the work to my editor. If there are sections that pull me out of the story, I know I still have work to do."

Caroline Hatton knows when a project is ready "after setting aside the manuscript long enough (weeks to months), so that the next time I read it, I feel like I'm discovering it anew. If I can't think of what else to change, it's ready to submit, or at least I'm ready to submit."

space out or try to read through quickly because I'm not hooked."

O'Dell is on the same page as Cecile Goyette, the Executive Editor at Alfred A. Knopf who currently edits O'Dell's YA novels and also edited O'Dell's Agnes Parker novels when she worked at Dial Books. Goyette suggests that writers ask these questions as they revise: "Have I made it so that it would be absolutely unbearable not to turn to the next page? What hits an emotional bull's-eye right away? Is every scene compelling, interesting, and entertaining? Does every scene contribute something new and crucial?"

Open Minds

Such painstaking self-revision pays off when an editor responds to a submission with interest. But a writer's excitement at receiving such a response can be tempered with dismay at the editor's further revision requests, especially if the writer disagrees with them. If that happens, Boyles advises, "Try not to take it personally. Take some time to cool down if necessary, and come back with a reasoned response. The author should know much more about the subject than I do and should be able to educate me and help me see the wisdom of his or her approach. I'm

open to that, and I expect authors also to be open to my views."

"Receive all requests with an open mind and a willing heart," Hatton says. She reminds fellow writers, "Your editor is the biggest fan in the universe of your work-in-progress. Help him or her help you make your book the best it can be."

Even when a submission is "nearly perfect," as Boyles describes Hatton's manuscript of *The Night Olympic Team*, revision still comes into play. He e-mailed her questions and suggestions about passages he thought needed adjustment, "and one by one, we talked through each point until we reached agreement."

Hatton says, "We exchanged the most substantial e-mails after he asked me to draft an introduction to reveal upfront that I was one of the scientists on the team. My concern was that disclosing this, and therefore that the team was composed of scientists, would spoil a revelation in another part of the book." She was reluctant until Boyles explained the danger of alienating readers who might feel that the author hadn't been forthright with them. "Andy's eloquent analysis convinced me that he knew better."

The key is maintaining focus on the end result. Boyles says, "Throughout the process, Caroline kept the quality of the final book as her main criterion."

Give and Take

Wheeler recommends against reacting quickly to an editor's revision request. "I find that by waiting a few days for the editor's suggestions to soak in, I either begin to see what they are asking for, or if I totally disagree, I can take time to explain my reluctance and perhaps ask them a few questions."

Reynolds notes that revision is a give and take process. "Revision must always be a dialogue that retains the author's vision while at the same time solving the difficulties that the experienced editor can foresee coming at the next stage." Often, she must ask authors to revise to make a story work in picture book format. "I send the author the paginated manuscript with comments in the margin, explaining what I'm after and why. The author responds with his or her thoughts, and we go back and forth from there until we feel we have a text that will allow the artist to concentrate on art rather than the practical aspects of making the script fit."

Keeping the end goal in mind sometimes means making painful changes, as it did with *Dino-Hockey*. Reynolds reveals, "We had to cut some fabulous scenes, but Lisa totally understood that cutting was preferable to jamming two elaborate scenes onto a spread, and so did it cheerfully and promptly. Neither of us wanted to lose the material, but both of us understood what was required to make a good book."

Trying on Ideas

O'Dell acknowledges that an editor's revision requests can seem overwhelming. She recommends that writers let the suggestions soak in for a few days. "Next, don't think you have to do everything at once. Pick one aspect of the story to improve. I try to remember that one of the most difficult parts of a revision is the actual opening of the laptop."

Goyette prefers that writers take time to consider her suggestions. "I'd like them to try things on, and where they don't fit and we don't agree, to try and be creative about an alternative option—to glean the intent of an edit, rather than feel bound to accept it literally. If after trying this they feel something that I've questioned should stay as it is, so be it."

O'Dell testifies to the benefits of this method. "There are very few times that I've found it necessary to say no to changes. I've found that if you try the editorial suggestions, you can more readily see the rationale for them. Cecile and I have engaged in horse-trading, however. I'll say, 'I'll give up the line about _____, if I get to keep the chapter's opening sentence.'"

Goyette believes one reason she and O'Dell make a great team is their willingness to learn from each other. "In the original draft of *Agnes Parker . . . Girl in Progress,*" Goyette says, "she had created a really funny opening scene that we both loved, but it just didn't serve as an effective introduction. It was hard to give it up because it was very well-written and enjoyable and I remember feeling nervous about asking her to cut it and come up with something else after I had already expressed my admiration for the scene. But it was the right call to make and she crafted a wonderful alternative, by gum."

O'Dell points out that both writer and editor have the same goal. "Your editor is there to help make the best book possible. She has a stake in its success."

When writer and editor work together to reach the end of the rainbow, they may discover a pot of gold better than either imagined. Goyette says, "I think it's important to both editor and author to acknowledge the inherent tension in the revision process and to keep in mind the benefits it should yield if handled with creativity, faith, enthusiasm, and stick-to-it-iveness. The work will not stay the same, but will become better, and even fabulous."

Business

Queries: Sell Yourself, Sell Your Editor

By Mark Haverstock

With shrinking staffs and looming deadlines, editors have a difficult time keeping up with submissions. Given the large number of manuscripts they receive, the query letter remains the most effective way to break into many magazine markets, especially nonfiction markets.

Editors would rather read a one-page query than a multi-page manuscript. The brevity allows them to spend considerably less time wading through slush piles and to be more timely in communication. "Queries are also of value because they expose editors to fresh story ideas and provide opportunities to get in touch with new writers," says Alison Phillips, Editor of *InSite*, published by the Christian Camp and Conference Association.

Writers also benefit from writing queries. They're short and relatively painless to produce. You don't have to invest large amounts of time in research or write a finished piece until you get the go-ahead from the editor.

What Queries Tell About You

Your query is both your introduction to an editor and your sales pitch, so presentation is everything. "Each of our editors has different requirements. Some still like to see paper queries, others prefer e-mail," says Lou Waryncia, Editorial Director of Cobblestone Publishing, a division of Carus Publishing Company. "The general rule is to make

185

sure it's well-written, and your basic structure fits on one page. We want to know that you can write, that you can think out a story in a matter of a few sentences, and can explain it well."

A query also has to show some direction and creativity compared to others the publisher receives. "Say we're doing a story on Plymouth Rock. We might receive fifteen queries on that subject. How are you going to differentiate yourself?" says Waryncia. "Give me the story behind the story or some interesting tidbit, or maybe something that isn't even about the rock at all, but is related to it, and how it had an effect. Don't just give me the obvious; answer the questions that are surrounding it."

Where you send your queries reveals if you've actually done market research. Poorly targeted ones suggest that you haven't done the basics, like looking at writers' guidelines or back issues. "Just this morning I received a query from a corporate consultant related to an article on a

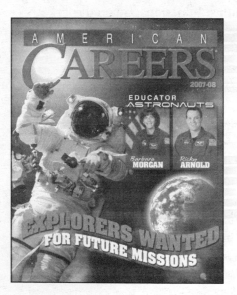

business topic of concern to executives," says Mary Pitchford, Editor in Chief of *American Careers*. "The proposed article would be of little interest or concern to readers in grades eight to ten or to the teachers and school counselors who work with them. I suspect he sent the query to hundreds of editors and wasted a lot of money and effort in the process."

"From the query, I can tell if a writer has done his or her research about our publication, and I can also glean some information about the individual's writing skills," says Phillips. "I can usually tell if someone isn't a good fit for our magazine, but it is harder to tell from the query alone if he or she is going to be a successful writer with the publication."

Formulas for Successful Queries

Writer and editor Moira Allen suggests in her writings and on her website, Writing-World.com, that a successful paper query includes five basic components: the hook, the pitch, the body, the credentials, and the close.

When it comes to the *hook*, your very first line, or at least the first paragraph, should grab an editor's attention. It needs to demonstrate clearly that you can write effectively and that you understand the market. Use a fascinating fact, an interesting quote, a unique angle.

Once you have the editor's attention, the next step is the *pitch*. This is generally your second paragraph, and it explains exactly what you're offering. "If possible, your pitch should include a working title for your article, a word count, and a brief summary of what the article will cover," Allen explains.

The *body* then gets into the details of your article. Your editor will want to know exactly what the article will cover, so you should have a tentative working outline in mind. Presentation may be in block paragraph form or bulleted items. "There's no rule on best style. Choose a style that makes your query visually appealing and easy to read," she says.

A list of *credentials* tells the editor why you're the best person to write the proposed article. These don't necessarily need to include writing credits. Professional experience, degrees or training, personal experience, and interviews with experts will also help you build credibility. Once you've pulled these together, the final paragraph—the *close*— should thank the editor for reviewing your proposal, give a tentative completion date upon approval, and perhaps give one more nudge to encourage the editor to respond.

Waryncia has a query pack that he often hands out at conferences containing both good and bad examples. "One that I use as a good example is from a writer who queried about writing a story about *Anne of Green Gables* author L. M. Montgomery and her life on Prince Edward Island," he says. "We were doing a whole issue on the Maritime Provinces and right from the start her query indicated why the subject of *Anne of Green Gables* was important. Then she gave us examples, and told what she was proposing for the article in short, concise form. Next, she went on to list her credentials. In four short paragraphs, she wrote with confidence everything I needed to know to make the decision to run that article. Then, of course, she provided a very detailed outline and references—where she would research her material. It was just an exceptionally good query."

Turning Rejections into Sales

We've all gotten the bland form rejections: "Thanks, but this doesn't meet our needs." But what if you get a more positive and encouraging response like, "Feel free to pitch more ideas" or "I like your idea, but it's not quite right"?

Follow up soon, especially if you have another idea that would fit the targeted publication. If you can't respond with something new right away, when you do, don't forget to remind the editor about that prior contact. Cobblestone Publishing Editorial Director Lou Waryncia mentions how a favorite query with a pitch about the writing of *Anne of Green Gables* was the result of an author coming back several years after an initial submission.

The author wrote, "Does this query sound familiar? You might remember that I proposed this same article for the January 1999 *Faces* issue on Canada. Although you had expressed interest in the proposal, you couldn't use it because the focus of that issue had changed. You mailed the proposal back to me and asked that I resubmit when *Faces* did an issue that was

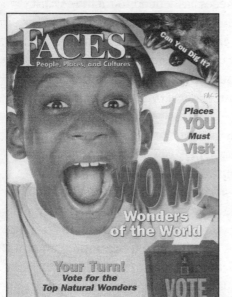

more closely related to the subject matter."

"Once again, the author followed through, and she reminded the editor that we had talked," says Waryncia. "The query was accepted and the article was published. Later it won an SCBWI (Society of Children's Book Writers and Illustrators) award. This is a perfect example of good query writing follow-through. Don't hesitate to remind us of the things we say."

Pitchford also appreciates complete and concise queries. "Good queries mention the topic, describe the approach, and mention the source or sources of information," she says. "We reject queries that ramble, display poor writing skills, and lack knowledge of our publications."

The E-mail Alternative

While some publishers prefer print queries sent by regular mail, an increasing number, especially electronic publications, now accept or even prefer e-mail queries. E-mail queries save postage and paper, and arrive within seconds rather than days.

According to Allen, the most common format for an e-mail query is the same as a traditional paper query. But many editors prefer shorter queries by e-mail. "This is partially a display issue," says Allen. "The less the editor has to scroll to read your query the better. Thus, more writers are turning to brief, one- to three-paragraph e-mail queries." The hook is often eliminated, with writers going directly to the pitch, followed by a single-paragraph description, and ending with the writer's credentials. The final product should be a concise summary of what you would write in the longer paper query.

Formatting is a bit different. Instead of a letterhead-style block of contact information at the top of the page, you'll include this information at the end of your query, below your typed signature. The body should be in plain text at a minimum size of 12 points (not HTML or text pasted from a word processor) to help keep *garbage characters* from appearing along with the text. Avoid sending attachments, such as article clips, outlines, submissions, or other supporting information unless the publication's guidelines say it's acceptable or you have the editor's okay. Use a header such as Query or Article Submission, followed by the title or subject.

Who Gets the Query?

It's always best to get your query directly into the hands of the decision makers, not just blindly submit. Start by looking at the magazine's website under Contacts, or consult writers' market directories, either in print or online. Often, specific editors' names and e-mail information can be found.

Another approach is to look at the magazine masthead of a recent

Query as a Feedback Tool

Sometimes a query is more than just a query. Editors may use one as an opportunity to provide feedback on article ideas or guide the writing process if an idea piques their interest. Here's what three editors say.

➤ "If we like an article idea, we talk with the writer about approach, length, and other matters." Mary Pitchford, Editor in Chief, *American Careers*.

➤ "If I'm interested in an article topic, I do sometimes ask the writer to re-shape the original idea to some degree. I always provide a word count, point the writer to past issues, and offer insights about our readers and style." Alison Phillips, Editor, *InSite*.

➤ "We give authors feedback on their queries all the time; it's often how we select new writers because we see the potential in the query. Maybe it's not the direction we want to go, or perhaps we've already assigned that topic. It could be any number of reasons. But we frequently will go to a person and say, 'We like what you presented, but could you change this for us?' In most cases, people are willing to work with the editor and I think it's a great way of establishing a relationship." Lou Waryncia, Editorial Director, Cobblestone Publishing.

issue. Scan the list of editors and determine who is the best for your purposes. For example, if you're pitching a feature, look to see if there's an articles editor or features editor and direct the query to that person. See if any e-mail addresses are listed.

Within reason, you might also call, but with care. If you call the magazine's main switchboard and ask for the editorial department, you will likely be routed to an editorial assistant. Simply tell her the subject of your query and ask for the name of the appropriate editor to address. "Editorial assistants get these calls all the time; it's part of their job to handle inquiries from writers," says author Linda Formichelli in *Query Letters that Rock*, written with Diana Burrell (Marion Street Press). "Ninety-five percent of the time you'll get the information you need in a minute or less." Again, take this advice with a caveat. Many editors and editorial departments do not in fact want to be contacted by phone about queries; it could open too many floodgates.

Formichelli says if that strategy doesn't work, post your question on a freelance writers' bulletin board like Mediabistro (www.mediabistro.com) or Freelance Success (www.freelancesuccess.com). It will often get you a response and a name to go along with the address.

If you're going the e-mail route, you may find an editor's specific e-mail address published on the website, or the address may be very general (editorial@ourmagazine.com), or it may be conspicuously absent. You could ask for this information when you're calling for the name of the appropriate editor, or include the question when you post on a bulletin board. Another way is to visit the magazine's website and look at contact information for the advertising department. From that

> # "More often than by query, I find a new writer by reading their attached clips. It's their style, a unique spark, a turn of phrase, a sense of humor."

you can often figure out the magazine's e-mail format. For example, if the magazine's ad sales representative is listed with the address John.Smith@ourmagazine.com, you can assume that editors can be reached using the same pattern: firstname.lastname@ourmagazine.com.

Strutting Your Stuff

Along with queries, editors often ask for published clips. "More often than by query, I find a new writer by reading their clips," says Catherine Hughes, a Senior Editor at *National Geographic Kids* magazine. "It's their style, their creative approach to a story, a unique spark, a turn of phrase, a sense of humor." One writer caught her attention with a clip titled "A Shark Is Not a Toy," which made Hughes want to read more—and this author is now a regular with *National Geographic Kids*.

Both Hughes and Pitchford prefer clips in printed format. "Personally," says Hughes, "I am far more likely to read a hard copy than go to a website," where some writers display their clips. "I'll read something that comes to me in the mail, but I am not nearly as likely to pay attention to an e-mail from someone I don't know with references to websites. I just get too many and do not have the time."

Phillips is open to electronic clips in any format, including attachments in PDF or Word formats and Web links. "I accept hard copy as well, but this of course is more costly to the writer," she says. "I do recommend sending clips or links to clips. It gives the writer some credibility and allows me to determine if his or her work is suitable for our publication."

Waryncia says many of the editors in his group also look at links. "I think websites are fine if you have a story posted there," he says. "We take chances on new writers all the time, and the ones that we do [respond positively to] have not only a good cover letter but also show us some of their writing."

Following Up

Whether you send your query by regular mail or e-mail, the worst part is the wait. You open your mailbox only to find the utility bills and a 20 percent off coupon from Spatula City. Clicking on your e-mail inbox only brings up a batch of Canadian Pharmacy ads and a pitch for timeshare vacations.

You figure an e-mail query would yield a quicker response. Your impatience builds. But just because your query may arrive in seconds doesn't mean an editor is going to read it immediately, or even respond the same day. "Nothing annoys an editor so much as a writer who starts nagging for a response within days (or hours) of sending an e-mail query," says Allen.

Despite the instancy of communication technology, business at most magazines still moves at a snail's pace. "Even if your editor has had a chance to read your pitch, he still needs time to consider it—not to mention that assigning a story is usually not a one-person job," advises Formichelli. "He'll probably forward your query to other editors for approval."

So how long is long enough? If you find that the writers' guidelines or one of the market guides state a reply time, then respect those parameters. If the guide says, "responds in six to eight weeks," then allow at least that much time before contacting the editor again. If there's no time frame stated, decide what feels comfortable and reasonable, but above all, professional, to you.

Waryncia notes that the magazine editors at Cobblestone Publishing generally approve article queries about five months before the publication date, which may be several months after the query due date stated in their guidelines. "If you do not hear from us by that time, you can assume your query has been rejected," he says. Most editors are now following this policy, and the author guidelines are being revised to reflect this. However, according to Waryncia, there's no problem sending a quick e-mail to the editor when in doubt.

Formichelli knows of a few successful writers who follow up on an e-mail query in five business days if there's no response. Others may wait two or three weeks, or more if it's an evergreen topic. "If your idea is time-sensitive, you indeed should follow up in a day or two," she says. In this case, you should stress in your original query that the story is time-sensitive and that you would appreciate a prompt response.

Queries Forever?

Will you always have to write queries? Once you've established yourself with a few magazines, you'll find that you won't always have to. And even if you do, you'll find the process more streamlined. You'll only need to sell your idea, not yourself. Sometimes just a short e-mail or phone call will do.

After you've done several pieces for an editor and proven yourself to be reliable and easy to work with, you might even find the editor calling on you with ideas and assignments. You've arrived! Querying won't be the necessity it once was.

Acquisition = Achievement

A Look at the Acquisitions Process at Six Publishers

By Judy Bradbury

Most authors are familiar with the famed black hole that swallows unsolicited manuscripts. We all lament when editors move to another company because we know that submissions are destined to pile up in an abandoned cubicle or converted supply closet. But more the mystery is what happens when the content of our manila envelope meets with a better fate. What transpires between an editor's initial interest in a manuscript and the green light to publish?

The answer to that question, like the answer to *what if?* when you're crafting a plot, varies. At an independent house with an intimate core staff or at a conglomerate consisting of several imprints with discrete editorial, sales, and design teams, the path a manuscript travels from interest to acquisition can be direct or circuitous—and it's not relative to the size of the house. Let's have a look at the acquisition process at a handful of representative publishing houses, big and small, that currently are open to unsolicited submissions.

Reading It All

The acquisition process at Philomel, an imprint of Penguin Young Readers Group, is "fairly standard" according to Editor Courtenay Palmer. "We read all the mail that comes to us, and if we like a concept or see potential in an author's writing, we ask to see more." The type of response given to submissions varies. "If it's an agented submission, we work with that agent and give feedback or more direction about what we are seeking. If the agented submission doesn't work for us, we send it back with an explanation and/or comments or criticisms," Palmer explains. "Regardless of whether we take the book or not, we always respond to agents. As far as unsolicited manuscripts go, we do accept them, but are unable to respond unless interested, even if there is an SASE. We simply discard the manuscripts or queries we do not care for. This is due to an overwhelming volume of submissions and a physical inability to respond to every author unless we're interested in continuing the process."

If the response to submitted work is positive, says Palmer, "Sometimes we will make an offer based on the first submission, but this is rare for slush. Usually it goes a few rounds, and then we decide whether the work in question will be a good fit for our list. If so, we offer a contract." Before that offer is made, however, there is a process to be followed at Philomel. "We take potential books to an editorial meeting and get general feedback. If the feedback is good, we do the work on the book, and either bring it back to a meeting, or present it to the publisher if we feel it's ready. When he agrees, we do a P&L [profit and loss] statement to determine advances/royalties, etc., get it signed, and then go to the author with an offer," explains Palmer. "Usually, even after a contract is signed, there are several rounds of editing that happen before a manuscript is ready for publication."

Palmer cautions that telephoning Philomel about the status of your manuscript is discouraged. "We're doing the best we can. If you are in doubt whether something has arrived, you can send it again, but we will respond only if we're interested in your work." When asked who reads unsolicited submissions, Palmer says, "Most editors at Philomel read mail addressed specifically to them; that is, interns or junior members do not read or reject a specific editor's mail." Palmer offers this tip: "If a manuscript has our name on it, we try to deal with it personally. But anything sent to 'submissions editor' is possibly going to be read by an assistant or intern. It pays to do research on an imprint before sending a manuscript out" so that you can direct a submission to a specific editor by name.

Simple, With Options

Senior Editor Timothy Travaglini explains the process at G. P. Putnam's Sons, another imprint in the Penguin Young Readers Group. "When a manuscript is first being considered for publication, either I read it or my assistant reads it and passes it along to me. If I believe that something is worth pursuing, I take it to the publisher for approval. If she agrees, we sign it up. It's as simple as that."

If the publisher does not agree, Travaglini has options. "I may choose to pass on the project without further ado. If the publisher is on the fence, or I am particularly passionate about something that the publisher does not feel the same about, we will solicit the opinions of the rest of Putnam's editorial staff. Those opinions may set the publisher's concerns at ease, or they may not. Beyond that, there is no acquisitions meeting." According to Travaglini, "The publisher makes the ultimate decision, no matter how the review process plays out. And the editor who is acquiring the work typically calls the author as soon as possible after the green light has been given to sign the book up."

For acquisitions where large sums of advance money may be involved, he says, "We present the project to both Sales and Marketing to see if they feel comfortable with the number of books we estimate we need to sell in order to justify the advance money. The heads of the sales and marketing departments attend such meetings. And often, if we are in an auction situation bidding against another house, we may request that Marketing draw up a preliminary marketing plan. But such acquisitions are the exception, not the rule."

Colleagues' Opinions Count

Senior Editor Erin Clarke explains standard procedure for incoming mail at Alfred A. Knopf Books for Young Readers. "I read agented submissions. My assistant reads unsolicited submissions addressed to me. If he likes them, he will then pass them on to me." If Clarke is interested, the process moves forward. "There are two ways I go about acquiring a manuscript. I may circulate copies for our editorial meeting, which is attended by the seven editors in our house, the three assistants, and all six Knopf designers. I get their opinions on whether the project is worth pursuing. Or, I talk directly to our editorial director about the submission. We do not have acquisitions meetings." If the

Submissions

Within the past few years, many publishing houses have adopted the procedure of not responding to unsolicited submissions unless interested, so be sure to check current submission guidelines before including an SASE with your manuscript.

➤ **Boyds Mills Press** requests that authors submitting a manuscript include "a cover letter of relevant information, including your own experience with writing and publishing." Label the package Manuscript Submission and include an SASE if you would like the manuscript returned. Unsolicited manuscripts for both children and young adults are accepted, including poetry and nonfiction. www.boydsmillspress.com

➤ **Alfred A. Knopf Books for Young Readers** is currently accepting unsolicited submissions. There is no need to include an SASE. If the editors are interested in the submission, they will respond within six months. If you are submitting a picture book, send a cover letter and the full manuscript. If you are submitting a novel, send a cover letter, a one-page synopsis, and 25 pages of text. Do not send original art and do not send the only copy of your manuscript, as Knopf will no longer return submission materials. E-mail or disk submissions are not accepted, only hard copy. www.randomhouse.com/kids

➤ **Philomel Books** accepts picture book manuscripts in their entirety, and a maximum of ten pages for longer works. When submitting a longer work, include a cover letter that briefly describes the plot, genre (i.e., easy-to-read, middle-grade, or YA novel), the targeted audience age, and any publishing credits. Philomel no longer responds to unsolicited submissions unless interested in publishing the work, in which case a reply will be made within approximately four months. www.us.penguingroup.com

Submissions

➤ **G. P. Putnam's Sons** is open to unsolicited manuscripts, but no longer responds to such submissions unless interested in acquiring the project. According to published submission guidelines, "You will not hear from Putnam regarding the status of your submission unless we are interested in publishing it, in which case you can expect a reply from us within approximately four months." www.us.penguingroup.com

➤ **Walker Books** publishes three lists a year, each consisting of approximately ten picture books and four to five middle-grade and/or YA projects, for a total of 40 to 45 titles annually. According to the website, "At the moment, our strongest needs are for middle-grade and YA novels and for well-paced picture book manuscripts for both the preschool and early elementary age levels. We do not publish folktales, fairy tales, textbooks, myths, legends, books in series format, novelties, science fiction, fantasy, or horror. Submissions that fall within these categories will be returned unread." Include a cover letter that contains your current address, phone number, and a brief description of your manuscript. Be sure to include your name, address, and phone number on the first page of your story as well. Walker responds to manuscripts if an SASE is enclosed. www.walkerbooks.com

➤ **Albert Whitman & Company** accepts unsolicited submissions and requests that an SASE be enclosed for response, which typically takes three to five months. Because the editors work so closely together, Whitman requests that authors do not resubmit a manuscript that has been rejected by one of its editors. www.awhitmanco.com

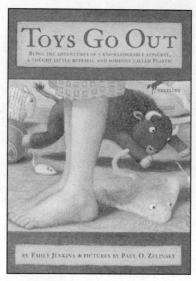

TOYS GO OUT

BEING THE ADVENTURES OF A KNOWLEDGEABLE STINGRAY, A TOUGHY LITTLE BUFFALO, AND SOMEONE CALLED PLASTIC

YEARLING

BY EMILY JENKINS • PICTURES BY PAUL O. ZELINSKY

response is positive, Clarke makes an offer to the author directly by phone. Currently, Clarke acquires picture books, middle-grade, and young adult books, "but at the moment I am desperate to find quality middle-grade in the vein of *The Penderwicks* or *Toys Go Out*." Clarke stresses, "We publish very literary books on the Knopf list, so superior writing is an absolute must." She is not interested in fantasy or issue novels.

From Emotional Response to Business Sense

Associate Editor Stacy Cantor has worked at both Bloomsbury and Walker Books, sister imprints of Bloomsbury USA. Although the imprints share sales, marketing, publicity, and design departments, the editorial teams are separate and distinct. The two imprints also have different submission guidelines. They both accept unsolicited submissions, but Bloomsbury does not respond unless interested. Walker, where Cantor currently is an editor, will respond if an SASE is enclosed.

Cantor, who likes "a little bit of everything" editorially, brings a manuscript she favors to one of the weekly editorial meetings. Three editors are in attendance, and they discuss the merits of the writing, how the project would fit on the list and in the marketplace, how the manuscript compares to others like it that are already published, whether it can stand on its own, how it fits in the genre, and most important, if it "does something new" within the genre or the market. "We decide if the story is too derivative versus something that breaks out," says Cantor.

If the consensus is positive, the project moves on to the acquisition meeting, also held once weekly. "Here it's all about the business," explains Cantor. "While in the editorial meeting we might talk about how much we love the book, in the acquisition meeting, we consider bullet points indicating why the book should be published, whether it might be a big seller, what would drive its publicity, how much money to offer the author, and so on. We also look at comparison titles and how they did or are doing." This meeting includes sales and marketing staff, the head of design, the school and library marketing director, publicity and rights people, and the editors. "Not all projects get passed, although it's not an actual vote," notes Cantor. Even though an editor can still consider publishing a project that gets a lukewarm response in this meeting, "if there isn't excitement among the various departments about a proposed book, it's hard to muster support for its success down the

> ## "We decide if the story is too derivative versus something that breaks out."

road." When the buzz is there, though, the editor moves forward and makes an offer. "I either go through the agent via e-mail, or I initiate the face-to-face relationship with the author by making a phone call." Contact with the author may occur prior to the acquisition meeting, says Cantor, in order to gather information that could help the book's cause, such as whether the author has won awards for other titles.

Tight Team Works as One

Senior Editor Wendy McClure has been with Albert Whitman & Company for 10 years. She finds the working relationship within this small independent house to be comfortable, intimate, and efficient. One of three editors who share the work of putting out a list of 30 titles per year, McClure says, "We don't have assistants. We're each other's assistants." The editors cull through submissions directed specifically to them and also share the sizeable slush pile. "I put aside those manuscripts I am interested in," explains McClure, "and then go back in a couple of days and read them again. I may show a manuscript to another editor if I am unsure. If I am certain of its merit, I put it in another pile to take to the editorial meeting." This is the first tier of the acquisition process at Whitman.

At the editorial meeting, the editors read each other's piles and discuss the manuscripts. "Many will get returned or may go back to the author for revision at this point," notes McClure. If the team feels strongly about a project, it moves on to the acquisition meeting. "Here the whole company gets involved," says McClure. This includes the president, vice president, production manager, marketing and advertising staff, editors, and the person who keeps an eye on sales figures. The manuscripts are circulated and discussed, and then a decision is made. "We may request a revision at this level," notes McClure. Once a project is cleared for acquisition, Editor in Chief Kathleen Tucker typically contacts the author. "How fast the project moves along is dependent upon which list it is targeted for, whether the illustrator is in line or we are still looking for one, and other key factors that ultimately impact the timeline of a project."

McClure reveals that, unlike the process at many larger houses, "At Whitman each editor plays a part in the production of every book on the list. Even though I may initially have pulled the manuscript from the slush or received it from an author I have worked with in the past, I may not head that project. The assignment depends on a variety of factors, such as which editor has previously worked with the illustrator, or who is best matched to the writer's work style and tempo." That said, the editors work closely together throughout the production of each book, offering suggestions, giving feedback, and generally assisting one another. "We honestly think as one," muses McClure. "We all have different points of view, but it's a mistake to think there's only one editor who understands you as the author and will make your book happen. My colleagues need to like the project, too. If a book doesn't do well, we all feel it, and if a book is successful, we all revel in that, too."

And that's something about which authors as well as acquiring editors at houses both big and small resoundingly agree.

How to Negotiate a Better Contract

By Chris Eboch

You just got a contract offer. Hooray! You dance on your desk, call all your friends, toast with champagne. And sign the contract when it comes.

When an editor wants a book, many authors are so ecstatic and grateful that they are willing to sign just about anything. But if you want to be a professional writer, you have to consider the business side of the business. That means fighting for the best contract you can get.

Agent Advantages

If you have a good agent, much of the work is done for you. Stephen Barbara, Agent and Contracts Director at the Donald Maass Literary Agency, says, "A book publishing contract is a complex, at times arcane document, and if you don't know what's in it, what to look for, and what you're licensing to the publisher, you're putting yourself in a very disadvantageous situation. A lot of that fine print in a contract has big import in the real world."

An agent brings knowledge and experience to the negotiations. "The best agencies have negotiated author-friendly boilerplate agreements with the major publishers," Barbara says. "They have in their favor knowledge, experience, and a client list, which taken as a whole acts as a kind of leverage against the size of the publisher. These are real advantages."

Specifically, he notes, "Good agents aim to narrow what is licensed and to raise the monies being offered. So while the author without representation might license all the rights for a small sum, a good agent is looking to hold onto translation and audio and film/TV rights, while getting a stronger advance up front and maybe even better royalties at the back end."

Jamie Weiss Chilton, Associate Agent at the Andrea Brown Literary Agency, says, "Part of an agent's job is to understand publishing contracts and to stay up to date on publishers' changes. An agent often has precedent for what they have negotiated with an editor or a publishing house in the past, and can use that information to negotiate a better deal."

Tracy Barrett, author of the Sherlock Files series (Henry Holt), sold several books on her own before getting an agent. "I acquired an agent only when I was offered a contract to write a series for a packager. She was great. Then she helped place a different novel and negotiated the contract. It's the same publishing company and even the same editor who's done two of my other novels, but the advance my agent got was three times the advance on my previous novel. She also retained more rights and even got some things that I didn't know existed—and I've frequently attended sessions on contract negotiation and participated in phone seminars on the topic with the Authors Guild. They're mostly bonuses if the book gets on the *New York Times* bestseller list, wins a Newbery, etc. But hey, why not have them in the contract? Stranger things have happened."

Can an agent always do better than an unagented author? According to Barbara, "It has a lot to do with how clever the agent is, how much leverage he or she has, how good his or her agency is. I don't think anybody gives you more money or a better contract just because you call yourself an agent. You still need to do the work of asking for the right things and fighting for them. Does that mean writers can get the same results if they're equally tough and smart? I don't know if I would say that. It can be very fraught, a negotiation, and the publisher probably needs you less than you need it. So it's good to have an agent handling this role for you. It takes away a lot of the anxiety and allows you to focus more on the creative side of things."

"It's not a matter of negotiating harder, it's a matter of knowing what to ask for and how to ask," Chilton says. "Getting the best deal means different things for each client, and for each book. Authors often focus only on their advance, and that's a mistake in my opinion. There are many other important aspects of the contract to consider, and royalties and subsidiary rights can be significantly more important than the advance."

Nice, but Not Necessary

Despite the advantages of having an agent, some authors choose to go without one. Kersten Hamilton, author of *Red Truck* (Viking) worked happily with an agent for years, but when that person closed her agency, Hamilton decided to go it alone. "I thought, if an agent has 50 clients, how much time each week can she spend on me? How much time can I spend on me? It's a lot more." Hamilton spends one week each month on marketing, essentially acting as her own agent.

Alexis O'Neill, author of *The Worst Best Friend* (Scholastic), says, "When I started out, it was easier to find an editor than an agent for my picture books, so that's what I did. I also felt it was important for me to learn this business from the inside out and earn some negotiating stripes in the process. And to be frank, it's nice not to have to share 15 percent of my earnings.

"The biggest challenge was going one-on-one with the different publishing houses' contract negotiators and standing firm on which clauses would be deal-breakers for me. It's possible that a dedicated agent—

who also has clout and connections—could help me get better deals. But with a flooded picture book market, I'm not sure that my books would get as much attention from an agent as I can give myself. After all, I live with my books 24/7 while agents have to divide their focus among many clients. Who could blame agents for promoting authors who might be the biggest breadwinners for them?"

Shirley Smith Duke, author of *No Bows!* (Peachtree Publishers), doesn't have an agent either. For her first negotiation, she says, "I had a standard, boilerplate contract used with many first-time authors. I knew I could ask for a few things, but didn't get up enough nerve to ask for much. I think an agent might have gotten more."

Still, she improved her negotiating technique over time. "I've learned to ask for what I'd like and not be offended if I don't get it, because asking for more sometimes gets you what you want. I have improved, because I know more and I've gained more backbone about selling and promoting my work."

Other Options

Even if you don't have an agent, you can get professional help. "If an author or illustrator is negotiating the contract without an agent, he or she may want to consult an attorney who specializes in book publishing contracts," Chilton says.

O'Neill joined the Authors Guild and made use of its contract review service. "The Authors Guild staff reviewed my contracts and made recommendations for negotiating more equitable deals," she says. "I also read everything I could find on book contracts and negotiating, the most helpful being Mark L. Levine's book, *Negotiating a Book Contract.* Friends shared their contracts with me and I compared them with mine. For one contract, I hired an agent on an hourly basis to review the contract and make recommendations."

This may even be the best time to look for an agent, Chilton notes. "It's never too late to approach an agent,

The Authors Guild

Published writers, or those with a contract offer from an established American publisher, can join the Authors Guild (www.authorsguild.org). Among other benefits, members can get free book contract reviews from experienced legal staff.

and having an offer in hand will put you at the top of every agent's list in terms of the speed of our response time."

Going It Alone

If you are negotiating on your own, take your time. "When the editor makes their first offer do not accept it straight away," Barbara suggests. "Be nice and thank the editor for their enthusiasm, but ask for some time to think over the terms. That way you can look at the offer later with a clear head and really mull over what's important to you in the negotiation. If, in your excitement at being made an offer, you say 'Yes! of course!' then the negotiation is over and you have a deal. Finis."

> **"If a publisher pressures you to say yes immediately, and won't give you a few days to consider the offer, that's a red flag."**

Chilton agrees. "Getting an offer is extremely exciting, and the tendency can be to say yes right away, but I encourage authors to carefully consider any offer before accepting. If a publisher pressures you to say yes immediately and won't give you a few days to consider the offer, that's a red flag."

Be prepared before you enter into negotiations. Know what you want, and what's fair. "Talk to other authors who've had a book or two published and ask what they did," Duke suggests. "Get a ballpark figure from them, too. Learn what each part of the contract means. Read a book [on contracts] and make certain you understand every item. Don't feel bad about asking for changes."

Michael Barker, a journalist with Highlighting Writing, an Australian program in which professional authors help train children to write, offers a reminder. "All clauses in a contract are negotiable, though some more than others of course. Publishers expect professional writers and illustrators to make changes to the contract. Negotiating contracts is not a fight. This is part of the business of writing. If you want respect, and more money, either get an agent or learn to negotiate."

A Negotiator's Reading List

➤ Tad Crawford. *The Writer's Legal Guide: An Authors Guild Desk Reference* (Allworth Press); *Business and Legal Forms for Authors and Self Publishers* (Allworth Press, 2005).

➤ Richard Curtis. *How to Be Your Own Literary Agent: An Insider's Guide to the Business of Getting Your Book Published* (Houghton Mifflin, 2003).

➤ Jeff Herman. *Guide to Book Publishers, Editors & Literary Agents 2008: Who They Are! What They Want! How to Win Them Over!* (Three Dog Press, 2007).

➤ Ellen M. Kozak. *Every Writer's Guide to Copyright and Publishing Law* (Holt, 2004).

➤ Martin P. Levin. *Be Your Own Literary Agent: The Ultimate Insider's Guide to Getting Published,* third edition (Ten Speed Press, 2002).

He suggests practicing before you face a serious negotiation. "Go down to your local weekend market about half an hour before closing time. Pick a box of fruit/vegetables/fish—whatever you would like to take home. Now start haggling." He also suggests that writers practice mock contract negotiations with other writers. Have your opponent play it tough, and see how firm you can be in return. You won't feel as nervous when it's time to face the editor.

No matter how much you prepare, sometimes you just can't get what you want. "What if a contract is not good?" Barker asks. "Or actually exploitative? What if the publishers won't budge? This is a time when you look deep into your heart and decide. Is this your first book? Perhaps you might need the kudos of a published book even if you don't make money. Is this a small publisher? Maybe bigger ones would be more reasonable.

"Publishing is a gamble," he adds. "For authors, publishers, and even the book buyers. If a contract is not good, you have to weigh up the risks, consider the benefits, take a deep breath, and make a decision. The most important factor of all is this: Are you prepared to walk away? If you don't have that, then you don't have real power."

With an agent or without, authors need to maintain a professional attitude. "The bottom line is that this is a business, it's not personal,"

O'Neill says. "Ask for changes in the contract, but keep it businesslike. Don't get bent out of shape when the negotiator says, 'No.' But be clear about which clauses will be deal-breakers for you, and be willing to walk away from the table if you're not satisfied. When you learn how to negotiate, it helps in all kinds of life's situations!"

Author, Promote Thyself!

By Christina Hamlett

Writing your book was the easy part. Easy, that is, compared to shopping it to the world. Many a new author has been surprised to be asked during the contract negotiation phase, "How do you plan to promote this title?" The combination of a troubled economy and the corporate downsizing of marketing divisions at even the largest publishing houses has put the onus of aggressive public relations on the writers themselves. The following experts are media-savvy when it comes to starting a buzz, and have graciously shared their best tips.

Thousands of Drops

"Marketing books is like filling a bucket with water until it overflows when your only tool is an eyedropper," says Steve Mettee, Publisher of Quill Driver Books and author of *The Fast-Track Course on How to Write a Nonfiction Book Proposal*. "It takes a thousand small things to happen before a book takes off on its own. Don't pass up any chance to put another drop in that bucket!"

Mettee believes book signings at bookstores have gotten a bad rap recently because many result in few sales. He suggests making the signings into events—at bookstores and anywhere else writers can find. "An event billed 'Learn the Five Fastest Ways to Build Passive Income from Bill Dork, author of *Dork's Surefire Investments*' will likely draw a crowd. Even if it doesn't, the bookstore will still display your book and you'll

Blogs and Business Cards

Author Yvonne Perry is owner of Writers in the Sky Creative Writing Services (www.writersinthesky.com), a team of freelance writers and editors in Nashville, Tennessee. "Never underestimate the power of a book blog!" she says. "A book blog can serve as a point of purchase, provide information, share book excerpts and author interviews, and provide a stopping place for your online virtual book tour." She recommends getting a dozen bloggers together to participate in a fun group activity. "Each blogger visits all the blogs on the chain within one week, leaving comments and their respective URLs. Each blogger gets eleven links to their blog, and eleven new comments." She also points out that many people need content for their newsletters and websites. "Be the expert and send them an article with your byline that includes a link to your site." If you have bookmarks about your book, Perry suggests including them in envelopes when you pay your bills. "There's a reader in every nook of the world!"

Companies such as VistaPrint (www.vistaprint.com) offer low-cost bookmarks, business cards, postcards, and brochures that allow you to upload your own design. You can even customize return address labels to include "Author of (latest book)" as the line below your name. Specialty magnets, pens, calendars, t-shirts, and eye-catching signs are also available.

get to meet the store's clerks who, if they like you, will hand-sell it. You'll also likely get a mention in the local paper, which may be read by a writer for a large magazine, who might write an article that's read by the buyer at Costco, who might . . . . Well, you get the idea." Mettee suggests that a writer stop promoting their book when they want to stop selling it. "Think of all the Coca-Cola signs everywhere. Everyone already knows about Coca-Cola. So why do they keep promoting it?"

Paper PR

When YA author Kirby Larson set out to promote *Hattie Big Sky* (Delacorte Press), she recruited a friend to help create a promotional pamphlet. "We called it a 'first-chapter teaser,' and it included a letter from my editor about why she'd bought the book, a letter from me, and the first chapter. Several hundred of these were professionally printed up and handed out or sent to booksellers. Since advanced reading copies (ARCs) are produced in limited numbers [by publishers], this was a nice way to give booksellers and others a taste of the plot. When the website (www.hattiebigsky.com) launched, people could also download the pamphlet. I felt this was a solid investment of my personal marketing dollars." Larson's latest book is *Two Bobbies: A True Story of Hurricane Katrina, Friendship, and Survival*, written with Mary Nethery (Walker Books).

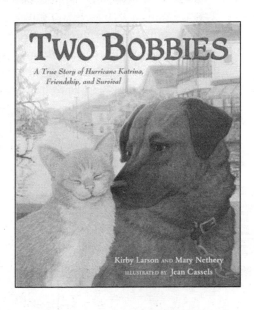

Janet Elaine Smith has 14 novels to her credit and offers monthly marketing advice as a staff editor for *Writers' Journal*. "If you have or know children in school," Smith recommends, "give them a copy of your book and autograph it just for them. Ask them to show it to their friends and teachers, who might even read it to the class or ask you to come speak to them." Volunteering to read one's book at the local library or bookstore for its children's reading day is another promotional tool that has served her well. "Always carry two copies of your book wherever you go—one to show people and one to sell."

Consistent Presence

When C. Hope Clark launched Funds For Writers (www.fundsforwriters. com), her strategy for success was to market herself on a daily basis, "one article at a time, one ad-swap at a time, one chat at a time." Her site is a writing resource that gives "direction on funding streams"—in other words, markets, competitions, awards, grants, publishers, agents, and jobs.

Clark says that the competitive business of being a writer calls for diligence, steadiness, and passion to endure and make work succeed financially. "When you can be considered a reliable and genuine expert, you develop that all-important platform of readers who love who you are. That connection springboards your reputation and, ultimately, sales."

Readers can tell if an author really cares for them and wants to deliver the best information and entertainment, says Clark. "Good promotion isn't about marketing whims, gimmicks, or the YouTube frenzy. Good promotion is a consistent infusion of presence across the Internet and in the circles of your subject matter. The successful young adult author appears in hundreds of different newsletters, websites, and magazines, not just a handful, and participates in interviews, online chats, and school visits. He writes a phenomenal amount of articles, placing a well-honed, brief bio at the base of the piece, directing readers where to find him at a professional website. These may not sling hundreds of readers his way, but will initiate a word-of-mouth, grassroots movement that infiltrates the worlds of many potential readers. Finally, the successful author cherishes the reader and the buyer. He

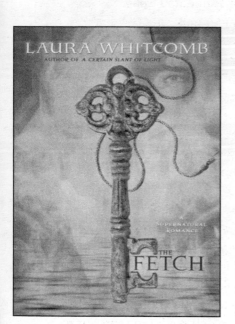

answers all e-mail thoughtfully and provides a regular newsletter, whether monthly or quarterly, but often enough to let the reader know that the author cares and wants to stay in touch. Readers love being a part of the writer's life. The writer who relates to his readership, who stays connected, and who proves he's in this business for the long haul is the writer who makes a writing hobby a career."

Polite Contact, Traditional and New

Laura Whitcomb, author of the middle-grade novel *The Fetch* (Houghton Mifflin) and *Novel Shortcuts: Ten Techniques that Ensure a Great First Draft* (F&W), among others, not only has a long memory but puts it to good use in hyping her upcoming releases.

"I send publicity materials to the libraries in my own town as well as the libraries in all the cities where I've ever lived," says Whitcomb. "I do the same for the colleges I've attended and the junior and senior high schools where I used to teach." She keeps an extensive contact list of every place where she has spoken, taught a workshop, or visited a book club. "I keep track of everyone I've met in the industry, too—bookstore owners, librarians, teachers, fans, fellow writers—and send them post-cards of my upcoming books and/or information on my appearances if they're close enough to attend." In addition to teaching writing work-shops at least five times a year and saying yes to every request for book signings and speaking engagements, Whitcomb is diligent about an-swering every fan letter or e-mail, often on the same day it arrives. "I've also contacted my old English and writing professors to let them know I broke in and am doing well. I thank them for their help." Acknowledg-ing authors who have inspired her over the years is important to Whit-comb, too. "I send them short letters or cards just to say thanks."

On a Platform

Having a professional looking and regularly updated website is an excellent way to promote one's work and credentials, says Cynthia Roberts, the owner of Delphinius Talent Management. "It costs only pennies a day to maintain and presents a much sharper image than throwing together something trendy on YouTube." Roberts is particu-larly drawn to new clients who include a website link as part of their signature block. "With one click, this lets me view their credits and available projects in a single place rather than all over the Internet."

When author and speaker Stephanie Chandler first pursued publica-tion for *The Business Startup Checklist and Planning Guide* (Aventine Press), prospective agents and editors kept asking what her *platform* was. "One well-known agent told me I needed to be speaking to tens of thousands of people annually. I took this as a challenge and decided that the quickest way to build an audience was online." She proceeded to launch BusinessInfoGuide.com and offered free resources to her target audience of entrepreneurs. "I filled it with valuable links, articles, and information so visitors would have a reason to keep coming back. I also began publishing a monthly e-newsletter. The debut edition went out to eight people. Today I have thousands of subscribers." She has also re-cently published *The Author's Guide to Building an Online Platform: Leveraging the Internet to Sell More Books* (Quill Driver).

Websites

➤ **Amazon Guides:** www.amazon.com/gp/richpub/syltguides/create. A place to share information on subjects you know about—and therefore a good way to promote your "product"—in an Amazon profile.

➤ *American Chronicle:* www.americanchronicle.com. Click on "Send Us Info" for various possibilities including submitting press releases, articles, and commentary.

➤ **BookSpoke:** www.bookspoke.com. Bookspoke is a platform specifically designed for writers to communicate with readers about their work and themselves.

➤ **Stephanie Chandler:** www.stephaniechandler.com

➤ **Delphinius Talent Management:** www.delphinius-management.com

➤ **Funds for Writers:** www.fundsforwriters.com

➤ **Gather:** www.gather.com. Social networking for people over 30. It includes thousands of shared interest groups.

➤ **Kirby Larson:** www.hattiebigsky.com, www.twobobbies.com

➤ **Novelspot:** www.novelspot.net. Book reviews, forums, columns, interviews, chats, and more for lovers of books.

➤ **Quill Driver Books:** www.quilldriverbooks.com

➤ **Kathryn Raaker:** www.kathrynraaker.com

➤ **Janet Elaine Smith:** http://janet_elaine_smith0.tripod.com/

➤ **VistaPrint:** www.vistaprint.com

➤ **Laura Whitcomb:** www.laurawhitcomb.com

➤ *Writers' Journal:* www.writersjournal.com

Although Chandler's first title was published via print-on-demand, the popularity of the online platform she established resulted in her two subsequent books attracting the attention of traditional publishers. "Every author has the same opportunity to create a publishing career. It's all about finding out who your target audience is and what kind of information they want. Be creative! Children's book authors can create fun short stories, tips for parents, activities for kids, contests, and much more." Launching a website, blog, or electronic newsletter is a must, she says. "I built my site on a $20 template!" Chandler also stresses the importance and ease of learning how to optimize a website with search engines. "Always keep the wheels of your career in motion. If you can do two or three things a day to build your platform and promote your book, success is sure to come along."

On the Air

Syndicated radio and TV personality Kathryn Raaker (www.kathryn-raaker.com, www.bornb464.com) is enthusiastic to have authors as guests on her show. She also recommends that they pursue quarterly radio or TV spots as part of a promotional campaign. "Take advantage of things like MySpace and YouTube to do upbeat one- or two-minute spots about your latest release and what inspired you to write it. See if your local access station has talk-show slots where you can get an interview." Raaker also suggests that authors register at RadioTimes (www.radiotimes.com) and establish themselves as an expert through participation in its forums and blogs.

All-Around Effort

Freelance writer and editor Lisa Marguerite Mora (www.barring-toneditorial.com) has found no shortage of promotional opportunities through participation in Yahoo groups for writers and artists, advertising on Craigslist (www.craigslist.org), and maintaining contact with anyone she has ever worked with. "I keep my business cards handy, and my e-mail signature includes my business name and my website. I was corresponding with a longtime acquaintance about something nowhere in the realm of work when she e-mailed me with, 'Editor? You're an editor? Oh, I have a manuscript I'm working on . . . .' I generally do something every day toward promoting myself. The only cost is time."

That's a strong lesson: Do something daily, and keep your eyes open to new possibilities. If you've previously only thought about Amazon.com as a 24/7 virtual bookstore, think again. Features such as So You'd Like To Guides and Listmania, as well as regular participation in online discussion groups, can help establish you as an expert in your field. Use Inside the Book as a teaser to reel in readers. And, of course, you'll want to collect as many reviews of your latest release as you can from friends and relatives.

Clubs and schools are always looking for guest speakers for meetings, special events, and career days. They'll welcome the addition of your name, a local success story, on their rosters! Too shy to talk? Let technology be your voice by sharing your views and building a network through interactive Internet channels such as *American Chronicle*, BookSpoke, Gather, and Novelspot.

Start a ripple, create some waves, and employ all the imagination and tenacity that you can to make your new book the splashing success it deserves to be.

Schmoozing for Fun and Profit

By Chris Eboch

Networking successfully can turn a freelancer's talent and hard work into a lucrative career. Writers may schmooze casually at conferences, through blogs, or on listservs. Some push the schmoozing further by forming groups designed specifically for professional networking in which peers share contacts, advice, and publicity, and everyone benefits.

Food for Thought

Some branches of the Society of Children's Book Writers and Illustrators (SCBWI) have professional networking groups. The Illinois chapter's Food for Thought program is intended to help members with the business side of writing. Meetings are open to all published members, and those close to being published. "After all, the best time to learn about contracts, publicity, etc., is often prior to publication," says Sara Shacter, author of *Heading to the Wedding* (Red Rock Press), who has helped plan Food for Thought meetings. The group meets about three times a year. Members choose a topic of interest and then someone volunteers to set up the meeting: securing the venue, contacting a speaker if necessary, coordinating food, and so on. At the end of each meeting, members consider more topics.

The format varies. At one meeting, people delivered parts of their school visit presentations. "I got some great ideas—and great feedback —from my peers!" Shacter says. "First, I saw the range of possible programs. I also learned more about the business end of school visits— fees, contracts, thank you notes after the fact, setting up book sales, etc."

Wife and husband writing team Mary and Rich Chamberlain, authors of *Mama Panya's Pancakes: A Village Tale from Kenya* (Barefoot Books), comment, "We organized a Food for Thought program last year that brought in an expert webmaster to speak to SCBWI members on setting up a Web presence. Some areas we found helpful were a review of some member websites online during the program; how to set up keywords, including an interactive group exercise; how to accommodate slow browsers in the set-up; and lots of other practical advice."

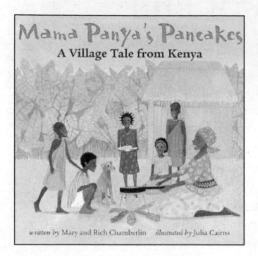

Mama Panya's Pancakes
A Village Tale from Kenya

written by Mary and Rich Chamberlin   illustrated by Julia Cairns

Sallie Wolf, author of *Truck Stuck* (Charlesbridge) is another member of the Illinois SCBWI who benefited from Food for Thought meetings. "At one that occurred before the publication of my book, we discussed publicity and what other authors were doing to promote their books. This was really helpful to think about before I actually had the book in hand."

Can-do

Other networking groups have sprung up independently of a larger organization such as SCBWI, wherever someone saw a need. In 2008, Kersten Hamilton, author of the Caleb Pascal and the Peculiar People series (Standard), invited published children's book authors in New Mexico to monthly lunches. At one meeting, the ten attending writers and illustrators discussed the advantages and disadvantages of agents, and how to negotiate contracts on your own. They shared tips on changes at publishing houses, including warnings about a difficult editor. Hamilton also offered to share contact information for the head librarian of a local school district, who was looking for people to do school visits. The meeting encouraged camaraderie, and most people walked away with at least one professional tip.

The Children's Authors Network! (CAN!) began in 1995 as a forum for writers and illustrators to discuss the business side of the profession.

Members try to meet at least quarterly and have a listserv to stay in touch via e-mail. The 12 members have hosted dinners with experts such as librarians, book representatives, publicity experts, Web designers, media interviewers, and even a counselor to talk about the psychology of success. They also use the expertise present in the group. Member Alexis O'Neill, a former teacher and a supervisor of teachers, led a session on teacher workshops. Evelyn Gallardo showed how to put together a press kit. Teachers Jeri Chase Ferris and Michelle Markel explained how to link books with educational standards.

CAN! members pay $50 a year for dues and use that for promotional activities. They may buy booth space at teaching fairs. They produced a cooperative brochure to advertise their school visits. When one does a school visit, they leave a brochure and a copy of their "Guide to Author Visits" so the school knows about the other authors. In the early days, they did free group showcases at libraries and schools to get the word out, and they refer jobs to each other. Finally, they recently created a cooperative website at www.childrensauthorsnetwork. com.

O'Neill, author of *The Recess Queen* (Scholastic Press), says, "In addition to wanting to talk about the business of publishing, the thing binding us all together is our shared commitment to doing high-quality public presentations for kids. We have all seen each other's presentations and can recommend each other without reservation. More and more hosts are telling me that they found me via the CAN! website."

Mamas and Sisters

Not all groups focus just on writing for children. Journalist and author Dawn Yun founded the Writing Mamas five years ago. "It began when I was with my toddler and another mother asked me what I did," she explains. "I said I was a writer. She had such a longing look in her eye and said that writing was what she always wanted to do. I told her

Writer Websites

➤ **Toni Buzzeo:** www.tonibuzzeo.com
➤ **Mary and Rich Chamberlain:** www.richnmarywriters.com
➤ **Phillis Gershator:** http://phillis.gershator.com
➤ **Kersten Hamilton:** www.kerstenhamilton.com
➤ **Alexis O'Neill:** www.alexisoneill.com, www.childrensauthorsnetwork.com
➤ **Sara F. Shacter:** www.sarafshacter.com
➤ **Jennifer Ward:** www.jenniferwardbooks.com
➤ **Sallie Wolf:** www.salliewolf.com
➤ **Jane Yolen:** www.janeyolen.com
➤ **Dawn Yun:** www.writingmamas.com

she could. It was never too late.

"Shortly after that, I thought, why not start a group for women who are mothers who write or want to learn how? It began as a series of classes I taught on writing and has since morphed into the Writing Mamas. We're a group of women ranging in age from their twenties to their seventies, from one child to five. People who join the Writing Mamas want to write, get paid for their writing, and become published. Some have never published before, others have, still others are getting published now that they have joined the salon."

The Writing Mamas has chapters starting nationwide. The original group meets twice a month, with a guest speaker one of those times—usually an author, but sometimes literary agents and editors. "In addition to becoming a good writer," Yun says, "the Writing Mamas very much concentrate on the business side of writing. Having the speakers come helps us make connections with writers who often will share with us names of agents or editors at magazines."

Yun started "The Mama Monologues" as a showcase for members to learn to read and perform their work in public, and to raise money for charities. "I media train Writing Mama members beforehand," Yun says. "The idea is when your books are published and you are touring, you will not be just a reader of *X* book, but of an *entertaining* one." The group has a daily blog, essays, and articles on its website (www.writingmamas.com), with information on writing, connecting, and getting published.

Even small critique groups can help members with the business side of writing as well as the creative side. Jane Yolen's writers' group meets once a week. "We read aloud and critique," Yolen says. "It was through the writing group that the father in my picture book *Owl Moon* (Philomel) became Pa, and the old man in *The Seeing Stick* (T. Y. Crowell) became blind. It was because of us that Patricia MacLachlan's picture book, *Sarah, Plain and Tall* (HarperCollins), became a novel. We give one another tough love. We talk about the marketplace. We help ourselves change agents, find new editors, and get through life's uncertainties. I wouldn't be where I am now without these smart, sassy, caring, brilliant women holding my back."

Virtual Support

For people who can't find or start a local group, the Internet offers an alternative. Phillis Gershator, author of *Sky Sweeper* (Farrar, Straus and Giroux), is a member of Bookartists, an invitation-only Yahoo group. "In my group, there's a policy of nondisclosure," she says, "so we feel free to be upfront about money, contracts, negative experiences (which publishers are submission black holes, for example), and to share good news, too, balancing off any bad. I live in the Virgin Islands, which is a bit isolated, so I feel when I read the daily digests that I'm not alone, and feel supported, uplifted even. A lot of sharing of ideas and career information goes on, including technical information. Visiting writers and artists on their websites, I was finally persuaded to get busy and create a website, so the group has encouraged me in my professionalism and outreach. I've also gained more courage to (sometimes) negotiate for better contracts."

Online groups can form as strong a community as live ones. "When people have had trouble with a plot point, or a title, or need professional information, there's give and take," Gershator says. "Everybody is generous and supportive. I got the chance to meet some good people in real life. The virtual friends are great too, witty and funny—I laugh out loud at the posts."

Jennifer Ward, author of *Because You Are My Baby* (Rising Moon), and Toni Buzzeo, author of *Adventure Annie Goes to Work* (Dial), connected through an online forum of published children's authors and illustrators.

Ward says, "From this forum, a discussion presented itself regarding what everyone earned in one fiscal year in royalties, advances, speaking gigs, etc. Everyone was really frank and honest, and it was an eye opener, for certain! Especially to see a breakdown specific to each area of income—school visits income, for example, versus advances.

"The overlying frustration that surfaced from the discussion was how challenging it was to support oneself as a writer. Yet, there were several folks in the discussion who were indeed making a good living as writers —and I hate to say this, but the men predominated!"

This realization offered inspiration. Ward says, "So Toni and I (and another writer who actually started the forum conversation) started thinking: Why are the men earning more? Because often they are primary wage earners and must. And what are they doing, from a business angle, in regard to negotiating contracts, accepting speaking gigs, etc., in this business that is so different from what women do that allows them to earn more?"

Ward and Buzzeo formed an online club. They write independently, but work as a team to support one another to achieve common goals.

With a laugh, Buzzeo says, "We began to ask ourselves WWGD? (What would a *guy* do?) We became excellent supporters of each other's efforts by asking hard questions. Why are you doing this piece of work? How much time will it take? How much is your time worth? What will you have to earn to make it worth your while? And we also were brutally honest with each other when we thought the other was heading in a wrong direction or making a mistake. Of course, if the other person had a deeply personal reason for making that decision, and could defend it, we respected personal choice."

The results show in their income. "I have doubled my income in the time we have worked together," Buzzeo says, "and I have shifted the portion of my income that comes from writing versus that which comes from speaking to strongly favor writing, an annual goal of mine. I could not have done this without our partnership. Writing and speaking is lonely and sometimes isolating work. But it needn't be if we are wise in choosing business partners for support, encouragement, and good advice."

Ward adds, "I have tripled my income in the time we have worked together and I, too, have shifted my earning revenue toward advances and royalties versus income from speaking in schools." That is professional networking at its best.

These groups vary in terms of their focus, financial and time requirements, and openness to new members, but all are helping their members advance their careers. O'Neill of CAN! says, "I would encourage other children's authors to form a collaborative like CAN! I have learned so much about presentations, promotion, and the workings of the publishing business through the generosity and skills of my colleagues. Knowledge is power. And I believe that our shared knowledge has led to our greatest accomplishment of all—doing powerfully great things for kids through our books and presentations."

Ideas and Inspiration

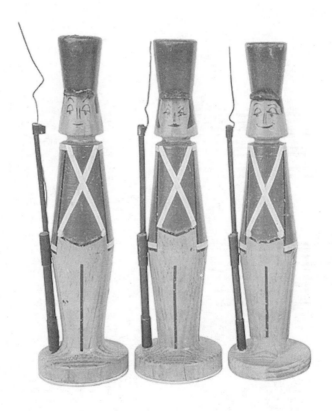

Cultivating the Seeds of Memory

By Sue Bradford Edwards

When you finish one project, do you already have another idea ready to go? If not, learn to dig through and cultivate your memories and you'll have enough ideas to write a shelf full of fiction. Many successful writers use this technique to come up with everything from short stories to articles to picture books to novels.

Family Tales

People who come from a family of storytellers may have a natural edge in the nurturing of stories, but everyone has inspirational memories if they just start looking. The trick is to have ready access to them.

"My parents and grandparents told stories of their pasts around the dinner table and I soaked them up like a sponge," says Andrea Cheng. "Some centered on World War II and the Holocaust. These stories became the seed of my first novel, *Marika* (Front Street). I imagined my mother as an 11-year-old girl. Her father and her uncle ask her to forge a document that may save their lives. She knows, and they know, that forgery is wrong, yet in this case, it is of vital importance. This seed became the first chapter."

What stories did you weave in your mind after hearing about your aunt's exploits or your grandpa's adventures? If their stories inspired you as a child, they can inspire you and young readers today.

Don't limit yourself to mining memories just for plot. After all, you have to create a full-fledged story that is more than a string of events. Leslie Wyatt says, "For *Poor Is Just a Starting Place* (Holiday House), I used family stories for characters, scenes, and setting. My grandmother

229

told many tales of growing up in Kentucky during the Great Depression. I wanted to capture not only family history but the lush, green hills of Kentucky, the struggle of families in that very difficult era, and the over-arching idea that who we are matters—that we are part of our ancestors before us and that who we are will be passed on in some measure to those yet to come." In mining her grandmother's tales, Wyatt drew on what happened, but also who made it happen, where it happened, and why it was important.

Not every family story naturally yields such a complete picture. Even stories that only hint at what happened can spark a full, well-rounded tale. "When I learned that my great-grandmother had homesteaded by herself as a young woman in eastern Montana, I was astonished," says Kirby Larson, author of the Newbery Honor book *Hattie Big Sky* (Dela-corte). "I had no idea people were still homesteading in 1914; I thought that was only in covered wagon times. I couldn't imagine that tiny, shy woman doing anything so gutsy. Originally, I just wanted to learn more about her experience, one which she never talked about with our family. But as I read and researched, it be-came clear there was a great story to tell." Her great-grandmother's past provided the inspiration that led to *Hattie Big Sky*.

The memories that lead to good stories have an undeniable emotional pull. "A family vacation inspired both the setting and characters for 'Hot Rocks and Icy Water,' a story I placed with *Skipping Stones* magazine," says Tina Dybvik. "The plot is loosely based on two separate visits to a Finnish friend's home on Minnesota's North Shore. Her beautiful property and old-world customs made a lasting impression on me. It's a story I told many times before I began to write." Dybvik says she has learned to pay attention to those stories that seem to demand being told often. Consider the true story you begged your great uncle to retell, or one your children repeat for anyone who will listen. These memories have demonstrated their emotional pull. Now learn to fictionalize them.

Tilling, but Altering, Fertile Ground

Creating quality fiction based on something that really happened can be difficult for writers who hesitate to alter that reality, however. "If you can get over the hurdle of feeling that family stories are sacred and meant to be left untouched, it can free you to treat them much as you would any other idea you get as you craft your book," says Wyatt. You must be willing to rework the memory into solid fiction to make a sale.

The memories that lead to strong stories have an undeniable emotional pull.

"Tweak any details—dates, ages, people involved, etc.— that don't fit or further your plot." Few memories are publishable without these kinds of changes; some elements essential to successful fiction will need development.

Pat McKissack grew up in Nashville in the 1950s. "Everything was segregated in downtown Nashville, except the library," says McKissack, who used these memories to write *Goin' Someplace Special* (Simon & Schuster, illus., Jerry Pinkney). "I didn't want to use Nashville because Nashville is a well-known city," says McKissack. Instead, she set her story in a generic city in order to lead her character from one segregated location to another before reaching the library. "No sane person would take that route in Nashville," McKissack says with a laugh, but that fictitious route propelled her character out of segregation.

Other memories must be changed because they simply aren't complex enough to sustain a plot. "My daughter and I found a turtle on the road when she was young and we decided we needed to let it back into the wild," says Kathryn Lay. "We went straight to a pond at a nearby park where we'd seen other turtles and set it free. That would've been a boring story without a conflict," says Kathryn Lay. "So in 'A Turtle Home' (*Pockets*, June 2001), I had the girl try to help three times with

What Is That?

Objects from the past can inspire stories.

Kathryn Lay wrote "Voices in the Storm" *(Boys' Life)* because of a gift. "My daughter had a doll that her grandfather gave her, bless him. If you spoke to it, it repeated the same words back in an annoying, high-pitched voice. Sometimes she'd say a phrase and let it repeat over and over. Drove me nuts!" says Lay. "I had an idea about a boy who was irritated with his sister and her doll that repeated things over and over. During a bad storm, he threw it out the door, and then a tornado hit. The roof of the house fell in and he and his sister were trapped, trying to find the stairs. Then he heard that stupid doll. He remembered it had landed at the top of the stairs. He was able to lead his sister out safely by following the doll's voice."

An object can also inspire a full-length novel. Andrea Cheng shares this

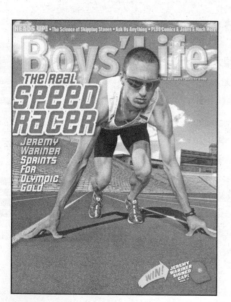

example: "My aunt has an exquisite lace tablecloth framed in her apartment. When I asked her about it, she told me that her mother commissioned the piece from a lace maker in a small town in Hungary that was famous for this sort of handiwork. My grandmother was poor, but she thought it would be important for her daughter to have this lace as part of her dowry. My aunt's tablecloth became the seed for the *The Lace Dowry*, most of which is fiction."

What heirlooms does your family treasure? Grandpa's cane fishing pole or Aunt Mary's crocheted shawl can hook a new story idea.

something happening to the turtle: It falls down a hill and lands on its back, and is messed with by a cat. Ultimately the girl realizes the pond is the best place for the turtle." Fictional scenes created conflict.

Other dramatic memories contain no character growth. "When I was little, I learned to ride a bike that belonged to the woman across the street," says Anne Marie Pace. "I always asked first, but one day, when she wasn't home, I rode the bike anyway. When she came home and saw me riding, she stopped the car and screamed at me, calling me a thief. While I realized I should have asked, I didn't understand why she was so angry." Pace never borrowed the bike again nor learned why her neighbor became angry. "In the story 'Mrs. Benson's Bike' (*My Friend*, September 2002), the girl learns that the woman lost her temper because she was disappointed that her own granddaughter's visit was canceled. The girl then plans a party at which the neighbor will be adopted as a class grandmother. To make it an effective piece of fiction, I had to add the antagonist's motivation, the protagonist's movement from hurt and anger to understanding, and solve the problem."

Over time, you may realize you are drawn to certain kinds of memories that require specific changes to become successful fiction. "Often, I begin with an emotionally charged negative experience, and then resolve it with a happy ending," says Dybvik. "'Hot Rocks and Icy Water' ends with the main character running downhill to jump in Lake Superior. Lake Superior is freezing, and as a child I neither witnessed nor experienced that level of courage in my sister or myself. A happy memory, on the other hand, requires the creation of a conflict that never occurred. For me, it's a more natural process to begin with the conflict."

Too True to Be Good?

Writing about conflict based on real events panics some writers. What if your antagonist reads the story?

Most authors write their way out of this problem. "When I write, I don't think about the audience," Cheng says. "If I did, I would be paralyzed. I can only think about the character, what she says and does, how she moves and talks. With *Marika*, I was concerned that some of the people who are still alive might be upset. But my relatives in Hungary loved the book, and my aunt translated it into Hungarian. I am lucky that my family members know that all my stories are fiction even if the seeds are true." Fictionalizing real people well makes it more difficult for a real person to see themselves, negatively, as an antagonist.

McKissack solves the problem by not basing a character on one person. "I do composites. I had an uncle who did this and an uncle who did that and I combine them to create a very familiar character. Everyone claims it is them. Most people see themselves in the story that they want to be in." And they perceive other people as the bad characters, even saying such things, says McKissack, as "'I see who that nosey lady is you were talking about.' I've never had a problem because I changed them enough to make a story."

Inside Views

Most memory-based stories require research to flesh them out. This is especially true for historical fiction such as Wyatt's *Poor Is Just a Starting Place.* "I did a tremendous amount of research on the era—politics of the times, societal norms, fashions, radio programs, anything I could think of to immerse myself in the culture and mindset of that time. For historical writing, you've got to get inside the worldview of that era. You can't have a character with a 2008 attitude in 1939."

Just as belief systems must be researched, so must tiny details. "*Hattie Big Sky* represents more than four years of research; the new book about the same. I had to learn about everything! Clothes, homestead requirements, train schedules, planting crops," Larson says. "For instance, I called the Selective Service System to find out exactly how the draft worked in WWI. People are generally thrilled to share their knowledge and expertise with you."

Like Larson, Lay turns to experts for help. "'Cave-a-Phobia' in *Spider* dealt with when my daughter was young and we went into a public access cave. I didn't know much about caving," says Lay. She has a technique for maximizing expert input. "I have an Expert Box where I keep index cards noting people and their interesting jobs and hobbies." One included the perfect person for the cave article. "The father of a friend of my daughter's did a lot of spelunking and let me interview him and told me about good websites to check out."

Taking a memory seed and growing it is far from just transcribing people's stories. "When I was a child, my sister used to accuse me of changing the truth when I told stories of past events, and I think she was right. The truth is often not as interesting or compelling as a fictionalized retelling," says Cheng.

Cultivating, nurturing, and seeing stories come into full bloom isn't a short process, but it can yield beautiful crops. Inspiration is just a recollection away.

Inspiration to Speak, Reason to Read: Ways to Find Voice

By Mindy Hardwick

S tory voice: It is almost as individual as fingerprints, or more relevantly, as voiceprints. A short story or novel must have a distinct sound and feel if editors and readers are to fall in love with it. Voice has to do with your own authorial style, but it is also the unique *speaking* of a particular story or novel—the way a narrator tells the tale or a protagonist's way of talking, all working in combination with the time and place and pace of the story.

"The voice is the soul of the book," writes Cheryl Klein, Senior Editor at Scholastic's Arthur A. Levine Books, on her website, Talking Books (www.cherylklein.com). In a series called "The Rules of Engagement," she explains, "The narrative voice is a person the reader wants to spend time with."

Sometimes voice comes to a writer almost fully formed. Laurie Halse Anderson has related how her character Melinda, in the novel *Speak*, just started talking to her. Anderson woke in the middle of the night to hear a girl sobbing. After she checked on her daughters, who were sleeping peacefully, Anderson realized that the girl was in her head. She quickly sat down at her computer and allowed the crying girl to tell her story. But if a character doesn't just start talking to us, how do we find this elusive thing called voice?

The process of finding a story's voiceprint is not unlike solving a mystery. Writers may need to become their own story detectives—to uncover the voices that are meant to speak, and to capture the personalities of characters who resonate through every part of the story.

Raw Voice

I can often begin to detect a story's voice through writing exercises. Every week, three other writers and I meet for an hour at a local cafe and have timed group free-writes. We each bring an open-ended writing prompt written on a small piece of paper. Our prompts might be "I opened the door and . . ." or "Let me tell you my side of the story . . . ." We also use lines of poetry and picture prompts. We place the prompts in the center of the table and set a timer. Someone picks one of the prompts, reads it, and we all write on that lead for five minutes. We each then read aloud what we wrote. Although it's not always comfortable to share off-the-cuff writing, it is important to listen for the raw voice behind what we've put down. Perfection isn't the point here; hearing is. It's okay to have imperfect writing, but this exercise allows us to hear and find a direction. Writing gems may emerge, and sometimes, well, sometimes we all just get a good laugh and move on, but we are left with clues to follow.

We repeat this process, but in the next rounds we write for 10 or 15 minutes, and continue to share our work aloud each time. It's amazing to see what happens by the later rounds of timed writing, when the mind is loosened and the words are flying. By the time the session is over, I always have new ideas and almost invariably a fresh voice begins to emerge for one of my works-in-progress.

Hearing a Character Speak

You can also slip on your voice detective hat with exercises on your own. For one of my favorites, I keep supplies at the ready in the form of a small bin containing scissors, glue, old magazines, colored pencils, index cards, and heavy cardstock paper. For five or ten minutes at a time, I use one of the following techniques to generate ideas and develop voice in the context of the other elements of my story.

Character portraits: Voice starts with character. It's important to spend some time getting to know our characters, especially those things about them they want to keep hidden. If one were sitting beside you, how would they sound? What would they tell readily? What would they avoid saying but ultimately reveal?

As a story detective, create a file of possible suspects and their qualities loosely based on character trading cards, an idea borrowed from artists. Gather a stack of blank index cards and on each card ask, and then answer, the following for a character in your story. Set the first pile aside and do the same for each character in the story. The questions range from large to small, and there are many others you may add.

> What is your secret?
> What do you love?
> Whom do you love?
> Whom do you hate?
> What do you fear?
> What do you want?
> What clothes do you wear?
> How do you fix your hair?
> What do you look like?
> Whom do you resemble?
> What unique habits do you have?
> Where do you live?
> Where were you born?
> How old are you?
> Who are your friends?
> What makes you laugh?
> What do you do on a Saturday afternoon?
> What is your most prized possession?

Character Cards

To flesh out some of your characters, you can borrow an idea from artists, using Artist Trading Cards (ATCs). Mixed-media artists often create and carry these illustrated trading cards, sometimes for promotion and sometimes just for the pleasure of collectible trading. For a more detailed look at these fabulous creations, check out the book, *1000 Artist Trading Cards,* by Patricia Bolton (Quarry Books). ATCs are made using a small number of items such a piece of text, lace, an embellishment, and an image. The cards are then mounted on a painted playing card. For your characters, use card stock and miscellaneous items to create a card representative of their life, interests, and personality.

➤ What do you sound like when you speak, when you sing, when you laugh?
   ➤ What is likely to make you cry?
   ➤ What do you like to eat, and what do you detest?

Each character card pile will begin to add up to a portrait of a full person with a real voice. Keep the cards close at hand as you write. By creating character cards, you might just find that the most interesting character is not the one who you have selected to tell the story; perhaps your story would be better told through the eyes of a different character. Or you may learn that the character didn't sound quite like you thought they would. Maybe a character is so fearful, her voice is a raspy whisper, or he stutters. With these attributes coming to the surface, the course of the story may become more clear.

Magic character boxes: Another exercise to develop a character and begin to hear his or her voice uses visuals. Remember shadow boxes? Ever have a treasure box? In your supply bin, keep issues of magazines such as *National Geographic, Smithsonian,* or history, science, fashion, sports, or niche magazines. Cut out pictures of small items you think might interest a developing character. You might devote a shoebox to that single character. Fill it with the cut-and-paste pictures, or with pieces of pottery, glass, jewelry, small illustrations, rocks, bugs, animals, foods—anything at all that you feel represents this unfolding person.

➤ What do these items tell you about the character?
➤ Does he or she have a collection of these items?
➤ Did someone give the character the items? Why?
➤ Did he or she ever lose an item? Which? How? Was it found?

When you are feeling stuck for ideas, pull out one of the pictures or items. Pretend that your character has been handed the item and ask yourself the following questions:

➤ Imagine the item has magic powers. What are they?
➤ Why was this character given this item?
➤ Who wants this item besides your primary character?

Character blog: Many of us now blog (or try to!). But maybe your characters blog or journal too. A fun way to discover how passionate your character is about a subject is to give your character a blog!

> ➤ What would they post on their blog?
> ➤ Is there a subject they feel passionate about?
> ➤ How often would your character post?
> ➤ Would they be an obsessive poster or maybe someone who forgets and only remembers at the last minute?
> ➤ Who would comment on the blog?
> ➤ Who would disagree with your character's blog posts?

Try to write a blog in your character's voice for a week to see what you discover. Who knows, you might start a blog in a character's voice and find that an editor lands on your blog and loves it.

Sounding out the Setting

While a story's voice largely arises from how a character sees the world, writers (and ultimately, readers) often need to know more about the place a character lives if they are to understand the character's motivation and actions. As a story detective, you can search out where an event occurred, and why the location matters to those involved. Try these setting exercises to detect the echoes of your character's voice in a particular place. They can help you map out a real or fantasized globe, create a town, or style a room. Within any of those places, people speak.

Draw a map. Many a reader of many an age loves a map, whether for real or imagined places. A location can give an accent to characters, a cadence, and a culture or philosophy that helps explain motivations and actions. Is the character located somewhere in the contemporary or historic U.S.—Northeast, Midwest, South, Northwest, other? Is he or she from the U.K.—Cornwall, London, Scotland? Or from other parts of Asia, Africa, Australia, Latin America? Or does your character live on Mars or in some unnamed place? Wherever your characters live, ask:

> ➤ What does the story place mean to the protagonist, or other characters in your story?

> ➤ Even if the location is not at the forefront of the story, how does it inform characters as background?

> ➤ How do characters get from here to there in your story? Walking? Bike? Train? Bus? Horse cart? Ship?

> ➤ What does the place a character lives have to do with the tone and the sound of who they are?

Not every important location is large-scale. Sketch out a map of your main character's home, school, favorite park, street names, and even the tree that might hold a tree house, or—in a certain kind of story—their galaxy, even if it's all for background and doesn't make its way into your story.

Collage a room. Imagine the bedroom your hero, villain, or the best friend next door returns to each night. Does a patchwork quilt from Aunt Lucy cover the bed, or did Dad build a blue race car bed? Or is the room spare and worn? Is it never empty, always noisy? Is it kept pristine, or is there always clothes and *stuff* everywhere? What kind of stuff? Gather a collection of shelter magazines: *Cottage Style, Martha Stewart Living* (or some of the Martha Stewart special issues on kids). Clip images and create a collage of an imaginary bedroom for your character.

Doorways. Have you ever thought about the doors in your story? Where are the doorways that your character steps through? Take a few minutes to sketch out a couple of the doorways in your story. They might be actual doors or they might be portals to other lands. Then try writing to these prompts:

> ➤ When I stepped through the door, I saw . . .
> ➤ I opened the door and . . .
> ➤ I did not open the door and...

Plot Away

Voice is also heard through plot. One of the best ways to hear our characters is to toss obstacles before them. How will your character respond when confronted with his or her greatest fear? How will your character respond in a situation in which he or she is asked to choose between two difficult choices? Try the following exercises and see what emerges.

Playing with photos: Photographs are all around us—in newspapers, on the Internet, in art museums, and on library walls. Photos peer back at us from high school gymnasiums and school hallways: teams winning and teams losing, classes that passed through the school building years before, star students. What story do these photos tell? How would the people in them speak?

➤ If you feel like your writing time could benefit from a field trip, take a trip to a school or other location where you know there will be pictures of children or teens, and listen for the voices that emanate from them.

➤ Gather issues of the local newspaper, with pictures of events at schools, churches, and athletic fields.

➤ If you're writing historical fiction, go to your library to find books of photos (or, for earlier periods, drawings and paintings), like those famously taken by Dorothea Lange during the Depression. Or, find a photography exhibition to attend.

➤ Look to your own family: Do you have old photographs of people you can identify and some you can't?

Spend a few minutes studying a chosen picture or set of photos, and ask these questions:

➤ Who are these people?
➤ What is their history?
➤ What do they want?
➤ What do they fear?
➤ Whom do they love?
➤ What obstacles do they face?
➤ What is the next action they will take?
➤ What do they regret? What are the consequences of that regret?

➤ What are they proud of? How does that impact the way they live?

In what voice would your character tell you the answers to these questions? With strength or shame? Openly or resistantly? How would they tell a friend the answers? A stranger? An enemy?

Secrets: Everyone, including your character, has secrets. But, how do you get your character to tell you his or her secrets? Try looking in your character's closet. Close your eyes and picture yourself standing in front of a character's closet. Open the door. What is inside? Are the clothes neatly folded and hanging in a row or are they messy? Push your way past the clothes. What is on the shelves? Is there a secret hiding place inside the closet? Is there a secret object inside the closet? What is your character hiding or treasuring?

Try drawing your character's closet. What does the door look like? The inside? The back of the closet? The walls? What is the secret in your character's closet? What secret would you never tell anyone?

If you want inspiration to find more secrets, log onto the blog kept at Post Secrets, where secrets are written anonymously and mailed in on postcards: http://postsecret.blogspot.com.

Plot a timeline: When and where do the important events of your story take place? How does that impact tone, accent, vocabulary? This exercise is similar to drawing the setting map, but with the added dimension of time. Mark when and where key events happen.

➤ Where is your main character when she learns about the problem of the story? What emotions does she feel and how does she express them?

➤ Where is your antagonist when complications arise?

➤ Where is your protagonist when he solves the problem?

➤ How old was your character when a key event happened?

➤ Did your character experience a significant life event that does not take place in the course of your story—for example, perhaps a beloved pet died, or a parent died?

A story's voice is a mystery at some point in your writing process, but it's one that can elicit great creativity in solving. By following a few clues, you'll soon find a distinct voiceprint, and your story will be filled with the heart and soul we call voice.

Making a Good Idea Great

By Jane Landreth

W hen you were a child, you made up stories. You invented characters and situations and perhaps had a saga running in your mind. No matter what happened in your real life, in your imagined world, you were the hero. You made up these stories because they were fun, or perhaps they offered you a place of safety. They made you feel good.

As an adult, your stories and your reasons for imagining them changed. The demands of the practical world have made the story world become more than just fun. You have learned about writing style, skills, and techniques. You have learned about strange new forces, such as editors and market trends. Having moved away from the source of your imaginative power, your stories now seem flat or mechanical. They have lost the zest that once made your stories seem to live.

How can you re-enliven an idea that will capture the eyes and heart of an editor? More important, how will your story take hold of the eyes and heart of a young reader?

Imagining

Ideas may originate within or without. Some of the ones that you'll use to write exquisite work are already inside you, in your memory or sub-conscious, or in your foundation of knowledge. Even those ideas that are in the world around you and waiting to be found will blossom into life as they connect with your imagination. Only in being responsive to what you know, feel, and have experienced will you find the great ideas that already belong to you. Search your mind for images and events, people, and places. Discover your thoughts and feelings. Allow yourself to respond automatically to the ideas that come to mind, and at this stage of the idea development process, don't censor anything.

➤ *From within:* Ginnie Gail based her picture book, *The Great Pigeon Race* (PublishAmerica), on a memory of her and her brothers helping their grandparents to release pigeons at a train depot. This idea led to researching facts about trains, homing pigeons, and telegraphs. Gail says, "I was impressed with the use of homing pigeons to deliver messages during wartime."

➤ *From without:* Perhaps you prefer to explore the world outside yourself, looking into issues and ideas that interest you, such as current

or historical events or scientific processes. If a subject is interesting to you, it's possible to make it interesting to others. When Sherry Fiscella was a homeschooling consultant, two of her students shared a history lesson about George Washington praying at Valley Forge. "What a great starting point for a children's story," Fiscella thought. She was surprised to learn in her research that children assisted the troops during the American Revolution—and that was just the idea she needed for a child protagonist in her story, "A Christmas Hero." *(Focus on the Family Clubhouse,* December 2008)

➤ *From imagination:* Fantasy and science fiction may be your interest, with characters, scenes, and conflicts that are completely imaginary. But even in these genres a story must have a foot in reality to be believable and relatable for readers. Think about creating a dream family you always wanted, a place you dreamed of going, a sport you always wanted to try, and place it in a far-off world. One night as Ronica Stromberg was putting her resistant four-year-old son to bed, she said, "What about your guardian angel? Don't you think he's a little tuckered out from watching over you all day?" She wondered "if anyone had written a bedtime story involving a rambunctious child and a tuckered-out angel." Because she thought she had heard all the excuses to avoid going to bed, she wrote *The Time-for-Bed Angel* (Lion Hudson Publishing), with the make-believe angel.

Try one or more of these prompts to explore as you investigate your inner and outer worlds.

> ➤ Make a list of at least five important memories, good or bad. Focus on experiences that made a difference in your life. Choose one or more and explore it by writing a page about it.
>
> ➤ Write a paragraph about an event or issue, current or historical. Now write a paragraph about some personal connection you have to the event or issue.
>
> ➤ List some facts that interest you from your own foundation of knowledge. Select one and explore it for who, when, why, where, how.

Enlivening

Generating ideas doesn't have to be so tough, does it? The tougher part may be bringing the idea to life on the page, sustaining the magical elements throughout the grunt work of completing the piece.

You may ask yourself how to know if an idea is worth pursuing. There is no magic key that unlocks that answer door. It all depends on what you think and how you decide to make the idea work. Explore possibilities. Get something on paper. Write down a bare bones description of the idea, list character names, compose a bit of dialogue—anything to set the story in motion. For nonfiction, write down what you know about a subject, or where you could go for interviews. You don't need much to get an idea breathing. The important part is to have started, to give your idea life outside your mind.

Sometimes an idea is no longer of interest. You may have begun it long ago, and it's been worked to death. Yet you are hesitant to let it go; you've grown attached to it because you've invested so much time and energy that would be wasted. Relegate the idea to a *hold* file. You're not trashing it, but you're allowing yourself to move on to other work that, for right now, has more spark. At another time you can come back, and perhaps then a good idea will move more steadily to a great one.

> ➤ If you have an idea you've been carrying around in your mind for a while, put something on paper. Describe the story or article in one paragraph. Write two titles. Name characters. List potential sources.

> ➤ Sift through ideas that have been brewing for a while. If you haven't written them down in a notebook or file, do so. Brainstorm other ideas based on them. Keep a running list of ideas.

> ➤ In a short paragraph, evaluate an idea you are questioning. What are its strengths and weaknesses? Pros and cons? Why do you want to pursue the idea? How will you achieve what you want? Who would be interested in reading what you are planning to write about? Why?

You can think of a dozen ideas for stories, but if you don't put them on paper and take time to push them around a bit, you will have nothing to show for your creativity. The act of writing down the idea plants it more firmly in your mind.

Exploring

Once you've committed to the worthiness of an idea, continue to open yourself to possibilities. Follow an idea intuitively, waiting for the characters to assert themselves, a conflict to reveal itself, a shape to form, or a voice to rise from the page. Allow these things to happen; don't force them. Pursue, but don't push. Give yourself time to brainstorm and move in various directions, even if they don't seem to be related at first.

At the same time, begin to pull the idea into focus: Listen to it and play with it. Keep putting words on paper, keep adding ideas. Look for complications and possibilities and levels, but begin to see the shapes that form. If you have found a direction you want to follow, but find yourself struggling with the first couple of paragraphs, skip them. Start anywhere. Move around and let the words spill from you. Some writers focus on characters first. Others move to conflict and then allow the characters to develop as the plot unfolds.

Sometimes an idea seems to go stale. That great idea that sent you racing to a notepad in the middle of the night, the one that seared your brain through stimulating sessions at the computer, now lies unfinished on the page, and is less than what you hoped it would be. Step back and evaluate how you've developed and complicated the initial idea. Be subjective, and search your feelings. Does the idea still speak to you? Next, look at it objectively: Is your idea fresh? Have you read a piece like this before? How is yours unique?

For an idea to work well, it needs to grow, to complicate itself with more ideas that extend or enlarge the first. For example, I wanted to write a story about moving to a new town, but this idea is tiresome to many editors. I needed a new, unique situation. Telling the story from the point of view of a child who is doing the welcoming, rather than the moving, unfolded as I developed my idea. In my story, "Monica's Good Neighbor Gift" (*Primary Treasure*, August 2008), Monica greets the new neighbors with a basket of gifts—flowers, garden produce, fresh baked cookies—which she gathered from her neighbors.

> Brainstorm a list of complications, additions, or changes for your idea. Make it a big list.

> Describe your story idea in two sentences. Now add a third sentence, introducing a new element. Write another third sentence, that goes in a different direction. Do this as many times as you can.

> Rewrite a scene to change the tone in a significant way—from anger to humor or from predictable to shocking, perhaps.

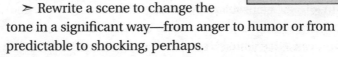

Christopher Visits Grandpa

Exploding

At some point you may just need to acknowledge that an idea isn't working. Naturally, there's no step-by-step formula to determine that, but there are noticeable signs that an idea is in trouble.

Sometimes an idea isn't bad at all, but it resists your attempts to develop it. You write a story about a family picnic, taking the idea from an event in your own past. You remember the happenings, have real descriptions, but the story feels prosaic. Distance yourself from the true events.

Sometimes you come up with an idea that seems great, to yourself and to others. As you work on the piece, you find yourself less and less interested; you have no passion for it. Avoid situations that force you to be untrue to yourself. It might be right for someone but not right for you.

At other times, you find yourself shifting from one idea to another in what seems an endless series of discoveries. Continuing research causes you to change the concept in significant ways, hindering the development of the idea. You are in an endless chain of new beginnings.

> Write a few pages about the idea, its meaning and interest for you, and your connection to it. Be as honest as you can be as you analyze the connections. Is this idea right for you to pursue?

> If the idea in question is a small one, add a new character or scene to the story, or pull a character or scene from the narrative and review how the absence affects the story. Is the character or scene superfluous? If so, let it go. If you're still drawn to it, explore it in a page or two of writing. It might be the start of a different prospect.

> Take time away from developing the idea. When you return, review the idea, reading the pages you've already written. Are new possibilities presenting themselves or do you find you have little interest?

Getting an idea isn't a problem. Knowing what to do with it, knowing how to turn it into something substantial, intriguing, and unique is the challenge. You can force yourself to write, to assess and develop your ideas, to the point where you destroy any fun or creativity that might make the ideas better. You can put pressure on yourself, blocking your use of imagination. Think back to creating stories as a youngster. Remember the fun you had being the hero, the good feeling in the adventure. Challenge yourself to that same delight as you create stories for children in today's world.

Fight the Good Fight Against Writer's Block

By Sue Bradford Edwards

O nly one thing is more frustrating than sitting down to write and discovering that the words won't flow. That is hearing the advice so often given about how to *cure* writer's block: "Put your butt in the chair and write."

Write? Isn't that already the problem? Writer's block is a part of writing. You don't need to feel guilty about it as if it were something for which you are responsible. You're only responsible to yourself for finding the way to work through it. Learn how to prevent it, how to solve writing problems that lead to it, and when, for a little while, to surrender.

Prevention

"Put your butt in the chair and write" may be annoying to hear, but it does have a large dose of truth—the cure is just not miraculous or sudden. Writing is like working out. Do it seldom, and you'll sweat and strain. Do it often, and there may still be hard work, but you will write with more strength, rhythm, and breadth. The key is to find a method that works.

"I had a routine of writing in the morning in a coffee shop. That felt critical for me," says Laurel Snyder, whose titles include *Up and Down the Scratchy Mountains* (Random House). "Something about the other people around me forced me to work. As though they'd know I was a slacker if I quit. They expected me to arrive and to keep my head down. For me, a total extrovert, finding a way to make the solitary work of writing into a group activity is important."

You can still write without a fixed schedule. With two toddlers, Snyder no longer gets mornings at the coffee shop. "I write whenever the house is quiet, and sometimes in the bathtub or over the crockpot. I've become a good multitasker. But that's its own kind of routine. Writer's block is a luxury I can't afford right now, because I usually have a list of things to work on 'when I get a chance.'"

Be ready to adapt your expectations. "Any given schedule will only work for me for so long, and will then need changing," says Janni Lee Simner, author of *Bones of Faerie* (Random House). "Sometimes I alternate days of fiction writing and day job freelance work. Right now I've been recommitting to touching base with my story six days a week. Some days I'll write a few paragraphs, some days pages and pages, but every day I have to write something."

> ## "Living by a schedule reminds me that my need to write is stronger than my temptation to procrastinate."

For this to work, hold yourself accountable. "When your mind says, 'It's 6:00 AM, time to write something,' you know that you have become serious about your work," says David L. Harrison, who has published more than 70 books, among them *Pirates* (Wordsong) and *Paul Bunyan: My Story* (Step Into Reading/Random House). "Living by a schedule reminds me that my need to write is stronger than my temptation to procrastinate. By showing up for work on a regular basis, I rarely find myself at a loss for words or thoughts."

At times the writing doesn't flow nonetheless. The next step is to see if, despite a writing routine, your work habits have caused the problem.

Fixing a Problem

Sometimes a well-developed writing habit is part of the problem.

Perhaps it's time to write and, fortunately, you're eager to start your new project. You fly through the first page. The second comes more slowly. Then you sit. You get a snack. You check your e-mail. How could you freeze up this quickly?

When the words won't come, science writer Fiona Bayrock examines her writing plan. Does she know where the manuscript is going? If not, she knows what to do. "I step away from the keyboard to do the prep work I should have done before sitting down in the first place: researching and thinking about things to the point of feeling totally comfortable with the material, time period, characters, and the desired style, voice, and story." Only then is she ready to write. Among her titles is *Bubble Homes and Fish Farts* (Charlesbridge).

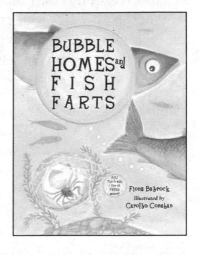

Planning can also be the problem when a rewrite bogs down. Laura Purdie Salas, author of *Stampede! Poems about the Wild Side of School* (Clarion) offers an example: "When an editor whom I admire and trust asked for a revision recently with some vague suggestions, I was totally blocked. If she had said specifically what she wanted, I could have done that. But that's not how trade publishing works. The editor wants to raise questions, make the writer think, but let the writer create a new version."

Don't begin the minute you get the revision request. Instead, consider the comments. Find a solution natural to you and this particular story. Then write.

Salas couldn't even begin rewriting. "I kept second-guessing myself." Her solution came with a fixed deadline in the form of an upcoming holiday. "I knew I wouldn't be able to relax on vacation with that project hanging over my head," she says. "The deadline forced me to do lots of brainstorming, and I found an approach to try."

Second-guessing yourself also can become an impediment when you're reworking a section of a manuscript. The first thing to do may be to banish perfectionism. "I write really messy first—and second and third—drafts anyway, so I remind myself that the words and the story don't need to be perfect yet. I just need to get them down," says Simner.

If messy is okay, and the words still won't come, you may need to examine if you're truly ready to take on a particular project. Simner admits, "I have a book that took me 12 years to write. I wrote the opening chapter, loved it, and had no idea what to do next. I realized that part of what was going on was simply that I wasn't good enough a writer to finish that book yet. I could have spent 12 years doing nothing but failing to write that one book. Instead, I wrote a bunch of other books and short stories, all of which helped me become a better writer, a writer who could finally finish that book, *Bones of Faerie.*"

The longer-term cure here is one that anyone who is exercising their best career health takes seriously: Study your craft. Read what others have done. Write to hone your skills. Eventually, you will possess the skills you need to get the job done.

Brain Freeze

Even with healthy writing habits, developed skills, and the right project, you may sometimes freeze up. Try an ice breaker.

➤ *Do anything to fill that blank page.* "The mind cannot revise a blank piece of paper. If nothing comes at first, I doodle, scribble non-

sense, put down a word (any word) and make a list of situations I associate with it, dive into my idea files, describe objects I see around the room, reminisce about a favorite trip, jot down a few childhood memories, compose a few what-if questions, list and describe five things that are important to me—anything to get some marks on my piece of paper," says Harrison.

➤ *Turn to past inspiration.* "Whenever I have an idea for a book, I jot it down on a piece of paper. Sometimes it's just a title or a concept or a character," says Susanna Reich, author of *Painting the Wild Frontier: The Art and Adventures of George Catlin* (Clarion Books). "When I'm stuck, I pull out those pieces of paper to see if there are any ideas I want to pursue. Sometimes I play around with one of those ideas for a day or a week. If nothing comes of it, that's okay."

➤ *Switch writing gears.* "First, work on a different project, or simply

Don't Try Too Much

Writers are notorious multitaskers, often committing to much too much.

"During a period of six years, the quality of most of my work became too lackluster for publication," says David L. Harrison, whose published books number more than 70 and counting. "I kept writing, but only a couple of books were good. This was a time when I added a six-year term on our school board to an already busy schedule which, in addition to writing, included being husband/father, running a company, and remaining active in community affairs. Maybe the stress of one more responsibility was what overwhelmed my muse. When I finished my term of office, I spent the next three years writing in a new genre—poetry—and that got me off to a fresh start."

If you simply don't have the energy to write, pull back. Take a look at your schedule and evaluate how important your writing is. Something else may have to go.

work on a different poem within the same collection. My brain keeps working on the stalled one without my knowing about it, and I usually come back to the stalled one fresher and with words flowing," suggests Salas.

➢ *Take a break.* If you've tried other options and only sit and fidget, take a break. "My most recent experience took place with a picture book revision I was working on for Margery Cuyler at Marshall Cavendish. I simply couldn't produce the words to make the story click," says Jennifer Ward. "It is a story in rhyme, so word choice was limited—very frustrating! I got through it by taking a break and stepping away from the story for a few days. Using a fresh eye approach is something that often proves inspiring for me." The end product is *The Busy Tree*.

➢ *Get physical.* To gain a fresh eye, distance yourself by doing something not strictly writing-related. Simner says, "One thing that's important to me as a writer is getting in regular physical activity. Writing is a sedentary business, but being too sedentary saps our energy and makes it harder to push forward. A half hour away from the keyboard to go for a walk or a run may well buy me more than a half hour of writing time over the long term." Take a walk. Do yoga. Go dancing. The solution to your plotting problem may pop into your head. Even if it doesn't, regular exercise increases your energy level.

➤ *Remind yourself that creativity is fun.* Some writers find inspiration by setting their creativity loose in the kitchen. "I might do any number of things, including baking numerous meat loaves and distributing them to friends," says Ward. "I have earned the nickname Princess Meat Loaf."

Snyder also re-energizes in the kitchen. "I love to cook, slowly and spicily. There's a zen to chopping and mixing and tasting." If cooking is not your thing, try gardening, painting, woodworking, or knitting.

➤ *Sample the work of other talented writers.* "Reread some classics and sense the craft behind the words. Borrow some inspiration from a few masters, then pick up your pen with renewed determination," says Harrison.

Snyder turns to specific writers for inspiration. "I have a few books and authors I can go back to and they'll wake me up: John Berryman, Tomaz Salamun, Frank O'Hara, James Wright, James Thurber. Kind of a weird mix of things I've loved at different times for different reasons. This works especially well with poetry, which has such a quick, momentary effect. If I read a really great poem, I want to write a really great poem."

Reich is another who is moved to writing by reading. "I get constant inspiration from reading. I read every night before I go to bed, mostly children's and young adult books, but occasionally an adult novel. I also read the *New York Times* book review section every day at breakfast."

I Surrender!

Sometimes writer's block follows a personal tragedy. "I remember at one point, after a death in my family followed by an illness in my family," says Simner, "I spent six months working on the same short story, making really, really slow progress." Bayrock experienced something similar after suffering through three losses in two months. You must solve this type of burnout as an individual.

Bayrock had to pull back. "I hadn't had time to grieve and recover from the first death when the second and third happened. I simply could not write in a light, fun, spunky style for young children when I was feeling so far away from light, fun, and spunky," she says. "My well was completely dry. For many months, everything I wrote was unrecoverably flat. Finally, I stopped trying to fix things and just let go of the writing. For many months, I concentrated on living and life and filling my emotional vessel. Eventually, I did get the joy back, but it came at its own pace. For me, I just needed to be patient and allow time to heal."

Other writers, like Simner, must keep writing. "I forced myself to keep working on the story whether I wanted to or not, which was probably the right thing to do, but I was pretty depressed about it. Looking back, I think I'd forgive myself more for my slowness now than I did then. During hard times, I think maybe it's okay not to be too hard on ourselves."

Often, writer's block is avoidable. Re-invigorate by doing things you love mentally and physically. Keep healthy and maintain a doable schedule. When writer's block does strike, examine your work in progress. You've probably got the resilience and strength to break that block and start writing again.

Ideas Around the Globe: Starting with the A's

W e all know people who love to read almanacs or peruse the pages of atlases. They may be trivia hounds, or oriented toward data, but they may also be creative types. A simple fact fascinates them, and unfolds into many levels of significance. That is the reason behind this listing of countries, all beginning with A: See how tidbits of this and that from around the world, facts of geography, culture, history, science, people, and more can send your ideas and writing traveling far.

Afghanistan

Geography

▓ About the size of Texas, with approximately 30 million people, the Central Asian nation of Afghanistan is landlocked.

▓ Kabul is the capital. It is located in a valley and is connected by a tunnel through the Hindu Kush mountains to neighboring Tajikistan. The city has existed for 3,500 years.

▓ Much of Afghanistan remains unsurveyed because of its terrain and its history of ethnic clashes and unstable governments.

▓ The Hindu Kush Mountains, part of the Himalayas, divide the eastern and western parts of a nation that is largely mountains and desert. Less than one-eighth of the land is arable, and about half of that is used for agriculture.

▓ The famous Khyber Pass in the Hindu Kush leads from Afghanistan to Pakistan and the Indian subcontinent. The word *khyber* means *across the divide*.

▓ Resources include natural gas, coal, iron, copper, and precious and semiprecious stones. Crops include opium, wheat, sheepskins, and nuts. Among exports are handwoven carpets, gems, and hides.

History & People

▓ The word *Afghan* can be traced to the third century AD. The official languages are Pashto and Dari, both Indo-Iranian languages. The word Pashto is thought to derive from the Persian word for *border people*. Dari is a Farsi, or Persian, dialect. Both use modifications of the Arabic alphabet.

▓ Invasions of Afghanistan have been frequent for millenia. Darius I and Alexander the Great traveled through Afghanistan to India. Leaders over the centuries coveted the country's trade routes, including what came to be called the Silk Road.

▓ The region has historically been home to Dravidians, Indo-Aryans, Greeks, Scythians, Arabs, Turks, and Mongols.

▓ Islam came to Afghanistan in the seventh century.

▓ Genghis Khan conquered the country in the thirteenth century, and Tamerlane in the fourteenth.

▓ In the nineteenth century, Russia and Britain fought imperial wars in Afghanistan. Rudyard Kipling wrote of the struggles he called the "Great Game."

▓ Britain declared the country fully independent in 1919, and Afghanistan was then ruled by a monarchy. Its neighbor, India, gained independence from Britain in 1947.

▓ In 1973, the monarchy was overthrown and a republic declared. Its legislature is called the Loya Jirga, or Grand Assembly.

▓ The Soviet-backed Afghan government in the 1970s was opposed by ongoing guerrilla resistance, resulting in a Soviet invasion that lasted until 1989.

▓ In the 1990s, Afghanistan came under fundamentalist Islamic rule in the form of the Taliban. In the first decade of the next century, it has been shelter to Osama bin Laden and his group, al-Qaeda.

Culture & Daily Life

▓ Islam is the religion of about 99 percent of Afghanis, with about three-fourths of the population Sunni Muslims and the rest Shi'a. The mystical Sufism has had a large impact on the nation's religion.

▓ The many ethnic groups of Afghanistan include Pashtun, Tajik, Hazara, Kyrgyz, Uzbek, and Turkmen.

▓ *Persian lamb*, a glossy and tightly curled wool, comes from the Karakul sheep native to Afghanistan. They are probably the oldest domesticated sheep, dating to 1400 BC.

▓ Common Afghan proverbs include: The first day you meet, you are friends; the next day you meet, you are brothers. A tree does not move unless there is wind. There is a path to the top of the highest mountain. Don't stop a donkey that is not yours. He who can be killed by sugar should not be killed by poison. A liar is forgetful. There is blessing in action. Debt is the scissors of love. No one says his own buttermilk is sour.

▓ The life expectancy in Afghanistan is 42.9 years.

▓ A little more than a third of Afghanis can read. Fewer than a quarter of children go to school. Newspapers are often read aloud in public places, since so few people read.

▓ Farming villages often take the form of small mud forts. Some Afghan ethnic groups are nomads who herd cattle or sheep with camels and donkeys. The nomadic peoples live in yurts or other tents.

▓ Potable water is not accessible in most of the nation.

▓ When they ruled, the Taliban would not allow women to serve as health care workers.

▓ Living in a highly tribal society, Afghans are identified by their *qawm*, which may define a clan or village group.

▓ *Naan*, a flat bread, is a staple. Other foods include *qabli pulao*, which is steamed rice, carrots, and raisins, often accompanied by lamb; kababs; *quorma*, which is fried onions with meat, fruit, or vegetables, and spices; and *mantu*, steamed dumplings.

▓ Clothing and entertainment are dictated largely by Islamic practices. These have been more or less strictly regulated in recent decades depending on who was in power.

▓ Traditional dress for men consists of baggy trousers, a long shirt, and vest. Women generally wear the *chadri*, a form of the *chador*.

The birth rate is 6.75 children per woman, and the infant mortality rate is 163 children per 1,000 born.

Buzkashi might be considered the national game. It is played on horseback with the carcass of a goat or calf, not unlike polo. Other games and sports played are competitive kite flying and wrestling.

Arts

Early cultural influences in Afghanistan came from Persia, India, and Greece.

The *attan* is the traditional public dance. Dancing has long been central to Afghan celebrations, except when banned under strict Islamic rule such as the Taliban.

The great ancient statues of Buddha, found in caves in Bamiyan, were lost in 2001 under an order by the Taliban that all pre-Islamic statues and objects be destroyed.

The Timurid school of the fourteenth and fifteenth centuries was a high point in art and architecture. It was named for the Mongol leader Timur, also known historically as Tamerlane. One of the strengths of the school was manuscript illumination. The period continues to influence Afghan art.

Afghanistan's literature belongs largely to the Persian tradition and its poetry has been notable. The thirteenth-century poet Jalaleddin Rumi, who wrote in Persian, was also the founder of the mystical Islamic order, the Whirling Dervishes. Another mystical poet, Jami, wrote in the fifteenth century. The seventeenth-century chieftain Khushal Khan Khatak is sometimes considered Afghanistan's national poet; one of his themes was the noble tribesman. In contemporary times, Haidery Woojudi struggled, through his writing, to maintain Afghan culture during the Soviet occupation.

Among the country's traditional instruments are drums called the *daira* and the *zerbagali*, a stringed instrument called the *richak*, and a flute called the *tula*.

Science & Nature

Trees are rare in southern Afghanistan. Monsoons make the north more fertile, but forests still make up only three percent of the land area.

Tigers, once indigenous, are no longer found in Afghanistan.

Among the region's animals are ibex, mongooses, jerboas, hyenas, jackals, and pelicans.

Business & Economy

▦ The unit of currency is the *afghani.*

▦ Large reserves of natural gas have drawn outside interests to Afghanistan.

▦ Most of the population farms. In small towns are artisans, traders, and government workers; very few Afghanis work in industry.

▦ The country has less than 2,000 miles of paved roads, and about 11,000 miles unpaved. There are virtually no railroads.

▦ There is one telephone per thousand people, and one television per hundred people in Afghanistan. Radios are much more common.

Famous People

▦ The widely influential philosopher and physician Avicenna (Ibn Sina), was born in Afghanistan in 980, but lived his entire life in Iran.

Albania

Geography

▦ Albania is on the Balkan Peninsula along the Adriatic Sea and borders Greece, Macedonia, Montenegro, and Serbia.

▦ Tirana is the capital of Albania. Shkodra is one of the oldest European cities, having originated as an Illyrian fort. Apollonia and Butrint are other ancient cities.

▦ Internally a mountainous country with severe winters, coastal Albania has the hot summers and mild winters of the Mediterranean.

▦ A fifth of Albania is cultivated. A third is pasture. A third comprises forests and swamps. The mountains historically isolated the country.

▦ Crops include citrus fruits, figs, and olives.

▦ Resources include natural gas, petroleum, coal, copper, iron, and chromium. Tobacco and wine are exported.

▦ Nature preserves protect animals such as boar, chamois, jackals, and bear. Birds include storks and pelicans.

History & People

■ The ancient name for Albania was *Illyria*. The region was known for its mines in classical times. Some linguists believe Alabanian derives from Illyrian, while others argue that it came from Thracian.

■ Among the ancient Illyrians, women were nearly the equals of men and could became tribal leaders.

■ Albanians call their nation *Shqipëria*, and themselves *shqiptarë*, which means *sons of eagles*.

■ Ptolemy of Alexandria first wrote of the Albanoi tribe in the second century AD.

■ The country was part of the Byzantine Empire from about the fifth century to 1204. In this period, the Slavs integrated into the population.

■ Several coastal cities in Albania were founded by Venetians in the eleventh century as centers of trade.

■ From the fifteenth to the twentieth century, Albania was part of the Ottoman Empire. Conversions to Islam began in the sixteenth century, to avoid reprisals by the ruling Turks. The Ottoman system included feudal estates called *timars*, and rulers were *pashas*.

■ An Albanian nationalist movement accompanied a cultural renaissance in the mid and late nineteenth century.

■ Albania became independent in 1912 after the First Balkan War.

■ The country became a monarchy between World War I and World War II. The nation was assaulted by feuds, poverty, illness, illiteracy, and inequalities.

■ As World War II geared up, Italy annexed Albania in 1939. It became communist in 1944, but was more allied with Chinese than Russian communism. Under the leadership of Enver Hoxha, the country began to modernize but continued to be extremely isolated. The government was marked by political purges and squashing of dissent.

■ Albania began a slow movement toward democratic reform and openness to other nations around the time of the fall of communism in 1989.

Culture & Daily Life

■ Tosk is the official Albanian dialect, and the second major dialect is Geg. The language is generally believed to descend from Illyrian, though some linguistic scholars believe it comes from the language of ancient Thrace.

▦ A national written alphabet for Albanian wasn't formally developed until 1908.

▦ Seventy percent of the population of Albania is Muslim. Twenty percent is Orthodox and 10 percent Roman Catholic.

▦ The literacy rate in 1945 was 20 percent. Today it is 100 percent.

▦ Schools stress technical education.

▦ The infant mortality rate is 25 deaths per thousand births. The ratio of doctors to population is 20 per 10,000.

▦ Albanian food is a mix of Eastern and Western dishes. It typically includes lamb, yogurt, mint, eggplant, tomatoes, and walnuts. *Mezes* are savory appetizers.

Arts

▦ Albanian folksongs and oral poems were often accompanied by a lute-like instrument called the *lahuta*. The *ciftelia* is a small two-stringed mandolin with a thin neck.

▦ The oral tradition of epics, legends, and ballads is strong in Albania. Common themes are heroism and loyalty.

▦ A unique Albanian style of religious icon developed in the eighteenth century and remained in use through the twentieth century.

▦ The first Albanian play ever written was Anton Santori's *Emma*, dating to 1887.

▦ Albania has many archaeological museums, including the National Museum of Archaeology in Tirana.

▦ The mythological tradition of Albania dates back to the Illyrians and through the Middle Ages. The king of gods and father of mankind was Tomor, who was called En in the Middle Ages. He gave his name to Thursday, which is *enjëtë* in Albanian. Tomor's attendants were the wind spirits. The fairy of beauty and happiness, E Bukura e Dheut, was his lover. Her sister was Bukura e Detit, which means beauty of the sea. Others in the mythology were Perendi, the thunder god; Perendi's wife Prende, a goddess of beauty who in the Middle Ages was believed to be a saint; the deaf god of hail, Shurdi; and Djall, the devil or god of evil and death.

Business & Economy

■ The monetary unit is the lek.

■ Albania is the poorest country in Europe, with a per capita income of $4,900.

■ The country is primarily agricultural.

■ In 1997, Albania experienced a run of pyramid schemes that ultimately collapsed. Albanians blamed the government. The country fell into anarchy until elections replaced the president.

■ In 1999, Albania took in 440,000 ethnic Albanians when war was waging in Serbia.

Famous People

■ Albania's national hero is Gjerg Kastrioti-Skenderbeg, later called Iskender Bey or Lord Alexander. He fought against the domination of the Turks in the fifteenth century.

■ Ali Pasha ruled Albania in the early nineteenth century.

■ Naim and Sami Frasheri were brothers who furthered the literature of Albania in the nineteenth century.

■ Ismail Kadare is the nation's most famous contemporary novelist and poet.

■ Mother Teresa was an ethnic Albanian born Gonxhe Bojaxhiu in 1910 in Macedonia. She founded the Missionaries of Charity and is on the path to official sainthood. Her beatification was the fastest that has ever occurred under the current procedures of the Roman Catholic Church.

Algeria

Geography

■ Algeria is about 3.5 times as large as Texas, and 85 percent of its land area consists of the Sahara desert. It is the second largest African country, after Sudan, and it is the eleventh largest in the world. The Mediterranean makes its northern border.

■ The coastal north also has mountains, valleys, and plateaus; the heartland is called the Tell. Southern Algeria is desert. The country has no navigable rivers. Daily temperatures vary widely, but there is little change in seasons.

■ Virtually all cultivation is along the Mediterranean coast. Only about three percent of the land is not arable; about 2,200 square miles are irrigated.

■ The *sirocco* begins as a dry wind that blows across the Sahara, often at gale force, and affects Algeria's agriculture.

■ Less than two percent of its land is forest. Soil erosion is a major problem.

■ The capital city of Algiers numbers nearly 4 million people, while the Sahara region of Algeria is virtually uninhabited.

History & People

■ Ancient names for the region of North Africa that includes Algeria were Numidia and Mauretania. It is also called the Maghrib. The area was settled by Phoenician traders, with ports on the trading route between their home cities in what is now modern Lebanon to Spain. It became a Roman colony in 145 BC, after the Punic Wars.

■ The Berbers are the indigenous Caucasian people of North Africa. They still live widely scattered throughout Algeria, Egypt, Libya, Morocco, and Tunisia. Egyptian tombs provide proof of the Berber culture that dates to at least 2400 BC. The word *berber* comes from the Roman *barbarian*, and is the source of *Barbary Coast*.

■ The Vandals conquered Algeria in the fifth century AD, and the region didn't return to Arab rule until two centuries later.

■ Algeria was part of the Ottoman Empire from the sixteenth to the nineteenth centuries.

■ The Barbary pirates were Muslims whose home ports were on the North African coast, and especially in Algiers and Tunis, from the 1500s into the 1800s.

■ In 1830, France occupied Algeria in part to control the pirates. The nation was under French colonial rule for 130 years.

■ During its rule of Algeria, France modernized agriculture and industry, but society remained divided between Europeans and Arabs. A nationalist movement grew in until uprisings in 1954 and 1955 led to open war with France. Algeria gained independence in 1962.

■ Fundamentalist Muslims sparked civil war in Algeria in the 1990s, with about 100,000 killed by terrorists. The nation today may be described as a socialist government based on French and Islamic law, and

269

also a military dictatorship, still subject to militant violence and to protests by ethnic minorities.

Culture & Daily Life

◾ Arabic became the official language in 1990, though it did not replace French as the instructional language in the schools until 2000.

◾ Half of the Algerian population is under 19.

◾ Algeria is 99 percent Sunni Muslim. Four-fifths of the population is Arabic and one-fifth is *Amazigh*, made up of various ancient tribes mainly related to the Berbers.

◾ The literacy rate is 70 percent.

◾ Unemployment is about 25 percent.

◾ The infant mortality rate is 3.1 percent.

◾ Women in Algeria remain subject to restrictive family and fundamentalist Islamic codes.

◾ Algerian food is a combination of Arabic, Turkish, and French influences. Among its now well-known staples is couscous. Other traditional dishes include a meat pastry called *brik*, sausage called *merguez*, and lamb or chicken stew called *tajine*. Figs, dates, almonds, honey, mint, coffee, cumin, cinnamon, coriander, paprika, and fennel are common in the Algerian diet.

Arts

◾ The Algerian city of Oran is home to a music form called *raï* (pronounced *rye*). The word means *viewpoint, advice,* or *plan*. The music developed in the 1930s, paralleling an urban migration, though its roots are older. It might be described as danceable instrumental poetry. A related style is called *wahrani.*

◾ Among contemporary writers is Assia Djebar, who called Algeria "a dream of sand." Others are Jean Amrouche and Mouloud Feraoun.

◾ Conflict between traditionalist Muslims and the modern artistic community in Algeria has been extreme, to the point of assassinations. In the 1990s, novelist Tahar Djaout, musician Lounès Matoub, and the director of the National Museum were murdered. Many in the cultural community emigrate, often to France.

◾ The movie industry in Algeria is strong. Among the films of the last decade was *Living in Paradise,* about Algerians in France.

Science & Nature

▦ More than 2,000 people were killed in an earthquake near Algiers in May 2003.

▦ Because of the dry, hot climate, plants that survive in Algeria are drought-resistant, even those nearer the temperate Mediterranean.

▦ Animals native to Algeria include boar, mouflons, Barbary deer, Barbary macaques, gazelles, fennecs, hyenas, jackals, gerbils, desert hare, scorpions, storks, and flamingos.

Business & Economy

▦ The *dinar* is Algeria's monetary unit. The word comes from the Latin *denarius*, which was a small silver coin worth 10 bronze coins. The first dinars were gold, struck in the late seventh century.

▦ Vineyards and a wine industry were once mainstays of the Algerian economy, but political unrest and Islamic fundamentalism have dramatically reduced their part in the economy.

▦ Since the 1960s and independence, manufacturing has shifted toward heavy industry such as steel, zinc, and petroleum production. Most industries were state-run until the 1980s, when private businesses began to be allowed partnerships with the government.

▦ European and South Korean car companies have opened factories in Algeria since the 1990s.

▦ The Algerian National Navigation Company runs one of the world's largest merchant fleets.

Famous People

▦ One of the greatest thinkers of Western culture, and one of the Doctors of the Church, Saint Augustine was born in what is modern-day Algeria in 354. His important writings included *City of God* and his autobiography, *Confessions*.

▦ Albert Camus, the existentialist writer from the mid-twentieth century, was born in Oran when Algeria was under French rule.

▦ Although born in Martinique, Frantz Fanon left for France to fight with the underground during World War II, and later lived in Algeria. There he practiced psychiatry, but became known internationally for his anti-colonialism and revolutionary writings, including *The Wretched of the Earth*.

▓ Hassiba Boulmerka was the first Algerian to win an Olympic medal, in 1992, in the women's 1,500-meter race. Noureddine Morceli won the men's 1,500-meter race in the 1996 Olympics.

Angola

Geography

▓ Angola is a republic located in southwestern Africa. It borders the Democratic Republic of the Congo, Namibia, and Zambia, and has a coastline on the South Atlantic.

▓ With 481,351 square miles, Angola is slightly less than twice the size of Texas and more than three times the size of California.

▓ The highest point in the country is Morro de Moco. Its lowest point is sea level at the Atlantic Ocean. The terrain ranges from a semidesert coastal area to an interior rainforest, highlands, and river valleys.

▓ The capital, primary business center, and port city is Luanda.

History & People

▓ Angola has been inhabited since prehistoric times. Some argue that the earliest language was Khoisan, but the dominant native language is Bantu. Portuguese has been spoken since explorers arrived and founded the Colony of Angola in 1575, and it remains the official language.

▓ Angola's first Portuguese church was the Church of Our Lady of Cabo, built in 1575.

▓ Administered from the Portuguese colony of Brazil, Luanda was central to the slave trade. The growth of the slave trade changed the history of the native governance, including the Lunda empire, the Loango Kingdom, the Ndongo Kingdom, and the Kasanje Kingdom.

▓ Portugal remained in control of Angola until well into the twentieth century. Not until a coup in the European nation did Angola obtain independence, in 1975. Later that year fighting between the Popular Movement for the Liberation of Angola (MPLA) and the National Union for Total Independence of Angola (UNITA) led to a civil war that lasted until 2002, when rebel leader Jonas Savimbi was assassinated. Four weeks later, rebels signed a cease-fire with the government.

▓ September 2008 marked Angola's first national elections in 16 years. The MPLA won approximately 82 percent of the vote.

Culture & Daily Life

■ Angola has a population of over 12 million. The life expectancy is 38.

■ Angola has a literacy rate of just over 66 percent.

■ The three major ethnic groups are the Ovimbundu, the Kimbundu, and the Bakongo.

■ Forty-seven percent of the Angolan people have indigenous religious beliefs; 38 percent are Roman Catholic; and 15 percent are Protestant.

■ Much of modern Angolan cuisine reveals the Portuguese influence, featuring spices and techniques used to marinate and roast. Other influences in cuisine come from India and Malaysia. Local dishes are usually based on fish and have a generous amount of spices. Traditional dishes include palm oil beans and meat *calalu*, which consists of layers of meat, fish, and vegetables.

■ Angolan tradition dictates that men and elderly family members receive the largest portions of meat at a dinner.

■ Angolan men make their own beer from honey and grains such as maize and millet. Wine is also made from the sap of certain palm trees. Traditionally, Angolan women prepare all the food and the men are in charge of providing the beverages.

■ In 2008, the UN World Food Program stopped aid to Angola citing the good economy from oil revenue. With a high level of corruption remaining in Angola after the years of war, the majority of its people still struggle to survive without that aid.

Arts

■ Wooden masks and sculptures play an important role in Angola's cultural and religious ceremonies and rituals. Artisans also work in bronze, ivory, malachite, and ceramic mediums to create masks representing life and death, the journey into adulthood, and celebrations such as harvest and hunting season.

■ Angola's music has roots in Portugal, as well as in other African countries, Cuba, and Brazil. Luanda is home to many different musical styles, among them Angolan merengue, kilapanda, semba, and rebita.

■ Although the country's music has seen little international success, one of the groups known outside the region is Orquestra os Jovens do

Prenda. The band featured a big band style with trumpets, saxophone, and guitars.

▨ Cokwe Thinker, an ivory statue, is one of the most famous pieces of Angolan art. It is named for an ethnic group that may have been its source, and probably was tied to a coming-of-age ritual.

Science & Nature

▨ Natural resources are abundant in Angola. They include oil, diamonds, iron ore, copper, gold, and agriculture and fishing resources.

▨ The fauna include lion, impala, hyena, hippopotamus, rhinoceros, and elephant.

▨ Angola's wet regions in Cabinda and Uíge are filled with thick forests. About 18 percent of the country is classified as forest and woodland.

▨ Food scarcity has led to the extermination of many animal species. In 2002, the Angolan government imported elephants and other wild animals to aid its ecological system.

Business & Economy

▨ Angola's monetary unit was the Angloan escudo (AE) until 1977, when the kwanza (Kw) replaced it.

▨ Oil production and its supporting activites contribute about half of the gross domestic product, and 90 percent of exports.

▨ Angola is America's third largest trading partner in sub-Saharan Africa. The U.S. is also Angola's top investor.

▨ Angola's main agricultural exports include coffee, sisal, and cotton. Agriculture was the mainstay of the economy, but the years of war took a toll on the country and its conditions.

▨ Angola is the world's fourth largest diamond producer.

▨ Extensive unemployment affects more than half of the population.

Famous People

▨ António Agostinho Neto (1922-1979), a poet and physician, served as president of the MPLA and president of Angola from 1975 to 1979.

▨ Jonas Malheiro Savimbi founded and led the anti-Communist rebel group UNITA in 1966. UNITA fought the MPLA in the Angolan civil war that resulted in the assassination of Savimbi in 2002.

▓ Famous Angolan singers include Mario Rui Silva, Angelo Boss, Eduardo Paim, and Elias Dya Kimeuzu.

▓ Antonio Ole is one of Angola's most famous artists. A painter, photographer, and filmmaker, his work is known well beyond the borders of Angola.

Argentina

Geography

▓ Argentina is the second largest country in South America, smaller only than Brazil, and the eighth largest in the world.

▓ The country is largely plains, though it also has forests and mountains, the Andes.

▓ The Pampas of Argentina are rich grasslands, home to farming and livestock that support much of a country that is 90 percent urban. The region of dry lowlands near the Andes is called the Chaco.

▓ Patagonia, the southernmost region, is a 260,000-square mile plateau of desert and steppes.

▓ Aconcagua, in the Andes, is the highest mountain in the world outside of Asia.

▓ Tierra del Fuego, which belongs partly to Argentina and partly to Chile, is the southernmost point of South America.

▓ The largest cities are Buenos Aires, with more than 13 million people, and Cordoba and Rosario, each with well over a million.

▓ Argentina runs north-south from the subtropics 2,360 miles to the subantarctic. The climate, however, is almost exclusively temperate.

▓ Iguaçu Falls is a horseshoe of about 275 waterfalls. They are wider than either Niagara Falls or Victoria Falls.

▓ Lago Nahuel Huapi is a glacial lake of about 62 miles with Isla Victoria at its center. The island is home to rare species of trees and animals.

History & People

▓ *Argentina* means *land of silver.*

▓ The Diaguita and the Guarani were the two primary indigenous peoples in Argentina before the Europeans arrived. They successfully resisted Incan incursions.

▓ The population is 97 percent Caucasian, primarily Spanish and

Italian; and only 3 percent Native peoples and other. In 1810, about 30 percent of the population was Indian. In the mid 1800s, European immigration exploded the population of Argentina.

▓ Legend is that Magellan named the region Patagonia because the Native peoples he encountered, the Tehuelche Indians, reminded him of a monster named Patagon from a Spanish or Portuguese chivalric romance, *Amadis of Gaul*.

▓ Argentina was part of Spain's Viceroyalty of Peru until 1776, when it became part of the Viceroyalty of the Río de la Plata, with Buenos Aires as the capital.

▓ A movement for independence began in 1806 and continued over decades, with military leaders often in control in various provinces, and proponents and opponents of federalism at odds.

▓ Jose de San Martin was among those who, with Simon Bolivar, furthered separation from Spain in the early nineteenth century.

▓ In 1824 a national government was formed, but it later foundered. In 1829, federalist Juan Manuel de Rosas became governor and had wide support. In and out of office, he dominated the political scene for years. Between 1852 and 1880 was a period of national consolidation.

▓ In 1833, a British warship took the Falkland Islands, located off the coast of Argentina.

▓ A farming colony was founded in 1856 at Esperanza by about 200 families from Switzerland, Germany, France, Italy, Belgium, and Luxembourg.

▓ The constitution, established in 1853, was based on the U.S. Constitution. Though it was updated in 1994 to allow for presidents to serve consecutive terms, Argentina's constitution remains essentially the same.

▓ In 1881, Chile and Argentina agreed on the Andes as a boundary.

▓ Hipólito Irigoyen was the first president elected by popular vote, rather than named by the previous president.

▓ Juan Perón rose to power in the 1940s. He led a secret military lodge that was behind a 1943 coup. At that point he took a labor department position, working with unions and establishing many social services. He lost his position and clout, but later regained public approval, ultimately becoming president in 1946. Perón and his wife Eva (Evita) were popular with the *descamisados*—shirtless ones, or lower class workers. Perón was overthrown in 1955, and he went into exile.

Perónism continued to weave in and out of Argentinian politics through the 1960s, and Perón was re-elected in 1973. He died in 1974 and his second wife, Isabel, then became president—the first woman president anywhere in the world. She was deposed in 1976.

■ After the coup that removed Isabel Perón the *Guerra Sucia,* or Dirty War, began. It is estimated that as many as 15,000 were killed, and even more imprisoned and tortured. Argentina called it a civil war, but the rest of the world pointed to horrific violations of civil rights, especially as the Mothers of the Plaza de Mayo attracted international attention. They were the mothers of the *desaparecidos*, those who had disappeared.

■ The Falklands War took place in 1981 when Argentine troups landed on one of the islands and subdued the British marines. The British navy was sent and took back the Falklands.

■ Democracy returned in 1983, though tentatively. The economy continued to deteriorate. The economy has been on an upswing since 2001.

■ Néstor Kirchner, a Peronist, was president of Argentina from 2003 to 2007. The current president is Cristina Fernández, Kirchner's wife and the first female president of the country since Isabel Perón.

Culture & Daily Life

■ Italian culture has had a strong influence on Argentina because of the large number of Italian immigrants in the nineteenth and twentieth centuries.

■ *Lunfardo* is a slang that developed in Buenos Aires in the late nineteenth century. It borrows from Italian, Portuguese, Spanish, French, German, African dialects, and others. Tango music often has lyrics in lunfardo.

■ Buenos Aires has often been called South America's Paris because of its sophistication and cultural amenities.

■ On the other end of the spectrum, housing has become a problem in Argentina. Shantytowns called *villas miserias* have arisen in its cities.

■ The National University of Córdoba was established in 1613, and the University of Buenos Aires in 1821.

■ Despite the highly urban profile of Argentina, the gaucho—the cowboy of the Pampas—remains a strong symbol of the nation's identity.

Polo is one of the most popular sports in Argentina, in part because of its gaucho tradition and its history of horse-raising. Another game played on horseback is *pato*, or *duck*, originally played with a duck in a basket instead of a leather ball.

Among the working classes, soccer is the most popular sport.

Among popular foods are breakfast sweet rolls called *medialunas* and grilled beef called *parrilla*. Argentinians eat twice as much beef as Americans, and are second in the world only to Uruguayans.

The literacy rate is 97 percent.

Argentina won soccer's World Cup in 1978 and 1986.

Arts

The tango began in the dockside district of Buenos Aires in the late 1900s, but eventually became a romanticized ballroom dance that still represents the national identity.

Among Argentina's most accomplished writers is the world-renowned author of prose and poetry, Jorge Luis Borges, who helped found the avant garde Ultraist movement. Other important modern Argentine writers include Julio Cortázar and Ernesto Sábato, who is also a physicist.

The movie industry is currently experiencing a renaissance in Argentina.

The National Library was founded in 1810; Jorge Luis Borges was for a time the National Librarian.

The opera house in Buenos Aires is the Teatro Colón.

Science & Nature

Lamoids—guanaco, llama, alpaca, and vicuña—are native to northwestern Argentina. They are part of the camel family. Bands of female guanaco and vicuña are led by a male.

Animals of the Chaco region include capybaras, the largest rodent in the world, typically weighing more than 100 pounds, as well as tapirs, jaguars, pumas, and ocelots.

Rheas are flightless cousins of the ostrich and emu; they herd in groups with guanacos and deer. Several females lay up to 50 eggs each in a single nest dug in the ground by a male. A male then incubates the eggs and herds the chicks.

■ The native Indians of the Pampas developed the bola to hunt the fleet-footed animals. The bola consists of two balls joined on a short rope. It is spun and thrown to catch the quarry's legs.

■ The pudu, the smallest deer in the world, is found in Patagonia.

■ Patagonia, the southernmost part of Argentina, is rich in fossils. The region was inspirational to Charles Darwin in his studies.

■ Magellanic penguins, also known as jackass penguins, breed at Punta Tombo from April to September.

■ The national park at Los Alerces has almost 50 major glaciers.

■ A citizen of Argentina although born in Hungary, László Bíró, invented the ballpoint pen, called the biro in many parts of the world.

Business & Economy

■ Argentina is the largest grain producer of South America. Cattle and tourism are second largest in the continent. Major exports are wheat, soybeans, meat, and hides.

■ Argentina was one of the wealthiest nations in the world in the 1920s. By 1980, it had become part of the economic third world. It is in a very weak economic state in the twenty-first century.

■ Oil and natural gas reserves are large in Argentina. Hydroelectric power is abundant, and the country has several nuclear power plants.

Famous People

■ Ernesto Guevara de la Serna—Che Guevara—was born in Argentina in 1928. The revolutionary was trained as a physician.

■ Bernardo Alberto Houssay won the Nobel Prize for Medicine in 1947 for his study of pituitary hormones. Other Argentine Nobel Laureates include Luis Federico Leloir (1970, for chemistry, in the study of carbohydrates) and César Milstein (1984, for the study of antibodies).

■ Adolfo Pérez Esquivel received the Nobel Peace Prize in 1980 for speaking up against the Dirty War and the government. At that point the war was winding down.

■ Diego Maradona was a great soccer player of the 1970s and 1980s.

■ Tennis star Gabriela Sabatini was born in Buenos Aires in 1970. Tennis star Guillermo Coria was born in Rufino, Argentina, in 1982.

■ Composer and conductor Daniel Barenboim was born in Buenos Aires in 1942.

■ *Gilmore Girls*'s Alexis Bledel claims Argentinian ancestry through her father.

Armenia

Geography

■ Armenia is the smallest of the nations that formerly belonged to the Soviet Union. It is about 11,000 square miles in area.

■ Yerevan is the capital and largest city, with about 1.5 million people in the metropolitan area. The next largest city, Vanadzor, has about 150,000 people.

■ Armenia is a landlocked Asian republic dominated by the Caucasus moutains. Its neighbors are Azerbaijan, Georgia, Iran, and Turkey.

■ Mount Ararat was in ancient Armenia, though the biblical mountain is now part of Turkish territory.

■ The country's geography is extremely varied, with semi-desert, steppe, forest, alpine meadow, and high-altitude tundra.

History & People

■ In the seventh century BC, the Greeks called an invading people the Araratians or Urartians, because they drove others east of Mount Ararat. The Armenians call themselves the *Hayk*.

■ Armenia was the center of a great Asian empire in the first century under King Tigranes the Great.

■ The Romans eventually gained control of Tigranes's empire; many Roman battles with the Parthians, Persia's rulers, took place in Armenia. The region came under Parthian control after Persia signed a treaty with Rome.

■ Armenia was divided between Persia and the Byzantine empire for centuries, but came under Arab control in 653 AD.

■ In 885, under Ashot I, Armenia became an independent kingdom. The Byzantine emperor again gained control, in 976. The Turks took over in 1071.

■ The Mongols invaded in the thirteenth century and ruled until the fifteenth.

■ Russia came to rule parts of Armenia and neighboring territories in the early nineteenth century. The Ottomans ruled the rest of what had been ancient Armenia. Armenian nationalism grew in the late nineteenth century.

▓ The Armenian genocide, and mass deportations that involved forced marches, took place at the hands of the Ottomans during World War I and after. Ninety percent of Armenians living in Anatolia were killed or deported when the Ottoman government claimed they were pro-Russian. The modern Turkish government disputes the genocide.

▓ Under the Treaty of Sèvres after World War I, the Ottoman government recognized Armenian independence. The Turks, led by Mustafa Kemal Atatürk, rejected the treaty, however, and invaded Armenia, but invading Bolsheviks limited Turkish control.

▓ Armenian nationalists and the Bolsheviks formed a coalition government, and Armenia became a Soviet republic in 1922.

▓ In 1992, Armenia declared itself independent of the U.S.S.R.

Culture & Daily Life

▓ About 65 percent of Armenians live in cities or towns.

▓ No other surviving languages are related to Armenian, though it has many dialects.

▓ Food and music are strongly Middle Eastern.

▓ The largest religious group, with 93 percent of the population, belongs to the Armenian Apostolic Church.

▓ The Armenian alphabet can be traced to the fifth century and has 38 letters.

▓ The literacy rate is nearly 100 percent.

▓ Health care is free in Armenia, provided by taxes.

▓ *Harissa* is a traditional stew of chicken and wheat. It is usually eaten on Easter.

▓ *Khash* is eaten in the winter—traditionally by men, during months that contain the letter *r*—made from cow's feet, garlic, and lemon juice or vinegar. The Armenian bread called *lavash* is often crumbled into it and the whole is served with hot peppers, pickles, radishes, cheese, herbs, and vodka.

▓ Two Armenians recently held boxing titles: Avetik Abrahamyan, or Arthur Abraham, is the middleweight champion of the International Boxing Federation, and Vic Darchinyan is the flyweight champion.

▓ Armenia has produced many chess grandmasters, including Levon Aronian, Vladimir Akopian, Gabriel Sargissian and Tatev Abrahamyan. Gary Kasparov's mother was born in Armenia.

Arts

▓ Rugs and metalwork remain important folk crafts.

▓ Stone carving is an ancient art of Armenia. In prehistory, menhirs were carved with various religious symbols. Among them was the fish, which may have been related to a water goddess. In the Middle Ages, *khatchkars* were stones highly decorated with crosses; they are still created today.

▓ Armenian literature dates to the fifth century, with the *History of Armenia* and *Refutation of the Sects.*

▓ The first great poet was Grigor Narekatsi, a mystic and bishop of the tenth century.

▓ In the sixteenth century, troubadors wrote lyric poems called *ashugh*, and many remain popular love songs.

▓ Under the pseudnym Raffi, Hakob Melik-Hakobian wrote novels in the nineteenth century.

▓ The renowned classical composer Aram Khachaturian was Armenian. Native folktales influenced some of his work.

Science & Nature

▓ Armenia has more than 3,000 species of plants, more than the vastly larger Russian Plain.

▓ The forests include beech, oak, hackberry, pistachio, honeysuckle, and dogwood trees.

▓ Among Armenia's native creatures are the Syrian bear, wildcat, lynx, bezoar goat, mouflon, mountain turkey, horned lark, and bearded vulture.

▓ Sergey Mergelyan is an Armenian mathematician who developed theories involving functions of complex variables, approximation, and potential and harmonic functions. He is known for Mergelyan's theorem.

▓ An ethnic Armenian, Boris Artashesovich Babaian pioneered supercomputers in the U.S.S.R.

Business & Economy

■ The country moved away from agriculture and was highly industrialized under the Soviet Union.

■ Armenia struggled economically with the breakup of the Soviet Union, which followed hard on a 1988 earthquake that destroyed a third of its industry. Today, the economy has begun to turn around.

■ Fruits and vegetables are high-quality exports, though little was exported during the 1990s because of blockades by Turkey and Azerbaijan and civil unrest in Armenia's northern neighbor, Georgia.

■ Armenia continued to use the Soviet ruble after the dissolution of the U.S.S.R., and didn't issue its own currency, the *dram*, until 1993.

Famous People

■ Andre Agassi, the tennis player who was ranked number one in the world in 1995, is of Armenian descent.

■ Actor and author Eric Bogosian has an Armenian background. Among his movies is *Ararat*, a movie about the Armenian Genocide.

■ Cherylin Sarkissian—Cher—is of Armenian descent. She went to Armenia to help after the 1988 earthquake.

■ Classical composer Alan Hovhaness is an American of Armenian and Scottish ancestry. He explored Armenian culture in his music.

■ Children's performer Raffi Cavoukian was named for a famous Armenian poet. He was born in Egypt to Armenian parents.

■ American playwright William Saroyan was the son of immigrant Armenians.

Australia

Geography

■ The smallest continent but one of the largest countries in the world, Australia (including Tasmania) is about equal in size to the continental U.S.

■ The Great Barrier Reef to the northeast of Australia is about 1,250 miles long, at a distance ranging from 10 to 100 miles from the coast.

■ The waters around the island of Australia are the Timor Sea, the Arafura Sea, the Torres Strait, the Coral Sea, the Tasman Sea, the Bass Strait, and the Indian Ocean.

▓ Western Australia is mostly desert.

▓ Australia is one of the flattest places in the world, consisting mostly of plains and an average elevation of only about 1,000 feet. Mount Kosciusko is the highest point in Australia, at 7,308 feet. It is located in the mountains along the east coast.

▓ Australia was originally part of the supercontinent of Pangaea, and then part of the southern portion that broke away, Gondwanaland, which also contained South America, Africa, India, and Antarctica. The continent divided completely when Tasmania separated from Antarctica about 35 million years ago, relatively recent in geological terms. Australia is now drifting back toward Southeast Asia and will eventually join that continent.

▓ Australia has the oldest known geologic material on Earth— possibly more than 4 billion years old.

▓ The topography ranges from deserts to tropical rainforests, from desert plains and red rocks (such as Ulura, also called Ayres Rock), to fertile plains with sheep and sugar plantations.

History & People

▓ The first aboriginal peoples arrived in Australia from Asia, 50,000 to 60,000 years ago. By 20,000 years ago, they had spread throughout the mainland and Tasmania.

▓ Australia was the last continent to be explored by Europeans. In 1616, the Dutch named it New Holland. The British arrived in 1688, and Captain James Cook claimed it in 1770. The first permanent British settlement, in 1788, was a penal colony at Port Jackson, which was to become Sydney, in New South Wales.

▓ From 1788 to 1839, Britain transported some 161,000 convicts to Australia.

▓ The Aborigines, the indigenous Australian people, were nomadic hunter-gatherers. At the beginning of the nineteenth century, the population spoke about 250 languages, in hundreds of aboriginal groups. Many people were multilingual.

▓ Diseases brought from Europe contributed to a rapid decrease in the aboriginal population.

▓ Only 200 years ago, the vast majority of Australia was still in a primal state, its land untouched by human modifications.

▓ Tasmania was originally called Van Diemen's Land. It was one of Australia's six colonies, which joined together in 1901 in a confederation of states under a constitution. Australia remains part of the British Commonwealth of Nations. It is a federal parliamentary democracy that recognizes the British monarch, represented by a governor-general, as the head of state. The Australian prime minister, however, is the head of government.

▓ About 300,000 Australians fought in World War I, most famously in the Battle of Gallipoli during the Dardanelles Campaign. Under Prime Minister William Morris Hughes, Australia strongly supported the war, in large measure because of growing concerns about an attack by Japan. Hughes was a controversial figure in a turbulent time.

▓ Because of the remoteness of some of the population, the Flying Doctor Service began in 1928, to provide health care services to people in the outback and other remote regions. It consists of air ambulances and medical bases where trained staff can communicate with those in need of medical health.

▓ The Great Depression in the 1930s was particularly bad in Australia because much industry had been subsidized. A quarter of all workers lost jobs. During the worst years, emigration from Australia was greater than immigration.

▓ In 1931, Britain's Statute of Westminster declared Australia, and the other members of the Commonwealth, "autonomous communities within the British Empire, equal in status, in no way subordinate one to another in any aspect of their domestic or external affairs, though united by a common allegiance to the Crown, and freely associated as members of the British Commonwealth of Nations." Australia did not ratify the statute until 1942.

▓ Australia generally supported the policy of appeasement in the years before World War II, but then contributed strongly to Britain's defense during the war, especially in North Africa.

▓ During the war, the United States became Australia's primary ally, and the continent-nation moved somewhat away from ties with Britain.

▓ The first Olympics ever held in the Southern Hemisphere took place in Melbourne in the summer of 1956.

▓ A political movement involving land and other rights for the Aborigine was marked by a national referendum in 1967. Until the 1960s, most lived rural lives, often in the outback. Today, more than 70 percent of Aborigines and Torres Strait Islanders live in towns and cities. The national census did not include aboriginal peoples until 1971.

■ Discriminatory policies of all kinds against non-Europeans dating from the nineteenth century were officially ended in 1973. After that point, immigration from Asia increased markedly.

■ A court decision in the Mabo case in 1992 led to the Native Title Act. The court and the legislation recognized that land had been taken from the indigenous peoples when Australia was settled. They directed that aboriginal title to pastoral land could co-exist with ownership of the property by others.

Culture & Daily Life

■ Australia is the least densely populated continent, at seven people per square mile. About 92 percent of the 20,265,000 Australians live in cities.

■ Ninety percent of Australians have European ancestry, especially British and Irish. The culture has therefore been largely Anglo-Celtic.

■ Twenty percent of the population was not born in Australia. Immigration is increasing, especially from China, Vietnam, Hong Kong, the Philippines, New Zealand, and South Africa. The aboriginal population is more than 400,000 and growing.

■ With a modern history that began as a British creation of a penal colony, Australians have developed an egalitarian, pragmatic, humorous, friendly persona. They are generally proud to have made something of themselves out of a population of convicts, immigrants, and laborers.

■ Music, food, and style tend to be similar to those of Europe and North America, with an Australian twist.

■ Traditional aboriginal food included kangaroo, wombat, turtle, eel, emu, snake, and witchetty grubs.

■ Holidays include Australia Day, on January 26, for the day in 1788 when the British landed in Port Jackson (Sydney); and ANZAC Day, on April 25, commemorating the 1915 Battle of Gallipoli, fought by Australia and New Zealand against Turkish forces allied with Germany in World War I. ANZAC stands for Australian and New Zealand Army Corps.

■ Because Australia's shores are heavy with sharks, beaches have bells, sirens, or lookout towers for warnings to swimmers. Nets are also strung along the coast to catch sharks nearing the shore.

In the 1970s, Miriam Dixson and Germaine Greer were at the center of a strong Australian feminist movement. In the years that followed, the number of women in government, medicine, law, and literature increased considerably.

The most popular summer sport is cricket, which British sailors brought to Australia in 1803.

Australian football is something like Gaelic football, but began in Melbourne in 1858. Rugby is also a popular sport.

Arts

Australia provides many subsidies for the arts, most obviously reflected in the building of museums and theaters such as the Sydney Opera House.

The National Library of Australia was founded in 1960.

Australian festivals include the music, theater, and fireworks of the Sydney Festival in January and others in Adelaide and Melbourne. Festivals dedicated to the aboriginal arts are the Barunga and Cultural Sports Festival and, in Broome, the Stompin Ground.

Music and story are core to Aborigine culture, and are strongly spiritual. They are often based on the belief that the past exists in an eternal present, that what is simply is. The person and place are part of and affected by *Alcheringa*, the Dreaming. Songs and stories of the Dreaming come from spirits of the past, and tell of ancestors, the land, journeys, and the past, but they are also seen as being in the present. These are often sung, and danced, during gatherings called *corroborees* where the *didjeridu*, a wind instrument, is played.

The first Australian novel was *Quintus Servinton,* written by Henry Savery in 1831. In 1874, Marcus Clarke wrote a powerful depiction of Australian convict life in *His Natural Life*. In the nineteenth century, journals of exploration by writers such as Charles Sturt and Edward John Eyre were popular.

Winner of the Nobel Prize for literature in 1973, Patrick White is often considered the greatest Australian novelist and playwright. His works include *Voss, Riders in the Chariot, The Solid Mandala,* and *The Twyborn Affair.*

■ Banjo Paterson was a poet and journalist whose works included *The Man from Snowy River and Other Verses* (1895), and most famously, "Waltzing Matilda."

■ D. H. Lawrence visited Australia in 1922 and from that came the novel *Kangaroo*, in part dealing with fascism.

■ Two opposing literary movements developed in Australia in the 1930s: the extremely nationalistic Australia First, and the Catholic Social Movement, consisting of young Roman Catholic intellectuals who supported social justice issues and opposed communism.

■ Other important modern Australian writers include Arthur Boyd, Thea Astley, Peter Carey, Elizabeth Jolley, Thomas Keneally, David Malouf, Hal Porter, Janette Turner Hospital, and Tim Winton.

■ Australia has been widely known for its operatic voices in modern times, from Nellie Melba to Joan Sutherland. Classical composers and artists have included Percy Grainger, Arthur Benjamin, John Henry Antill, Peggy Glanville-Hicks, Richard Mills, and Peter Sculthorpe.

■ Evidence of ancient aboriginal art in the form of rock carving and painting, bark painting, wood sculptures, and sand sculptures continues to influence some artists today. Boomerangs were often decorated with paintings of stories from the Dreaming.

■ The Heidelberg School of painting in the mid-1800s was the first quintessentially Australian art movement, often focusing on landscapes. Into the mid-1900s, painter Sidney Nolan often depicted Australian life in the outback. Nolan was especially known for a series on Australian bushranger Ned Kelly (also the subject of biographies and novels such as Peter Carey's *True History of the Kelly Gang: A Novel).*

■ A 1906 film, *The Story of the Kelly Gang,* was Australia's first narrative feature film; other bushranger films followed. The movie industry didn't truly gain momentum and a personality of its own for decades. Australians have had a strong presence in modern film at home and abroad, however, since the 1970s. Director Peter Weir became known for *Picnic at Hanging Rock* (1975). Popularly, Crocodile Dundee became a phenomenon in the 1980s. Among other well-known films are *Mad Max* and *Mad Max 2: The Road Warrior; My Brilliant Career; Muriel's Wedding; Priscilla, Queen of the Desert; Shine;* and *Moulin Rouge.*

■ The famous Sydney Opera House was designed by Danish architect Jørn Utzon.

Science & Nature

▦ Australia made important contributions to the growth of anthropology.

▦ Australia is the driest of the continents, apart from Antarctica, with an annual average of 18 inches of rainfall. Only about six percent of the land is arable. The continent's aridity has made irrigation, dams, and other methods of conserving and providing water critical. One means has been to form artificial freshwater lakes, and another to draw on deep artesian supplies. Such means have been so successful, Australia is a world leader in agriculture.

▦ Most Australian lakes are salt water. Some southern lakes are the remnants of a large inland sea.

▦ Several gold rushes marked Australia's history. In 1904, four million ounces of gold were produced.

▦ Minerals include bauxite, coal, diamonds, gold, iron, nickel, and uranium. Australia is also rich in petroleum and natural gas.

▦ The Australian continent is known for many unique species of plant and animal. Among the plants are varieties of the eucalyptus, some varieties of pine, kangaroo paws, and blackboy. Among the animals are the kangaroo, platypus, koala, dingo, spiny anteater, wombat, bandicoot, Tasmanian devil, kookaburra, and emu.

▦ Mulga, a variety of acacia, covers about 20 percent of the land; in the dry climate the mulga extracts and uses water with great efficiency. The Aborigines long used its seeds as a major source of food and for medicine.

▦ The Queensland lungfish has remained essentially the same since the Paleozoic or Mesozoic eras.

▦ Over the centuries, the Aborigines did *firestick farming*, setting fires to clear land for new grazing grasses. The practice attracted kangaroos and other animals, but it has been argued that it also permanently destroyed much vegetation and animal life. Others argue that the fires kept an environmental balance.

▦ The Europeans brought many plants not indigenous to the continent, which have made incursions on native species. Among the most intrusive has been mimosa. As a result, the environment is a source of much debate today.

▦ Wild horses, originally brought from Europe, are called *brumbies*.

■ Seventy species of shark swim in the waters of Australia.

■ The Royal Botanic Gardens in Melbourne include a research center, the National Herbarium. The Herbarium has 1.4 million specimens, including some that date back to collections by naturalists on Cook's voyage in 1770. Other plants of historical interest were gathered by Matthew Flinders during a circumnavigation of Australia in 1801 to 1805.

■ The only father and son team to be awarded the Nobel Prize were Australian physicists William and Lawrence Bragg, for x-ray crystallography. Lawrence was 25 when the prize was awarded in 1915, and remains the youngest recipient.

■ Australian Dr. David Warren invented the flight data recorder.

Business & Economy

■ Australia has the world's largest wool industry, which has been an important part of the economy since colonial times. The number of sheep hit a high point in 1970 but today is a third of that number. Nonetheless, Australia produces a quarter of the world's wool.

■ An infestation of rabbits, which were introduced to the continent in 1788, negatively impacted grazing land for sheep and cattle. The difficulties really began in 1859 when Thomas Austin released two dozen wild rabbits on his land. It is estimated the population once reached 500 million rabbits. Today, attempts are made to control their numbers.

■ Despite poor land over much of the Australian continent, the nation is also one of the world's important producers of grain, sugar, fruit, meat, dairy products, and cotton.

■ In recent years, the government has estimated that one-fifth of Australia comprises native forests and that a third of that is privately owned. One-fifth of the total is used commercially. Environmental groups oppose rainforest harvesting for wood pulp.

■ Despite the extensive waters under Australia's jurisdiction, the marine industry is relatively small. It began growing, however, in the 1990s.

■ Mining is now a larger industry than agriculture. Australia has about one-fourth of the world's known uranium, but it is not extensively mined. It does produce large amounts of iron, tungsten, zinc, lead, and bauxite.

■ Foreign investment in Australian manufacturing and other

businesses began to increase in 1950 and has had a major impact on the economy. Among the largest businesses affected is the automobile industry, with strong influences from the U.S. and Japan.

▤ Australia's largest growth has been in communications, education, finance, health, government, insurance, real estate, and recreation and tourism.

▤ Australia has about 650 newspapers, among them 65 daily papers.

Famous People

▤ Famous Australians in the film industry have included Cate Blanchett, Jackie Chan (an Australian citizen born in Hong Kong who emigrated in 1960), Russell Crowe, Judy Davis, Errol Flynn, Mel Gibson, Barry Humphries (Dame Edna), Hugh Jackman, Nicole Kidman, Heath Ledger, Baz Luhrmann, Geoffrey Rush, Naomi Watts, and Peter Weir.

▤ Internationally known popular musicians have included Peter Allen, Natalie Imbruglia, Kylie Minogue, Olivia Newton-John, Keith Urban, and the bands AC/DC, INXS, and Midnight Oil.

▤ Tennis has seen many Australian champions, including Margaret Court, Evonne Goolagong, John Newcombe, Rod Laver, and Ken Rosewall.

▤ International-level golfers from Australia include Greg Norman and Jeff Ogilvy.

▤ Rupert Murdoch was born in Australia.

▤ The top grossing Australian entertainers have included the children's group the Wiggles, who feature a collection of CDs, DVDs, and other merchandise appealing to very young children.

Austria

Geography

▤ Austria is a landlocked country bordered by Germany, the Czech Republic, Slovakia, Slovenia, Italy, Switzerland, and Liechtenstein.

▤ The total area of Austria is 32,000 square miles, about twice the size of Switzerland and slightly smaller than the state of Maine.

▤ Austria consists of nine independent federal states: Burgenland, Carinthis, Lower Austria, Upper Austria, Salzburg, Styria, Vienna, Tyrol, and Vorarlberg.

▓ The western and southern parts of Austria are mostly mountains (Alps), while the eastern and nothern regions are mostly flat.

▓ The Austrian Alps make up 62 percent of the country in three major Alpine ranges: the Northern Alps, Central Alps, and Southern Alps.

▓ The Danube River is one of the most well-known features of the Austrian landscape. It flows from southwestern Germany through Austria, and empties into the Black Sea. It is the only major European river that flows eastward.

History & People

▓ In Roman times, the region that is now Austria saw the growth of important towns along the river Danube. They included Vindobona, or Vienna. The Danube served as a Roman defensive border with the Germanic tribes. By the fifth century, the Huns had overcome the defenses.

▓ The Magyars began to move into the region in the ninth century, with a battle against the Franks near Vienna in 881. In other areas, the Germanic and Slavic tribes dominated. The German Otto I, who would become Holy Roman emperor, won a victory against the Magyars around 960. Vienna became Austria's capital in the twelfth century.

▓ Among the dynastic families to battle over the region that today comprises Austria, Germany, and Hungary were the Babenbergs, the Welfs, and the Hohenstaufen. Frederick Barbarossa controlled some of their feuds, as Holy Roman emperor.

▓ The Austrian flag is one of the oldest in the world, dating back to 1191. It consists of three equal horizontal stripes of red, white, and red. According to legend, the flag's design was created by Duke Leopold V of Austria, when, after a battle, his white uniform was drenched in blood. When he removed his belt, that area of his clothing remained the stark white. The color combination then served as inspiration for the flag.

▓ In 1282, the Habsburgs came to rule. While their power diminished at times, they dominated the region for centuries. In the sixteenth century, the Habsburgs began in real earnestness a drive to unite Austria, Bohemia, and Hungary. The height of Habsburg rule was from the seventeenth century until the death of Charles VI, and the succession of his daughter Maria Theresa, who was left to fight off Prussia's claims to power in the War of the Austrian Succession, from 1740 to 1748.

Prussian Prime Minister Otto von Bismarck forced the Austrian Habsburgs to war again in the nineteenth century. After the Austro-Prussian War of 1866, the Habsburg monarchy reorganized, and it negotiated with Hungary. Eventually a Dual Monarchy—Austria and Hungary—was created.

In June of 1914, the Archduke Francis Ferdinand, heir to the Austro-Hungarian throne, and his wife were assassinated in Sarajevo, Bosnia by Gavrilo Princip, a Serbian nationalist. With German support, Austria-Hungary declared war on Serbia in July 1928. Following Germany's declaration of war on Russia and France in August, the conflict turned into World War I.

The Habsburg Empire ended when Austria was reduced to a small republic after its defeat in World War I. Germany declared Austria and itself a united "democratic republic."

In March 1938, Adolf Hitler pressured Austria into unification with Germany, called the Anschluss.

After World War II, Austria's status remained uncertain for over a decade until a state treaty was signed in 1955 recognizing Austria's independence. October 26 is considered National Day commemorating the passage of the law on permanent neutrality.

Culture & Daily Life

Ninety-eight percent of the people of Austria speak German.

Approximately 74 percent of Austrians are Roman Catholic.

The population of Austria is more than 8 million, with 1.6 million people living in the capital, Vienna.

The city of Vienna is known for its own unique cuisine, especially its pastries. Popular desserts include apfelstrudel, kaiserschmarren, and sachertorte. Typical Austrian main dishes include wiener schnitzel, schweinsbraten, knödel, and tafelspitz.

Austria is known for yodeling, or throat singing, which originated in the Alps. Yodeling was developed as a method of communication across the mountains.

With the Alps as a prime location, skiing is one of the most popular sports in Austria. Other common sports are soccer and ice hockey.

In June 2007, Austria's Parliament passed a law lowering the voting age to 16.

▓ According to legend, Austrian children are visited yearly by Saint Nicholas (Santaklausen) and the devil (Knect Reprecht) on December 4. Together, they ask each child if they have been good or bad. If the child confesses to bad behavior, legend says that the devil tries to strike them with a stick, but Saint Nicholas sends the child running. The pair returns on December 6, Saint Nicholas Day, to reward the good children with gifts and candy.

Arts

▓ The movie *The Sound of Music* was based on the true story of the Austrian von Trapp family and their escape from Nazi Austria to Switzerland. A setting for this popular film, Salzburg holds an annual, world-famous theater and music festival.

▓ The Vienna Boys' Choir is one of the most well-known boys' musical groups in the world. It was established in July 1498.

▓ The Vienna State Opera employs more than 1,000 people and has an annual operating budget of 100 million euros. The capital city is also home to one of the world's finest concert halls, the Musikverein.

▓ Folk music is very popular in Austria. Modern performers include Roland Neuwirth, Karl Hodina, and Edi Reiser.

▓ Austria is famous for its folk dances, which include the ländler, schuhplattler, polka, zwiefacher, and waltz.

▓ Although he was from Munich, composer Richard Strauss is linked to Vienna. Even more tied to the city were the Johann Strausses, father and son, who wrote operettas and waltzes.

▓ Austrian painter Gustav Klimt was part of the Art Nouveau movement, a Viennese school of art. Other Austrian painters of the past century are Egon Schiele and Oskar Kokoschka.

Science & Nature

▓ Tiergarten Schönbrunn is the oldest zoological garden in the world. It was founded in 1752 in Vienna.

▓ Grossglockner is Austria's highest mountain. It is 3,798 meters above sea level. The country's largest natural lake is Neusiedler Lake.

▓ Austria's greatest natural resource is water, which supplies two-thirds of its electrical energy through water power.

▓ Austria is one of Europe's most heavily wooded countries. The climate and topographic conditions account for the country's lush and rich flora, which includes edelweiss, gentian, alpine carnation, alpine rose, and heather. Nature parks amount to three percent of the country.

Business & Economy

- Austria is one of the 10 richest of the world's nations.
- With its prime location in Europe, Austria was a major player in the economic, military, and political arenas during the Austro-Hungarian Empire. This role diminished significantly after World War I, when a much smaller Austria began to take form.
- Germany has historically been Austria's main trading partner, but since becoming a member of the European Union (EU), Austria's exports and imports with other EU countries have grown to account for approximately 66 percent of its trade. Exports include machinery and equipment, vehicles, paper, metal, chemicals, iron, steel, textiles, and foods.
- Many Austrian companies hold a high position in the international market including Swarovski, Red Bull, Glock, and Doppelmayr.
- PEZ candy was invented in Austria.
- Austria produces both white and red wines, and has about 125,000 acres of vineyards.

Famous People

- The father of psychology, Sigmund Freud, was born in Moravia, which at the time was part of Austria, although it is now a part of the Czech Republic.
- Arnold Schwarzenegger, governor of California, actor in *Terminator* and *Kindergarten Cop,* and former Mr. Universe, was born in Graz, Austria.
- Austria was the birthplace of many famous composers, including Wolfgang Mozart, Joseph Haydn, Franz Schubert, Franze Liszt, and Wilhelm Bruckner.
- Austrian-born Ferdinand Porsche was the founder of German sports car company Porsche, and also designed the Volkswagen.
- Gregor Mendel, the monk and botanist who is considered by most to be the father of the study of genetics, was Austrian.
- Adolf Hitler was born in Braunau am Inn, Austria.

■ Actress Hedy Lamarr, famous for such movies as *Boom Town*, *Ziegfeld Girl*, and *Tortilla Flat*, was born in Austria.

■ Austria was also the birthplace of many famous athletes, including Hermann Maier, Thomas Muster, Eva Pawlik, and Michaela Dorfmeister.

Research

The Truth Is Out There

Random, Fun, Informative, Serious,
Crazy Websites to Add to Your Bookmarks

By Christina Hamlett

To a student's ears, there is probably no phrase more welcome than *open book test*. The catch, however, is that an open book can be next to useless if you don't know which chapter holds the answer or how to interpret and apply the information to a fresh problem. Adult writers aren't that far off from high school test takers.

For writers on a quest, technology has placed the biggest open book imaginable in our hands: the Internet. The plus side of this virtual repository of knowledge, news, entertainment, and opinions is that it's open 24/7 and can satisfy even the most persistent midnight musings—like the one that keeps you from sleeping until you've successfully tracked down the name of Joan of Arc's horse. The downside is that the parameters defined for a specific search can often create obstacles to discovering many scholarly, interactive, or offbeat websites we could never guess existed. Or a search turns up so many inaccurate or off-point sites we become frustrated.

Once you've bookmarked a few of our favorites from the list below, your research days will never be quite the same, nor will you lack for inspiration in finding ideas, topics, plots, characters, settings, and scintillating dialogue for your future projects.

Who Are You?

➢ *Anecdotage:* www.anecdotage.com

This site offers much fodder for biographies and profiles, with its funny and inspirational true stories about famous people. Or, if you're writing about fictional characters interacting with historical figures, you might orchestrate their encounters via a documented anecdote. Madame Curie, for instance, coveted her privacy and once pretended to be her own housekeeper in order to advise an aggressive American reporter to be more curious about ideas and less nosy about people. You'll also find a tale about Beethoven, who once threw an entire plate of roast beef at a waiter's head because it wasn't what he had ordered.

➢ *Behind the Name:* www.behindthename.com/random

If you're stuck on what to call your latest characters, this website allows you not only to generate first, middle, and last names but also specific nationalities and historic, literary, mythological, biblical, rapper, and fantasy monikers. *Examples:* Valeriya, Sveta, Riley Cassian Finch, Jamar Skye, and Bubblebroom Bristlecape.

➢ *Medieval and Ancient Names:* www.lowchensaustralia.com/names/medievalnames.htm

If your book's setting is eleventh-century Castile, it's not likely you'd find a Brad or a Hannah running around. You might know more than one Fagildo and Estefania, however. In addition to hundreds of medieval first and last names, you can also look up Arabic, Norse, Babylonian, Jewish, Chinese, Aztec, and Mongolian names (just to name a few).

➢ *Find a Grave:* www.findagrave.com

Did you know Mata Hari's body was donated to medical science after her death by firing squad? Or that Anton Chekhov and the founder of Bloomingdale's died in 1904, the year Salvador Dali was born? Find the final resting places of the famous, the infamous, and any workaday Joe.

Where Am I? What Time Is It?

➢ *ePodunk City Profiles:* www.epodunk.com

This site features comprehensive county and community profiles, maps, calendars, weather, history, demographics, and anything else you might want to know about places in the U.S. It is a resource for nonfiction topics—from history to science to family travel—and can help make your story settings accurate, interesting, and realistic. It can also help you locate places for further research. Categories include airports, cemeteries, colleges, libraries, museums, and newspapers.

➤ *World Time Server:* www.worldtimeserver.com

If your plucky girl detective in San Francisco makes a telephone call at noon to her favorite pen pal in Sri Lanka, what is the latter likely to be doing? Unless she's a party girl, she's probably asleep; in Sri Lanka, it's 12:30 AM the following day. This site not only calculates time zones anywhere in the world but also gives you news and weather.

The Past Is Present

➤ *Ellis Island Records:* www.ellisislandrecords.org

Genealogy tips, vintage photos, immigration timelines, and stories of newcomers whose first glimpse of America was from a ship in New York Harbor are available on the Ellis Island site. You can search for relatives who arrived through Ellis Island, and even see their ship manifests, pictures of their ships, and more.

➤ *Archiving Early America:* www.earlyamerica.com

Want to participate in a town crier forum on whether to throw British tea into Boston Harbor? Sneak a peek at Ben Franklin's *Pennsylvania Gazette,* circa 1750? How about kicking up your heels to favorite tunes of the Revolutionary War? You'll find America's early past preserved at this address.

➤ *Rulers:* http://rulers.org

Who was in charge of the Bahamas in 1710? With a database that covers more than three centuries of leadership, this is the place to learn about heads of state, royalty, territorial governors, foreign ministers, and dictators. The answer to the Bahamas question, by the way, is pirates. *Arghghgh.*

➤ *EyeWitness to History:* www.eyewitnesstohistory.com

Letters, diary excerpts, photographs, film clips, and vocal recordings of speeches and radio broadcasts bring the past to life in a you-are-there "ringside seat to history," from ancient times through the twentieth century. Learn what Victoria's first day on the job was like when she became queen. See the courtship rituals of eighteenth-century New England. Find out how World War I soldiers spent Christmas in the trenches.

➤ *dMarie Time Capsule:* www.dmarie.com/timecap
Plug in any date as far back as the 1800s and this website will generate a list of newspaper headlines, top songs, movies, books, toys, and the prices that people paid for milk, bread, houses, and transportation.

➤ *History in Song:* www.fortunecity.com/tinpan/parton/2/atoz.html
Looking for the 1914 lyrics to *Come and Take a Joy-Ride in my Aeroplane*? If your characters plan to break into a vintage tune, this site will ensure they've got all the words right. In addition to an alphabetical listing of songs with dates—from *The King's Own Regulars* (1775) to *Last Thoughts on Woody Guthrie* (1963)—the distinct History in Song page categorizes by topics and artists.

See more history resources in the article beginning on page 309, "Back in Time with History Research."

What Are You Wearing? What's for Dinner?

➤ *Food Reference:* www.foodreference.com
Sink your teeth into culinary quotes, trivia, recipes, and a food timeline that dates to 10,000 BC. Here you can discover that the first Olympic champion in 776 BC was a cook, that the Visigoths demanded 3,000 pounds of pepper as ransom for Rome, and that England's King Henry I died from eating a moray eel. Many of the fun facts found here can spur nonfiction ideas: A 279-pound alligator gar fish was caught in Rio Grande in 1951, the largest on record. *Gnocchi* are also known as *strangolapreti* because of a story of an Italian priest who loved the dumplings so much, he ate them too fast and choked.

➤ *The Household Cyclopedia:* www.publicbookshelf.com/public_html/The_Household_Cyclopedia_of_General_Information
How did people manage their households in the nineteenth century?

If they had this nifty resource guide, they would know how to avoid drowning, how to tell the age of cattle, how to make ink, and how to get sugar from a beet root. You never know. Such knowledge could come in handy someday.

➤ *The Costume Gallery Research Library:* www.costumegallery.com/research.htm

Everything from hats to shoes is covered in this fashionable resource directory. It includes textile and color references, etiquette primers, designers, paper dolls, vintage photos, needlework, and film costumes. The information spans Byzantine, medieval, Renaissance, and later centuries, plus topics such as the *Titanic*, German fashion, and British occupations.

Let's Get Scientific, Here

➤ *EurekAlert!:* www.eurekalert.org

The latest breaking news in science covers chemistry, biology, archaeology, medicine, mathematics, education, outer space, geology, technology, social behavior, Earth science, and more. On a recent day, the stories highlighted were "Pre-cancerous condition linked to chronic acid reflux faces several hurdles" and "For the birds or for me? Why do conservationists really help wildlife?"

➤ *Robert Niles, Statistics:* http://nilesonline.com/stats

Links to every statistical study imaginable will enjoy heavy use by non-fiction authors penning books and articles related to law, politics, agriculture, health, education, government, and world populations. There's even a link to an online rhyming dictionary for poetry and song lyrics.

A Matter of Semantics

➤ *Surfing for Slang:* www.slanglinks.cjb.net

This is one of the most comprehensive slang databases I've ever found and includes common colloquialisms from the U.S., U.K., Australia, Scandinavia, South Africa, the Caribbean, and many others. In addition to colorful insults, you can also find specialized jargon related to the military, sports, journalism, truckers, technology, chess, and alternative lifestyles.

➤ *The Phobia List:* http://phobialist.com

Does your hero suffer from alliumphobia (fear of garlic), anuptaphobia (fear of being single), or arachibutyrophobia (fear of peanut butter sticking to the roof of one's mouth)? Conflict derives from characters having to face their worst anxieties, even if they involve a fear of chopsticks (consecotaleophobia), a fear of otters (lutraphobia), or a fear of really long words (hippopotomonstrosesquippedaliophobia).

So Odd!

➤ *Eccentric America:* http://eccentricamerica.net/links.cfm

A plethora of links to roadside oddities, quirky landmarks, iconic architecture, kitschy hangouts, unusual museums, and chatty journals of intrepid road-trippers are to be found on Eccentric America. For starters, visit the World's Largest Catsup Bottle, the Starship Pegasus, or Carhenge (a Nebraska homage to Stonehenge constructed out of cars).

> # Find roadside oddities, quirky landmarks, iconic architecture, kitschy hangouts, unusual museums, and chatty journals.

➤ *The Dumb Network:* www.thedumb.com

Ridiculous laws, kooky facts, silly photos, and stories of stupid crooks are available for perusal on this site. In Wisconsin, for example, it's illegal to serve apple pie in public restaurants without a slice of cheese. In Finland, taxi drivers have to pay royalties on radio songs they play if their cabs are in service. And don't even think of changing a light bulb in Australia unless you're a licensed electrician.

➤ *Snopes: Rumor Has It:* www.snopes.com

This large collection of urban legends, *fauxtography*, frauds, scams, and old wives' tales can provide plenty of fodder for creative minds. The amusing site details the stories and provides evidence if there is any truth behind them.

➢ *Absolutely Totally Useless:* http://home.bitworks.co.nz/trivia/index.htm

Don't let the name of this website fool you. If you're trolling for trivia for your characters to expound on, this is the place. The site explains, for instance, that the American national anthem is the only one in the world that doesn't identify its country by name. Picasso used to burn his own paintings to stay warm when he was poor. Monaco's national orchestra outnumbers its army. Writers, of course, will appreciate the ironic revelation that Albert Einstein's final words died with him; the attending nurse didn't understand German.

➢ *Andy's Anachronisms:* www.timetravelreviews.com

If you're a fan of time travel themes, this extensive website addresses every spin on time travel, alternative universes, and temporal anomalies as found in novels, films, plays, short stories, TV, and music. It also includes links to scientific theories in case you want to compare your own methodology for getting from here to there.

➢ *Tru-TV Crime Library:* www.crimelibrary.com

Everything you ever wanted to know about scandalous murders, gangsters, conspiracy theories, spies, and mysterious workings of the criminal mind is available here. Now, whether the subject is appealing or appropriate for a young audience? Take care.

Serious Footnotes

➢ *WorldCat:* www.worldcat.org

Want to be connected to 10,000 libraries throughout the world? The free registration at this website allows you to track down books, authors, and publishing houses; locate the nearest library that carries a particular edition; and automatically generate proper citations according to the APA, Chicago, Harvard, MLA, and Turabian style guides. Searches can be run on individual articles, CDs, and DVDs, too.

➢ *Libweb:* http://lists.webjunction.org/libweb

Regional, state, national, academic, and public libraries in almost 150 countries can be accessed from this site. This global gateway allows you to peruse collections, tap into library webcasts, view archival images, search databases, participate in distance learning programs, and ask librarians for advice even if they're half a world away.

➤ *University of Virginia Electronic Text Library:* http://etext.lib.virginia.edu/collections/languages

The verbatim transcripts and depositions of the Salem witch trials are only one example of the academic treasures to be found at this extensive electronic library. Literary masterpieces in multiple languages, medieval and modern literature, poetry, and handwritten letters from luminaries such as Mark Twain, Thomas Jefferson, and Alexander Hamilton will turn your casual browsing into an addictive hobby.

➤ *Project Gutenberg:* www.promo.net/pg

Don't have time to go to the library and brush up on Shakespeare, Dante, or Sir Arthur Conan Doyle? The ambitious founder of Project Gutenberg has compiled a full spectrum of famous texts predating the 1920s and made them all available as electronic downloads.

➤ *Online Newspapers:* www.onlinenewspapers.com

What in the world is going on? Whether it's the *Blairgowrie Advertiser, Daily Yomiuri, As-Sabeel Weekly, Oakland Tribune,* or *Nassau Guardian,* there's never a shortage of hot story ideas dominating the headlines. The website is also useful from the standpoint of perspective, to see how different entities report exactly the same event based on their frames of reference.

➤ *Database of Award-Winning Children's Literature:* www.dawcl.com

This is an excellent resource for combing the shelves of children's literature all the way back to 1921. Age-specific searches based on setting, historical period, format, genre, and even protagonist gender invite you to explore how your own topic has been handled by the world's best authors.

➤ *McGill Humanities and Social Science Library:* www.mcgill.ca/hssl/collections/links/subject

This research site focuses on history, social science, and pop culture topics and walks users through its extensive catalogue of publications, databases, Internet sites, citation guides, classes, and one-on-one assistance with librarians.

> *All Experts:* www.allexperts.com

If you don't know an answer, you should always seek out an expert. This website neatly assembles experts of many kinds under one umbrella. Just reading some of the existing message board chatter on any given topic will ignite your imagination.

Back in Time with History Research

By Mary Northrup

For those who love to write about history, either as nonfiction or fiction, one of the most rewarding parts of the process is the research into the time period. There is certainly no shortage of sources, print or electronic, in this discipline. In fact, the amount of information can be overwhelming.

You can research in a well-stocked library, in archives, at your computer, or at a historical location. Perhaps your writing project will require all of these research locations. But no matter where you research, of prime importance is getting the facts straight. The following tips and sources will help.

Initial Steps

Begin by reading an overview of the time you are researching. Specialized encyclopedias are good for this purpose, such as *The Oxford Classical Dictionary,* on the ancient world, or perhaps the *Encyclopedia of the Renaissance* or *Encyclopedia Africana.*

Take a look at chronologies, too, which will give you a feel for what was going on in politics, arts, technology, and society at that time. Or try a book about research, written especially for anyone (not just students!) delving into history.

➤ Grun, Bernard. *The Timetables of History: A Horizontal Linkage of People and Events,* 4th ed. New York: Simon & Schuster, 2005.

➤ Mellersh, H. E. L. *Chronology of World History*. Santa Barbara, CA: ABC-CLIO, 1999.

➤ Presnell, Jenny L. *The Information-Literate Historian: A Guide to Research for History Students*. New York: Oxford University, 2007.

When you are ready to move on to specific sources, use your public library's online catalogue as your map. The most efficient way of searching is by subject. Use *history* as a subheading under any topic. For example, try China—history, or Women—history.

Don't forget about interlibrary loan. You can request books to be sent to your library from other institutions. If you have not used interlibrary loan before, ask a librarian how to do it.

You may want simply to browse the stacks for books, too, because many a researcher has come across a perfect source by relative chance. History is in the 900s; for example, the 930s contain books on the ancient world: China, Egypt, the Middle East, India, and Europe.

E-Books and Primary Source Texts

The Web is a great source for old historical books and documents that are in the public domain; that is, no longer under copyright. Many websites have been developed to make the searching easy and to bring numerous sources together in one place.

➤ *Hanover Historical Texts Project:* http://history.hanover.edu/project.html

Read letters of Crusaders, accounts of witch hunts, books on the Scientific Revolution and the Enlightenment, and royal decrees. All time periods from ancient to modern are represented.

➤ *Internet History Sourcebooks Project:* www.fordham.edu/halsall

Three main sourcebooks comprise this extensive site: Ancient History, Medieval, and Modern History. Here you can find histories, travel accounts, works of literature, medical texts, laws and decrees, and letters from all time periods. Each sourcebook also contains a section on using primary sources and provides links to other sources of information.

➤ *The Perseus Digital Library:* www.perseus.tufts.edu

The classics of Greek and Latin culture are here, as well as books from the English Renaissance by authors such as Bacon, Marlowe, and Shakespeare.

➤ *Project Gutenberg:* www.gutenberg.org

This is the biggest and the oldest collection of the free e-books sites, with more than 25,000 titles. You can search or browse in this remarkable collection.

History comes alive when you use sources that were written at the time of the event or by the person involved. Find diaries, letters, journals, eyewitness accounts, or oral histories for personal expressions of the people of the time. Official documents, such as decrees, laws, or party platforms, are also considered primary sources. To find primary sources in books, use your library's online catalogue and select (1) your subject, and (2) a subheading such as *personal narratives, diaries, correspondence, speeches, addresses,* or *laws and legislation,* depending on your need. Ask a reference librarian for further guidance.

Primary documents may also be found on the Internet. Many collections have been digitized. With some, you can even view the original document rather than a transcript. For an excellent site to get you started, take a look at:

➤ *Using Primary Sources on the Web:* www.lib.washington.edu/subject/History/RUSA/

Find definitions of primary sources, links to major collections and aids for locating documents, and a section on evaluating websites.

Maps

Maps provide an invaluable representation of the political and geographical state of the nation or region that you are researching. Look for historical atlases, which illustrate particular time periods. A good library should have several of these, some for particular countries or historical events (a war, for example), and some for the entire world. Several excellent websites offer comprehensive collections, too.

➤ *Atlas of World History.* New York: Oxford University, 2002.

This book offers maps throughout prehistory and history—where people settled, patterns of agriculture, first cities, religions, political divisions of countries, and population growth.

➤ *Mapping History:* http://mappinghistory.uoregon.edu/english/index.html

Explore four main areas on this site: American, Latin American, African, and European. Under each are modules that contain explanations and maps of historical events or developments.

➤ *Odden's Bookmarks: The Fascinating World of Maps and Mapping:* http://oddens.geog.uu.nl/index.php

The home page of this site is spare, but hidden behind those links are thousands of maps. Start by clicking on *maps and atlases*, then click on *old*.

➤ *Perry-Castañeda Library Map Collection:* www.lib.utexas.edu/maps

This is a good source for current maps, but look down the list on the first page until you find Historical Maps. This will take you to maps of the world, continents, and countries over a variety of time periods.

Checking Credentialed Sources

Few would argue that the Web has expanded the study of history and benefitted both scholars and interested laypeople. Many museums and libraries have digitized their collections, so that everyone may have access to historical materials.

History books and articles have greater or lesser value depending in part on the author's credentials, and it is even more important to evaluate the websites you use for research—anyone can put up a website. Find out what you can about the source, whether an individual or an organization, and the purpose or perspective of the site. On the following sites, experts in the relevant fields selected the links.

➤ *BUBL Link:* www.bubl.ac.uk

This site divides its resources using the Dewey Decimal system, so click on 900: Geography and History.

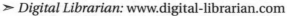

➤ *Digital Librarian:* www.digital-librarian.com

The home page features many subject areas, including architecture, archives and manuscripts, art, classics and the ancient world, medieval and Renaissance, as well as history. Click on the subject to find lots of links.

➤ *INFOMINE:* http://infomine.ucr.edu

For scholarly sources, this is the website to use. Click on one of the subjects on the home page; for historical subjects, that would mean the social sciences and humanities link. You can then search by key-word, or select one of the browse options to go to a list of subjects.

➤ *Librarians' Internet Index:* http://lii.org

Drill down through this directory-style site from the first page. The arts and humanities selection covers history.

➤ Daccord, Thomas. *The Best of History Web Sites.* New York: Neal-Schuman, 2007.

This book contains more than 400 pages of websites, divided gener-ally by time period. Although geared for teachers, researchers in history will find much here that is very useful. The information is also available at www.besthistorysites.net

For more focused historical searches online, try one of the following.

➤ *Ancient Mesoamerican Civilizations:* www.angelfire.com/ca/ humanorigins/index.html

Content on the Maya, Mixtec, Zapotec, and Aztec groups, as well as links to other websites can be found here. For research into the govern-ments or religions of these Mesoamerican peoples, this site is a good source. It also contains information on the Mayan calendar.

➤ *The Avalon Project at Yale Law School: Documents in Law, History and Diplomacy:* www.yale.edu/lawweb/avalon/avalon.htm

If you need a treaty, charter, grant, or law, this is the site for you. The pre-eighteenth-century section goes back to before the Common Era, although the majority of the documents on the site in that category

History Associations

Sometimes contacting an expert for an interview is the best way to get the information you need. Experts in history can be found at your local college or university. You may also want to contact an association whose members may be willing to answer your questions.

➤ *American Historical Association:* www.historians.org
This organization, the largest historical society in the United States, includes members whose specialties cover all historical time periods and areas. Its website also includes a directory of history journals.

➤ *Association of Ancient Historians*: http://associationofancienthistorians.org
The specialty of this organization is the ancient Mediterranean, especially Greeks and Romans.

➤ *National Council on Public History:* www.ncph.org
This association promotes making history accessible to everyone, and so includes museum curators, archivists, film and media producers, and other historians, as well as educators.

➤ *Encyclopedia of Associations*. Detroit: Gale, annual.
Consult this set of books, found in most libraries, to find thousands of associations, societies, and organizations, with description and contact information. May also be available as an online database at your library.

date to the 1600s. Other sections cover each century, including the twenty-first. Some documents have been gathered into collections, such as African Americans; World War II; or ancient, medieval, and Renaissance.

➤ *BBC History:* www.bbc.co.uk/history
Need information on the Vikings? Check the ancient history section of this media site. How about the Normans? Try the British history collection. The site includes biographies of historical figures, virtual tours of historical architecture, and loads of information on all time periods of history.

➤ *Digital History:* www.digitalhistory.uh.edu

For United States history. Contains textbook information, primary sources, an interactive timeline, and virtual exhibits, plus links to articles and websites.

➤ *Diotima: Women and Gender in the Ancient World:* www.stoa.org/diotima

This scholarly site contains articles, selections from books, translated texts, and images. Includes an extensive bibliography and list of images.

➤ *Exploring Ancient World Cultures:* http://eawc.evansville.edu

For research into the ancient Near East, India, Egypt, China, Greece, Rome, Islam, or Europe, try this site on early historical cultures. Each section contains numerous links to essays, images, texts, and other sites.

➤ *EyeWitness to History:* www.eyewitnesstohistory.com

Explanations and contemporary accounts of historical events are available on EyeWitness to History, from happenings in the ancient world to the modern. The site also includes audio and film clips from the twentieth century.

➤ *Library of Congress:* www.loc.gov

The Library of Congress is the largest library in the world, followed by the British Museum. The LOC also offers one of the largest digital collections of historic documents. Highlights of the website include American Memory, a collection of primary sources, photos, ads, sheet music, and recordings; Thomas, for laws and legislation; Global Gateway, for sources on world culture; and Veterans History Project, for personal narratives, letters, and photos from World War I to the present.

➤ *NetSERF: The Internet Connection for Medieval Resources:* www.netserf.org

Thousands of links to sources of information on all aspects of the long medieval period—from the fifth to the fifteenth century— are available on NetSERF. It includes a research center with links to libraries, museums, organizations, and maps.

➤ *The Orb: Online Reference Book for Medieval Studies:*
www.the-orb.net

On this scholarly site, all articles are peer-reviewed. It contains many documents, both primary and secondary, and writings from the medieval period.

➤ *Voice of the Shuttle:* http://vos.ucsb.edu

Numerous links to sites in all areas of the humanities are accessible on this website, which calls itself "a website for humanities research." The reference in the website's name is classical, invoking the shuttle of Philomela's loom, as described in Ovid's *Metamorphoses.* Check out the website's history section, which includes links to general history, prehistory, and countries by time period, as well as military history, the history of science and technology, and more. Other sections may be valuable for history, too, such as classical studies, archaeology, and religious studies.

Databases

Your local public library may provide access to online databases you can use either in the library or at home. For history research, databases provide access to reference material over a broad category range. Here are some that may appear in your library. Website addresses are included, for your information, but these sites require subscriptions.

➤ *ABC-CLIO history databases:* www.socialstudies.abc-clio.com

Explore an era or search through entries, including biographies, subject information, images, and maps in American History, World History: Ancient and Medieval Eras, and World History: The Modern Era.

➤ *Facts on File history databases:* www.fofweb.com

Facts on File is a print and online publisher that, among many other categories, in history provides biographies, subject coverage, primary sources, and images. Its sites include African-American History Online, American History Online, American Indian History Online, American Women's History Online, Ancient and Medieval History Online, and Modern World History Online.

➤ *Greenwood Daily Life Online:* http://dailylife.greenwood.com
For a look into the everyday life of people in countries and eras throughout history.

➤ *History Resource Center:* www.gale.cengage.com
Gale Cengage offers many resources, including the History Resource Center for the U.S. and for the world. They include articles and primary documents related to individuals and events from pre-colonial times to the present, or pre-antiquity to the present.

Making the Most of Markets

By Chris Eboch

Y ou've heard the stories about the enormous slush piles at publishing houses. No doubt you've heard editors talk about what's in those piles: Sometimes as many as 90 percent inappropriate submissions, ranging from novels sent to a house that only does picture books to nonfiction submitted to a publisher that solely offers fiction, or vice versa. Now, you would never make such a beginner's mistake. You understand the importance of market research. But are you doing the best possible job of targeting markets?

Eleni Beja, an Associate Editor in the Trade Publishing division of Scholastic, sees few submissions that are perfectly targeted, even though she only reviews submissions from agents or writers with whom she has had personal contact. "For every ten" submissions, she says, "I'll see about two that are right for Scholastic. Of the two, I'll see nil to one that are right for Scholastic and me."

Dial Books Editor Alisha Niehaus says, "I've only seen something truly inappropriate a couple of times. More commonly, someone sends a project that's too commercial for Dial, or on a topic in which we have a strong backlist—things which, no matter what their merit, won't fit on our list."

The same *close, but not quite* situation holds true for magazines, according to Marileta Robinson, Senior Editor at *Highlights for Children*. "The majority of submissions we see are in the ballpark of meeting our guidelines. That's not to say that the majority are right for *Highlights*. Tone, length, writing quality, age-appropriateness, and subject matter have a great deal to do with a manuscript's chances of success."

319

Digging Deeper

A more than casual use of updated market guides is an important step. The guides list hundreds of publishers, with details about what the editors want. Use the tools provided in the guides, and the market research becomes more effective. For example, look for a category index. According to Marni McNiff, Editor of *Book Markets for Children's Writers* and *Magazine Markets for Children's Writers* (both from Writer's Institute, the publisher of *Children's Writer Guide*), "Using the extensive cat-

> # The majority of submissions may be in the ballpark of meeting needs. But what's needed is a home run.

egory indexes in the back of the directories can help you to narrow your market selections based on age range and topic. Writers should read through several listings that they feel would be a good fit for their piece. Then study the needs of the publisher well, including reading its articles, stories, or books, and follow the writers' guidelines carefully."

After identifying a few publishers, Robinson agrees, authors should do more targeted research. "Reading the guidelines and current needs posted on our website and studying several issues of the magazine can help a writer learn what we are and are not looking for," particularly currently. Needs can change rapidly at magazines and book publishers.

Edward Necarsulmer IV, Director of the Children's Department at literary agency McIntosh & Otis, says he does some research "the old-fashioned way"—over drinks or lunch with editors. Authors don't have that option, but they can use other techniques Necarsulmer recommends. "Publishers' catalogues are enormous resources for us. I can really see an imprint's style." Catalogues also let him know about the publisher's other policies, such as what rights they're buying. Authors can find publishers' catalogues online, request them from the publisher, or ask bookstores and libraries to pass along the ones they've used.

Janet Fox describes the research she did to sell *Get Organized Without Losing It* (Free Spirit Publishing). "My book idea was nonfiction, for

middle-graders, and for kids who have trouble getting and staying organized. I looked at existing books on organizational skills for older kids and adults, talked with teachers and librarians, and analyzed the demand for the type of book I proposed." She checked *Books in Print* and found nothing current for her target audience.

"Then I researched publishing houses. I was looking for a publisher that specialized in books for kids and adults, whose focus was on self-help. That is Free Spirit's mission statement. Of course, I looked at their online and paper catalogue, and had already seen a number of their books, and felt that the manuscript I was drafting fit hand in glove with their other offerings, which included a book for older teens on study skills."

Molly Blaisdell, author of *Rembrandt and the Boy Who Drew Dogs* (Barron's Educational Series), starts market research with "a reader's approach. I keep a book journal. I learn about books all over—by networking at conferences, going to bookstores, chatting with folks online. I don't look at trends. I don't care how much the advance was. I only look at what I like. Did I care enough to read this book? If I did, I might want to do business with these people."

After gathering this information, Blaisdell keeps it organized with a submission spreadsheet. "I start a new line every time I learn the name of a new house or editor that I am interested in.

Market Moves

➤ Develop a system for researching, maintaining, and updating the market information you will gather. Consider creating a spreadsheet or database.

➤ Talk with teachers, librarians, kids, to find out what is in demand.

➤ Review market directories to gather and review potential book publisher or magazine targets for your writing project. Also research in library databases and reference books such as *Literary Market Place*.

➤ Study a book publisher's catalogue, or magazine issues, to get a sense of (1) categories, (2) style, and (3) what has been published recently by the company. Do the same with a magazine's editorial content.

➤ Review—and follow—publishers' submission guidelines.

➤ Read the articles, stories, and books themselves. Analyze them.

➤ Determine if you want to target a general or a specialized publisher.

➤ Learn the appropriate editors' names by doing research online and in trade publications.

➤ Attend conferences to meet and listen to editors, to learn more about what they need now, and to develop relationships.

➤ Do an overall analysis of the current demand for the book you are proposing, or a comparable analysis for articles and stories. It will help you develop insights to use in a query or proposal.

After some research I add the proposed book title that I think best connects with that house. I gather hard, concrete evidence about what these editors and agents like: books, genres, etc. That stuff goes in the comments."

The system has worked well for Blaisdell. "If I glance down my spreadsheet, my last 20 submissions all led to personal responses, such as requested manuscripts or at least a wish to see more work." She gives an example. "I wanted to write an art book. I looked into what houses sell those kinds of books. Then I heard a tip at a conference, from a writer, that one house was considering publishing more art books. I wrote a one-paragraph query letter on the basis of my research and that conference tip. I was able to convey in very few lines that I knew exactly what kind of books this house published and I was aware of the publishing house's goal." The query led to the sale of *Rembrandt and the Boy Who Drew Dogs*.

Online and In Person

All this research sounds like a lot of work, but, Blaisdell says, "You have to be pretty lazy these days not to target houses. Just Google the editor's name! Don't know the editor? Google it by searching *editor* and the book title and the author's name. Nine times out of ten you are done. Research has become very simple. I have several bookmarked websites that I check on a regular basis. If the editor or agent that you are interested in has a blog, you need to become a faithful reader and post on it sometimes."

"A great way to make contact with editors, especially those who aren't generally open to submissions, is to attend writers' conferences," McNiff says. "Spending the extra money for a one-on-one chat with an editor can be invaluable to a writer. It's your chance to jump from the slush pile right into an editor's hands."

Shutta Crum, a retired librarian and author of *A Family for Old Mill Farm* (Clarion), says, "I am always amazed by how little some writers use their public libraries for research. Not only are the important titles, like *Literary Market Place,* in most reference collections, but many libraries subscribe to databases that are worthwhile for authors. Often these databases are available to home users who simply input their library card number and a pin number."

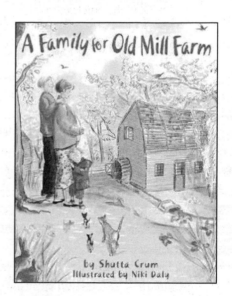

A Family for Old Mill Farm
by Shutta Crum
Illustrated by Niki Daly

With all the information available, beware of getting carried away by market research. "The tricky thing is not wasting your time," Blaisdell says. "You should be working toward creating a list of targeted editors. Do not collect any information about anyone that is not a real connection. Do not put a name in your spreadsheet without a reason!"

The reasons can vary. If you make a personal connection with an editor, you might want to keep in touch even if you don't currently have a suitable submission. I met Mark McVeigh at a conference when he was an editor at Dutton Books. We had a good rapport, and continued to visit at conferences over the next few years. Some of my writing friends thought I should take advantage of the connection by sending him something—anything. But I was writing historical fiction and fantasy at the time, the two genres he dislikes.

Later, McVeigh moved to Simon & Schuster as Editorial Director at Aladdin Books. When I again saw him at a conference, he said he was looking for original paperback series. I had just finished writing a book for a new series and quickly sent him the proposal and first manuscript. A month later, he called to express his interest in my Ghost Trackers series, and the first book, *The Haunted Hotel,* will come out next summer. In this case, networking paid off—but only because I waited until I had something an editor wanted, and didn't waste his time with a string of inappropriate submissions, just because we had met.

To maintain good relations, Necarsulmer is also careful not to send submissions to the wrong editor. He typically sends picture books exclusively, and may send a novel to a handful of editors at a time. If you think your project is right for 50 different publishers, you're not being realistic. Necarsulmer says, "Meeting with editors, reading the catalogue, studying what's out there, all leads to that *ah-ha* moment that this is right for a specific editor."

Making it Pay Off

Once you have all the market information, you can use it in your queries to show that you understand an editor's needs. "My queries are always specific," Blaisdell says. "I met you at the XYZ conference. I read about you on XYZ blog. You edited XYZ book. I love that book and feel a connection to my work because of XYZ. I'm sending to you because you like XYZ."

"I made sure my submission fit Free Spirit's format," Fox says of *Get Organized Without Losing It.* "They like e-mail queries as opposed to snail mail. I learned the name of the submissions editor and used it. I tailored my cover letter to Free Spirit. I let them know they were my first, and at the time only, choice for submission."

"I get a sense from the submission whether the writer or artist is familiar with Scholastic's trade division," Beja says. "If they mention why

Stepping into the Marketplace

➤ *Book Markets for Children's Writers* and *Magazine Markets for Children's Writers* (Writer's Institute) list hundreds of publishers, with information about submission policies and needs. www.writersbookstore.com

➤ *Children's Writer's and Illustrator's Market* (F&W) offers similar information. www.childrenswritersandillustratorsmarket.com. Find an online subscription option with a searchable database at www.writersmarket.com.

➤ The Society of Children's Book Writers and Illustrators (SCBWI) has many market guides, updated yearly and available online to members at www.scbwi.org. "Edited By" lists books edited by particular editors. The Bulletin newsletter has frequent updates.

➤ *WorldCat* lists books in collections around the world (nonfiction and some fiction). Do a subject search to see what has already been written on your topic, at www.worldcat.org.

➤ *Books in Print* and *Books Out Of Print* (Gale Research) are also good places to check on titles and subjects, available through many libraries.

➤ *NoveList* is a fiction database from EBSCO Publishing with reviews, annotations, and more, searchable by author, title, plot, and series. It's available at many libraries.

they're submitting to Scholastic, and to me, and those reasons make sense, then they'll have my attention, and gratitude. If I love the project and choose to pursue it, my efforts to get support for it can only be helped by an author's convincing pitch." She gives an example: "I know you're interested in politics and Moviolas, and Scholastic published *The Invention of Hugo Cabret.* So, my illustrated novel about a girl who fixes radios, set against the backdrop of Watergate, seems like a perfect fit for you."

Niehaus says, "I don't need to hear about Dial or Penguin and what we publish—I know that. I want to know what makes your story exciting, original, and publishable, in as concise and entertaining a fashion as you can say it. For me, since Dial accepts full picture book manuscripts and the first ten pages of a novel, the shorter the cover letter the better." If you've done your research, that will speak for itself.

For Necarsulmer, if someone mentions a book he agented, it makes an impression. You can use your research on publishers here as well, but only if you have something special to say. "I don't really care what the writer says about where they want to publish," Necarsulmer says. "But if you've met an editor at a conference or retreat, and they've asked about your work, absolutely tell me."

Robinson says, "Information that is useful in a cover letter includes any experiences or background that make the writer especially qualified to write the story or article, and reference to any research the writer did beyond the ordinary. Although we publish many first-time authors, a writer's published credits, especially in similar markets, make an impression."

Even extensive market research doesn't guarantee success, Blaisdell notes. "I think it is important to realize that we actually have no control over the sale of books. What we can control is who we offer our books to and the execution of those offers. I believe that this marketing focus will get you out of slush piles and open doors that would otherwise be closed to you."

One-on-One with Today's Teenagers

By Susan Sundwall

How old is Huckleberry Finn in *The Adventures of Huckleberry Finn?* How old is Tom Sawyer? Having read the book some time ago, I didn't remember. Good old Google. With just a few key words I found the answer; Huck is 13 and Tom is about 12. My curiosity was satisfied, but I had another thought. How would these two staple characters of the literary world get along with present-day teens? What's the same about adolescents then and now? What's different? The answer to both questions is, a lot.

Culture Shift

The term *teenager*, a word coined just after World War II to describe the upcoming generation of consumers, would have been unfamiliar to Mark Twain. His research about adolescents may have consisted only of candid observations of people at a certain stage in life, coupled with personal childhood memories. But things are a bit different in our time, and anyone wanting to write for and about teens needs to do a variety of research—much more than a trip or two down memory lane. That trip will aid you very little, for the world that today's teens inhabit seems to change at the speed of light.

"Youth culture shifts at an amazing rate," says T. Suzanne Eller, author of *Real Issues, Real Teens: What Every Parent Needs to Know* (Life Journey). "Today's 13-year-old is experiencing different pressures, technological advances, and issues than the college freshman who was 13 just 5 years ago. If you don't know several teens (not just your own), then maybe it's not appropriate to write for them until you do. Know their culture. Know what they listen to, watch, how they relate. Listen. Learn about the issues they face and the things they desire to learn."

In other words, set out to find out. Begin by checking out one of the most profound technological advances of our age—the Internet. Teens everywhere join *social utility* websites such as Facebook and MySpace to connect with their peers in cyberspace. These sites have teens all

over the world visiting to chat, share ideas, listen to music, and expand their horizons. Writers who have an account with one or both can pick up scads of information on current teen culture. Eller advises joining these sites "or one of the myriad social communities if you really want to reach teens; I'm connected in both."

So is Rachel Vail, author of *Lucky* (HarperTeen). "Facebook in particular is an almost addictive part of the lives of many teens I know, as are texting and IMing. I am on Facebook and have recently set up a MySpace presence. It's fun to connect with readers that way, too."

Hanging Out

Once you've plumbed the depths of all that's online, go a step further and get nosy. Hang out and take notes. While you may dislike the idea of lumping teens into a kind of cultural petri dish with your microscope and inoculation needle at the ready, some picking, probing, and examining is essential.

"I go on the Internet, read books, and talk to experts," says Alden Carter, author of *Love, Football and Other Contact Sports* (Holiday House). "Often the experts are kids, usually my own children, one of my numerous nieces and nephews, or one or more of their friends." Carter believes that, though the world has advanced in so many ways, Twain's readers would have recognized many timeless young adult qualities. "Kids haven't changed," he says. "They're still the same uncertain, overly sensitive, confused, hormone-driven people they were in the time of Aristotle." Or maybe Huck and Tom. "Only the details of life have changed," Carter continues. "Teens are wonderful, tough, funny, resilient, and courageous."

"In addition to using my own imagination, memories, and theater training, I rely on correspondence with readers (now mostly by e-mail) and visits to schools to connect with kids and teens," says Vail. "I also have a number of friends and relatives who are teens themselves with

> ## "Teens are wonderful, tough, resilient, and courageous."

whom I check to make sure I am not saying anything obviously stupid in my books, as well as to keep sharp my ear for the way they talk and for they way they interact. I love to listen for what they are trying not to tell."

Writer/director John Cosper works with teens in a theater setting. "Listen to them. Be around them. You can read books and magazine articles about youth culture and what's hot, but half of that stuff is out of date before it ever hits the shelf. You need to be in touch with kids and be willing to listen without prejudice." Cosper appreciates a one-on-one approach. "Another good idea is to get their input. Let them read what you're writing and give you feedback. Let them help you see the world through their eyes, and you will improve your communication with them."

Being in Touch

Being in touch and being in the thick of things often amounts to the same thing. "I hang around teens and listen to their talk," says John Coy, author of *Box Out* (Scholastic Press). "I spend my time watching, listening, and talking to teens. I walk the halls of schools, eat in cafeterias, and go to games and practices." *Box Out* is the story of a teen finding his voice and his way in the world of high school basketball. "I also visit classrooms and ask teens questions and have them write down their answers. They do this anonymously and tend to be very honest. I ask them what adults don't understand about being a teen now and what aspects of their lives they feel are underrepresented in books."

"There are a number of ways to keep in touch with teens," says Eller. "I am a community mentor in my city, going into four area high schools to speak, and also to join them in community projects." Look for opportunities in your town or city that involve teens, and if you're a parent of teens, invite kids into your home. "I also research youth culture, not just because I have a youth culture column, but because it keeps me in touch," she adds.

"For years I announced our high school baseball games for fun," says Carter. "I'm a member of the committee advocating passage of local school referendums, which requires frequent contact with school personnel and the student committee that works for passage." His involvement includes school concerts, plays, and hundreds of school visits in the last 25 years. "Always both fun and informative."

"I learn a great deal from teens," Eller enthuses. "This is true whether I'm writing for them or for their parents. Teens are open, contrary to popular belief, and if they think you'll listen, they'll open up. I love that."

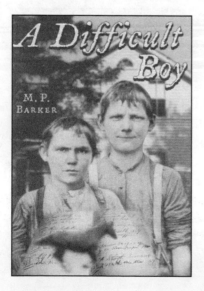

Staying in Balance

Authors writing nonfiction about teens in other times—even ten years ago—must chart a dual course when researching. They must be aware of differences in the era they are writing about, and still understand the modern sensibilities of their current teen audience.

M. P. Barker, author of *A Difficult Boy*, (Holiday House) was surprised when she discovered that young adults turned out to be her audience. "I didn't set out to write for a particular market. The characters I chose (or rather, who chose me) just turned out to be that age, and all I thought about during the creation process was following them and finding out how they ended up, not who the market was going to be." Soon, though, people who read the manuscript were telling her who her audience was. "I figured I needed to find out what was out there. And boy, things have changed since I was that age."

Barker's book is historical fiction, and she had the advantage of having worked in a living history museum setting, Old Sturbridge Village in Massachusetts, which was a great aid to her research. Juxtaposed between two eras she had to be careful to walk between the two worlds.

"It can be a tricky balancing act to create characters with whom readers can relate (especially teens) while also retaining that sense of a different place and time," says Barker. "It's important to include little details of everyday life—what people wore, ate, how often they bathed—especially for young readers who are going to be less familiar with the time period than adults. You need to convey that [the historic teens'] thoughts and beliefs were different than ours, even though they might have shared many of the same problems and values. You also want the dialogue to sound appropriate to the time period without seeming stiff and unnatural."

Gail Jarrow, author of the biography *Robert H. Jackson: New Deal Lawyer, Supreme Court Justice, Nuremberg Prosecutor* (Calkins Creek), had a similar situation. "Since my recent work has been nonfiction and most sales are to libraries, I'm aware of school curricula. I look for general subjects that tie into what teens study, but I choose specific topics that haven't been covered much in previous books. I'm always looking for an angle teens will find interesting. Based on teens I know and on my own teen years, I think history and science come alive for readers when they can connect the material to real people."

Websites for and about Teens

In addition to the sites everyone knows about—MySpace and Facebook—that are frequented by teens, here are others of interest.

➤ **By Parents For Parents:** www.byparents-forparents.com. Articles and resources for parents raising teens, from CRC Health Group, a company that specializes in recovery, disorders, and behavioral issues.

➤ **Gaia Online:** www.gaiaonline.com. A place to build avatars, enter contests, talk in forums about poetry, politics, celebrities, and more.

➤ **Parenting Teens Online:** www.parentingteensonline.com. A helpful source of information for parents raising teens.

➤ **Teens Safe Sites:** www.funsites.com/ki-teens.html. Links to safe sites for kids and teens. Note that some of the links are outdated.

➤ **Teen Central:** www.teencentral.net. Features an anonymous help line, and was developed by a teen counselor. Also includes stories by teens and materials on school, celebrities, and other teen interests.

➤ **LoveToKnow Teens:** http://teens.lovetoknow.com. Covers fashion, health, relationships, school, working, and issues of growing up for teens. See the article on teenager websites for more information on where teens like to surf.

➤ **Lyrics.com:** Find the latest music teens listen to, and read comments on it. This is also a social site that includes forums and messaging, and publishes poetry.

➤ **RollingStone.com:** The site of the still going strong publication about music, politics, and culture.

➤ **SparkNotes.com:** The study guide site also offers pages on college searches, music, books, movies, television, and news of interest to teens.

➤ **TeenChat:** www.teenchat.com. A free chat room site for teens.

➤ **TeensHealth:** http://kidshealth.org/teen. Created by the Nemours Foundation, this site gives teens accurate health information in an appealing way.

➤ **Teen Voices Online:** www.teenvoices.com. A companion to a print magazine for teen girls.

➤ **TeenWire:** www.teenwire.com. From Planned Parenthood, this site focuses on sexual health for teens, and also covers entertainment, school, careers, relationships, and activism.

➤ **Wet Seal:** www.wetseal.com. The site of the clothing store that caters to teens and can help writers incorporate the cool and current.

Gasping, Sudden Truth

Whether writing contemporary fiction, fantasy, historical novels, drama or nonfiction, there's across-the-board writer agreement that responsible writing and respect for your reader are crucial.

"Kids want and deserve good stories," says Carter, "and the writer for teens has, if anything, a greater responsibility to his or her readers than writers in any other genre. Don't lie to the kids. Reality isn't always pleasant. They need to be ready for it."

> ## The anonymity of age allowed one writer to overhear teens talking— but also led to the surprising discovery of just how disrespected by adults teens feel.

Vail declares, "Most important when writing, whether for teens or kids or adults, is to tell the truth. There may be a temptation on the part of an adult writer to make sure every bad choice is punished, every good kid is ultimately vindicated." It's a hoped for result but not consistent. "One thing we crave as readers is that moment of gasping, sudden truth: *Yes! That is just how it feels! How did the author know that about me?*"

More often than not, teens will "get it" without a preachy attitude, too. "Your characters can learn lessons, change, and make the right choices without having someone preach to them," says Cosper. "Give your audience credit, remembering that a lesson they put together for themselves makes a deeper impression than one you spell out for them."

A complication of the massive quantities of information available via technology today, however, is that teens may not *get* what is accurate and what is not. "I'm concerned when it comes to any kind of nonfiction," says Jarrow. "Young people get more and more of their information from sources that aren't carefully researched. Teens don't always realize this. As writers, we owe it to our teen readers to supply

Shattered Times Three

"How does it really feel when your world falls apart and you have to put it back together yourself? That shattering question at the heart of adolescence itself was and continues to be the genesis for my new trilogy: *Lucky, Gorgeous,* and *Brilliant*." So says author Rachel Vail. In the trilogy, three teenage sisters are living the American Dream but each must cope with its sudden loss. These are stories of upheaval, humiliation, passion, and discovery in a year when teenagers face unexpected loss.

"The impetus for writing these books was a conversation I had with a friend," says Vail. "We were having one of those great girlfriend talks, covering topics from past indiscretions to secret thoughts, politics to religion, homosexuality, sex, racism, and mothers-in-law to illicit drug use. We were sharing everything without any hesitation, as only really close friends can. Until the question of how much a pair of sunglasses cost arose. Sudden tension: 'Do you mind if I ask approximately how much you paid? You don't have to tell.' We had finally stumbled onto a taboo! Money? We laughed at the absurdity.

"But the conversation kept replaying in my mind. When I was a kid, reading under the covers with a flashlight, books by Paula Danziger and Judy Blume that dared to address issues of teen sexuality, divorce, and politics felt absolutely revolutionary. I loved them. *Catcher in the Rye* and *A Separate Peace* dared to show people my age feeling rage, helplessness, jealousy, passion—all the taboo subjects. I couldn't get enough of them. Today, so many books and magazine articles and TV shows chronicle the lifestyles of the rich. But I became fascinated with the question of what happens when someone from that group can no longer live that way."

Vail came to the eventual conclusion, "Money matters. How do you cope when it's gone?" These inspiring thoughts led to her chronicles of three teen sisters, Phoebe, Allison, and Quinn Avery. For more information on Vail's life and books visit www.rachelvail.com.

the best, most accurate information we can."

The question of trust arises despite, or because of, a secret adult weapon: The anonymity of (ahem) advanced age. (Any teens trusting, or noticing, anyone over 30 these days?) Coy says, "I hang around teens and listen to their talk. I'm at an age where it's very easy for them to ignore me, so I can just listen." On the far side of that divide has been a surprising discovery. Coy says he learned "how used to being disrespected by adults many teens are." That is an essential piece of information for YA writers to learn and counter.

"Teens aren't blind," says Eller. "They see I am way older than them, so if I try to be something I'm not, it turns them away. They just want someone to be real. *Authenticity* is a buzz word that many people believe is overused, but that doesn't make it any less important."

Coy also acknowledges how greatly he has benefitted from real teen reactions to his books. "Teens have been generous and honest with me in their feedback and I am honored and grateful to write books they like."

Every generation metamorphoses. Every generation needs to feel—and is—unique, but builds on the experiences of preceding times. Young adults pick up and carry forward, even if they don't want to admit it. Young adults create their own world, even if their parents and grandparents find it difficult to acknowledge it.

Huck and Tom, and old Samuel Clemens, would understand the emotional complexities of their peers in this age. But they'd surely also be confused and amazed at the challenges, choices, numbers, and speed of life today. Writers for teens must, and can, measure *mark twain* in the river of researching and writing for the next new age, the next stage, of young adulthood on the brink.

Conferences & Contests

Chautauqua Workshop: The Nurturing of Children's Writers

By Mark Haverstock

I n 1985, Kent L. Brown Jr. organized the first Highlights Foundation Writers Workshop, which took place at the Chautauqua Institution near Jamestown, New York. Now Executive Director of the Foundation, Editor in Chief Emeritus of *Highlights for Children,* and Acting Publisher of Boyds Mills Press, Brown chose what many feel is the perfect location to foster creativity and conduct a program to inspire participants to become better at their craft. Chautauqua itself is like no other place. For more than a century, this unique summer retreat has been a center for intellectual growth, artistic endeavors, and creative renewal of all kinds.

"Our workshop's philosophy is directly connected to the foundation's mission, which is to increase the quality of writing and illustrating for children," says Kim Griswell, Senior Editor of Special Projects. "You do that by keeping it small, limiting attendance, and having a really low faculty-to-student ratio. Within the confines of this beautiful place, we nurture and support writers on their journey to becoming better at what they do."

Something for Everyone

The Writers Workshop doesn't try to be one-size-fits-all. Because there are so many different classes—45 different workshops related to writing and illustrating—the program touches on just about everything connected to children's writing. Attendees have the option of choosing

339

Chautauqua at a Glance

➤ **Where:** The Highlights Foundation Writers Workshop is held at the Chautauqua Institution near Jamestown, New York. Founded by John Heyl Vincent and Lewis Miller in 1874, Chautauqua is a small lakeside community dedicated to culture and education. The quiet rural setting makes it an ideal retreat for writers and illustrators.

➤ **Who:** Writers and illustrators at any stage of their career will benefit from the variety of workshops, low student-to-faculty ratio, and individual attention available at the conference. The conference is limited to 100 participants.

➤ **When:** The Highlights Foundation Writers Workshop is held from Saturday to Saturday, the third week in July. The 2009 conference dates are July 11 to 18.

➤ **Cost:** The 2008 fee, which included everything except housing and transportation, was $2,400 (or $1,985 for first-timers who register by the end of February). Scholarships are available from the Highlights Foundation for those who might not otherwise have the opportunity or resources to participate. Application forms and additional information can be obtained by calling 570-253-1192 or by e-mailing Kent L. Brown Jr. at klbrown@ highlightsfoundation.org.

➤ **Website:** www.highlightsfoundation.org

those workshops that best fit their individual needs. Explore what the program calls the Core: point of view, a selection of workshops on character and plot, theme, a sense of place, beginnings and endings, and writing dialogue. Exploring Genres includes workshops that delve into fiction, nonfiction, picture books, biography, and magazines, with specific topics ranging from writing humor to writing globally. A third group of workshops come under the heading of the Publishing Business: contracts, submissions, getting out of the slush pile, and book promotion. Participants can also select Advanced Techniques sessions, covering interviewing, finding ideas, research, thinking like an editor, and other topics. In addition to the workshops are one-on-one manuscript sessions with editors, authors, and other faculty members.

With this range of selections, writers at every stage can come away with something valuable. Griswell says, "If you're a beginner, you really benefit most from the core workshops because you're going to get basics on plot, characterization, point of view, and all the essentials. Those people who are well published probably benefit most from their manuscript critiques." More advanced writers work with experienced authors or editors who will help them to reach the next level. *Face time* with these seasoned writing professionals is more important to them. Even past attendees who return to Chautauqua can find what they need to move forward in their writing and illustrating careers.

"Chautauqua has a way of getting writers over that next hurdle."

Faculty members who have been at several Chautauqua conferences often say that the quality of the attendees' work seems to improve every year. "I worked with several accomplished writers this year, quite widely published already," says Rich Wallace, author of the Winning Season series from Viking. "I also saw quite a few unpublished writers who are just about ready. Chautauqua has a way of getting writers over that next hurdle."

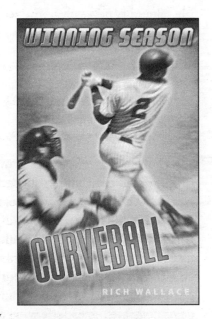

Recipe for Faculty

Brown chooses conference faculty based on an incredible amount of experience in the publishing field and his personal knowledge of each faculty member's ability to nurture writers and illustrators. "He tries to have a range of experience in different genres, so he wants to have nonfiction people, poets, novel writers, and picture book writers and illustrators," says Griswell. "Also, he wants to have a mix of editors, authors, and people in other areas of publishing."

Past conferences have included top editors from such publishers as Philomel, Scholastic, Clarion, Henry Holt, Charlesbridge, Cricket Magazine Group, National Wildlife Federation magazines, and *National Geographic World*. Of course, editors and publishing professionals from *Highlights for Children* and Boyds Mills Press join the faculty. Writers have numbered many award winners, such as Jerry Spinelli, Richard Peck, and Sharon Creech. Illustrators such as Brian Pinkney, David Small, and Floyd Cooper have also shared their talents. The faculty has included distinguished educators, book packagers, librarians, reviewers, bookstore owners, and members of prestigious national award committees.

But what really makes the mix of faculty work is Brown's commitment to inviting people who are accessible, supportive, and nurturing of others in the field of children's literature—those who want to help other writers and illustrators take the next step. "All of them are incredibly talented and easily approachable," says Sue Heavenrich, a first-time attendee. "The environment is one of support."

"There are no egos" at Chautauqua.

Real People

"There are no egos," says Brown. "We don't separate the faculty out or put them on a pedestal." The faculty members are truly a part of the conference on a day-to-day basis. During the entire week, you not only go to their workshops and listen to their general sessions, you eat breakfast with them, go for walks with them, and you get to know them as people.

Attendees are immersed in this conference for seven full days and evenings. "Kent Brown invites faculty members whom he knows are eager to share the experience, so the line between faculty and conferees is effectively blurred," says Wallace. "There's never anything like a head table. In fact, the faculty is encouraged to mix at every opportunity."

You're paired with a faculty member who acts as a mentor, one who has read and critiqued your manuscript and meets with you in one-on-one sessions. He or she may ask for a rewrite during the week and meet with you to review your changes; you may also mutually agree to work on other manuscripts you've brought.

Throughout the conference, you'll also connect with other mentors, among attendees and faculty, who can help you with manuscript submissions, career guidance, and other writing issues. This living and interacting together is what makes Chautauqua different from other writers' conferences. "A big part of it is the way Kent does things, in terms of connecting people with people—writers with other writers, writers with editors, illustrators with working illustrators," says Griswell.

The Chautauqua Magic

Attendees often mention the Chautauqua magic: an attitude, atmosphere, and place that's difficult to describe. By the end of the week, it's hard to imagine this conference being held in any other location. "Why this works so well here is that as you walk the grounds, you hear opera, you hear public speakers, and you hear the symphony. It's the beauty of the place," says Griswell. "All of that creates a synergy among writers working on their craft and the arts in general. It takes you out of your current world into a kind of utopian world." Job and family pressures fade. The pace is slowed. There is time to take a leisurely walk around the lake or admire the Victorian architecture on the grounds.

Most people who attend get that experience of finding their *tribe*. "It feels like home," says Griswell. You find yourself in the midst of a group of people who are totally focused on the same thing and totally understand what you say when you talk about your passion for children's literature. "People in the world don't get what we're about—not even our family members understand us," she says. The first thing attendees notice is that sense of community, of people who understand how they think, why they care, and what they love about writing and illustrating for children.

Griswell sees this as a huge benefit, because it's something most writers don't get enough of in the real world. "With a group like this and a place like this, that sense of community and finding others who think like you do is a big thing," she says. "A lot of people connect with other writers who live near them that they've never met before. They form critique groups, both in-person and online. Many take away a long-term support system that they didn't have before." They also leave with the personal interactions with faculty they've met during the week, and that experience carries over to the practicality of the publishing business. When you submit something to a faculty member you met who happens to be an editor, the editor now knows you as a person, not just another name in the manuscript pile. They'll still judge your work on its merits, but they're now judging the work of someone they know.

Getting the Most From Your Experience

With all the available workshops and open access to faculty and fellow writers, some attendees feel they need to take advantage of everything. By midweek, it can become a bit overwhelming. Sometimes it's best to go with the flow, stop at the Refectory in Bestor Plaza, and sit down with some fellow writers over ice cream. Some of the best shared ideas happen during these in-between times. Take advantage of them.

Writer M. LaVora Perry, who attended the workshop two years ago, feels that the best way to maximize the Chautauqua experience is to enter the Institute's fairy tale-like grounds with an open mind and heart. "Don't be afraid to ask for the help you need, and help others however you can," she says. "If one person is unable to provide what you're seeking, someone else will. The spirit of honestly sharing and caring from one's heart pervades the entire conference. This spirit is perhaps what Chautauqua's magic is really all about."

Most attendees find that the one-on-one manuscript critiques or portfolio reviews are among the most important parts of the experience. Choose your materials carefully, rather than waiting until the last minute and grabbing whatever's handy. "Make sure that the manuscript you choose is one that will take you a step closer to your writing goals," suggests Griswell. "If you're an illustrator, prepare a portfolio that will give your reviewer a good sense of your abilities."

You might also want to bring along an extra manuscript or two to share with other attendees, or perhaps with a faculty member you've met who is willing to take a look. "My roommates worked on revisions and brought other short pieces," says Heavenrich. "I think bringing a couple extra short pieces that you feel are ready to send out is a good idea."

Over the last decade, Lunch and Learn has been added as an unofficial part of the program. Selected faculty teach optional mini-lessons to small groups during the lunch hour, covering topics that might interest attendees. These sessions are much more casual and conversational than the workshops, with lots of back and forth between the facilitator and the attendees. Most are planned in advance, but occasionally a faculty member will be inspired more immediately to present one during the week. Some of the 2008 offerings included an Ask the Editor session, with Charlesbridge Editor Randi Rivers; The Future of Publishing, with Boyds Mills Press President Clay Winters; and Why Write for Magazines? with Mary Dalheim, Editorial Director for three children's nature magazines published by the National Wildlife Federation.

Continuing the Magic

Many Chautauqua graduates credit the conference with their writing success stories. Some, like Newbery Medal winner Sharon Creech, even come back later as faculty members because they want to share their knowledge and insights with aspiring writers. This year's faculty includes several more successful graduates, such as award-winning authors Mary Casanova and Sue Beckhorn.

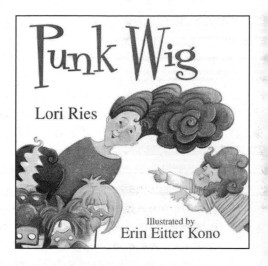

Punk Wig
Lori Ries
Illustrated by
Erin Eitter Kono

Attendees leave with polished articles that they will pitch to *Highlights for Children, Cricket, Boys' Quest* or one of hundreds of periodicals in the children's markets. Others will pursue publication of their picture book ideas or middle-grade novels, or hook up with a publisher to illustrate the next Caldecott contender. "When author Lori Ries first came to Chautauqua, she had not published a book yet. Like many attendees, she was a bit quiet and shy as the week began, but she made a connection at Chautauqua that allowed her to publish her first book," says Griswell. "And now she's confidently teaching writing workshops herself." Ries's books include *Punk Wig,* illustrated by Erin Eitter Kono; (Boyds Mills); *Mrs. Fickle's Pickles,* illustrated by Nancy Cole (Boyds Mills); and *Fix It,*

Sam, illustrated by Sue Rama (Charlesbridge).

Each day, from the minute you wake up until you fall asleep, you think, talk, read, write, and breathe children's literature. But even experiences like these must end. When the week is over, what happens next? You'll likely take the sum of your experiences and maybe a little of that Chautauqua magic home with you. You'll take along lasting connections to new friends, both workshop graduates and faculty members. You'll take a bag full of autographed books and pages filled with workshop notes and ideas. Most of all, you'll take the inspiration and experiences you gained during the week and apply them to your work.

Next year will be the twenty-fifth anniversary of the Chautauqua Writers Workshop. "It's going to be a really big year for us," says Griswell. "Kent is considering some ideas about bringing back faculty members from past conferences—including the very first in Chautauqua in 1985. Twenty-five years is a long time to refine things—and I think we have a handle on what components really make this work."

The X-Factor: What Makes a Prize-Winning Story?

By Jacqueline Horsfall

"**W**e're looking for the X-factor," announces the judge on a popular TV singing competition. "Something fresh, original, electrifying." The same preferences could be echoed by writing contest judges.

In a typical fiction contest, submissions are distributed among a panel of judges made up of editors, authors, and/or educators. They read and sort stories into two categories: finalists versus others. Finalists are re-read and ranked by all the judges, who each make the case for their favorites. This might seem a time-consuming and potentially contentious process, considering each judge's differing tastes and interests. In fact, the prize-winning selection process often takes less than an hour, in congenial agreement.

The reason for the speedy selection is simply this: Judges tend to choose the same winners. In most writing contests—short story, novel, poetry—the winners emerge like lotus flowers from the muck. Out of hundreds, even thousands, of submissions, the same few submissions rise to the top. What is the magical X-factor? How do you determine if your story has this special something that will carry it from the slush pile to the finalist stack? The X-factor isn't as elusive or mysterious as it sounds. There's a sound logic behind its workings, and a systematic method of crafting fiction any writer can understand and apply. Let's take a behind-the-scenes look at a typical annual short story contest.

Hurdle One

Soon after the contest deadline, all stories are divided equally among the judges. Because breaking contest rules is grounds for instant disqualification, here's the first threshold to cross and improve your chances in the contest. Many manuscripts are rejected at this point, not because of weak storytelling skills, but simply because the author either did not follow directions or did not submit clean, error-free copy. You can use this stage of the culling process to your benefit by being professional and paying close attention to the details of the rules. At this hurdle, a high percentage of competitors will be eliminated.

Let's assume you have followed the submission rules exactly: You've adhered to word count, written to theme, used proper manuscript format, provided your contact information (a common but costly omission), included an SASE if required, and submitted before the deadline. You've proofed your copy for typos, grammatical errors, and dialogue punctuation. You've presented a professional package with no flashy gimmicks, one that doesn't flash *amateur!* You've passed the first hurdle.

Hurdle Two

Judge A now holds your masterpiece in her hands. Let's peek into her mind and see what she's looking for in the X-factor department.

➤ *Originality.* Did a spectacled boy wizard sneak into your plot? Is a spider-suited superhero saving a city from destruction? Have zombies raided a Mayan temple? Judges label stories that are based on TV shows, movies, best-selling novels, or video games as derivative. Even if you didn't copy word-for-word—which is plagiarism—a story deemed derivative will not make the cut. Originality is highly valued by judges, as by editors, who see the same tired, hackneyed plots year after year. If you must write a story about a neighborhood witch who turns out to be a kindly old woman, rev up your creativity and tell it in an insightful, fresh way: The woman is an Asian acupuncturist who sticks needles in people to heal, not hurt them.

➤ *Structure.* Have you written a witty character sketch? An essay full of delightful nature observations? A conversation between two characters at a murder scene? Then you haven't written a story. A story has a recognizable plot with a beginning, middle, and end. It must have a story problem (a conflict or dilemma) with rising action, climax, and resolution. Every story has a main character who wants something and an obstacle blocking the way. Stories are about growth and change. Does your protagonist come to a startling realization about himself? Does she change her behavior in some subtle or drastic way, seeing the world differently because of what has happened to her? If there is no trouble, there is no story. Scenes, essays, and character sketches are not stories.

If your story has proper structure and originality, you've caught the judge's eye, survived the cut, and passed the second hurdle. On to the third.

> Have you written a witty character sketch? An essay full of delightful nature observations? A conversation between two characters at a murder scene? Then you haven't written a story.

Hurdle Three

With the basics covered, the judges will pay greater attention to pacing, characterization, plot development and consistency, dialogue—all the elements of good fiction—but to the following in particular.

➤ *Prose.* Judges are language-lovers. They prize writing that is clear, direct, and simple, yet powerful, aesthetic, and visual. Have you used sensory details and active verbs in your story, showing instead of telling? Instead of writing in a flat, lifeless way (*The snake ate the tiny mouse*) have you sent shivers down the judge's spine (*The python unhinged its jaw and swallowed the mouse in slow gulps*)? Instead of bland, emotionless scenes (*Emma grew angry after reading Ted's letter*) have you depicted gripping feeling (*Emma crumpled Ted's letter and pitched it into the gutter*)? If you felt the need to modify every verb with an adverb (*walks slowly and stealthily*), did you use a thesaurus to find a stronger verb that could stand alone (*creeps*)? Have you cluttered up your story with flowery, overwritten passages (*Her face reddened like the*

A Wind-up with a Wallop

Textbooks and other books on writing are full of advice on how to craft skillful endings. Note *endings*—in the plural. And that's exactly how you should attack your story close, by writing several trial endings. Endings are challenging for all writers, including screenwriters. In movie production, directors often film two versions of the ending. Test audiences preview these endings before the movie is released, voting for their favorite. Sometimes you can view alternate endings on the DVD. So why shouldn't you try the same technique? Brainstorm two endings—or ten! Test them on your writer friends or critique group and select the one that gets rave reviews.

first flush of a budding rose) instead of more concise constructions (*She blushed*)? Did you banish clichés? Make no bones about it, clichés make your judge madder than a wet hen and stubborn as a mule—and your story will end up deader than a doornail.

➤ *Realism*. Characters, settings, and dialogue must be believable and dilemmas must be challenging yet age-appropriate. Judges have keen ears for authentic patter, favoring dialogue that's chatty and familiar (*I've gotta ask my mom*) instead of stilted and pedantic (*I must request my mother's permission*). Judges expect characters to be consistent in thought and action, period details to be accurate, and scene changes marked with clear transitions. If you make a judge roll her eyes in disbelief, your story will roll off her radar. Even though J. K. Rowling's Harry Potter series presented a fanciful world with whimsical creatures, the world was structured, the characters developed and memorable, and the exploits and situations believable within their imaginary framework.

So, your story is structured, original, and believable, with fresh vivid language and a conflicted protagonist. Weak competitors have toppled.

Hurdle Four

One final hurdle to go, and it's a biggie.

➤ *Satisfying ending*. You're running your story race, picking up speed, carrying the judge along for an exhilarating ride. The end of this journey is near, and the judge is looking forward to a satisfying wind-up. Stride, stride, stride. . . whump! What happened? You choked before reaching your final destination.

Judges mourn the fact that the majority of nearly perfect stories fall flat at the end. They use terms like *predictable, weak, disappointing, preachy, no surprises.* Since the ending can make or break a story, it's imperative to end with a wallop. The ending not only clarifies the meaning of your story and reveals the change in your characters, but it's the part that lingers with the judges. Did you leave your protagonist miserable and despondent, without hope *(. . . and since no one loved her, Jenna decided to jump off a cliff)*? Did you sum up your story in one sentence *(So, the naughty piglets gobbled their slop and promised never again to wallow in the mud)*? Or an abrupt cliffhanger *(The doctor told Matt he might live—with brain surgery)*? Have you moralized, using a character as a preachy mouthpiece *("Children who steal honey deserve to be stung," Mama Bear scolded)*? Did you wield a *deus ex machina,* the sudden coincidental arrival of an outside force *(Nick cheered as a Black Hawk helicopter arrived to rescue him from the oak tree)*? Then you haven't written a satisfying ending.

Satisfying is not synonymous with *happy.* A satisfying ending may be thought-provoking, irreverent, tragic, or humorous—but it must grow logically out of your plot and your characters' personalities. There's no simple formula for crafting an ending that catapults your story to the top. It's more of a heightened feeling of completeness and authenticity, the deep emotional gut wrench you get at weddings and graduations and births. Shivers and tingly goosebumps are sure signals that your ending is approaching perfection.

Which leads to the ultimate goal in the X-factor race: Like all readers of fiction, judges want to be entertained. They adore surprises, the un-expected twist. They love to laugh. To weep. To gasp in delight. To be caught off guard. To empathize with your protagonist and see the world from a different viewpoint. That's exactly what your reader wants too, a story that's memorable. Think about all the stories and movies you love, the ones etched in your memory, with unforgettable story lines and characters. As the judges re-read the finalists, they're looking for that same soul-stirring quality, for a story that resonates. If your story stays with the judge, sticks in her mind after she's left the office, whirls through his head as he's watching his son's soccer game, sifts through

X-Factor Checklist

Take an honest look at your story. Is it fresh, original, and electrifying? Will it stand up to countless readings? Before submitting your story to a contest, make sure you've cleared all the hurdles:

➤ **Hurdle 1:** Have I followed the contest rules exactly?
- Word count (didn't exceed stated limit; didn't undershoot by too much)
- Spacing (usually double, but sometimes single)
- White paper
- Typed
- Included contact information (name, address, phone, e-mail)
- SASE or SASP
- Themed (if so requested)
- Easily-readable font (not italics or bold)
- Deadline (check whether "postmarked by" or "received by")

Is my copy error-free and grammatically correct? (No typos—especially in the title!)

➤ **Hurdle 2:** Is my plot original, not similar to any current TV show, movie, video game, or book? Is my story structured, with a beginning, middle, end, and with a conflict/resolution scenario?

➤ **Hurdle 3:** Have I revised any purple prose, cut excessive adverbs and adjectives, deleted clichés? Have I used active verbs and sensory details, showing vs. telling? Are my characters, settings, and dialogue believable within their story framework? Is my story problem age-appropriate?

➤ **Hurdle 4:** Is my ending logical and convincing, yet not preachy? Surprising and unexpected, yet realistic and hopeful? Is my overall story entertaining and memorable? Will readers remember my story tomorrow— or even for the rest of their lives?

her thoughts as she prepares for bed—you've captured the essence of the X-factor. Your story is not only skillfully crafted and beautifully worded, but compelling and memorable.

When the panel of judges convenes, each with a short list of finalist recommendations, now familiar titles elicit compliments and praise: "Oh, I remember that one!" "I love that character!" "I laughed until I cried!" After briefly discussing the merits of each finalist and comparing ranking lists, the judges come to a quick consensus as to grand prize winner and runners-up.

Each finalist story has its particular strengths and weaknesses, but all have one thing in common—the strong appeal of the X-factor.

Writers' Conferences

Conferences Devoted to Writing for Children— General Conferences

BYU Writing and Illustrating for Young Readers Workshop
348 HCEB, Brigham Young University, Provo, UT 84602
http://ce.byu.edu/cw/writing

This five-day workshop features full-day or afternoon sessions for beginning to advanced writers looking to publish children's and young adult fiction or nonfiction. Workshop highlights include writing and illustrating critique groups led by award-winning professionals, and seminars covering every aspect of children's fiction and nonfiction.
Date: June.
Location: Provo, Utah.
Cost: See website for cost information.

Highlights Foundation Writers Workshop at Chautauqua
814 Court Street, Honesdale, PA 18431
www.highlightsfoundation.org

Now in its twenty-fourth year, this workshop was created specifically for children's writers. Topics explore a range of genres, writing techniques, and the publishing business. Group or one-on-one sessions, workshops, critiques, and informal activities are available.
Date: July.
Location: Chautauqua, New York.
Cost: $1,785-$2,200 (includes meals).

The Loft Festival of Children's Literature

1011 Washington Avenue South, Suite 200, Minneapolis, MN 55415
www.loft.org

Children's book writers, illustrators, publishing professionals, and educators come together at this annual conference that combines workshops, full-group sessions, and breakout sessions. It also provides opportunities to share writing in small groups with an editor and other writers.
Date: April.
Location: Loft Literary Center, Minneapolis, Minnesota.
Cost: See website for cost information.

Oregon Coast Children's Book Writers Workshop

7327 SW Barnes Road, Portland, OR 97225
www.occbww.com

This is an intensive workshop designed for writers of all skill levels, offering a high degree of one-on-one coaching from other writers, editors, and literary agents. Participants learn to improve their writing through presentations, group manuscript sharing, and instructor consultations.
Date: July.
Location: Oceanside, Oregon.
Cost: $745.

The Pacific Coast Children's Writers Workshop

Nancy Sondel, Founding Director
P.O. Box 244, Aptos, CA 95001
www.childrenswritersworkshop.com

This three-day workshop is for middle-grade and YA novelists specializing in character-driven, realistic fiction. The program is for writers of literary novels, and focuses on craft as a marketing tool. Includes individual and group faculty critiques, pre-workshop readings, keynotes, panels, and focus sessions. University accredited.
Date: August.
Location: Hilton Hotel, Santa Cruz, California.
Cost: $299–$599.

Pacific Northwest Children's Book Conference
PSU School of Extended Studies
P.O. Box 1491, Portland, OR 97207-1491
www.ceed.pdx.edu/children

Sponsored by Portland State University, this weeklong conference for writers and illustrators covers all genres of children's writing and includes lectures, workshops, critiques by publishing professionals, first-page analyses, faculty readings, and open-microphone sessions.
Date: July.
Location: Cannon Beach, Oregon.
Cost: See website for cost information.

Conferences Devoted to Writing for Children— Society of Children's Book Writers and Illustrators

Alabama
Southern Breeze Fall Conference
Regional Advisor
P.O. Box 26282, Birmingham, AL 35260
www.southern-breeze.org

The Southern Breeze Fall Conference offers children's writers and illustrators 30 inspirational and educational workshops. Critiques of manuscripts, portfolios, or marketing packages are also available.
Date: October.
Location: Birmingham, Alabama.
Cost: See website for cost information.

California
SCBWI Writing and Illustrating for Children
8271 Beverly Boulevard, Los Angeles, CA 90048
www.scbwi.org

Sponsored by the world's largest children's writing organization, this conference allows writers to network and learn from publishing powerhouses. Events include workshop sessions, master classes, juried art showcases, manuscript/portfolio consultations, and a poolside gala.

Date: August.
Location: Los Angeles, California.
Cost: See website for cost information.

North Central California SCBWI Spring Conference
Tekla White, Regional Advisor
P.O. Box 307, Davis, CA 95617
www.scbwinorca.org

Sponsored by the North Central California chapter of SCBWI, this spring event presents a single day of networking and educational opportunities for children's writers. It features workshops and presentations from industry professionals on all aspects of children's writing. Writers may submit one manuscript prior to the conference for a critique.
Date: March.
Location: Veterans Memorial Center, Davis, California.
Cost: See website for cost information.

Ventura/Santa Barbara SCBWI Writer's Day
Alexis O'Neill, Regional Advisor
www.scbwisocal.org

The SCBWI-Ventura/Santa Barbara region and the California Lutheran University School of Education present a full day of activities on children's publishing, including first-page critiques, manuscript/portfolio critiques, a writing contest, illustration displays, a book sale, and presentations by newly published authors and editors.
Date: October.
Location: Thousand Oaks, California.
Cost: $85 for members; $95 for non-members. Additional fees for manuscript and portfolio critiques.

Canada
SCBWI Canada East Annual Conference
Lizann Flatt, Canada East Regional Advisor
505 Highway 118 West, Suite 454, Bracebridge, Ontario P1L 2G7 Canada
www.scbwicanada.org/east/

This one-day annual writing conference offers children's writers the opportunity to hear from a variety of industry professionals, as well as the chance to participate in one-on-one manuscript critiques and first-page manuscript readings. A book sale features works by published SCBWI authors. Visit the website for complete conference information and 2009 speakers.

Date: May.

Location: Ottawa, Ontario, Canada.

Cost: $85 for members; $100 for non-members. Additional fees required for manuscript critiques.

Carolinas

SCBWI-Carolinas Fall Conference

Stephanie Greene, Regional Advisor

www.scbwicarolinas.org

This annual event offers a dozen workshops to choose from as well as numerous opportunities to connect with editors, including an Editors' Evening, a buffet celebration, and first-page critiques. Visit the website for complete workshop list and conference information.

Date: September.

Location: North Carolina.

Cost: See website for cost information.

Florida

SCBWI Florida Regional Conference

Linda Rodriguez Bernfeld, Regional Advisor

10305 SW 127 Court, Miami, FL 33186

www.scbwiflorida.com

Attendees of this regional conference may participate in informal critique groups, first-page critiques, a dinner ball, a reception with authors and editors, and manuscript/portfolio critiques (for an additional fee). The conference is open to SCBWI members and non-members. Visit the website for complete conference schedule.

Date: January.

Location: Wyndham Miami Airport Hotel, Miami, Florida.

Cost: See website for cost information.

SCBWI Florida Mid-Year Writing Workshop
Linda Rodriguez Bernfeld, Regional Advisor
10305 SW 127 Court, Miami, FL 33186
www.scbwiflorida.com

This one-day workshop allows participants to focus on one of four tracks: picture book, middle-grade, young adult, or poetry. The day's events include first-page critiques, writing exercises, and market information for each genre. Informal critique groups and manuscript/portfolio critiques are also available.
Date: June.
Location: Disney Coronado Springs Resort, Orlando, Florida.
Cost: See website for cost information.

Kansas
SCBWI Kansas Fall Conference
Sue Ford
P.O. Box 3987, Olathe, KS 66063
www.kansas-scbwi.org

Open to SCBWI members and non-members, this conference was created to inspire writers of all skill levels, connect them with publishing professionals, and enhance their writing and marketing skills. Along with keynote addresses, panels, and breakout sessions, the conference will offer manuscript critiques and a first-page critique session.
Date: September.
Location: McCoy Meetin' House, Park University, Parkville, Missouri.
Cost: See website for cost information.

Maryland/Delaware/West Virginia
SCBWI MD/DE/WV Summer Conference
Mona Kerby, Regional Advisor
www2.mcdaniel.edu/scbwi/

Open to writers of all skill levels, this regional conference offers attendees the chance to network with editors, authors, illustrators, and agents through a series of seminars, critiques, and informal gatherings. Conference scholarships are available for a limited number of participants.

Date: July.
Location: McDaniel College, Westminster, Maryland.
Cost: See website for cost information.

Missouri
SCBWI Children's Writers Conference
Sue Bradford Edwards, Regional Advisor
www.scbwi-mo.org/

This annual one-day conference covers all aspects of writing and illustrating children's literature. Participants must register and submit their work early to take part in manuscript critique sessions with editors.
Date: November.
Location: Cottleville, Missouri.
Cost: See website for cost information.

New England
SCBWI-New England Annual Conference
Marilyn Salerno, New England Regional Coordinator
www.nescbwi.org

Aspiring and experienced children's writers benefit from the range of workshops offered at this annual conference, which covers the craft of creating books for children, marketing your work, and practical information. The day's events include a mix of presentations and workshops.
Date: April.
Location: Crowne Plaza Hotel, Nashua, New Hampshire.
Cost: See website for cost information.

New Mexico
Handsprings: A Conference for Children's Writers and Illustrators
Chris Eboch, Regional Advisor
www.scbwi-nm.org

The annual conference of the New Mexico SCBWI chapter offers a day of information on how to break into the children's book business or advance your career. Attendees may participate in a 15-minute private critique with an editor, a first-page critique panel, or peer critique groups.

361

Date: May.
Location: Albuquerque, New Mexico.
Cost: See website for cost information.

Tennessee
SCBWI Midsouth Annual Fall Conference
Tracy Barrett, Regional Advisor
www.scbwi-midsouth.org

This weekend-long conference offers writers of all skill levels a chance to network and learn from well-known industry professionals. The conference program includes meet-and-greet sessions, manuscript critiques, and numerous breakout sessions, as well as 15 one-hour morning and afternoon workshops that include a Q&A session. Conference participants may also attend group critique sessions.
Date: September.
Location: Nashville, Tennessee.
Cost: See website for cost information.

Texas
SCBWI-Houston Editor Day
P.O. Box 19487, Houston, TX 77224
www.scbwi-houston.org

This annual one-day event offers Houston-area SCBWI members access to editors from a variety of publishing houses. Conference attendees may participate in manuscript critiques, speaker seminars, and meet-and-greet sessions. Visit the website or send an SASE for current conference information and workshops.
Date: February and/or November.
Location: Houston, Texas.
Cost: SCBWI members, $90; non-members, $120.

Virginia
SCBWI Mid-Atlantic Fall Conference
Ellen Braaf, Regional Advisor
www.scbwi-midatlantic.org

This one-day conference features a mix of keynote speakers, writing workshops, and a meet-and-greet with editors and agents. A limited number of manuscript and portfolio reviews are offered to members only. Early registration is recommended.

Date: October.

Location: Arlington, Virginia.

Cost: SCBWI members, $95; non-members, $125.

Conferences with Sessions on Writing for Children— University and Regional Conferences

Antioch Writers' Workshop
P.O. Box 474, Yellow Springs, OH 45387
www.antiochwritersworkshop.com

Organizers of this annual workshop strive to provide inspirational activities for professional and personal growth among writers of all genres. The weeklong program offers a mix of classes, lectures, intensive seminars, panel discussions, manuscript critiques, and more. Serious writers of all skill levels are welcome.

Date: July.

Location: Yellow Springs, Ohio.

Cost: See website for cost information.

Arkansas Literary Festival
4942 W. Markham, Suite 1, Little Rock, AR 72205
www.arkansasliteraryfestival.org

Arkansas' largest literary event includes author readings and discussions, writing workshops, booktalks, and a book fair to benefit literacy councils throughout the state. Writers can meet and talk with others who have had success in the industry, including best-selling children's authors. The festival also offers a children's breakfast, storytime, and craft centers, and writing workshops for teens.

Date: April.

Location: Little Rock, Arkansas.

Cost: Free.

Aspen Summer Words
110 E. Hallam Street, Suite 116, Aspen, CO 81611
www.aspenwriters.org

Book lovers and writers alike find stimulation at this five-day retreat, which is a combination literary festival and writers' workshop. Literature appreciation classes, writing instruction, professional consultations, and daily writing exercises make up the educational aspects of this program.
Date: June.
Location: Aspen, Colorado.
Cost: See website for cost information.

Bear River Writers' Conference
Department of English Language and Literature
3187 Angell Hall, University of Michigan, Ann Arbor, MI 48109
www.lsa.umich.edu/bearriver/

With a focus on creative writing, this annual four-day conference offers attendees a chance to connect with nature while at the same time be inspired in their writing. Directed at writers of all levels, the program combines recreational activities with a variety of workshops, faculty readings, panel discussions, and free time for writing.
Date: May/June.
Location: Walloon Lake, Michigan.
Cost: Check the website for cost information.

CanWrite! Conference
Canadian Authors Association
P.O. Box 419, Campbellford, Ontario K0L 1L0 Canada
www.canauthors.org

Created to support the Canadian writing community, this yearly conference is sponsored by Canada's national writing organization. Publishers, agents, and authors participate in writing workshops and readings, an annual short story contest, and manuscript evaluations.
Date: July.
Location: Edmonton, Alberta.
Cost: See website for cost information.

Cape Cod Writers Conference

Cape Cod Writers Center
P.O. Box 408, Osterville, MA 02655
www.capecodwriterscenter.com

This conference has been hosting distinguished writers and poets since 1963. It offers specific tracks in all genres from children's books to memoirs, and includes classes, workshops, and panel discussions. Manuscript evaluations are also available for a fee.

Date: The third week of August.
Location: Cape Cod, Massachusetts.
Cost: $35 registration (waived for CCWC members), $165 per course, $150 mentoring, $125 manuscript evaluation, and $125 master class.

Central Coast Book & Author Festival

P.O. Box 12942, San Luis Obispo, CA 93406-2942
www.ccbookfestival.org

Created to celebrate "reading, writing, and libraries," this one-day festival provides a venue to meet authors, find out about new books, and participate in free author workshops. The family-friendly event also features musical entertainment and children's games and crafts.

Date: June.
Location: San Luis Obispo, California.
Cost: Free.

Clarksville Writers' Conference

Arts and Heritage Development Council, Box 555, Clarksville, TN 37041
www.artsandheritage.us/writers/

This conference offers two full days of writing workshops and author presentations in historic Clarksville, Tennessee. In addition to the workshops, events include a bus tour of area writers' homes and related locations, manuscript evaluations, keynote luncheons, and a banquet.

Date: July.
Location: Clarksville, Tennessee.
Cost: See website for cost information.

Columbus Writers Conference
P.O. Box 20548, Columbus, OH 43220
www.creativevista.com

At the sixteenth annual Columbus Writers Conference, writers can "learn, network, and be inspired." The two-day conference includes more than 40 breakout sessions, a literary agent panel, editor panel, special programs, and open mics, as well as presentations by writers, editors, and agents on a variety of topics. One-on-one consultations, agent/editor chat sessions, and panel discussions are also included.
Date: August.
Location: Columbus, Ohio.
Cost: See website for cost information.

Far Field Retreat for Writers
Mary Ann Samyn, Director
Far Field Retreat for Writers, Rochester, MI 48307
www2.oakland.edu/english/farfield

Writers of varying skill levels attend this four-day conference on the campus of Oakland University to study writing with a faculty of committed teachers and prominent writers. Attendees participate in workshops, readings, and craft/publishing sessions, and are allotted free writing time.
Date: May.
Location: Rochester, Michigan.
Cost: $375 includes some meals, lodging (commuter).

Georgia Writers Association Workshops
1000 Chastain Road, Mail Stop 2701, Kennesaw, GA 30144
www.georgiawriters.org

Industry professionals come together for full-day sessions on everything from agents and contract negotiation to freelancing and the writing life. Manuscript evaluations are available, as are writing resources such as magazines, market information, and publishers' guidelines.
Date: March, April, May, and September.
Location: Smyrna, Georgia.
Cost: $45-$250.

Harriette Austin Writers Conference
Georgia Center for Continuing Education Conference Center & Hotel
University of Georgia, Athens, GA 30602
http://harrietteaustin.org/

Created in honor of Harriette Austin, a writing teacher at the
University of Georgia Center for Continuing Education, this two-day
conference is in its 15th year. Attendees participate in any combination
of workshops, manuscript evaluations, Q&A sessions, and opportuni-
ties for networking such as informal dinners and book signings.
Date: July.
Location: Athens, Georgia.
Cost: See website for information.

Indiana University Writers' Conference
464 Ballantine Hall, Bloomington, IN 47405
www.indiana.edu/~writecon

This annual conference offers attendees a choice of taking classes in
poetry, fiction, or creative nonfiction, or participating in manuscript-
specific workshops. Staffed by prominent writers and teachers, the conference also features panel discussions, readings, and social events.
Date: June.
Location: Bloomington, Indiana.
Cost: See website for cost information.

Iowa Summer Writing Festival
University of Iowa, C215 Seashore Hall, Iowa City, IA 52242-5000
www.uiowa.edu/~iswfest

Attendees sign up for the festival's series of weeklong or weekend
workshops covering all genres, from memoirs to children's writing to poetry. Workshops are devoted to critiquing original work. Also offered are
daily presentations on craft, the writing life, process, and publishing.
Date: June/July.
Location: Iowa City, Iowa.
Cost: See website for cost information.

Manhattanville College Summer Writers' Week
2900 Purchase Street, Purchase, NY 10577
www.manhattanville.edu

This weeklong writing program is for established and aspiring writers who want to create a work or revise a work-in-progress. Faculty members of editors, agents, and authors cover various aspects of writing and editing; additional activities include private conferences, readings, and social events. Participating writers can earn college credits.
Date: June.
Location: Purchase, New York.
Cost: See the website for cost information.

Maryland Writers' Association Annual Conference
P.O. Box 142, Annapolis, MD 21404
www.marylandwriters.org

Beginners and published writers alike attend this conference to hone their craft and learn more about the business of publishing. Book signings and networking opportunities are also offered.
Date: May.
Location: Linthicum Heights, Maryland.
Cost: See website for cost information.

Mendocino Coast Writers Conference
College of the Redwoods
1211 Del Mar Drive, P.O. Box 2739, Fort Bragg, CA 95437
www.mcwc.org

This conference is committed to writing for social change, because "honest words make a better world." It focuses on all genres for all age groups, and offers writing workshops (for work submitted prior to the conference), presentations, professional consultations, readings, and networking opportunities.
Date: July/August.
Location: Fort Bragg, California.
Cost: Check the website for conference costs.

San Francisco Writers Conference

1029 Jones Street, San Francisco, CA 94109

http://sfwriters.org

Designed to "Build Bridges to Better Tomorrows," this conference welcomes more than 100 agents, authors, and editors. Writers have access to publishing professionals through how-to sessions, panels, and workshops, including one-on-one "speed" sessions that provide a chance to pitch work directly to agents and editors.

Date: February, August.

Location: San Francisco, California.

Cost: See website for cost information.

Southeastern Writers Workshop

161 Woodstone Drive, Athens, GA 30605

www.southeasternwriters.com

Writers of all skill levels from around the country attend this annual workshop to hone their craft and be inspired. The conference includes classes, evening speakers, writers roundtables, open mic night, and an awards banquet.

Date: June.

Location: St. Simons Island, Georgia.

Cost: $395 ($350 early bird), $100 per day. Lodging from $400-$650, includes meals.

Whidbey Island Writers Conference

P.O. Box 1289, Langley, WA 98260

www.writeonwhidbey.com

This weekend conference, sponsored by the Whidbey Island Writers Association, combines an inspiring island atmosphere with a varied agenda of writing classes, workshops, "author fireside chats," and literary readings. Individual manuscript critiques are also available.

Date: February, March.

Location: South Whidbey Island, Washington.

Cost: $375-$395 includes luncheons & Saturday night reception. Volunteer, early bird, and membership discounts available.

Writers Retreat Workshop

5721 Magazine Street, #161, New Orleans, LA 70115

www.writersretreatworkshop.com

Visiting authors, agents, and industry professionals present an intense week of workshops, meetings, lectures, writing exercises, and more for novelists. Writers attend in-depth morning classes on how to craft a novel for publication, focusing on their individual works-in-progress.

Date: May, June.

Location: Erlanger, Kentucky.

Cost: See website for cost information.

Yosemite Writers Conference

6737 N. Milburn #160, PMB 1, Fresno, CA 93722

Top agents and magazine and book editors share their expertise at this two-day writers conference. The Yosemite Writers Conference includes lectures, social events, and workshops, as well as numerous writing contest opportunities. Visit the website for complete conference details.

Date: August.

Location: Fish Camp, California.

Cost: Not available.

Conferences Devoted to Writing for Children— Religious Writing Conferences

Delaware Christian Writers Conference

6 Basset Place, Bear, DE 19701

www.delawarechristianwritersconference.com

Designed to help Christian writers of all experience levels to meet their publishing goals, this three-day conference features editors, agents, and authors as instructors. In addition to workshops, it also offers manuscript critiques, appointments with editors, and a writing contest.

Date: April.

Location: Newark, Delaware.

Cost: See website for cost information.

East Texas Christian Writers Conference
East Texas Baptist University
1209 North Grove Street, Marshall, TX 75670
www.etbu.edu/News/CWC/

Created to encourage Christian writers, this annual conference offers a variety of activities to develop the Christian writer's craft. Participants attend presentations and workshops, network with other writers, and consult with agents and editors.
Date: June.
Location: Marshall, Texas.
Cost: $90 per couple, or $60 for an individual.

Florida Christian Writers Conference
Billie Wilson, Coordinator
2344 Armour Court, Titusville, FL 32780
www.flwriters.org

Now in its twenty-first year, this conference is packed with opportunities for aspiring and published Christian writers. It offers 56 workshops, continuing classes divided by genre, a book/magazine editor panel, "Manuscript CPR," and after-hours special interest group meetings.
Date: February/March.
Location: Bradenton, Florida.
Cost: See website for cost information.

Glorieta Christian Writers Conference
2201 San Pedro NE, Building 1, Suite 225, Albuquerque, NM 87110
www.classervices.com

Classes, roundtables, and writing critiques are all part of this annual four-day conference set in the mountains of northern New Mexico. Geared toward helping Christian writers communicate their specific message, the conference helps writers fulfill their writing, publishing, and speaking dreams. Manuscript critiques are available.
Date: October.
Location: Glorieta, New Mexico.
Cost: See website for cost information.

Mount Hermon Christian Writers Conference

37 Conference Drive, Mount Hermon, CA 95041

www.mounthermon.org/writers/

Called an "exhilarating laboratory" for training writers of all skill levels, the Mount Hermon Christian Writers Conference offers five days of intensive writers' workshops. Participants can choose from specific genre tracks and take part in any of 70 individual afternoon workshops. Free manuscript critiques are included.

Date: April.

Location: Mount Hermon, California.

Cost: $315 tuition only; see website for other cost information.

Oregon Christian Writers Conference

P.O. Box 20147, Keizer, OR 97307

http://oregonchristianwriters.org

This organization of amateur and professional Christian writers hosts several conferences each year. The one-day conference informs those who write for the ministry and other markets, and provides opportunities to meet with editors, agents, and other writers. The conference sets aside time for devotionals and prayer.

Date: July, August.

Location: Canby, Oregon.

Cost: $400-$500 depending on lodging.

St. Davids Christian Writers' Conference

87 Pines Road East, Hadley, PA 16130

www.stdavidswriters.com

For 51 years, this five-day conference has offered classes aimed at beginning, intermediate, and advanced writers. The agenda includes editor appointments, critique groups, meditation sessions, literary readings, and writing.

Date: June 22–27, 2009.

Location: Grove City College, Grove City, Pennsylvania.

Cost: See website for cost information.

Writers' Contests & Awards

Jane Addams Children's Book Award
Susan C. Griffith, Chair
Central Michigan University, English Department
215 Anspach, Mount Pleasant, MI 48859
www.janeaddamspeace.org

Since 1953, the Jane Addams Peace Association and the Women's International League for Peace and Freedom annually honor authors and artists of children's literature who reach standards of excellence while also promoting peace, social justice, equality of the sexes, and a unified world community. Books of fiction, nonfiction, or poetry for ages 2 to 12, published in the preceding year, are eligible.
Deadline: December 31.
Award: Winners, announced in April, receive an honorary certificate and cash award at a dinner in New York City.

Arizona Authors Association Literary Contest
Arizona Literary Contest Coordinator
6145 W. Echo Lane
Glendale, AZ 85302
www.azauthors.com/contest_index.html

Published and unpublished work for adults and children may be entered in this contest, co-sponsored by Five Star Publications, Inc. Unpublished categories include short stories, poems, essays, articles, true stories, and novels. Published catagories include children's literature,

novels, nonfiction, and short story anthologies. Entry fees range from $10 to $30. Submit first 25 pages for novel entries.
Deadline: July 1.
Award: Winners in each category are announced at a banquet in November, and receive $100 and publication in *Arizona Literary Magazine*. Winners in unpublished categories are published by Five Star Publications, Inc.

ASPCA Henry Bergh Children's Book Award
ASPCA Education Department
424 East 92nd Street, New York, NY 10128-6804
www.aspca.org/bookaward

This award recognizes authors whose work promotes humane treatment of animals and helps children understand the interdependence of humans, animals, and the environment. Entries for children (to age 12) or teens (13 to 17) may be fiction, nonfiction, or collections of stories, essays, or poems by one author; illustrations are also awarded.
Deadline: October 31.
Award: Winners are announced in May and honored at an annual ASPCA conference in June.

AWA Contests
c/o Julie Hale, Department of English
1350 King College Road, Bristol, TN 37620-2699
www.king.edu/awa/awa_contests.htm

This program to preserve Appalachian literary heritage allows members of the Appalachian Writers Association to submit unpublished entries in the categories of poetry, essay, short story, and drama. Five-dollar entry fee. Submit two copies. Word lengths vary for each category.
Deadline: June 1.
Award: Winners are announced in the fall. First-place winners in each category receive $100. Second- and third-place winners receive awards of $50 and $25, respectively.

Baker's Plays High School Playwriting Contest
Attn: Associate Editor
45 W. 25th St., New York, NY 10010
www.bakersplays.com

High school students striving to become playwrights may participate in this annual contest. Full-length plays, one-act plays, theater texts, musicals, and collections of scenes and monologues that can be produced by students in a high school setting are welcome. Entries should have a public reading or production prior to submission, and must be accompanied by the signature of a sponsoring English or drama teacher. Submissions are also accepted by email.
Deadline: January 30.
Award: First-place winner's play is published. A $500 cash prize is awarded. Winners are announced in May.

John and Patricia Beatty Award
California Library Association
717 20th Street, Suite 200, Sacramento, CA 95814
www.cla-net.org

This award, co-sponsored by the California Library Association and BWI Books, recognizes children's book authors who promote an awareness of California and its people. A committee of librarians selects the winning title, which has been published during the year preceding the contest.
Deadline: February 10.
Award: The winner is announced in April during National Library Week. Winner receives $500 and an engraved plaque, presented at the California Library Association's annual conference in November.

Geoffrey Bilson Award for Historical Fiction for Young People
Canadian Children's Book Centre (CCBC)
40 Orchard View Boulevard, Suite 101, Toronto, Ontario M4R 1B9 Canada
www.bookcentre.ca

This annual contest honors outstanding works of YA historical fiction by Canadian authors or landed immigrants. Created in memory of Geoffrey Bilson, a respected historian and author, it is open to books published in the preceding year. Winners are chosen by a jury appointed by the CCBC. Picture books, short story collections, plots involving time travel, self-published books, and books produced by a vanity press are not eligible. Six copies of each title are required.

Deadline: January 15.

Award: Winner receives $5,000 and a certificate.

The Irma Simonton Black and James H. Black Award for Excellence in Children's Literature

Linda Greengrass
610 West 112th Street, New York, NY 10025
http://streetcat.bankstreet.edu

Created in honor of Irma Simonton Black, a writer and editor of children's books and founding member of the Bank Street Writers Laboratory, this award is given to a children's book that exemplifies an outstanding union of text and illustrations. A panel of authors, librarians, and educators choose 20 to 25 books as initial candidates. Copies are then sent to Bank Street and other schools, where students in grades one through three discuss the books and choose a winner.

Deadline: December 12.

Award: Winners are announced in May at a breakfast ceremony. Both author and illustrator, if they are different, receive a scroll designed by Maurice Sendak.

Waldo M. and Grace C. Bonderman Youth Theatre Playwriting Competition

Dorothy Webb, Contest Chair
1114 Red Oak Drive, Avon, IN 46123
www.indianarep.com/Bonderman

The Bonderman workshop, held every other year, creates an opportunity for playwrights to come together to discuss dramatic literature for young adults. The competition is open to all writers who are able to participate in the development and presentation of their work in Indianapolis. Only uncommissioned plays are eligible. Plays for grades one through three should not exceed 30 minutes; grades three and up must be at least 45 minutes. Submit three copies, a synopsis, and a cast list.

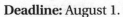

Deadline: August 1.
Award: Winners are notified in December. The top four winners receive $1,000 and a staged reading of their play.

The Boston Globe–Horn Book Awards
56 Roland Street, Suite 200, Boston, MA 02129
www.hbook.com

Among the most prestigious honors in children's and YA literature, these awards recognize excellence in books published in the U.S. during the preceding year. Publishers submit entries, and judges appointed by the editor of the *Horn Book* choose a winner and up to two honor books in the categories of fiction and poetry, nonfiction, and picture book.
Deadline: May 8.
Award: Winners are announced in June. They receive $500 and an engraved bowl. Honor recipients receive an engraved plaque.

Ann Connor Brimer Award
Alderney Gate Public Library
60 Alderney Drive, Dartmouth, Nova Scotia B2Y 4P8 Canada
www.nsla.ns.ca/

This award is presented to an author whose book constitutes an outstanding contribution to children's literature by the Nova Scotia Library Association and the Writer's Federation of Nova Scotia. Named for an advocate of Canadian children's literature, the award recognizes authors residing in Atlantic Canada who have written a book of fiction or nonfiction for readers up to age 15 during the preceding year.
Deadline: October 15.
Award: The winner, announced in May, receives $1,000 at a banquet in Dartmouth at the Atlantic Writing Awards ceremony.

Marilyn Brown Novel Award
Jen Wahlquist
English/Literature Department, Utah Valley University
800 West University Pkwy., Orem, UT 84058
www.uvu.edu/english/brownaward.pdf

Administered by Utah Valley University, Professor Jen Wahlquist, and the UVU English Department, and presented by the Association for Mormon Letters, this award is presented to the best unpublished novel submitted. No entry fee; one entry per competition.

Deadline: October 1.

Award: Winner receives a cash award of $1,000.

ByLine Magazine Writing Contests

P.O. Box 111, Albion, NY 14411

www.bylinemag.com/contests.asp

Writers may enter their work in numerous contests held monthly at *ByLine*. Contest themes change monthly and include children's stories, fiction, poetry, nonfiction, creative nonfiction, humor, and memoirs. Entry fees and word lengths vary per contest; all entries should be unpublished at the time of submission.

Deadline: Deadlines vary by category.

Award: Winners are announced in *ByLine* and receive awards ranging from $10 to $40 and publication in *ByLine*.

Randolph Caldecott Medal

American Library Association (ALA)

50 East Huron, Chicago, IL 60611

www.ala.org/alsc/caldecott.html

This prestigious medal, named in honor of nineteenth-century English illustrator Randolph Caldecott, is awarded to the artist of the most distinguished American picture book for children, by the Association for Library Service to Children, a division of the ALA. Open to citizens of the U.S., all illustrations must be original work published during the year preceding the award. Honor books are also recognized.

Deadline: December 31.

Award: The winner is announced at the ALA Midwinter Meeting and presented with the Caldecott Medal at an awards banquet.

California Book Awards
595 Market Street, San Francisco, CA 94105
http://commonwealthclub.org

The Commonwealth Club, with the goal of finding the best California writers and spotlighting the quality of literature produced in the state, annually awards 10 California authors with medals in recognition of outstanding literary works. Awards are presented in the categories of fiction or nonfiction for children up to the age of 10; fiction or nonfiction for children ages 11 to 16; and poetry. Submit five copies of entry.
Deadline: December 19.
Award: Winners are announced in May. Gold medal winners receive a cash award of $2,000; silver medal winners receive a cash award of $300.

Canadian Library Association's Book of the Year for Children Award
Jasmine Loewen, M.L.I.S., Assistant Librarian, Canmore Public Library
950 Eighth Avenue, Canmore, Alberta T1W 2T1 Canada
www.cla.ca

Any work of creative writing for children is eligible for this award, which recognizes excellence in Canadian children's literature that appeals to children age 12 and younger. Includes fiction, poetry, and retellings of traditional literature. Books must have been written by a citizen or permanent resident of Canada, and published in Canada.
Deadline: December 31.
Award: Winner is announced in the spring and presented with a leatherbound copy of the book and $750.

Canadian Writer's Journal **Short Fiction Contest**
Box 1178, New Liskeard, Ontario P0J 1P0 Canada
www.cwj.ca

Any genre of unpublished work not longer than 1,200 words is eligible for this contest, held in March and September by a journal that targets apprentice and professional writers. Each entry must be accompanied by a brief author biography. Entry fee, $5.
Deadline: Entries must be postmarked by September 30 or March 31.
Award: First-place winner receives $100; second and third place, $50 and

$25. Winning entries are published in *Canadian Writer's Journal* and in a chapbook called *Choice Works*.

CAPA Competition
Connecticut Authors and Publishers Association
223 Buckingham Street, Oakville, CT 06779
www.aboutcapa.com

Accepting entries of children's short stories (to 2,000 words), adult short stories (to 2,000 words), personal essays (to 1,500 words), and poetry (to 30 lines), this annual contest is open to everyone. Entry fee, $10 per short story/personal essay/children's story and $10 for up to 3 poems. Multiple entries are accepted. Each entry must be accompanied by an official entry form and four copies of the work.
Deadline: May 31.
Award: Winners are announced in October and receive $100; second place is $50. Winning entries are published in CAPA's newsletter.

Rebecca Caudill Young Readers' Book Award
P.O. Box 6536, Naperville, IL 60567
www.rebeccacaudill.org

This award for outstanding literature for young people is determined by students in grades four to eight at participating Illinois schools. Sponsored in part by the Illinois Reading Council, the award was developed to encourage children to read for personal satisfaction. Participating schools nominate books for initial consideration. Elementary and middle-school students make their final selections from a list of 20 titles.
Deadline: Tallied votes must be received by February 28.
Award: Winner is announced in March and receives a plaque.

Children's Writer Contests
95 Long Ridge Road, West Redding, CT 06896-1124
www.childrenswriter.com

All writers can submit unpublished material to the two contests sponsored each year by *Children's Writer*. Contest topics vary and have included poetry, preK, seasonal, sports nonfiction, folktales, fantasy, science, and historical fiction. The contests are judged by Institute of Children's Literature faculty. No entry fee for *Children's Writer* subscribers; $10 for non-subscribers (includes an eight-month subscription). Multiple entries are accepted.

Deadline: February 28 and October 31 of each year.

Award: Winners are announced in *Children's Writer.* First-place winners receive publication in the newsletter and a cash award. Second- through fifth-place winners also receive cash prizes in varying amounts.

Christopher Awards

5 Hanover Square, 11th Floor, New York, NY 10004

www.christophers.org

The Christophers is a nonprofit Catholic organization whose ministry is communications. The awards recognize artistic work in publishing, film, and TV that reminds people of their worth and power to create change. Profiles of courage, stories of determination and vision, and chronicles of constructive action and empowerment are recognized. Only original titles published in the preceding year are accepted.

Deadline: November.

Award: Winners are announced in March. They are presented with bronze medallions at a ceremony in New York City.

CNW/FFWA Florida State Writing Competition

P.O. Box A, North Stratford, NH 03590

www.writers-editors.com

This annual contest, open to all writers, honors authors of nonfiction, fiction, children's literature, and poetry. Children's literature entries must be unpublished or self-published; poetry may be free verse or traditional. Entry fees vary from $3 to $20. Multiple entries are accepted under separate cover. Word count should not exceed 5,000.

Deadline: March 15.

Award: Winners are announced by May 31. First- to third-place winners in each category receive prizes ranging from $100 to $50, and certificates.

Crossquarter Short Science Fiction Contest
P.O. Box 86, Crookston, MN 56716
www.crossquarter.com

Short stories that demonstrate the best of the human spirit in the genres of science fiction, fantasy, and urban fantasy are the focus of this contest sponsored by Crossquarter Publishing. Entry fee, $15; $10 for additional submissions. Entries should not exceed 7,500 words.
Deadline: January 15.
Award: Winners are announced in the spring. First place, $250 plus publication. Second to fourth place, $125 to $50 plus publication.

Delacorte Dell Yearling Contest
1745 Broadway, 9th Floor, New York, NY 10019
www.randomhouse.com

Sponsored by Random House, U.S. and Canadian writers of middle-grade novels are eligible for this annual award. The contest welcomes contemporary or historical fiction set in North America for ages 9 to 12. Entries should be between 96 and 160 pages and include a cover letter with a brief plot summary.
Deadline: Manuscripts must be postmarked between April 1 and June 30.
Award: Winners are announced in the fall and are given a book contract with a $7,500 advance against royalties and $1,500 cash.

Delacorte Press Contest for a First Young Adult Novel
1745 Broadway, 9th Floor, New York, NY 10019
www.randomhouse.com

This annual competition, intended to encourage contemporary YA fiction, offers a book contract to a winning author living in the U.S. or Canada who has not yet published a YA novel. Manuscripts must be between 100 and 224 typed pages. Limit two entries per competition. Stories should feature a contemporary setting suitable for readers ages 12 to 18.
Deadline: Entries must be postmarked between October 1 and December 31.

Award: Winners are announced no later than April 30. They are given a contract with a $7,500 advance against royalties and $1,500 cash.

Distinguished Achievement Awards
510 Heron Drive, Suite 201, Logan Township, NJ 08085
www.aepweb.org

The Association of Educational Publishers recognizes the best educational materials in many contest categories, including feature articles; poetry; plays; and editorials for adults, young adults, and children. Entry fee, $120 for AEP members; $240 for non-members. All eligible submissions must have been published in the year preceding the contest.
Deadline: All entries must be electronically submitted by February 14; hard copies must be received by February 15.
Award: Winners are notified by mail in April, and presented with a framed certificate at an awards banquet.

ECPA Christian Book Awards
9633 South 48th Street, Suite 140, Phoenix, AZ 85044
www.ecpa.org

Books that exemplify the highest-quality Christian literature are recognized by the Evangelical Christian Publishers Association. Established in 1978, the competition considers eligible books based on content, literary quality, design, and significance of contribution in six major categories: Bibles; fiction; children and youth; inspiration and gift; Bible reference and study; and Christian life. Books must be submitted by ECPA member publishers in good standing. Entry fee ranges from $175 to $299 per title.
Deadline: October 1.
Award: The finalists are revealed on January 25; winners are announced at an awards celebration each summer and acknowledged with plaques.

Margaret A. Edwards Award
50 East Huron, Chicago, IL 60611
www.ala.org/yalsa

Established in 1988 by the ALA's Young Adult Library Services Association, the Margaret A. Edwards Award honors a living author for a body of work and his or her special contribution to YA literature. The winner's writing will have been popular over a period of time and is generally recognized as helping teens to become aware of themselves and their role in society. Nominations are made by librarians and teens. All books must have been published in the U.S. no less than five years prior to the nomination.

Deadline: December 31.

Award: Winner is announced during the ALA Midwinter Meeting and receives $2,000.

Arthur Ellis Awards

3007 Kingston Road, Box 113, Toronto, Ontario M1M 1P1 Canada
www.crimewriterscanada.com

Canada's premier awards for excellence in crime writing, the Arthur Ellis Awards are sponsored by the Crime Writers of Canada, Sleuth of Baker Street, Book City, and McArthur and Company Publishing Ltd. Categories include best short story, best nonfiction, best first novel, best juvenile novel, best novel, best crime writing in French, and best unpublished first crime novel.

Deadline: January 31.

Award: Winners are announced in April and receive a hardcarved, wooden statue at the annual awards dinner in June.

Empire State Award

252 Hudson Avenue, Albany, NY 12210-1802
www.nyla.org

Since 1990, the Youth Services section of the New York Library Association annually recognizes a living author or illustrator residing in New York State who has made a significant contribution to the field of children's or young adult literature.

Deadline: December.

Award: An engraved medallion is presented to the winning author or illustrator at the annual conference of the New York Library Association.

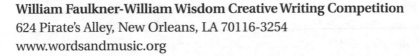

William Faulkner-William Wisdom Creative Writing Competition

624 Pirate's Alley, New Orleans, LA 70116-3254

www.wordsandmusic.org

The Pirate's Alley Faulkner Society sponsors this national competition to preserve the storytelling heritage of New Orleans and the Deep South. Prizes are awarded in seven categories for writers striving to be published: novel; novella; novel-in-progress; short story; essay; poetry; and short story by a high school student. Entry fees range from $10 to $35.

Deadline: May 1. Do not mail entries before January 15.

Award: Finalists are announced in July and August; winners are honored in November at the annual Faulkner Society gala. Winners receive cash awards ranging from $250 to $7,500.

Shubert Fendrich Memorial Playwriting Competition

P.O. Box 4267, Englewood, CO 80155-4267

www.pioneerdrama.com

Started in honor of the company founder, the competition encourages the development of quality theatrical material for educational and community theatres. Playwrights who have not yet been published by Pioneer Drama Service qualify for this annual contest.

Deadline: March 1.

Award: Winner is announced in June and receives a publishing contract and advance against royalties of $1,000.

Foster City International Writer's Contest

Foster City Parks and Recreation Department

650 Shell Boulevard, Foster City, CA 94404

www.geocities.com/fostercity_writers

All writers of original, unpublished fiction, humor, personal essays, children's stories, and poetry are eligible to enter this annual contest. Word lengths vary for each category. Entry fee, $15. Multiple entries are accepted.

Deadline: December 30.

Award: Winners are notified in late January. First prize in each category, $150; second prize, $75. Honorable mentions receive a ribbon.

H. E. Francis Award

Department of English, University of Alabama at Huntsville
Huntsville, AL 35899
www.uah.edu/colleges/liberal/english/whatnewcontest.html

Sponsored by the Ruth Hindman Foundation and the UAH English Department, this annual award accepts original, unpublished short stories that are judged by a nationally known panel of award-winning authors and editors. Entry fee, $15. Manuscripts must be unpublished and not exceed 5,000 words.

Deadline: December 31.

Award: Winners are announced in March. First place, $1,000.

Don Freeman Memorial Grant-In-Aid

8271 Beverly Boulevard, Los Angeles, CA 90048
www.scbwi.org

Members of SCBWI who intend to make picture books their primary contribution to the field of children's literature are eligible for this grant. It is presented annually to help artists further their training and understanding of the picture book genre.

Deadline: All entries must be postmarked between January 2 and February 2.

Award: Winners announced in August. Winner, $1,500; runner-up, $500.

Friends of the Library Writing Contest

130 North Franklin Street, Decatur, IL 62523
www.decatur.lib.il.us

This writing competition awards prizes in the categories of essay (to 2,000 words), fiction (3,000 words), juvenile fiction (3,000 words; no drawings), and rhymed/unrhymed poetry (40 lines). Published and unpublished writers may enter this annual contest. Main judging criterion is salability. Entry fee, $3; limit five entries per person.

Deadline: September 25.

Award: Winners are announced in December. First place in each category, $50; second and third place, $30 and $20, respectively.

Paul Gillette Writing Contest

c/o Pikes Peak Writers

4164 Austin Bluffs Pkwy. #246, Colorado Springs, CO 80918

www.ppwc.net

Writers looking for professional feedback, encouragement for producing a marketable piece, and the discipline of a deadline can find motivation through this contest, open to unpublished authors of book-length fiction and short stories. Categories include children's books, YA books, romance, and historical fiction, among others. Entry fee, $30 for members; $40 for non-members. Critiques are available at additional cost. For books, include the first 15 manuscript pages and a synopsis; short stories must be no longer than 5,000 words and accompanied by a description of the target market.

Deadline: November 1.

Award: Winners are announced at the Pikes Peak Writers Conference awards dinner in April. Winner receives a refund of conference fee, or $100. Second- and third-place winners receive $50 and $30, respectively.

Danuta Gleed Literary Award

90 Richmond Street East, Suite 200, Toronto, Ontario M5C 1P1 Canada

www.writersunion.ca

This award, sponsored by the Writers' Union of Canada, awards the best first collection of short fiction by a Canadian author. Entries must have been published in the year preceding the contest. Submit four copies of entry.

Deadline: February 2.

Award: Winners are announced on Canada Day, April 23. First prize, $10,000. Second and third prizes, $500.

The Golden Kite Awards

8271 Beverly Boulevard, Los Angeles, CA 90048

www.scbwi.org

Recognizing excellence in children's fiction, nonfiction, picture book text, and picture book illustration, the annual SCBWI Golden Kite Award is the only literary award presented to children's book authors and artists by their peers. SCBWI members are eligible for work published in the year preceding the contest. Editors and art directors of the winning titles are also recognized.

Deadline: December 15.

Award: Winners are notified by March 2 and are presented with a cash award of $2,500, in addition to a Golden Kite statuette. Honorable mentions receive plaques. The editor or the art director of the winning book will also be granted $1,000.

Governor General's Literary Awards

Canada Council for the Arts, Writing and Publishing Section
P.O. Box 1047, 350 Albert Street, Ottawa, Ontario K1P 5V8 Canada
www.canadacouncil.ca

Canada's national literary awards are given annually to the best English-language and the best French-language books in the categories of fiction, literary nonfiction, poetry, drama, children's literature (text and illustration), and translation (from French to English). Publishers submit books that have been written, translated, or illustrated by Canadian citizens or permanent residents of Canada.

Deadline: Varies according to publication date.

Award: Finalists are announced in October; winners are announced in November. The winner in each category receives $25,000 and a special bound copy of their book. Publishers of winning books receive $3,000 and finalists receive $1,000.

Lorian Hemingway Short Story Competition

P.O. Box 993, Key West, FL 33041
www.shortstorycompetition.com

Created in 1981, this international competition supports the efforts of writers who have not yet achieved major-market success. Writers of short fiction whose work has not been published in a nationally distributed publication (circulation of 5,000 or more) are eligible to enter. Original, unpublished fiction should be 3,000 words or less. There are no restrictions on theme, but only fiction is considered. Entry fee, $12 for entries postmarked by May 1, 2009; $17 for those postmarked between May 2 and May 15.

Deadline: May 15.
Award: Winners are announced by July 31 in Key West, Florida. First place, $1,000. Second and third place, $500.

Highlights for Children Fiction Contest
803 Church Street, Honesdale, PA 18431
www.highlights.com

Highlights designated its 2009 contest theme as contemporary world cultures stories. Work from published and unpublished authors over the age of 16 is welcome. Stories can be up to 800 words. Stories for beginning readers should not exceed 500 words. Indicate word count in upper right-hand corner of first page. All submissions must be unpublished. Clearly mark FICTION CONTEST on manuscript.
Deadline: Manuscripts must be postmarked between January 1 and January 31.
Award: Competition is announced in September; winners are announced in June. Winning entries are published in *Highlights for Children* and three cash prizes of $1,000 are awarded.

Insight Magazine Writing Contest
55 West Oak Ridge Drive, Hagerstown, MD 21740-7390
www.insightmagazine.org

Inspiring, uplifting, and thoughtful writing with a strong spiritual message earns attention in this contest, in which Bible texts are encouraged. Categories include student short story, general short story, and student poetry. Unpublished, true stories are eligible. Entrants in the student categories must be under 22. No entry fee. Short stories should be no longer than seven typed pages, and one page for poetry.
Deadline: June 2.
Award: Winners are published in *Insight*. First- through third-place winners receive prizes from $250 to $50.

IRA Children's and Young Adult Book Awards
800 Barksdale Road, Newark, DE 19714-8139
www.reading.org

The International Reading Association annually supports newly published authors who show exceptional promise in the field of children's literature. Eligible works include an author's first or second published book written for children or young adults (to age 17). Works are divided into three categories—primary, intermediate, or YA—and may be either fiction or nonfiction. Books published during the year preceding the contest are eligible, from any country or any language. Both authors and publishers may submit works for consideration.
Deadline: November.
Award: Winners are announced in January and receive a cash award of $500.

Barbara Karlin Grant

c/o Q. L. Pearce, 884 Atlantas Ct., Claremont, CA 91711
www.scbwi.org

The Barbara Karlin Grant is one of several grants offered by SCBWI, the largest children's writing organization in the world. To recognize and encourage aspiring picture book writers, this grant is given to SCBWI members who have not yet published a picture book. Works of fiction, nonfiction, or retellings of fairy tales, folktales, or legends are eligible. Length should not exceed eight manuscript pages. No entry fee. New applications and procedures are posted October 1 of each year.
Deadline: Completed applications are accepted between February 15 and March 15.
Award: Winners are announced October 1, and receive a grant of $1,500. Runners-up receive $500.

Coretta Scott King Awards

50 East Huron Street, Chicago, IL 60611-2795
www.ala.org

These distinguished awards are presented by the ALA to African American authors and illustrators for outstanding inspirational and educational contributions to children's and YA literature. Honoring Dr. Martin Luther King Jr. and his wife, Coretta Scott King, for their courage and determination, the award promotes the artistic expression of the African American experience through literature and graphic arts. All

entries must have been published in the year preceding the contest.
Deadline: December 1.
Award: Winners are announced each January during the ALA Midwinter Meeting. They are given a framed citation, an honorarium of $1,000, and a set of *Encyclopaedia Britannica* or *World Book Encyclopedia*.

Magazine Merit Awards

8271 Beverly Boulevard, Los Angeles, CA 90048
www.scbwi.org

In recognition of outstanding original magazine work, SCBWI sponsors this annual award for magazine writing published for young people. Four plaques are presented in the categories of fiction, nonfiction, illustration, and poetry. No entry fee. Submit four copies of the published work, showing proof of publication date. Only SCBWI members are eligible.
Deadline: December 15.
Award: Winners, announced in April, receive a plaque.

Maryland Writers' Association Novel Contest

P.O. Box 8262, Silver Spring, MD 20910
www.marylandwriters.org

The Maryland Writers' Association sponsors this contest for aspiring novelists throughout the U.S. to promote the art, business, and craft of writing. The contest's submission package is patterned on materials commonly requested by agents and editors. Categories include action/adventure/horror; mainstream/literary; mystery/suspense/thriller; romance/historical; and science fiction/fantasy. All entrants receive a detailed evaluation of their submission from two judges. Entry fee, $37 per submission for MWA members; $40 for non-members. Submissions should be a minimum of 50,000 words.
Deadline: February 28.
Award: Winners are announced in June. The overall contest winner receives $150. First-place winners in each category receive $100 and second-place winners receive $50.

Mayhaven Awards for Children's Fiction
P.O. Box 557, Mahomet, IL 61853
www.mayhavenpublishing.com

Mayhaven Publishing established this competition to encourage the writing of high-quality material for children. The competition is open to all writers and accepts entries written in English only. Entry fee, $50.
Deadline: December 31.
Award: Winners are announced in May. First-place manuscript is published by Mayhaven, which pays royalties. Second- and third-place winners receive $200 and $100, respectively.

Michigan Literary Fiction Awards
839 Greene Street, Ann Arbor, MI 48104-3209
www.press.umich.edu

This program is sponsored by the University of Michigan Press and is open to writers who have published at least one literary novel or story collection in English. It welcomes original submissions of short fiction collections and novels. No entry fee. Entrants should include a copy of their published book and the manuscript. Entries should be 100 pages minimum.
Deadline: Entries must be postmarked between February 1 and July 1.
Award: Winners, announced in November, receive a $1,000 advance and publication.

Mythopoeic Society Fantasy Award for Children's Literature
P.O. Box 320486, San Francisco, CA 94132-0486
www.mythsoc.org

This award honors outstanding fantasy books for young readers that are written in the tradition of J. R. R. Tolkien and C. S. Lewis. Picture books and early readers up through YA novels are considered. Books or collections by a single author are eligible for two years after publication.
Deadline: February 28.
Award: Winners are announced in August and presented with a statuette.

National Book Award for Young People's Literature

National Book Foundation
95 Madison Avenue, Suite 709, New York, NY 10016
www.nationalbook.org

One of the nation's foremost literary prizes, the National Book Award recognizes outstanding literature for young people as well as adults. Fiction, nonfiction, and collections of single-author short stories and essays are eligible; all books must be published in the U.S. in the year of competition, by U.S. citizens. Entry fee, $125. No translations or anthologies. Entries must be submitted by publishers.
Deadline: Entry forms due June 16; books or bound galleys due in August.
Award: Winners are announced in October. In each genre, $10,000 is accorded for first place and 16 finalists receive $1,000.

National Children's Theatre Festival

280 Miracle Mile, Coral Gables, FL 33134
www.actorsplayhouse.org

The Actors' Playhouse at Miracle Theatre sponsors a yearly competition for playwrights. Submissions should be unpublished scripts, appropriate for children ages 5 to 12, featuring a cast no larger than 8 adults, who may play multiple roles. Works that have received limited production exposure, workshops, or staged readings are encouraged, as are musicals with simple settings that appeal to both adults and children. Entry fee, $10. Running time should be 45 to 60 minutes. Include sheet music and a CD of music with vocals for musicals.
Deadline: April 1.
Award: Winners, announced in November, are awarded $500 and a full production of the play.

The John Newbery Medal

50 East Huron Street, Chicago, IL 60611
www.ala.org/alsc

The ALA's Association for Library Service to Children awards its prestigious Newbery Medal to honor the year's most distinguished contribution to American literature for children up to age 14. Eligible books are written by a U.S. author and published in the year preceding the contest. Genres include original fiction, nonfiction, and poetry. Books are judged on literary quality and overall presentation for children. Nominations are accepted from ALSC members only.

Deadline: December 31.

Award: The Newbery Medal is presented to the winning author at the Midwinter Meeting banquet.

New Millennium Writings Award

P.O. Box 2463, Room M2, Knoxville, TN 37901
www.newmillenniumwritings.com

This journal places no restrictions on style, content, or number of submissions for its annual contest. Entries are accepted in the categories of short-short fiction, fiction, nonfiction, and poetry; previously published works are accepted if published online or in a print publication with a circulation of less than 5,000. Entries should total no more than 6,000 words; short-short fiction, to 1,000 words; poetry, up to three poems, five pages total. Reading fee, $17. Simultaneous and multiple entries are welcome.

Deadline: July 31.

Award: Winners are published in *New Millennium Writings* and receive cash prizes ranging from $1,000 to $4,000.

New Voices Award

Lee & Low Books
95 Madison Avenue, New York, NY 10016
www.leeandlow.com

The New Voices Award encourages writers of color who have not published a children's picture book to submit their work. The competition specifically looks for submissions that address the needs of children of color, ages five to twelve. Fiction and nonfiction entries are accepted, but folklore and animal stories are not considered. No entry fee. Entries should not exceed 1,500 words and must be accompanied by a cover letter with the author's contact information and relevant cultural/ethnic information. Up to two submissions per entrant.

Deadline: Manuscripts are accepted between May 1 and October 31.

Award: Winners are announced in January and receive a publishing contract from Lee & Low, plus $1,000. Honorable mention, $500.

NWA Nonfiction Contest

10940 S. Parker Road, #508, Parker, CO 80134
www.nationalwriters.com

Established to recognize and encourage the writing of high-quality nonfiction, the National Writers' Association nonfiction contest grants the best unpublished works with this award. Submissions are judged on originality, marketability, research, and reader interest. Entry fee, $18. Multiple entries are accepted under separate cover. Entries should not exceed 5,000 words.
Deadline: December 31.
Award: Winners are announced by March 31. First-place winners receive $200. Second- and third-place winners receive $100 and $50.

NWA Novel Contest

10940 S. Parker Road, #508, Parker, CO 80134
www.nationalwriters.com

This annual contest encourages creativity and recognizes outstanding ability in novel writing. It is open to all writers and accepts original, unpublished novels in any genre. Multiple entries are accepted under separate cover. Entries should not exceed 10,000 words and must be written in English. Entry fee, $35.
Deadline: April 1.
Award: Winners are announced in June. First place, $500. Second and third place, $250 and $150, respectively. Fourth- through tenth-place winners receive a book and an honor certificate.

NWA Short Story Contest

10940 S. Parker Road, #508, Parker, CO 80134
www.nationalwriters.com

This contest looks for entries of well-written short stories. It accepts original, previously unpublished work only. Entry fee, $15. Multiple entries are accepted. Entries should not exceed 5,000 words.
Deadline: July 1.

Award: Winners are announced in the fall. First place, $250. Second and third place, $100 and $50, respectively.

Scott O'Dell Award for Historical Fiction
1700 East 56th Street, Chicago, IL 60637
www.scottodell.com

Named after a celebrated American writer of children's historical fiction, the Scott O'Dell Award is presented to a distinguished work of historical fiction for children or young adults. The award strives to encourage new authors to create historical fiction that boosts young readers' interest in history. Books published in the year preceding the contest are eligible. No entry fee. Entries may be submitted by authors who are U.S. citizens or publishers. Stories must be set in the Americas.
Deadline: December 31.
Award: Winner receives $5,000.

Once Upon a World Children's Book Award
1399 South Roxbury Drive, Los Angeles, CA 90035-4709
www.wiesenthal.com

The Museum of Tolerance recognizes and rewards books that inspire positive change. Books written for ages six to ten that convey messages of tolerance, social justice, social and personal responsibility, effective communication, or diversity are considered. Fiction and nonfiction titles are eligible. No entry fee. All entries must have been published during the year preceding the contest.
Deadline: April.
Award: Winners are announced in June and receive $1,000.

Orbis Pictus Award for Outstanding Nonfiction for Children
Literacy & Teacher Education, Husson College, School of Education
1 College Circle, Bangor, ME 04401
www.ncte.org

The Orbis Pictus Award recognizes excellence in children's nonfiction. Nominations may come from members of the National Council of Teachers of English (NCTE), as well as the general education community.

Winning books are useful in K-8 classroom teaching and are characterized by outstanding accuracy, organization, design, and style. Books must have been published in the U.S. in the previous calendar year. Textbooks, historical fiction, folklore, and poetry are not eligible. To nominate a book, write to the committee chair with the author's name, book title, publisher, copyright date, and a brief explanation of why you liked the book.
Deadline: December 31.
Award: Winners, announced in November, receive a plaque at the annual NCTE Convention. Five honor books receive certificates of recognition.

Pacific Northwest Writers Association Literary Contest
P.O. Box 2016, Edmonds, WA 98020-9516
www.pnwa.org

The Pacific Northwest Writers Association Literary Contest allows entrants to compete in multiple categories. It is open to previously un-published writers and includes the categories of young writers, screen-writing, poetry, mainstream novel, adult short story, juvenile short story/picture book, inspirational, romance, and adult short story. Each entrant receives two critiques. Entry fee, $35 for members; $50 for non-members. One entry per category.
Deadline: February 22.
Award: Winners are announced in July. First place in each category re-ceives $600 and the Zola Award. Second- and third-place winners, $300 and $150 respectively.

PEN Center USA Literary Awards
PMB 2717, 1420 NW Gilman Blvd, Suite 2, Issaquah, WA 98027
www.penusa.org

The Pen Center USA recognizes the literary achievements of writers living west of the Mississippi River. Entries are judged by a panel of distinguished writers, critics, and editors in the categories of children's literature, fiction, creative nonfiction, research nonfiction, poetry, trans-lation, journalism, drama, teleplay, and screenplay. All entries must have been published in the year preceding the contest. Entry fee, $35.
Deadline: December.
Award: Winners are announced in August and receive $1,000.

PEN/Phyllis Naylor Working Writer Fellowship
588 Broadway, Suite 303, New York, NY 10012
www.pen.org

Providing financial support for promising authors, the PEN/Phyllis Naylor Working Writer Fellowship is given annually to a writer of children's or YA fiction. Authors must have published at least two books but no more than five in the last ten years; likely candidates are those whose books have been well reviewed but have not achieved high sales. Nominations must be made by an editor or fellow writer via a detailed letter of support, accompanied by a list of the candidate's published work and reviews and a description of the nominee's financial resources. Three copies of no more than 100 pages of a current work must be submitted.
Deadline: Must be postmarked between September 1 and January 14.
Award: Winner is announced in May and is given a $5,000 fellowship.

Please Touch Museum's Book Awards
210 North 21st Street, Philadelphia, PA 19103
www.pleasetouchmuseum.org

Books that are distinguished in text, exceptionally illustrated, and that encourage a lifelong love of reading are recognized by this competition. Awards are given in two categories: ages three and under, and ages four to seven. Entries are judged by a panel of librarians, professors, and children's literature consultants.
Deadline: September 15.
Award: Winners, notified by December 1, receive a press release and are encouraged to hold a book signing at the museum. Awards are presented at the Early Childhood Education Conference in Philadelphia.

Pockets Annual Fiction Contest
P.O. Box 340004, 1908 Grand Avenue, Nashville, TN 37203-0004
www.pockets.org

Pockets sponsors this annual competition, open to all writers. It accepts previously unpublished manuscripts. Entries must be between 1,000 and 1,400 words. Biblical and historical fiction are not eligible. No entry fee.

Deadline: Entries must be postmarked between March 1 and August 15.
Award: Winner is notified November 1, and receives $1,000 and publication in *Pockets*.

Edgar Allan Poe Awards
Mystery Writers of America
17 East 47th Street, 6th Floor, New York, NY 10017
www.mysterywriters.org

The Edgar Allan Poe Awards are among the most prestigious awards for mystery writers. They are presented for published work in categories that include best fact crime, best young adult mystery, best juvenile mystery, best first novel by an American author, and best motion picture screenplay. No entry fee. All entries must have been published in the U.S. during the year preceding the contest.
Deadline: November 30.
Award: An "Edgar" is presented to each winner at an awards banquet in May. Cash awards may also be given.

Michael L. Printz Award for Excellence in Young Adult Literature
50 East Huron, Chicago, IL 60611
www.ala.org/yalsa/printz

The ALA's Michael L. Printz Award recognizes excellence in YA literature. Fiction, nonfiction, poetry, and anthologies that target ages 12 through 18 are eligible; books must have been published during the calendar year preceding the contest. ALA committee members may nominate any number of titles. Entries are judged on overall literary merit, taking into consideration theme, voice, setting, style, and design. Controversial topics are not discouraged.
Deadline: December 1.
Award: Winners are announced at the annual ALA Midwinter conference.

San Antonio Writers Guild Writing Contests
P.O. Box 34775, San Antonio, TX 78265
www.sawritersguild.org/contest_sawg-annual.html

Open to all writers, this multi-category contest revolves around fiction, nonfiction, children's literature, and poetry. Each writer may submit unpublished entries in up to three categories. Word limits vary by entry: novels and nonfiction books, first chapter, to 5,000 words; short story, to 4,000 words; essay, memoir, or article, to 2,500 words. Up to three poems may be entered for one $20 non-member entry fee ($10 for members).

Deadline: First Thursday of October.

Award: First prize, $100; second prize, $50; third prize, $25.

Science Fiction/Fantasy Short Story Contest

P.O. Box 121293, Fort Worth, TX 76121

http://home.flash.net/~sfwoe

The Science Fiction/Fantasy Short Story Contest was established by the Science Fiction Writers of Earth in an effort to promote short story writing in science fiction and fantasy. It is open to unpublished members. Entry fee, $5 for first entry; $2 for each additional entry. Manuscripts should be between 2,000 and 7,500 words.

Deadline: October 30.

Award: Winners are announced in February. First-place winner receives publication on the organization's website. First- through third-place winners receive awards ranging from $200 to $50.

Seven Hills Writing Contest

P.O. Box 3428, Tallahassee, FL 32315

www.twaonline.org

In this competition sponsored by the Tallahassee Writers' Association, awards are offered for best short story, memoir, essay, and children's literature. Only unpublished material is eligible. Judging criteria includes mechanics, technique, characters, dialogue, and use of language. Entry fee, $10 for members; $15 for non-members.

Deadline: Submissions accepted from January 1 through September 30.

Award: Winners are announced in December and published in the *Seven Hills Review*. First place, $100; second place, $75; third place, $50.

Skipping Stones Magazine Honor Awards

P.O. Box 3939, Eugene, OR 97403

www.skippingstones.org

These awards were established by *Skipping Stones* to recognize 26 books and teaching resources that promote diversity, peacemaking, environmental themes, and cooperation, and also serve as outstanding teaching resources for K-12 students. Entry fee, $50. Entries must have been published in the two years preceding the contest.

Deadline: February 1.

Awards: Winners are announced in April. Cash awards are given to the first- through fourth-place winners. Winning entries are reviewed in the summer issue of *Skipping Stones.*

Kay Snow Writing Contest

9045 SW Barbur Boulevard, Suite 5A, Portland, OR 97219-4027

www.willamettewriters.com

This annual competition of the Willamette Writers encourages writers to reach professional goals. Original, unpublished material is accepted in the categories of adult fiction and nonfiction, juvenile short story or article, poetry, screenwriting, and student writing. Entry fee, $10 for members; $15 for non-members. Word lengths vary by category.

Deadline: April 23.

Award: Winners are announced in August. Finalists are notified by mail prior to the announcement of winners. Prizes range from $50 to $300 in each category. A Liam Callen award with a cash prize of $500 is given for the best entry overall.

Society of Midland Authors Awards

P.O. Box 10419, Chicago, IL 60610

www.midlandauthors.com

Authors and poets who reside in, were born in, or have strong ties to any of the 12 Midwestern states are eligible to enter this contest, sponsored since 1915 by the Society of Midland Authors. Awards for excellence are presented for adult fiction and nonfiction, biography, poetry, and children's fiction and nonfiction. Entries must have been published in the year preceding the contest. No entry fee. Book entries must be at least 2,000 words. Multiple submissions are accepted.

Deadline: January 30.

Award: Winners are announced in May. Winners in each category receive a cash award and a recognition plaque.

SouthWest Writers Annual Contest

3721 Morris NE, Albuquerque, NM 87111-3611

www.southwestwriters.org

SouthWest Writers honors distinguished original and unpublished writing in a variety of genres: novel, short story, short nonfiction, book-length nonfiction, children's book, screenplay, and poetry. Entry fees range from $20 to $60; manuscript critiques are optional. Multiple entries are accepted.

Deadline: May 1.

Award: Winners are announced in the fall and receive awards ranging from $50 to $150. First-place winners in each category compete for the Storyteller Award with a grand prize of $1,000.

The Spur Awards

Deborah Morgan, Awards Chair

5552 Walsh Road, Whitmore Lake, MI 48189

www.westernwriters.org

The Spur Awards recognize distinguished writing about the American West. Open to all writers, entries must be set in the American West, the early frontier, or relate to the Western or frontier experience. Categories include best Western novel, best short story, best juvenile fiction and nonfiction, and best first novel. Entries must have been published the year preceding the contest.

Deadline: December 31.

Award: Winners are announced in March and awarded $2,500.

Stanley Drama Award
Wagner College, Department of Theater and Speech
631 Howard Avenue, Staten Island, NY 10301
http://leg.wagner.edu/stanleydrama/

Created to encourage and support aspiring playwrights, this contest accepts original full-length plays or musicals, or a series of two or three related one-act plays that have not been professionally produced or published as trade books. Entry fee, $20. Limit one submission per competition. Musical entries must be accompanied by an audiocassette.
Deadline: October 1.
Award: Winners are announced approximately 60 days after the deadline, with a first-place award of $2,000.

Sydney Taylor Manuscript Competition
Association of Jewish Libraries
315 Maitland Avenue, Teaneck, NJ 07666
www.jewishlibraries.org

Open to previously unpublished works of fiction containing Jewish content, the Sydney Taylor Manuscript Competition looks for universal appeal. Entries must be written for readers ages 8 to 11 and deepen children's understanding of Judaism. Manuscripts must be between 64 and 200 pages; short stories, plays, and poetry are not eligible. No entry fee. Limit one manuscript per competition.
Deadline: December 15.
Award: Winner is announced by April 15, and is awarded $1,000.

Utah Original Writing Competition
617 East South Temple, Salt Lake City, UT 84102
www.arts.utah.gov/literature/comprules.html

Honoring Utah's finest writers since 1958, this competition presents awards in categories that include YA book, novel, personal essay, short story, poetry, and general nonfiction. Only unpublished entries from Utah residents are eligible. No entry fee. Word lengths vary for each category. Limit one entry per category.
Deadline: Entries must be postmarked by June 27.

Award: Winners are contacted in September. Awards in each category range from $300 to $1,000.

Vegetarian Essay Contest

P.O. Box 1463, Baltimore, MD 21203

www.vrg.org

The Vegetarian Resource Group sponsors this contest that accepts personal essays highlighting any aspect of vegetarianism. There are three entry categories, determined by age: 14 to 18; 9 to 13; and 8 and under. Essays should be based on interviews, research, and/or personal opinion. No entry fee. Entries should be two or three pages. Limit one entry.
Deadline: May 1.
Award: Winners are announced at the end of the year and receive a $50 savings bond and publication in *The Vegetarian Journal* (all rights).

Jackie White Memorial National Children's Playwriting Contest

309 Parkade Boulevard, Columbia, MO 65202

http://www.cectheatre.org/

This contest is sponsored by the Columbia Entertainment Company to encourage the writing of scripts for children and families. Roles that challenge and expand acting talents are strongly encouraged. Only previously unpublished and unproduced material is considered. Entries should be full-length plays (60- to 90-minute running time) with well-developed speaking roles for at least seven characters. Entry fee, $10. Multiple entries are accepted. Include a cassette or CD of music, if appropriate.
Deadline: June 1.
Award: Winning entry is announced by August 31; playwright receives $500, plus possible publication or staged reading.

William Allen White Children's Book Awards

Emporia State University

1200 Commercial Street, Box 4051, Emporia, KS 66801

www.emporia.edu/libsv/wawbookaward/index.htm

This annual competition relies on children across the state of Kansas to vote for their favorite book from master lists chosen by the White

Awards Book Selection Committee. Entries must have been published during the year preceding the contest, and are judged by committee members for clarity, factual accuracy, originality, and respect for the reader. Two books are honored: one for third- through fifth-grade students and one for sixth- through eighth-grade students. The contest is open to North American residents only. Textbooks, anthologies, and translations are not eligible.

Deadline: May.

Award: Winners, announced in April, receive $1,000 and a bronze medal.

Laura Ingalls Wilder Medal

50 East Huron Street, Chicago, IL 60611

www.ala.org/alsc

The ALA's Association for Library Services to Children (ALSC) presents this award every other year to honor an author or illustrator whose body of work has contributed substantially to children's literature. Only books published in the U.S. are considered; nominations are made by ALSC members. The winner is chosen by a committee of children's librarians.

Deadline: December 31.

Award: Winners are announced in January at the ALA Midwinter Meeting. A medal is presented to the winner at the ALA conference in June.

Tennessee Williams One-Act Play Competition

938 Lafayette Street, Suite 514, New Orleans, LA 70113

www.tennesseewilliams.net

Playwrights around the world participate in this competition recognizing excellence in one-act plays. The winning script requires minimal technical support and a small cast of characters. Entry fee, $25. Multiple entries are accepted. Plays should be no longer than an hour and must not have been previously produced or published.

Deadline: Entries are accepted July 15 through November 1.

Award: Announced in April, winning entrants are granted $1,000 and full production of their play, as well as publication in *Bayou Magazine*.

Paul A. Witty Short Story Award

Kate Schlichting, Chair, Awards Subcommittee
4000 Hounds Chase Drive, Wilmington, NC 28409-3274
www.reading.org

Given to an author of an outstanding original short story published in the year preceding the contest, the Paul A. Witty Short Story Award is sponsored by the International Reading Association. Fiction or nonfiction, the winning entry demonstrates a high literary standard and provides an enjoyable reading experience for children. Authors, publishers, and IRA members may nominate a short story. No entry fee. Limit of three entries per competition.

Deadline: December 1.

Award: Winner is announced in the spring and is presented with $1,000 at the annual IRA convention.

Carter G. Woodson Book Awards

National Council for the Social Studies
8555 16th Street, Suite 500, Silver Spring, MD 20910
www.socialstudies.org/awards

These awards honor distinguished social science books relating to ethnic minorities and race relations. The winning titles portray these issues with accuracy and sensitivity, and show respect for ethnic and racial differences. Entries should be informational or nonfiction trade books. All submissions must have been published in the year preceding the contest.

Deadline: February.

Award: Winners are announced in the spring. In November, commemorative gifts and a medallion are presented to two winners at the NCSS annual conference. Additional books receive Honor Awards.

Work-in-Progress Grants

SCBWI, 8271 Beverly Boulevard, Los Angeles, CA 90048
www.scbwi.org

Each year SCBWI offers several grants to assist children's writers to complete projects not currently under contract. Grants are available to full and associate members of SCBWI in the categories of general work-in-progress; contemporary novel for young people; nonfiction research; and previously unpublished author. Requests for applications may be made beginning October 1. All applications should include a 750-word synopsis and writing sample of no more than 2,500 words from the entry.

Deadline: Applications are accepted between February 15 and March 15.

Award: Four grant winners are announced in September and are given $1,500. Four runner-up grants receive $500.

Writers at Work Fellowship

P.O. Box 540370, North Salt Lake, UT 84054-0370
www.writersatwork.org

Created to recognize emerging writers of fiction, nonfiction, and poetry, this annually presented fellowship is from Writers at Work, a non-profit literary arts organization. Writers not yet published in the genre of their entry are eligible to submit original works, though they may be self-published. Entries are judged by faculty members. Entry fee, $15.

Deadline: March 15.

Award: Winners receive $1,500 and publication in *Quarterly West*. Winners are annouced in May. Honorable mentions are also awarded.

Writer's Digest Annual Writing Competition

4700 East Galbraith Road, Cincinnati, OH 45236
www.writersdigest.com

Writer's Digest sponsors this annual competition for entries in many categories, including children's fiction, short stories, screenplays, and plays. It accepts previously unpublished work only. Entry fee, $10. Multiple entries are accepted.

Deadline: May 15.

Award: Winners are announced in the November issue of *Writer's Digest*. The grand prize is $3,000. Other prizes from Writer's Digest Books are given to winners in each category.

Writers' League of Texas Annual Manuscript Contest
611 S. Congress Ave, Suite 130, Austin, TX 78704
www.writersleague.org

This annual novel contest accepts entries in the following categories: mainstream fiction; middle-grade; YA; mystery/thriller; science fiction; historical or Western; and romance. Only original, unpublished material is accepted. Entry fee, $50. Include a one-page synopsis along with the first 10 pages. Visit the website or send an SASE for complete guidelines.
Deadline: March 1.
Award: Winners, disclosed in June, are invited to a meeting with an editor or agent at the Writers' League of Texas Agents and Editors Conference.

***Writers' Journal* Writing Contests**
P.O. Box 394, Perham, MN 56573-0374
www.writersjournal.com

Writers' Journal sponsors numerous contests year-round for writers of all experience levels and areas of interest. Categories include short story, ghost story/horror, romance, travel, fiction, and poetry. Word lengths and guidelines vary. All entries must be unpublished. Entry fees range from $3 to $15, depending on the category.
Deadline: Varies by category.
Award: Winners are announced in *Writers' Journal* and at the website after each contest deadline. They receive cash prizes and publication.

Writers' Union of Canada Writing for Children Competition
90 Richmond Street East, Suite 200, Toronto, Ontario M5C 1P1 Canada
www.writersunion.ca

Open to Canadian writers who have not yet had a book published, this competition helps discover and encourage new writers of children's literature. Multiple entries are accepted. Entries should not exceed 1,500 words. Entry fee, $15.
Deadline: April 24.
Award: Winner is announced in July and receives $1,500 and submission of their manuscript by the Writers' Union to three children's publishers.

Young Adult Canadian Book Award

Jessica Cammer, Collections Coordinator, Regina Public Library
2311 Twelfth Avenue, Regina, Saskatchewan S4P 3Z7 Canada
www.cla.ca/awards/yac.htm

Given to a work of YA fiction by a Canadian citizen or landed immigrant, this award honors an outstanding Canadian book in English. It is bestowed by the Young Adult Services Interest Group of the Canadian Library Association.
Deadline: December 31.
Award: The winner receives a leather-bound book embossed with the award seal in gold.

Paul Zindel First Novel Award

Hyperion Books for Children
P.O. Box 6000, Manhasset, NY 11030-6000
www.hyperionchildrensbooks.com

Honoring bestselling author Paul Zindel, this annual award honors works of contemporary and historical fiction set in the U.S. Manuscripts should reflect the cultural and ethnic diversity of the country for readers ages 8 through 12. Submissions should be between 100 and 240 typed pages. Limit is two entries per competition.
Deadline: April 30.
Award: Winners will be notified after July 15, and receive a book contract with Hyperion Books for Children, including an advance against royalties of $7,500, and an award of $1,500.

Charlotte Zolotow Award

Megan Schliesman, Chair, Cooperative Children's Book Center
600 N. Park Street, Room 429, Madison, WI 53706
www.education.wisc.edu/ccbc/books/zolotow.asp

This award is given to the author of the year's best picture book text. Honoring the work of distinguished children's book editor Charlotte Zolotow, this award was established in 1998 and is administered by the Cooperative Children's Book Center. Picture books eligible for review must be written in English and may be fiction or nonfiction.

Deadline: December 1.
Award: Winner is announced in January, and receives $1,000 and a bronze medal.

Index

413

416